Fodor's

ESSEN

ICELAND

T0268121

Contents

Welcome to Iceland

Iceland is like no place on earth. Glacier-topped volcanoes, black sand beaches, and towering sea stacks tell stories of Vikings and local folklore. The capital city of Reykjavík breeds immense artistic and musical talent. Residents embrace the cold (and are well equipped for it), and revel in ultragreen summers. Visitors come to party in the capital or venture through the interior Highlands to the edges of the sea, whether in ash-streaked snow or midnight sun. As you plan your upcoming travels to Iceland, please confirm that places are still open and let us know when we need to make updates by writing to us at editors@fodors.com.

TOP REASONS TO GO

★ **Art:** See live music in the capital and visit museums all over the country.

★ **Unique Cuisine:** The best lamb and langoustines you'll ever try.

★ **Protected Natural Wonders:** National parks here are UNESCO World Heritage sites.

★ **Year-Round Adventure:** Swim between tectonic plates; hike atop glaciers; horseback ride to waterfalls.

★ **Swimming:** From city pools to the world-famous Blue Lagoon and hidden hot springs.

★ **Night Sky:** Stargaze, seek out the northern lights, or bask in the midnight sun.

Chapter 1

EXPERIENCE ICELAND

14 ULTIMATE EXPERIENCES

Iceland offers terrific experiences that should be on every traveler's list. Here are Fodor's top picks for a memorable trip.

1 Northern Lights

The best opportunity to view the awe-inspiring Aurora Borealis is between September and March, as they require a dark sky to be seen. You'll also need to escape sources of urban light pollution, which can mask the celestial shimmers.

2 The Golden Circle

One of the world's best road trips, this loop of essential Icelandic sites includes Gullfoss waterfall, the Geysir hot spring area, and Þingvellir National Park. *(Ch.4)*

3 The Silfra Rift

You can snorkel or scuba dive the crystal-clear glacial waters of Silfra, a stunning fissure between the North American and Eurasian tectonic plates. *(Ch. 4)*

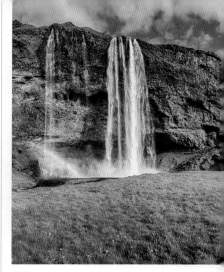

4 The Snæfellsnes Peninsula

This striking peninsula is blessed with waterfalls and lava fields, beaches with sand of gold and pink, and the ice-capped volcano from Jules Verne's *Journey to the Center of the Earth. (Ch. 5)*

5 Waterfalls

Don't miss the magic of Iceland's waterfalls: Gullfoss draws the most visitors while Skógafoss is close to the Ring Road and you can walk behind Seljalandsfoss. *(Ch. 4)*

6 Vatnajökull Glacier

One of Europe's largest glaciers covers some 8% of Iceland's surface. You can hike or go dog sledding on its surface. *(Ch. 10)*

7 The Blue Lagoon

No Iceland attraction is more iconic than the dazzling Blue Lagoon, a naturally heated seawater pool and spa. *(Ch. 4)*

8 Horseback Riding on a Beach

Two of Iceland's most famous features, its horses and its volcanic beaches, can be combined into one unforgettable experience. *(Ch. 4)*

9 Downtown Reykjavík

Home to nearly half of Iceland's population, Reykjavík is the political, cultural, and culinary hub of the country, with events that will delight every type of visitor. *(Ch. 3)*

10 Wildlife

Atlantic puffins can be seen on the cliffs at Látrabjarg in the Westfjords while the best place to spy the arctic fox is Hornstrandir nature reserve. Whale-watching tours are also plentiful. *(Ch. 3–6)*

11 Volcanoes

Iceland is alive with active volcanoes. Hike up Hekla, visit the freshly created lava fields in Fagradalsfjall, and explore the moonlike landscape of Askja Caldera where NASA astronauts trained. *(Ch. 4, 9)*

12 Music Festivals

Iceland's rich musical heritage is celebrated with numerous festivals including Dark Music Days in January, Þjóðhátíð in August, and Iceland Airwaves in November. *(Ch. 2)*

13 National Parks

Iceland is home to three national parks: Þingvellir, Vatnajökull, and Snæfellsjökull, each as spectacular as the next. *(Ch. 4, 5, 8, 10)*

14 The Ring Road

Iceland's Ring Road—also known as Route 1—runs all the way around the country, skirting the coast in the south and allowing access to all of Iceland's greatest sights.

WHAT'S WHERE

1 Reykjavík. The nation's capital sits on a beautiful bay, with the nearby mountains of Esja never far from view. Picturesque traditional houses dot the city center, and tourists throng the shops and restaurants downtown.

2 Reykjanes Peninsula and the South Coast. The moonlike landscape of Reykjanes is the first thing visitors see once they leave Iceland's main airport, and it's home to major attractions like the Golden Circle and the Blue Lagoon. The scenic South Coast features Vík í Mýrdal and its famous black beaches.

3 West Iceland and the Snæfellsnes Peninsula. Head north from Reykjavík to take in the towns of Borgarnes, Húsafell, Stykkishólmur, and the Snæfellsnes peninsula, home to the glacier-topped volcano Snæfellsnesjökull.

4 Westfjords. This region presents some of Iceland's most remote locations as well as numerous natural wonders such as the Dynjandi waterfall. The roads that wind around the Westfjords are most reliably navigable during summer.

20°W   10°W

Ittoqqortoormiit

N O R W E G I A N   S E A

Húsavík

Sauðárkrókur   6

5   Akureyri

Egilsstadir

3   7

ICELAND   8

rnes

REYKJAVIK   Vatnajökull

Golden Circle   Hofn

Selfoss

Vík

T H   A T L A N T I C   O C E A N

5 **Akureyri.** The nation's largest city outside the capital region, Akureyri sits on the west bank of a picturesque fjord and is an important port and fishing center.

6 **North Iceland.** Here, the coast features the Vatnsnes Peninsula to the west, the fishing village of Þórshöfn to the east, and Húsavík in the middle. This is where you can experience true solitude, and get as close to the Arctic Circle as you'll manage in Iceland.

7 **The Highlands.** Comprising Iceland's interior, the Highlands offer stunning natural wonders only accessible during the summer months. The campsites at Þórsmörk and Landmannalaugar are among the most magical in the country.

8 **Southeast Iceland and the Eastfjords.** The landscape of Southeast Iceland is dominated by the Vatnajökull glacier, which looms over the Ring Road as it hugs the coastline. The remote Eastfjords provide respite from the tourist hordes, with the pretty artistic town of Seyðisfjörður an underrated draw.

Iceland Today

Despite Iceland's relatively small population (around 376,000 people, roughly the same as Cleveland, Ohio), Icelandic society is complex and lively. Although first-time visitors might envision a nation of fisherfolk and sheep farmers in lopapeysa sweaters, the truth is that modern Iceland is way more diverse—and interesting—than that. Icelanders love to chat, so here are a few topics that might be useful around the local hot pots and coffeehouses.

TOURISM

Iceland chugged along quite nicely as a quiet Nordic backwater until two events brought it front of mind for the global tourism industry. First, in 2008, Iceland suffered an economic collapse that devalued the króna and made an expensive travel destination suddenly much more affordable. And then, in 2010, south Iceland's Eyjafjallajökull volcano erupted. The airborne ash pretty much shut down all air traffic in the northern hemisphere, making global headlines and forcing an uncomfortable crash course in Icelandic pronunciation on the world's newsreaders.

In the following years, visitor numbers rose steadily, reaching a peak of around 2.3 million in 2018 (that was more than six times the population of the country at the time) and placing a strain on infrastructure around tourist hot spots. As the pandemic loosens its grip and travelers return, tourism in Iceland looks set to pick up where it left off, especially with volcano Geldingadalsgos teasing a resumption of its fiery shenanigans. All this reignites conversations around how Iceland might best accommodate its very welcome influx of guests.

COVID-19 PANDEMIC

As robust as the tourism industry was at the start of 2020, it couldn't withstand the onslaught of COVID-19. Visitor numbers plummeted as the world shut down, and Iceland tightened its borders to protect itself. For many long-term residents of Reykjavík, the emptier streets were reminiscent of the city in which they grew up. But there was little nostalgia, as small businesses closed on the normally tourist-thronged streets of Laugavegur and Skólavörðustígur, and people felt the financial pinch of the pandemic.

The coalition government, led by popular left-green prime minister Katrín Jakobsdóttir, pursued a pragmatic, science-based approach to COVID-19, and Icelanders adopted pandemic response measures with little fuss. Coupled with the ease of controlling access to an island nation, all this resulted in remarkably few deaths, with Iceland suffering only 153 COVID-19 fatalities from the start of the pandemic to the time of writing.

ICELANDIC AIRLINES

Iceland's turbulent airline industry has had passengers and investors fastening their seat belts as operators have come and gone. WOW Air, the budget Icelandic carrier whose 2019 bankruptcy left over 1,000 workers without jobs and passengers stranded, has since been alleged several times to rise from the ashes. Despite some noise and posturing nothing has yet come of that, but a new Icelandic operator has emerged to fill the void. Play Airlines offers various international routes and is headed by CEO Birgir Jónsson, who is not only a former WOW Air executive but was also, until 2018, the drummer in Icelandic heavy rock group DIMMA.

Even Icelandair—the national flag carrier—had a bumpy ride while the pandemic was at its peak, and was forced to take government bailouts to survive. But now that tourism is returning, a new operator has arisen to rival Icelandair on European routes. The quaintly-named Niceair flies to Denmark, Spain, and the United Kingdom non-stop from Akureyri, allowing northern Iceland to be directly connected to the wider world for the first time.

IMMIGRATION

Connections with the rest of Europe have brought influences that are slowly changing Icelandic culture. Although it remains outside the European Union, Iceland is a member of the European Economic Area which means that most European citizens are free to settle in Iceland without restriction. In 2021, foreigners living in Iceland made up almost 14% of the population—twice the amount from only seven years earlier. This increase reflects the growth of tourism in Iceland, as many of these new residents work in the hospitality and construction sectors.

Despite the challenges this influx of new residents has brought, such as the availability of housing, Icelanders are very tolerant by nature and these "new Icelanders" generally find themselves welcomed into their adopted society. So don't be surprised if your waiter is from Warsaw or your bus driver is from Bratislava; Icelandic society is more diverse than you think.

THE ICELANDIC LANGAUGE

The shifting make-up of the population often focuses attention on the current state and future of the Icelandic language. Unlike some other Germanic languages like English, Icelandic has not undergone much grammatical simplification over the centuries, and for many immigrants getting their head around it can be a considerable challenge.

Another issue facing the Icelandic language is the creeping incursion of English through global cinema and music, and via digital spaces where it is the lingua franca. Iceland has pushed back by eschewing common globally-adopted English terms for certain items of technology, leading to uniquely Icelandic words such as *tölva* for computer and *sími* for telephone.

Nearly all Icelandic people—especially the younger ones—speak excellent English. However their native tongue plays an important part in their sense of national identity, and locals always appreciate visitors making an effort to speak a few words of it.

ICELAND IN POP CULTURE

Icelanders are a creative bunch, and artistry of various types is embedded in the national DNA. This fact has helped Iceland's creative industries achieve significant international recognition; long gone are the days when Björk was the only Icelandic artist known beyond the island's shores.

In recent years, Icelandic musicians have been well-represented at American award ceremonies. In 2019 composer Hildur Guðnadóttir won both a Grammy and an Emmy for her soundtrack to the HBO series *Chernobyl*, then the following year swept up a Grammy, a Golden Globe, and an Oscar for her soundtrack to the film *Joker*. Close behind Guðnadóttir, Ólafur Arnalds—a punk rock drummer who turned to neoclassical composition—had two of his tracks nominated for Grammys in 2021. And it's not only the nation's composers that have been wowing American audiences. The Icelandic-language film *Lamb*—a supernatural thriller shot in rural locations near Akureyri—grossed more than $1 million in U.S. cinemas over its opening weekend in 2021.

What to Eat and Drink in Iceland

Soup in a bread bowl

SOUP IN A BREAD BOWL
At Svarta Kaffið, a little upstairs café on Reykjavík's Laugavegur, two hearty soups are offered daily—one with meat, one without—and served inside loaves of bread hollowed out to make edible bowls.

HOT DOGS
Pylsur (hot dogs) are Iceland's go-to fast food. Bæjarins Beztu Pylsur serves up budget-friendly dogs, fresh and hot, at its historic kiosk in downtown Reykjavík. Order like a local and ask for *ein með öllu* (one with everything), to get yours with tomato sauce, *pylsusinnep* (a sweet brown mustard), and both fried and raw onions.

SKYR
Like yogurt but thicker and a tad more sour, skyr is a dairy product enthusiastically consumed by Icelanders, starting with its earliest settlers.

LAMB
The sheep which adorn the Icelandic landscape also grace its dinner tables with several of the nation's signature dishes. Whether

Lobster

as chops, cutlets, or *kjötsúpa*, (soup), the island's lamb is renowned for its high quality.

LOBSTER
In Iceland it's more likely to be a langoustine, but let's not split hairs; it's very close in appearance and flavor to its larger southern cousin. An annual lobster festival called Humarhátíð takes place in Höfn every June.

HARÐFISKUR
For most of the last millennium, the fishing industry has been a mainstay of the Icelandic economy. Harðfiskur is cod (or sometimes other fish) that's dried as a means of preserving the catch, and often eaten as a snack. These fish can be spotted air-drying on outdoor racks in more rural coastal areas (the stiff Icelandic breeze keeps the flies off).

ROTTEN SHARK AND TESTICLES
Iceland is often touted as a place to experience some unusual delicacies. Fermented shark and skate, boiled sheep's head, and ram's testicles all join the slightly less out-there offerings of puffin and whale on the list of historically odd Icelandic dishes. These days locals aren't tucking into such dishes on a daily basis, but some are still laid out for specific holidays. For example, *kæst skata* (ammonia-scented fermented skate) is eaten at the pre-Christmas celebration of Þorláksmessa. And *svið*, comprising half a sheep's head boiled with the brains removed, is associated with the Þorrablót winter festival.

ICE CREAM
Icelandic ice cream tends to be super creamy and very rich, and it's not just

for summer. It's enthusiastically consumed all year-round, whatever the weather.

BRENNIVÍN
Iceland's signature spirit, Brennivín is a clear drink distilled from grain and flavored with caraway. It is traditionally consumed during the winter feast of Þorrablót alongside *hákarl* (fermented shark).

AKUREYRINGUR
Akureyri has its own unusual culinary combination: Akureyringur, a hamburger with French fries cooked into it.

GULL BEER
This easy-drinking lager is Iceland's most prominent macrobrew. With mild flavors of grain and fruit, Gull has been around since beer prohibition was lifted in 1989.

Best Museums in Iceland

THE LAVA CENTRE, HVOLSVÖLLUR

Another of Iceland's remarkable immersive museums takes visitors inside of the country's famous volcanoes. Creative red lighting immediately conjures up the illusion of being surrounded by hot magma while exhibits showcase the powerful systems in place to track earthquakes, lava flow, and other seismic activity.

PERLAN, REYKJAVÍK

Perched high on a hill, this glass-domed exhibition center is unmissable. Explore the 100-meter ice cave, made from mountain ice, snow, and volcanic ash. Then experience Áróra, a high-resolution planetarium show on the northern lights. And when you're done, you can zipline off the roof down into the surrounding forest.

THE NATIONAL MUSEUM OF ICELAND, REYKJAVÍK

This museum presents the evolution of Iceland over the past 1,000 years, from the ships that brought the original settlers to the airport that Icelanders use today. Thousands of artifacts, including skeletons of ancient islanders and their horses, help to illustrate the story.

SKÓGAR MUSEUM, SKÓGAR

Skógar presents the architectural and technological history of the country, from turf houses to modern transportation. There's also a folk museum on-site dedicated to the collection and preservation of more than 15,000 individual items reflective of Iceland's cultural heritage.

THE ICELANDIC SEA MONSTER MUSEUM, BÍLDUDALUR

Located in the coastal village of Bíldudalur in the Westfjords, this highly interactive museum takes visitors through the stories and sightings of the various monsters in Iceland's nautical lore.

THE SAGA MUSEUM, REYKJAVÍK

Iceland's history has been on record since the first settlers arrived to find a barren land of ice and fire. Using lifelike animatronics, the Saga Museum takes visitors through 17 stories from different eras that have helped shape Iceland into the country we know and love today.

The Lava Centre

REYKJAVÍK ART MUSEUM, REYKJAVÍK
Down by the waterside, the oldest part of Reykjavík hosts a marvelous art museum in Hafnarhús, a former harbor warehouse. Stroll its spacious galleries for an overview of what is currently pushing the buttons of Iceland's art scene. The museum is also home to thousands of pieces of art by Erró, Iceland's most famous artist and friend to both Lichtenstein and Warhol.

THE MUSEUM OF ICELANDIC WITCH-CRAFT AND SORCERY, HÓLMAVÍK
This museum takes visitors back to a time when Icelandic witches (usually men, interestingly enough) were feared, persecuted, and commonly burned alive. On display are the runes and spells associated with the craft as well as a pair of necropants: the skin of the bottom half of a man, removed intact to be worn as a gruesome pair of trousers.

THE REYKJAVÍK MARITIME MUSEUM, REYKJAVÍK
Iceland's past and present are inextricably linked to the sea, and this museum in the capital's old harbor area presents a lively and informative account of that relationship. The Fish and Folk exhibit investigates how the fishing industry still sits at the heart of the nation's economy, and don't miss the chance to take a guided tour of Óðinn, a former coast guard vessel.

Iceland's Best Waterfalls

HRAUNFOSSAR

Hraunfossar is a series of falls created by rivulets streaming out of the Hallmundarhraun lava field, spread out over nearly 3,000 feet. The stunning color of the water changes daily: at times it's crystal-clear or turquoise, at other times a creamy white.

SVARTIFOSS

Svartifoss in Skaftafell National Park is flanked by tall columns of basalt rock. Don't step into the basin below the falls; the riverbed is full of sharp rocks, a hidden danger amid otherwise ethereal surroundings. A marked trail leads from the park up to the falls.

SKÓGAFOSS

This waterfall can be found on the drive between Reykjavík and Vik í Mýrdal (commonly known simply as Vík), just past Seljalandsfoss. Skógafoss—named after the Skóga River that feeds it—is visible from the main road, and there's a hostel and a restaurant within walking distance.

SELJALANDSFOSS

If you have only a few days (or even hours) in Reykjavík and want to explore the wilderness, consider visiting Seljalandsfoss. Fed by a river that starts in the Eyjafjallajökull volcano, it's the first major waterfall you'll hit on the route to Vík, less than two hours from the capital by car. The charm of Seljalandsfoss is that you can walk behind the falls, but be extremely careful: the rocks and mud are quite slippery at all times of year. And make sure to bring a waterproof layer if you plan on taking a stroll behind the falls; you'll absolutely emerge much wetter than expected.

GULLFOSS

This panoramic waterfall is located on the Golden Circle route in Þingvellir National Park, less than two hours from Reykjavík by car. Gullfoss means "Golden Waterfall," and it drops a total of 105 feet in two different sections. The nearby Gullfoss Café is the perfect spot to grab a cup of coffee after you've been awed—and probably soaked—by the waterfall's mighty display and the resultant mist. You'll encounter large crowds at Gullfoss, but the views are worth it.

ÖXARÁRFOSS

Unlike many of Iceland's waterfalls, Öxarárfoss is completely hidden from the Ring Road, despite being located quite close to it. The 44-foot cascade may be tiny, but its surroundings will steal your heart. Just a 40-minute drive from Reykjavík, there's a small parking lot on the side of

Seljalandsfoss

Route 36 and a set of stairs that leads down into the canyon. There, you'll find yourself between the two tectonic plates that make Þingvellir National Park so special. Legend has it that on New Year's Eve, this waterfall would run red with either wine or blood—revealing whether the year ahead would be full of prosperity or impending war. Some locals still celebrate the holiday with a toast near the falls.

DETTIFOSS
The most powerful waterfall in all of Europe can be found at the end of a gravel road in North Iceland. Dettifoss pushes 110,000 gallons of water to the ground every second.

GLYMUR
Set aside an entire afternoon to visit this impressive waterfall, as seeing it involves a four-hour hike there and back. Tumbling a full 643 feet, it is among the highest of Iceland's falls. Follow the yellow cairns to get to the falls, as there are other trails that lead away from the waterfall path.

HRAFNABJARGAFOSS
This impressive cascade is a hidden gem, tucked away in Iceland's north and certainly off the beaten track. It forms part of Skjálfandafljót, one of Iceland's longest rivers, and is located in the northern part of Vatnajökull National Park. Given its location off a gravel road, it's only accessible in the summer and even then only by 4WD vehicles.

GOÐAFOSS
With a name meaning "Waterfall of the Gods," Goðafoss has an interesting history. After the priest Þorgeir Ljósvetningagoði decided that Iceland should convert to Christianity, he traveled to this waterfall to throw his idols of the old Norse gods into the water.

Icelandic Wildlife

SEALS

Several species of seal spend time in Iceland, but only grey seals and harbor seals call the country home year-round. The most reliable place to look for them is the Vatnsnes Peninsula in northwest Iceland, which includes the Icelandic Seal Centre in the town of Hvammstangi.

WHALES

Although less active in recent years, Iceland still faces a lot of criticism for continuing its practice of commercial whaling. One way for visitors to oppose this practice is to support the industry of whale-watching. This shows the Icelandic government that there is more money in keeping whales alive than putting them on menus. Many whale, dolphin, and porpoise species call Iceland's rich waters home—in fact, Iceland is considered the whale-watching capital of Europe—and a multitude of whale-watching tours embark from the larger coastal towns. April through October is the best time to go, but tours are offered year-round.

MINK

Originally brought from Norway to Iceland in 1931, mink began populating the wild after escaping the cages that were supposed to hold them until they were harvested for fur. With plentiful prey and a total lack of predators, the North American mink has thrived in Iceland since its introduction. Unfortunately, its presence has negatively affected native wildlife, which happens when foreign species are left to run amok in a new environment. Mink are semi-aquatic creatures and can be found near seashores, river banks, and other concentrations of fresh water.

REINDEER

Another species introduced to Iceland, reindeer made their way from Norway back in the 18th century. These gentle invaders have done less ecological damage than their mink friends, remaining largely isolated in Iceland's east. In summer herds can be found gathering around Snæfellsjökull, in Vesturöræfi and Brúaröræfi, and even as far south as the Jökulsárlón glacier lagoon.

WHITE-TAILED EAGLES

Sometimes referred to as "sea eagles," these birds may be Iceland's most majestic species. With wingspans ranging up to a massive eight feet, the white-tailed eagle seems hard to miss but in fact it's one of the most elusive creatures on the island. The western area of Iceland (particularly the Breiðfjörður region) affords the best chances for spotting this massive raptor. Fortunately for bird lovers—and less fortunately for sheep farmers—the white-tailed eagle population is on the rise, making casual sightings more likely than ever.

Arctic foxes

ARCTIC TERNS

It's nearly impossible to visit Iceland without encountering the Arctic tern: a small seabird with striking coloration, most notably its bright orange legs and beak. These birds migrate farther than any other animal on the planet, summering in Iceland and other parts of the Arctic. It isn't just their beauty and their migratory prowess that makes these birds so remarkable; their ferocity is also widely renowned. Arctic terns are known to aggressively protect their nests, dive-bombing anything that steps close, regardless of its size. Arctic terns are ground nesters and their spotted eggs and chicks blend in very easily to Icelandic grasses, making them too easy to miss and accidentally tread upon.

Visitors should take care to avoid triggering a defensive response in these birds, as it requires them to use energy that could otherwise be used for foraging or warming their eggs.

ATLANTIC PUFFINS

It's true that Atlantic puffins are available for consumption at many restaurants in Iceland, but most visitors interested in puffins are looking to see them happily alive in the wild. After all, Iceland is home to the largest Atlantic puffin colony in the world, with huge numbers arriving to the Vestmannaeyjar (Westman Islands) off the southern coast in order to breed. The second-best place to spot them is the scenic Látrabjarg bird cliffs in the Westfjords.

ARCTIC FOXES

Iceland's only native land mammal is arguably its cutest. These little carnivores can be white, especially in the winter, though their brown and gray morphs are more commonly seen. The best opportunity to see arctic foxes is in the Westfjords, where their food supply is plentiful and human encroachment is minimal. Foxes are protected in the Hornstrandir Nature Reserve, making them relatively easy to spot in the wild. The Arctic Fox Centre in Súðavík offers a wide range of information, and sometimes they even rehabilitate orphaned kits or injured adults, offering visitors a chance to see them up-close.

Icelandic Musicians

BJÖRK

Arguably the most famous musician to come out of Iceland, Björk is weird in the most wonderful of ways. Her performances border on theater and her music is simply haunting. The Reykjavík-born singer released her first album when she was only 12, and went on to become a founding member of alt-rock band the Sugarcubes before going solo. Her 1993 debut album as an adult—entitled *Debut*—was a major international success, and provided a heads-up for many music lovers outside Iceland that there was something going on here.

OF MONSTERS AND MEN

Reykjavík's foremost purveyors of indie folk-rock came together in 2009 around the solo project of singer-guitarist Nanna Bryndís Hilmarsdóttir. Three studio albums later the band finds itself a firm favorite of fans around the world, with all three of those releases (*My Head Is An Animal* from 2011, *Beneath The Skin* from 2015, and *Fever Dream* from 2019) making it into the U.S. Billboard Top 10.

SIGUR RÓS

Sigur Rós has been filling our ears with their glorious avant-rock sounds since 1994. Formed in Reykjavík by singer and guitarist Jón Þór "Jónsi" Birgisson, bassist Georg Holm, and drummer Ágúst Ævar Gunnarsson, the line-up has shifted through the years with Jónsi and Georg the only constants. Multi-instrumentalist Kjartan Sveinsson is the band's third mainstay, and recently rejoined after a nine-year break. Their grand, ethereal soundscapes comprise some highly distinctive elements: Jónsi's guitar played with a cello bow; his pure, falsetto vocals; and lyrics in a mixture of Icelandic and Vonlenska, the band's very own made-up language. Visuals are highly important to the group, who painstakingly create beautiful videos for their songs and pay a great deal of attention to their stage sets. Sigur Rós recently made the wrong kind of headlines due to a protracted battle with the Icelandic authorities over alleged tax evasion (which the band won). A good entry point to the Sigur Rós catalog is *Með Suð Í Eyrum Við Spilum Endalaust,* their poppier-than-usual album from 2008.

EMILÍANA TORRINI

Chances are that you've already heard one of Emilíana Torrini's songs, even if you've never heard her name. The Italian-Icelandic singer-songwriter is the voice of "Gollum's Song" from the film *The Lord of the Rings: The Two Towers*. And in 2009 she released her biggest single—the very catchy "Jungle Drum"—to international acclaim. But her songwriting goes beyond her own releases, and she has her name on the Kylie Minogue songs "Slow" and "Someday" as a co-writer. Emilíana's adventurous approach to creating music has seen her work on two albums with the Colorist Orchestra, the Belgian ensemble who specialize in taking their collaboration partner's back catalog and giving it an entirely new spin.

ÓLAFUR ARNALDS

There's a distinct polymathic trait among Icelandic creatives, and Mosfellsbær musician Ólafur Arnalds is a fine example. Over the course of his career he has moved from drumming in hardcore punk groups to neo-classical piano composition, even managing to fit in a side gig as an inventor. He developed Stratus—a system of two self-playing, semi-generative pianos—in collaboration with composer and audio developer Halldor Eldjarn. The device features on Ólafur's remarkable 2018 album *Re:member,* but it was his next release (*Some Kind Of*

Peace) that delivered him global attention and two Grammy nominations. Either of these two records would make a fine introduction to his work, although you may already know it from the soundtrack to the TV series *Broadchurch.*

VÍKINGUR ÓLAFSSON
If you like your classical music in the more traditional style, then Reykjavík native Víkingur might be your man. The talented pianist has been awarded accolades around the world for his work, which he first released on his own label before moving to prestigious classical label Deutsche Grammophon. He has scored films and founded Reykjavík Midsummer Music, an annual chamber music festival. Interestingly Víkingur experiences synesthesia, a condition which causes a person to "see" specific colors when they hear particular musical notes.

SÓLEY
Sóley Stefánsdóttir studied Piano Arts at the Icelandic Art Academy, and those well-honed skills are front and center in most of her songs. Her compositions are introspective and often incorporate her personal fears, thoughts, and hopes. In fact, Sóley's 2017 album *Endless Summer* was inspired by a note the musician wrote to herself after waking up in the middle of the night: "Write about hope and spring." But if that album was about hope, her powerful 2021 album *Mother Melancholia* was less positive, musing on the retribution which Mother Earth is now meting out on the humans who have abused her. Sóley's imagination also leads to remarkable videos for her music; check out the short film for her song "Sunrise Skulls," which she made with filmmaker Samantha Shay.

GUSGUS
For close to three decades now, GusGus has been creating electronic music that has become loved around the world. Originally their intention was to create a film and music collective; the latter won out as a priority, and the rotating cast of creatives has since released some 11 studio albums. It was their second album *Polydistortion*—released on legendary British label 4AD, with vocal contributions from Emilíana Torrini—which launched them beyond Icelandic shores. The current incarnation of GusGus comprises founding members Biggi Veira and Daníel Ágúst, joined recently by vocalist Margrét Rán from electronica outfit Vök.

LAUFEY
Laufey Lin Jónsdóttir (known simply by her first name like many Icelandic musicians) came to prominence through posting videos of herself performing from her home during the pandemic lock-down. The young Reyjkavík resident has a classic jazz singing style reminiscent of Billie Holiday, and accompanies herself on guitar, piano, or even cello.

HATARI
This industrial techno BDSM bad boy goth trio have been around since 2015, when cousins Klemens Hannigan and Matthías Haraldsson got together with drummer Einar Stefánsson to make some noise. Since then the Icelandic alternative music scene has embraced the trio—whose name means "hater"—and their ironic, supercilious persona. Hatari grabbed the world's attention in 2019 by getting sent to Israel to represent Iceland in the Eurovision Song Contest, only to unfurl Palestinian flags on live TV in front of 20 million viewers. It's safe to say that their hosts were not impressed, but it certainly got Hatari noticed.

Icelandic Mythology and Folklore

Mythology pervades modern Icelandic culture. Widespread belief in elves proves Iceland's affinity with the supernatural, as does the revival of the ancient religion of Ásatrú. Norse mythology accompanied the first intrepid settlers of the island more than a thousand years ago, and plenty of lore has enriched the lives of Icelanders since then.

ELVES

Known as the *huldufólk* or "hidden people," Icelandic elves aren't that different from humans—just a bit more magical. They remain out of sight in enchanted caves and rocks except on special occasions, when a few lucky humans may spot them wandering. Keep an eye out on New Year's Eve and midsummer in particular; you never know what you may see.

THE YULE LADS

These 13 characters, the offspring of monstrous couple Grýla and Leppalúði, take turns visiting human children in the 13 nights leading up to Christmas. Each has a specific way of making mischief, reflected in their names, such as Door-Slammer or Skyr-Gobbler, and until recent times they were used by parents to frighten unruly youngsters into compliance. These days they're portrayed more as lovable rogues, and the prospect of their visits is more a source of seasonal wonder than nocturnal terror.

THE YULE CAT

Jólakötturinn or "the Yule Cat" is said to be owned by the Yule Lads and their half-ogre, half-troll mother, Grýla. The story goes that Jólakötturinn will devour anyone who does not receive new clothes for Christmas, so better ask Santa for some socks if you're going to be visiting over the festive season.

SEA MONSTERS

Vikings journeyed across the bitter Arctic waters to settle on this desolate island, and today Icelanders still rely on the sea for survival. The presence of sea monsters could spell disaster for those taking to the water, so there are seemingly endless myths that describe supernatural predators hunting fearful fishermen. The Sea Monster Museum in the Westfjords town of Bíldudalur is the best place to hear more about these encounters.

TROLLS

Many of Iceland's unique natural features are attributed to the actions of trolls, like Naustahvilft, or the Troll Seat. This hikeable mountain looks exactly like what would happen if a troll, with all his great weight, sat upon a mountain. In Reynisfjara, near the famous black-sand beach of Vík, hexagonal basalt columns rise 216 feet from the ground, a leftover from trolls dragging their ships to shore, getting there too late, and turning to stone in the sun.

THE LAND WIGHTS

One of the Icelandic sagas describes an incident in which the fearsome King Harald Bluetooth (yes, the wireless technology is named after him) intended to invade Iceland and had his sorcerer morph into a whale to find the island's weak spots. But each time the whale-sorcerer tried to land, a *landvættir*, or "land wight," fought him off, thus creating the four guardians of Iceland. A wight in the form of a dragon protected Iceland's Eastfjords, while North Iceland had an eagle; in the Westfjords a bull fought the whale off, and finally in South Iceland, a giant finished the job. Images of these wights are pervasive in Iceland, adorning the Icelandic coat of arms, certain coins, and government buildings.

Icelandic Beer

Given the popular international image of Vikings as boozy marauders, one might think that their Icelandic descendents would be born with beer for blood. But Icelanders' relationship with alcohol—and beer in particular— as not always been an easy one.

In 1915, prompted by the temperance movement, Iceland banned all alcohol. A mere six years later, when Spain refused to buy Icelandic fish unless the reciprocal trade in Spanish wine was reintroduced, reds and rosés quickly reappeared on Icelandic tables. The return of spirits followed in the 1930s, but full-strength beer remained forbidden; only low-alcohol (light beer) was allowed.

The beer ban persisted due to the fact that many Icelanders took a dim view of consuming the stuff. Beer drinking was closely associated with the Danes who, by ruling Iceland until 1944, had created resentment among the local population. Also, there seems to have been a belief that children were more easily tempted by beer than by other alcoholic drinks.

However by the 1980s, these attitudes had shifted, and in any case Icelanders had long been finding inventive ways around the ban, including creating a mock full-strength beer by simply dumping a shot of spirits in their léttbjör. The Icelandic parliament officially repealed the law effective March 1, 1989, a date now annually commemorated as Bjórdagurinn (Beer Day).

In the years since beer has become a staple booze for many Icelanders, with big breweries and craft beer producers popping up to slake Icelandic thirsts. Here's a guide to the best brews and brewers in the land.

ÖLGERÐIN EGILL SKALLAGRÍMSSON

This Reykjavík brewery is Iceland's oldest, starting production just two years before prohibition kicked in. It's also one of the biggest these days, and produces the ubiquitous Egils Gull (meaning "gold"), an easy-drinking lager with mild flavors of grain and fruit. It's the beer you're most likely to encounter by default in Iceland's bars and restaurants.

VIÍKING

Another major player in the Icelandic brewing industry, this subsidiary of Coca-Cola produces its wares in the northern town of Akureyri. Try their premium product Gylltur (another word for "gold"), a slightly bitter, fairly strong pale lager.

THE LADY BREWERY

When Ragnheiður "Raxel" Axel and Þórey Björk Halldórsdóttir started Reykjavík's Lady Brewery—Iceland's first craft beer producer to be owned and operated by women—only 3% of Icelandic breweries were female-owned. They hope that their initiative will help close the brewing industry's gaping gender gap. Groups can sample their wares, such as the excellently named Drink Like A Girl, at the House Of Lady in the city's harbor area.

EINSTÖK

Perhaps internationally the best known of Icelandic craft beer producers is Einstök, the Akureyri brewery with a Viking's head logo. Their line-up features lagers, pale ales, porters, and more, including a seasonal summer brew with hand-picked bilberries.

What to Watch and Read

GAME OF THRONES

Many scenes set in the frozen north of the blockbuster hit HBO television show *Game of Thrones* were filmed on location in the frozen north of Iceland. Perhaps the most memorable was the infamous subterranean hot spring scenario, in which Jon Snow finally got together with wildling Ygritte. You can visit the steamy site of that encounter in the Grjótagjá Cave near lake Mývatn.

THE NORTHMAN

American director Robert Eggers delivered this epic viking saga to the big screen in 2022, having co-written the screenplay with noted Icelandic author and poet Sjón. The plot, loosely based on a tale by the medieval Danish scholar Saxo Grammaticus, revolves around a 10th-century Norse prince who sails to Iceland to save his mother and exact bloody revenge on his uncle for killing his father.

But even the presence of legendary Nordic warriors couldn't prevent the pandemic from taking a battle ax to the film's production schedule, and the location shoots planned to take place around Iceland in the spring of 2020 had to be relocated to Ireland. Consequently only a couple of shots of genuine Icelandic landscape made the final cut, although the magic of digital post-production did allow a golden beach in County Donegal to morph into the iconic black sands of Reynisfjara.

EUROVISION SONG CONTEST: THE STORY OF FIRE SAGA

For reasons nobody really understands, Icelanders love the Eurovision Song Contest, the annual musical competition into which each European nation enters its champion artist to do battle by song. Iceland has entered the fray every year since 1986, and has never once won. But that doesn't stop it from trying.

This theme of hope against the odds runs through this Netflix movie starring Will Ferrell and Rachael McAdams, where they play a musical duo from Húsavík who luck their way into representing their nation at Eurovision. American clichés about Iceland abound throughout the film, but it's done with affection, and on the movie's release Icelanders appreciated its warmth and took it to their hearts. The film (and one of its main songs) also brought the town of Húsavík international attention, and its been reaping the rewards of a marked uptick in tourist interest ever since.

LAMB

This supernatural Icelandic film will be familiar to many Americans since it took in over a million dollars at U.S. theaters on its opening weekend in 2021. In Valdimar Jóhannssons's extraordinary directorial debut, a young childless couple farm sheep in a remote part of the north. They're taken aback when one of their ewes gives birth to something unusual, but they take a special interest in the lamb and decide to raise it themselves. However the strain of the bizarre situation which subsequently unfolds causes their carefully constructed world to unravel. This unsettling tale of nurture versus nature was shot around an abandoned farm near Akureyri, the beautiful but bleak locations powerfully conveying a sense of hidden malevolence in the wild Icelandic landscape.

RAMS

Another Icelandic film about sheep, but this time the cause of the drama is human rather than bestial. Two brothers live on neighboring farms, but haven't spoken to each other in 40 years. When their flocks are infected by scrapie, their very existence is threatened and they're forced to reconcile their differences to face a common foe. You may have seen the somewhat pointless Australian remake of this film, but don't let that put you off. The 2015 original has a slow-paced charm, providing authentic reflections of Icelandic character—self-reliance and fortitude with a streak of stubbornness—as well as some stunning rural locations.

CHILDREN OF NATURE
This charming Icelandic love story, released in 1991, was nominated for an Oscar in the best foreign language category. When Þorgeir becomes too old to continue his life as a farmer in the countryside, he moves to the city to join his daughter's family. However, he is not really welcome and ends up in a home for the elderly where he chances upon Stella, a love from his youth. Rekindling their relationship, he hotwires a jeep and they abscond to rediscover the lives that they once led when they were more connected to nature. The film affords a glimpse into an Iceland before mass tourism, one which visitors today are unlikely to see again.

DREAMLAND
Today Iceland is an advanced modern state, but only a couple of generations ago fishing and farming sustained the modest national economy. The natural resources now powering Iceland's buoyant times (tourism and cheap energy) comprised a sleeping economic giant back then. The relative newness of all this prosperity makes it natural for Icelanders to ask: what if it all falls apart?

Dreamland, which was released in early 2009, probes that particular national neurosis by shining a light on events just before the 2008 financial crash. Iceland's economically motivated attempts to retain American military bases on the island come under scrutiny, as does the highly controversial construction of the Kárahnjúkar dam and power station.

This project flooded huge expanses of untouched nature in the Highlands—affecting an area equal to around 3% of Iceland's surface—so that a foreign corporation could build an aluminum smelting plant.

TRAPPED
This excellent TV crime drama, produced by Iceland's public broadcaster RÚV, first debuted in 2015 and went on to become an international hit with three seasons to date. When the first was filmed (largely on location in Siglufjörður, Seyðisfjörður, and Reykjavík), it was the most expensive Icelandic TV show ever produced.

A Nordic-noir feel runs through each season as the murkier elements of Icelandic society— racism, corruption, human-trafficking, and the like—are brought to the surface. And great use is made of the brooding Icelandic landscape, with deep fjords giving up headless human torsos and avalanches cutting off communities with a murderer loose in their midst.

BLACKPORT
Another Icelandic TV series that was a smash hit at home, Blackport's first episode was watched by more than half the local population when RÚV screened it in 2021. This drama, set in the 1980s, follows the misadventures and machinations of four friends who find themselves riding the wave of an Icelandic fishing gold-rush. Money is made in huge amounts, leading to government-imposed quotas, fractious relationships, jealousy, and betrayal. The series won several international prizes and, in addition to being popular with Icelanders just for being a darn good yarn, it also received love from older viewers for its '80s nostalgia value. For non-Icelanders it's a fascinating glimpse into how today's complex Icelandic society has evolved, fairly recently, from its fishing and farming roots.

ÁRAMÓTASKAUPIÐ

If you're lucky enough to be in Iceland on New Year's Eve, then be sure to take part in the Icelandic television tradition of Áramótaskaupið. The truth is that you may have little choice, as pretty much every Icelander stops whatever they're doing at 10:30 pm to watch this satirical review of the year. In 2021, more than 70% of Icelanders tuned in.

A fixture in the national cultural calendar since 1966, this series of skits airs with English subtitles and is a great way to understand what has been on Icelandic minds over the past twelve months. If you're in Reykjavík you can tell when Áramótaskaupið has started: the barrage of fireworks set off by exuberant residents suddenly falls silent while they gather around their TVs, and only kicks off again once the show has finished.

THE LITTLE BOOK OF ICELANDERS BY ALDA SIGMUNDSDÓTTIR

Born in Reykjavík but raised and schooled in Canada, Alda Sigmundsdóttir returned to the country of her birth a foreigner after a couple of decades away. But Sigmundsdóttir still retained an innate understanding of the Icelandic people and their ways, a fact which eventually led her to pen this collection of pithy observations. Topics include Icelanders' driving habits, their profound fear of commitment, and how they manage to make social interactions really complicated.

THE HISTORY OF ICELAND BY GUNNAR KARLSSON

Gunnar Karlsson is a professor of history at the University of Iceland, a fact unlikely to be lost on those who venture into this scholarly tome. The content is precisely as described on the jacket, but among the statistics, dates, and tables, the author has sprinkled personal anecdotes and memories to lift the tone above that of a mere textbook. Probably best appreciated by those of an academic persuasion, it is nonetheless a good primer for any visitor to Iceland who desires a deeper understanding of its history.

INDEPENDENT PEOPLE BY HALLDÓR LAXNESS

This classic novel, written by Icelandic Nobel Prize–winning author Halldór Laxness in the 1930s, is Icelandic spirit distilled to its essence. The book is required reading for foreign students taking the Icelandic Culture course at the University of Iceland, and is recommended reading for any visitor seeking background material to enhance their trip.

Set against a bleak rural Icelandic backdrop, it's a tale of life, love, hardships, and betrayals as experienced by one farmer and his family in the early 20th century. The rich history of Icelandic culture is woven through the story, with characters living by the lore of hidden folk and ancient curses and the lead character, Guðbjartur, portrayed as a talented poet in the best Icelandic tradition.

THE EDDAS AND SAGAS

Thanks to the Norse people's rich storytelling tradition, Icelandic tales over the past thousand years have been diligently recorded in collections of stories known as the Eddas and Sagas. From dragon slayers to the complicated relationships of the Norse gods, the Eddas and Sagas provide invaluable context for this country.

Chapter 2

TRAVEL SMART

Updated by
John Pearson

★ **CAPITAL:**
Reykjavík

👥 **POPULATION:**
376,000

💬 **LANGUAGE:**
Icelandic

$ **CURRENCY:**
Icelandic króna

☎ **COUNTRY CODE:**
354

⚠ **EMERGENCIES:**
112

🚗 **DRIVING:**
On the right side

⚡ **ELECTRICITY:**
220 volts/50 cycles; electrical
plugs have two round prongs

🕐 **TIMEZONE:**
Four hours ahead of New
York during Daylight Savings
Time; five hours ahead
otherwise

🌐 **WEB RESOURCES:**
www.inspiredbyiceland.com
www.visiticeland.com

Know Before You Go

With a population of only around 376,000 people, there is a strong sense of community throughout Iceland. This makes it extremely easy and safe for visitors, but there are a few tips and tricks to remember when it comes to having a great trip.

EVERYONE SPEAKS ENGLISH.

The Icelandic language is a complex beast, and often touted as one of the hardest in the world to learn. So visitors should be grateful that the vast majority of Icelanders speak English, many of them fluently and in addition to other languages. It's common to hear locals using it, in particular younger people who are more likely to spend time in English-speaking digital environments. Many Icelandic websites will have a well-translated English option, (often accessed by clicking a British flag rather than an American one). Much credit for this proficiency can be given to schools, but a lot of American and British media is consumed in Iceland too, making colloquial (rather than formal) English the standard. Locals appreciate visitors trying out a few words of Icelandic, and may even offer an impromptu language lesson.

THE FOOD IS MORE DIVERSE THAN YOU THINK.

Food in Iceland is often portrayed as strange, with great emphasis on preservation techniques rather than flavor. It's true that traditional dishes like fermented shark (*hákarl*) and sour ram's testicles (*hrútspungar*) are eaten in Iceland, but this hardly captures the breadth of the Icelandic palate. Iceland's status as an island and three-time winner of the Cod Wars—fought against the United Kingdom over Atlantic fishing rights—ensures that its cuisine is rich in seafood. Meals can be hearty, delicate, land-based, sea-based, healthy, junky—there's so much to discover. And because Iceland has been largely self-sufficient for so long, much of its food comes from local sources: fresh ingredients are grown in greenhouses and livestock is farmed throughout the country. Note that while infamous Icelandic foods like whale and puffin are available (mostly in Reykjavík), most locals don't actually eat them.

STRIP BEFORE YOU DIP.

Americans often find themselves confronting their hang-ups about nudity when visiting Iceland, because Icelanders seem to have none—at least when it comes to going for a swim. One big frustration that locals have with visitors comes down to locker-room etiquette: in Iceland, it is customary to shower fully nude, washing the entire body before donning a swimsuit and heading into the pool. Tourists who try to get away with not performing this routine often learn that Icelanders are not shy about calling out rule-dodging bathers. Things aren't so strict at the Blue Lagoon, where it's predominantly foreigners in the water, but this just perpetuates a false idea that this behavior is acceptable at other public pools and hot springs in the country. And since visiting the community swimming pool is often an important activity in a town, it's important to take this custom to heart. If shower facilities are present near a shared body of water, do yourself—and all of Iceland—a favor, and get washing.

ALCOHOL IS HARD TO BUY.

Drinking in Iceland is notoriously expensive, which is why many travelers opt not to procure their liquor from bars and restaurants. What many don't plan for, however, is that drinks with alcohol content over 2.25% are not readily available, so party planning is imperative. Iceland's 52 liquor stores—called Vínbúðin—are all operated by the government, and they charge way more for wine, beer, and liquor than Americans are used to paying. Plus, to help restrict the consumption of alcohol, store hours are limited. Vinbuðin shops typically shut at 6 pm, although those in bigger towns might close an hour or two later on certain days. Those in small towns are sometimes only open for two hours, and none anywhere are open on Sunday. Wise visitors know that the best place to buy alcohol is from the well-stocked duty-free shop at Keflavík airport when they arrive (limits do apply; see ⊕ www.dutyfree. is/en/allowance-calculator).

ICELANDERS ARE PROUD OF THEIR CULTURE.

The first question Icelanders ask a stranger is often along the lines of "How are you liking Iceland?" This is both a custom and something of an inside joke, because there's only one answer: you love their country. Icelanders really like being Icelandic and aren't particularly interested in hearing from those who are less than enchanted with their visit (which frankly doesn't happen too often). Whether it's being home to the strongest men in the world, producing well-known musicians, or just having created a remarkably tolerant society, Icelanders are proud of who they are. And, out of respect, it's best not to bring critiques to the conversation.

THERE CAN BE TOO MUCH AND TOO LITTLE LIGHT.

Extremes are the norm in Iceland, and one which often shocks visitors is the shift in the amount of daylight through the year. Winter is the best time to see the northern lights as you need a nice dark sky, but that means you may see as little as four hours of daylight per day. In summer you can experience the midnight sun, when it seems to barely dip below the horizon at night and leaves the country in a state of "perma-daylight." Both experiences can be disorienting, and preparation is key for adapting to these unfamiliar daylight patterns. Depression and foul moods can be a side effect of diminished sunlight, so bring vitamin D supplements—or even a seasonal affective disorder (SAD) lamp—to fill in for the sun. Without darkness the body has trouble establishing an internal clock, so it's essential to simulate night—whether by wearing an eye mask or taking melatonin—or find another way of triggering sleep.

DON'T DISRESPECT THE ELVES.

The Icelandic reputation for belief in the supernatural is certainly exaggerated, but it's still important to respect that more than half of the population accept the existence of huldufólk (hidden folk), or elves. Iceland is a land of rich written history, with myths and stories forming an important part of Icelandic culture. Credence

in tall tales is therefore more widespread than in other places, and even if an Icelander doesn't subscribe to elf lore themself, they probably respect the fact that their countrymen might. Icelandic tolerance will lead them to see no reason to judge others for that, and visitors should follow their lead.

TAKE THE WEATHER SERIOUSLY.

Weather is a quaint topic of conversation for most Americans, but in Iceland it carries a lot more importance. Icelandic weather is unpredictable, wild, and often dangerous, so there's never a shortage of pertinent weather-related news to share. So much Icelandic culture is built around weather phenomena that it puzzles Icelanders when foreigners don't heed posted road conditions or weather alerts. Wind and rain akin to a tropical hurricane can spring up from nowhere in the winter, with walls of falling snow capable of obscuring vision entirely. Iceland is on top of warning people about these occurrences, and visitors can access this information through websites like ⊕ vedur.is and ⊕ road. is. Iceland has a stellar volunteer rescue service, but the rise in tourism has been accompanied by increasing national frustration as teams are deployed to fetch silly tourists who ignored weather warnings. In all circumstances, it's best to follow the advice of the experts.

Getting Here and Around

Getting into and around Iceland is an adventure in and of itself, but with proper planning, it can be easily mastered. You'll likely arrive at Keflavík Airport, the country's main port of entry. But if you've come by ferry from Denmark, you'll find yourself in Seyðisfjörður in the east, and if you've flown from some parts of Europe, you could even be in the northern town of Akureyri.

Internal flights are a convenient way to get between the main areas, and a popular mode of transport for locals. Although it means missing out on Iceland's rural attractions, flying remains an option for visitors. Public and private bus companies can be used for cross-country travel with some planning, and ferries ply the routes to offshore destinations such as the Westman Islands and Grímsey. A wealth of detailed information on public transit can be found at publictransport.is, an English-language resource created by cyclists but useful for any traveler.

The Ring Road (aka Route 1) conveniently circles the country. It's a popular choice for people traveling by car, bike, or even foot, and most of Iceland is accessible via this and a network of more minor roads. If you're driving yourself, you really should have a GPS navigation system to avoid becoming the latest tourist to needlessly inconvenience Iceland's volunteer rescue squad.

In Rekyjavík, you'll find that most locations of interest are within the downtown area, which takes no more than 30 minutes to cross on foot. Numerous companies scatter the capital's streets with hireable electric scooters and bicycles; simply download the relevant app and give it your card details to scoot off on one. Reykjavík has no metro system, but it does have buses that are convenient, clean, affordable, and widely used by locals. Strætó, the bus company, also offers routes elsewhere in the country. In Reykjavík, there are no services such as Uber or Lyft, but metered taxis are available.

 ## Air

The national flag-carrier Icelandair operates 15 routes to the U.S. and Canada as well as all over Europe and Greenland. During summer months, Air Canada flies from Montreal and Toronto, and both Delta and United—along with newer Icelandic airline Play—fly direct from New York City and Boston. Direct flights from the U.S. east coast take around six hours, whereas Icelandair's non-stop flight from Seattle clocks in at seven-and-half.

Connections from European cities are plentiful—Wizz Air flies from Budapest and twelve other European cities—and fast. EasyJet's London flight takes three hours, and Transavia's flight from Paris is only half an hour longer. Until recently, Icelandic international air traffic (other than the short hops to Greenland and the Faroe Islands) was restricted to Keflakvík Airport. However, recent startup Niceair now connects Denmark, Spain, and the U.K. directly with Akureyri in the north.

Icelandair operates domestic routes from Reykjavík to Ísafjörður, Akureyri, Egilsstaðir, and Vestmannaeyjar (the Westman Islands), sometimes branded as its former subsidiary Air Iceland Connect. Norlandair operates from Akureyri to Þórshöfn, Vopnafjörður, and Grímsey as well as Constable Point in Greenland. From Reykjavik, Norlandair flies to Bíldudalur and Gjögur. Eagle Air also connects Reykjavík to Bíldudalur and Gjögur as well as with Vestmannaeyjar, Höfn, and Húsavík. No domestic Icelandic flight is longer than one hour, but be aware that the smaller aircraft often used are more susceptible to in-air turbulence and cancellation by weather.

AIRPORTS

Iceland's main airport is Keflakvík (KEF), some 30 miles and a 45-minute drive outside Reykjavík. It's the airport travelers flying direct from the U.S. will use, and is not to be confused with Reykjavík Airport (RVK), which sits almost downtown in the city itself and handles domestic flights. When searching for tickets, you may find Keflakvík Airport referred to as "Reykjavík," but be aware of the distinction. Airport pickup services tend to know that when visitors say "Reykjavík Airport," they mean Keflavík, but will typically seek clarification.

In addition to Keflavík and Reykjavík, Iceland has two other small airports at Akureyri (AEY) and Egilsstaðir (EGS), both of which focus mainly on domestic traffic. The rest of the country is served by some 45 aerodromes and landing strips, indicating how important internal air travel is to a country where roads are regularly closed by snow.

Keflavík Airport—originally built by the U.S. military during World War II—is expanding to meet the massive increase in visitors seen over the last decade. The airport is modern, with plenty of food and shopping options. Of note for arriving passengers is the duty-free store: by far the cheapest place in the country to purchase alcohol. For more information about all Iceland's airports, consult ⊕ *www.isavia.is*.

GROUND TRANSPORTATION

It's rare for a hotel in Reykjavík to offer an airport shuttle service, but it's worth asking your hotel if they can help arrange one of the many high-quality shuttle services that exist. The most popular option is Flybus, which takes passengers in comfortable Wi-Fi-enabled buses from the airport to the city's BSÍ bus terminal for 3,499 ISK. You can walk to your hotel from BSÍ or catch a taxi, but a better option is a Flybus+ ticket for 4,599 ISK, which includes a transfer from BSÍ to your downtown accommodation in a minibus. It takes 45 minutes to get to BSÍ from the airport, then up to a further 45 minutes for the onward journey to where you're staying.

Your Flybus ticket is good for the day, so if your flight is delayed or you get caught up in the duty-free shop, just get on the next bus. You can buy tickets at the airport or online, but not on the bus itself. There is no fixed schedule for Flybus departures from Keflavík to Reykjavík; they shadow airline arrival times.

Airport Direct offers similar services to Flybus for slightly less money, but with slightly less flexibility; they run a fixed schedule, and tickets are only changeable if you pay extra. They also offer a premium service for 6,590 ISK, which gets you a minibus directly from the airport to your accommodation. You'll share the ride with other passengers, but you won't need to go via BSÍ and change buses.

Metered taxis will be waiting outside the airport and cost around 16,000 to 20,000 ISK to Reykjavík, depending on traffic and the time of day. Many car rental agencies are available at the airport, just be sure to book in advance.

Car drivers and bus passengers can stop at the famous Blue Lagoon hot springs, which sits about halfway between the airport and the city. Since Flybus operates a little like a hop-on, hop-off tour, passengers can pop out at the Blue Lagoon stop and get on the next Reykjavík-bound bus after they're done (this works going from Reykjavík to the airport, too). Note that purchasing this option does not include admission to the Blue Lagoon, which needs to be booked in advance. The Blue Lagoon offers bathing-suit and towel rentals, as well as left

Getting Here and Around

luggage, and has a restaurant and spa on-site. Many tourists stop here at the end of their trip, but bathing in these blue waters is an incredible jet lag cure and a great way to get into the Iceland spirit right after your flight.

At airports other than Keflavík, taxis are typically waiting outside after scheduled arrivals. The website of the Icelandic airport authority has information on taxis, buses, and car rentals serving any airport in the country.

🚢 Boat

If your plans for Nordic wandering include Denmark or the Faroe Islands, then you should consider taking the ferry that links Hirtshals in Denmark to Seyðisfjörður in Iceland, via Tórshavn in the Faroes. The Smyril Line operates this route— Iceland's only international ferry—with weekly departures that take two or three days, depending on the season. You can break up your journey when traveling in either direction to stay a few days in the Faroes. The ferry is cruise ship-sized, offering comfortable facilities and cabins for overnight accommodation. It also takes vehicles, so it's the ideal way to transport your car, motorbike, or motorhome from mainland Europe to Iceland. Foot passengers can get a bus onwards from Seyðisfjörður or fly from nearby Egilsstaðir.

A few domestic ferries operate all year-round to the more-traveled Icelandic islands, and major routes accommodate vehicles. If you are planning to travel by boat with a car, it's always a good idea to book ahead. In the west of the country, Seatours connects Stykkishólmur with Brjánslækur in the Westfjords via the island of Flatey, while Borea Adventures runs seasonal boats from Ísafjörður to Hornstrandir nature reserve. In the south Herjólfur runs from Landeyjahöfn to Vestmannaeyjar in the Westman Islands. In the north, the Sævar ferry sails frequently from Árskógssandur to the island of Hrísey, while Sæfari connects Dalvík to both Hrísey and the little island of Grímsey on the Arctic Circle.

Bus

Reykjavík-based bus company Strætó operates long-distance routes around Iceland, with services reaching across the island as far as Egilsstaðir and Höfn. It's more cost-effective than flying, and you can leave the driving to a professional while you enjoy the landscape. Reykjavík's main bus station, BSÍ, is just over a mile from the city center. It's a hub for local buses, long-distance lines, and many local excursions around the Golden Circle. However some long-distance buses may depart from Mjódd to the southeast of the city center, so do check before you travel.

Many larger towns have local bus services; in Akureyri and Egilsstaðir, they're even free of charge, courtesy of the local municipality. Reykjavík has a very comprehensive network operated by Strætó that goes pretty much everywhere you'll want to go in the city. Their large yellow buses are clean and comfortable, with clear written and spoken announcements of upcoming stops. Strætó has recently started trials of weekend night buses from the city center to the suburbs.

An adult fare within the Reykjavík metropolitan area is a flat ISK 490 which you can pay by cash, app, or via two types of smart cards. Note that drivers don't give change, so if you opt for cash try to have a ISK 500 bill at the ready (and say good-bye to your change of ISK10). Strætó's electronic payment methods are operated by a company called Klapp: their app (Klappið) and the rechargeable Klapp Card both need to be linked to a bank or credit card, while the Klapp Ten—a prepaid card loaded with ten journeys—is available at certain retail outlets, including the 10-11 convenience store. Note that none of the Klapp payment methods are valid on Strætó buses outside the capital.

If you're going to be busy sightseeing in Reykjavík, another good option for local travel is the Reykjavík City Card. This gives you 24, 48, or 72 hours of unlimited travel on the city buses, with a bonus of admission to certain attractions, thermal pools, and ferries.

Car

Driving is an extremely popular way to get around for Icelandic locals and visitors alike. With well-maintained roads, little traffic, and generally high standards of driving, it's an easy way to travel and enables greater exploration of the country. Route 1, also known as the Ring Road, goes by many of Iceland's most popular sights making off-road excursions unnecessary—a good thing, because off-road driving is illegal in Iceland.

Using a car in Reykjavík comes with the usual challenges of driving in an unfamiliar urban environment, but it's a breeze compared to some other capital cities. Local drivers are generally careful and courteous, for example often voluntarily stopping on smaller roads to allow waiting pedestrians to cross. Parking comes in the form of numerous underground facilities and the city's parking meter system, based on four

zones which reduce in cost the further you get away from the city center. Pay at the machine on the street, and enter your vehicle registration number.

CAR RENTALS

Many travelers pick up and drop off a rental car from one of the companies at Keflavík Airport. A wide range of vehicles is usually available, including camper vans which can provide very cost-effective accommodation in summer. But if you're there at any other time of year expect snow, so consider a 4WD vehicle and ask about studded tires. Insider tip: after picking up your car drive directly to a gas station and check the tire pressures—including the spare—as rental companies often don't. Note that you must be at least 20 years old to rent a car in Iceland, 23 to rent a camper van or 4WD, and, of course, it's wise to prebook any rental vehicle.

DRIVING

Remember to drive on the right, and use headlights at all times as the Icelandic weather can change in an instant. Speed limits are in kilometers per hour, the top one being 90 km/h (56 mph). The relative absence of speed cameras and patrolling cops can encourage locals to disregard these limits, and as you cruise the Ring Road diligently observing the law you may find that you have an enthusiastic tailgater. Don't be tempted into speeding up; they'll pass when it's safe. Also don't pull over to the side of the Ring Road to admire the scenery, unless using one of the designated pull-off areas. Even Iceland's main route is only wide enough for one vehicle in each direction at most points, and vehicles regularly smash into stationary tourists who have stopped for an Instagram shot.

Getting Here and Around

GASOLINE

Planning is essential when driving outside Reykjavík as gas stations can be limited in more remote areas, and the distance between tourist locations can be substantial. The main gas station brands are N1, Olís, AO, and Orkan, so search for these when planning your drive. In busier areas stations will probably have a shop and possibly some food options, but elsewhere they may be unmanned, only sell fuel, and only take payment by card. All gas stations, whether staffed or not, are self-service. Gas in Iceland costs around twice as much as you'd expect to pay in America, and is subject to the same price fluctuations as the rest of the world.

ROAD CONDITIONS

Weather and the state of road surfaces both have a big influence on the Icelandic driving experience. The local adage "if you don't like the weather, wait a minute" is a reminder that bright sunshine can change to blinding snow in an instant, and drivers need to be prepared. Check conditions on ⊕ *www. vedur.is* before you set out, and also as you go. City streets and the Ring Road are generally well-maintained, but smaller routes out in the country can be pot-holed or gravel-surfaced, raising the risk of punctures especially to improperly inflated tires. Seasonal and weather-related road closures are common, but fortunately you can keep tabs on these at ⊕ *www.road.is.*

Cruise

Taking an international cruise can be a relaxed way to visit Iceland, and a convenient way to group Nordic locations together in one trip without having to deal with too much air travel. Itineraries that include other countries typically stop only in Reykjavík, while Iceland-specific cruises may dock in many harbors, offering a chance to see parts of the country far from the capital. Ísafjörður in the west, Siglufjörður in the north, Seyðisfjörður in the east, and Vestmannaeyjar in the south all become more easily accessible this way, and there is often a wide range of excursions passengers can take while on shore. However it's worth noting that the number of guests aboard a ship can be more than double the population of the small towns that they're visiting, so the result can feel a bit like a mob invasion.

Taxi

Most towns will have a local taxi service, always using cars fitted with a yellow light on the roof saying "TAXI". In Reykjavík you can't hail them in the street, but you can make a booking ahead of time or pick one up at a taxi stand. They always use the meter unless you're leaving the city—such as to go to Keflavík Airport—in which case there will be a set price. Taxis are useful for short hops around the capital but alternatives such as Flybus exist for the journey to Keflavík, often working out as much more cost-effective and almost as convenient.

Essentials

Addresses

Street names in Iceland may seem confusing, as they don't have a separate word like "street" or "avenue" following the name (usually that definition is included in the name itself). Typical suffixes for Icelandic roads are -*gata* meaning gate, -*stígur* or -*braut* both meaning lane, -*vegur* or way, and -*stræti* meaning street.

Addresses are organized first by the name of the street, followed by the number of the building, the post (zip) code, the city, and finally the country. An example is Café Loki: Lokastígur 28, 101 Reykjavík, Iceland. If it's an apartment, the unit will follow the address, so Lokastígur 28a (if the café had a second unit).

Dining

For all the focus sometimes placed on the more unusual elements of Icelandic cuisine, the everyday food eaten by Icelanders is quite recognizable to most foreigners. Pizza is popular, the humble hot dog has been adopted as a national dish, burgers are everywhere, and potatoes and bread are the staple starches.

But the influence of immigration—and of international travel by Icelanders—has begun to show on local appetites and on the range of eateries available. There are now several excellent Thai, Chinese, and Indian restaurants in Reykjavík (admittedly these go easy on the spices for delicate Icelandic palates); befitting a nation built on fish, sushi and sashimi are now becoming popular; and flying in the face of that other Icelandic nutritional cornerstone (lamb), vegetarians and vegans are increasingly being thought of when menus are compiled. Fancier dining is

predictably more concentrated in urban areas, with a simpler approach taken in the farther reaches of the countryside, but the influence of imported cuisine continues to spread further into Icelandic culture.

Health and Safety

Good news: you're visiting the safest country on the planet. Crime is minimal, healthcare is plentiful and affordable, and the locals are generally respectful of each other and tourists. However, attention still needs to be paid to inclement weather and other natural hazards. Stay updated on swiftly changing weather, and always let someone know if a trip into the outdoors is on your schedule. For help, dial 112 to reach emergency services. There is also a 112 smartphone app that can locate users through GPS in an emergency.

In Reykjavík, things can get a little rowdy during drinking hours, so it's important to remain as aware as one would in any major European city. Pickpocketing does occur (although it's extremely rare), and locking valuables away is always a good idea. If a situation arises which requires the police, don't hesitate to dial 112 to get help—operators will usually speak English. And if you or someone you know has been the victim of sexual assault, the emergency room at the Landsspítali National Hospital has a special rape unit where specialized medical and psychological care will be provided, regardless of who you are or where you are from. You'll find that in the Reykjavík neighborhood of Fossvogur.

While healthcare is almost entirely subsidized for Icelandic citizens, non-European foreigners are liable for the full cost of their treatments. Europeans should travel

Essentials

with their European Health Insurance Card, while everyone else should consider getting travel insurance which can offset healthcare costs and has other benefits.

COVID-19

Most travel restrictions, including vaccination and masking requirements, have been lifted across the United States except in healthcare facilities and nursing homes. Some travelers may still wish to wear a mask in confined spaces, including on airplanes, on public transportation, and at large indoor gatherings, but that is increasingly a personal choice. Be aware that some local mandates still exist and should be followed. Since COVID-19-related quarantine requirements and other restrictions still exist in some destinations, it is wise to have travel insurance that will cover you for COVID-related cancellations and other expenses.

 ## Lodging

The burgeoning Icelandic tourism industry supports a wide range of accommodation types to suit all tastes and most budgets.

The lowest cost option is, of course, to camp. To protect the pristine natural locations that make Iceland so popular, it's illegal to just pitch a tent wherever you like. But there are some 200 campsites around the country for those looking to experience sleeping under the stars or the midnight sun. The cost varies, but is usually between ISK 1,600 and ISK 2,800 per person per night. Attempting to survive the Icelandic elements in a tent is recommended in the summer months only, although you might find a camper van provides a bit more protection in the spring and autumn.

Staying in a hostel is a very cost-effective way to get a solid roof over your head, and the Icelandic branch of hostelling international offers 24 locations with dorm beds from around ISK 3,100 per night. There are also independent hostels such as Reykjavík's legendary Kex Hostel, where you can grab a dorm bunk for as little as ISK 4,800.

The globally ubiquitous Airbnb has done very well in Iceland too. Enterprising locals have taken every opportunity to service the increasing demand for tourist accommodation, resulting in a useful proliferation of comfortable, purpose-built cottages dotted around the countryside. Self-contained Airbnb accommodations can also be found in towns and cities, often in apartments removed from the long-term rental market by landlords looking for a slice of the more lucrative vacation rentals sector. That practice isn't helping Iceland out of its acute housing shortage, but it does provide visitors with convenient urban *pied-à-terre* option and an alternative to hotels.

Speaking of hotels, you can certainly find the usual international chains—Hiltons, Marriots, and so on—around the capital region, should you choose. And Reykjavík offers a good choice of independently owned hotels, but perhaps of more interest to those venturing outside the capital are the Icelandic-owned Fosshotels, of which there are four in Reykjavík and eleven more scattered conveniently around the country. Particularly useful are Fosshotels Núpar and Glacier Lagoon, located in south Iceland on a long stretch of the Ring Road where campsites and Airbnbs are scarce.

Packing

The old Icelandic adage "if you don't like the weather, just wait a minute" is worth having at the front of your mind as you pack. Conditions can turn on a dime so flexibility is key, and layers are your best friends. However, one thing that you can rely on is that it will be cold and windy—even in summer, and even if the sun shines—but in some ways that makes packing easier. Bring a fleece or wool jacket, or buy a traditional Icelandic lopapeysa upon arrival. These sweaters are made from Icelandic sheep's wool, which is brilliant at keeping the weather out. A rain jacket is essential—you'll never see an Icelander using an umbrella—as are a beanie, gloves, scarf, warm socks, thermal underwear, and sturdy shoes (or better still, hiking boots) that can deal with rain, snow, and icy ground. High-quality outdoor clothing can be found in Iceland at 66° North stores, although your wallet will thank you if you come already kitted-out.

A swimsuit is essential for both planned and unplanned visits to pools and thermal springs; a road trip can reveal plenty of unmapped hot pots. Icelanders do sometimes dress up to eat out or go partying, so a smarter item of clothing might be useful in Reykjavík but there's no need to go overboard. There is rarely a "dress code," even at nicer bars and restaurants.

Horseback riders should know that Iceland strictly protects its purebred horses, making it forbidden to bring any leather riding gear into the country. When taking a tour by horse, riders will be provided with everything they need. So relax and leave equestrian equipment at home.

Tipping

Tipping is not the norm in Icelandic culture. Servers receive salaries which reflect that fact, and don't expect gratuities. Visitors from societies with a strong tipping culture are sometimes uncomfortable with this, but the best advice—as with any local custom—is to embrace it. However, if you feel that you have received unusually outstanding service, a tip of no more than 10% won't be refused. The best way to thank a tour guide is to offer to take them for a drink or a meal.

When to Go

The best time to visit Iceland is a matter of personal preference. For those seeking the northern lights (aurora borealis), winter is the best time as that season provides the prerequisite dark night skies. Visiting during the periods around the equinoxes in March and September adds to your chances of seeing aurora, as geosolar conditions for producing them are strongest then. But some activities and transport options are unavailable in winter, and the seasonal lack of daylight can be oppressive for some. The better weather offered by summer months might appeal, but then again the lack of nighttime darkness during an Icelandic midsummer can disturb sleep patterns. So there isn't really a bad time to visit Iceland: just decide what appeals to you about the country and then pick a season to match.

Helpful Icelandic Phrases

BASICS

Hello	Halló	hahl-lo
Yes/No	Já / Nei	yow / nay
Thank you	Takk fyrir	tak fear-ir
You're welcome	Verði þér að góðu	Vare-thee thear ahth goh-thu
I'm Sorry (apology)	Ég biðst afsökunar	Yehg bithst af-seh-kunar
Sorry (Excuse me)	Afsakið	af-sah-kith
Good morning	Góðan daginn	goh-thahn dahg-in
Good day	Góðan daginn	goh-thahn dahg-in
Good evening	Gott kvöld	goht kvuhld
Goodbye	Bless	bless
Mr. (Sir)	Herra	her rah
Mrs.	Frú	froo
Miss	Fröken	fruh-ken
Pleased to meet you	Gaman að kynnast þér	gam-an ath kin-nast thear
How are you?	Hvað segirðu gott?	kvahth seg-ir-thu goht

NUMBERS

one-half	hálfur	howl-ver
one	einn	ehnn
two	tveir	tvere
three	þrír	threer
four	fjórir	fyohr-eer
five	fimm	fim
six	sex	sex
seven	Sjö	syuh
eight	átta	owt-ta
nine	níu	nee-uh
ten	tíu	tee-uh
eleven	ellefu	elh-leh-vu
twelve	tólf	tulv
thirteen	Þrettán	Thret-town
fourteen	fjórtán	fyor-town
fifteen	fimmtán	fim-town
sixteen	sextán	sex-town
seventeen	sautján	soy-tyown
eighteen	átján	owt-yown
nineteen	nítján	nee-tyown
twenty	tuttugu	too-too-goo
twenty-one	tuttugu og einn	too-too-goo og ehnn
thirty	þrjátíu	thryow-tee-uh
fifty	fimmtíu	fim-tee-uh
sixty	sextíu	sex-tee-uh
seventy	sjötíu	syuh-tee-uh
eighty	áttatíu	owt-ta-tee-uh
ninety	nítíu	nee-tee-uh
one hundred	eitt hundrað	eht-hundrath
one thousand	eitt þúsund	eht- thoo-sund
one million	ein milljón	ehn-mill-yohn

COLORS

black	svartur	svar-ter
blue	blár	blaowr
brown	brúnn	broon
green	grænn	grine
orange	appelsínugulur	apple-see-nuh-guh-lur
red	rauður	roy-therr
white	hvítur	hvee-tur
yellow	gulur	goo-lur

DAYS OF THE WEEK

Sunday	sunnudagur	soon-new-dah-gur
Monday	mánudagur	mow-new-dah-gur
Tuesday	þriðjudagur	thrith-hue-dah-gur
Wednesday	miðvikudagur	mith-vik-oo-dah-gur
Thursday	Fimmtudagur	fim-too-dah-gur
Friday	föstudagur	fuhst-oo-dah-gur
Saturday	laugardagur	loy-gahr-dah-gur

MONTHS

January	Janúar	yah-new-ahr
February	Febrúar	feb-roo-ahr
March	Mars	mars
April	Apríl	ahh-preel
May	Mai	my
June	Júní	yoon-ee
July	Júlí	yoo-lee
August	Ágúst	ow-goost
September	September	sef-tem-ber
October	Október	og-toh-beer
November	Nóvember	noh-vem-beer
December	Desember	deh-sem-beer

USEFUL WORDS AND PHRASES

Do you speak English?	Talar þú ensku	tah-lahr thoo ehn-skuh
I don't speak [Language].	Ég tala ekki tungumálið	yehg tah-lah eh-kee toon-guh-mow-lith
I don't understand.	Ég skil ekki	yehg skill eh-kee
I don't know.	Ég veit það ekki	yehg veht thahth eh-kee
I understand.	Ég skil	yehg skill
I'm American.	Ég er ameríkani	yehg ehr ah-mehr-ee-kahn-ee
I'm British.	Ég er breti	yehg ehr breht-ee
What's your name.	Hvað heitirðu?	kvahth hate-er-thu
My name is ...	Ég heiti	yehg hate-ee
What time is it?	Hvað er klukkan?	kvahth ehr kluh-kahn
How?	Hvernig?	kvehr-nig
When?	Hvenær	kveh-nuyr
Yesterday	Í gær	ee guy-r
Today	Í dag	ee dahg

Tomorrow	Á morgunn	ow mor-guhn
This morning	Þennan morgunn	then-nahn mor-guhn
This afternoon	Þennan eftirmiðdag	then-nahn eftir-mith-dahg
Tonight	Í kvöld	ee-kvuhld
What?	Hvað?	kvahth
What is it?	Hvað er það?	kvahth ehr thahth
Why?	Af hverju?	ahf kvair-yoo
Who?	Hver?	kvair
Where is ...	Hvar er...	kvahr ehr
... the bus stop?	strætó stoppistöðin?	strie-toe stop-pi-stuh-thin
... the airport?	flugvöllurinn?	floog-vuhllh-uh-rinn
... the post office?	pósthúsið?	post-hoosith
... the bank?	bankinn?	bank-inn
... the hotel?	hótelið?	hotel-ith
... the museum?	safnið?	sabn-ith
... the hospital?	spítalinn?	speet-ahl-in
... the elevator?	lyfturnar?	lift-ur-nar
Where are the restrooms?	klósettin?	cloe-set-in
Here/there	hér / þar	here/thar
Left/right	vinstri / hægri	vin-stree/high-gree
Is it near/far?	Er það nálægt/ langt í burtu?	ehr thahth now-legt/ langt ee bur-too
I'd like ...	Ég myndi vilja	yehg mind-ee vil-yah
... a room	herbergi	hair-behr-gee
... the key	lykill	lIlI-kilh
... a newspaper	fréttablað	Fretta-blahth
... a stamp	stimpill	Stim-pilh
I'd like to buy ...	Ég myndi vilja kaupa	yehg mind-ee vil-yah koy-pah....
... a city map	kort af borginni	kort ahf borg-in-nee
... a road map	kort af vegunum	kort ahf veg-oo-num
... a magaine	tímarit	teem ar-it
... envelopes	umslög	um-sluhgh
... writing paper	blöð til að skrifa á	bluhth til ahth skriva ow
... a postcard	póstkort	post-kort
... a ticket	miða	mi-tha
How much is it?	Hvað kostar það mikið?	kvath koe-star thahth mikith
It's expensive/ cheap	það er dýrt / ódýrt	thath ehr deert / oh-deert
A little/a lot	Smá / mikið	smow / mi-kith
More/less	meira / minna	mare-ah / min-na
Enough/too (much)	þetta er nóg / þetta er of mikið	thetta ehr noeg / thetta ehr oh-fv mikith
I am ill/sick	Ég er veik / veikur	yehg ehr vake / vake-ur
Call a doctor.	Hringdu í lækni	hring-doo ee like-nee

Help!	Hjálp	hyowlp
Stop!	Stopp	stop

DINING OUT

A bottle of ...	flösku af....	fluhs-ku ahf
A cup of ...	bolla af....	bollah ahf
A glass of ...	glas af....	glass ahf
Beer	bjór	byore
Bill/check	reikninginn	rake-ning-in
Bread	brauð	broyth
Breakfast	morgunnmatur	morg-un-mat-ur
Butter	smjör	smyoore
Cocktail/aperatif	kokteill / fordrykkur	cock-tale for-dring-kur
Coffee	kaffi	kahf-fee
Dinner	kvöldmatur	kvuhld-mat-ur
Fixed-price menu	matseðill	mahts-ehthilh
Fork	gaffall	gahf-falh
I am a vegetarian/I don't eat meat	Ég er grænmetisæta	yehg ehr grine-meh-tih-sight-ah
I cannot eat ...	Ég get ekki borðað	yehg get ehk-kee bor-thahth
I'd like to order ...	Ég myndi vilja panta	yehg mind-ee vil-yah pan-tah
Is service included?	Er þjónustan innifalinn?	ehrr thyohn-uh-stahn in-nih-fahl-in
I'm hungry/ thirsty	Ég er svangur/ svöng // þyrstur/ þyrst	yehg air svahn-gur / svuhng. // thirst-ur / thirst
It's good/bad	Það er gott / slæmt	thahth air goht / sly-mt
It's hot/cold	Það er heitt / kalt	thahth ehr hayt / kahlt
Knife	hnífur	hnee-vur
Lunch	hádegismatur	how-dehg-is-maht-ur
Menu	matseðill	maht-seh-thilh
Napkin	þurrka	thur-kah
Pepper	pipar	pay-pahr
Plate	diskur	Disk-ur
Please give me ...	vinsamlegast gefðu mér	vin-sahm-leh-gahst geb-thu mare
Salt	salt	sahlt
Spoon	skeið	skathe
Tea	te	teh
Water	vatn	vaht
Wine	vín	veen

Great Itineraries

The Best of Iceland

Iceland has so much to offer a visitor, it can be difficult to find the time to do it justice. Hitting the Ring Road to tour all four corners of the country—taking it all in, and without rushing or skipping bits—can easily require four weeks or more. But by focusing on one area, and indulging in a little careful planning, it's possible to pack a great trip into only one week. But be warned: Iceland is addictive, and you may find yourself booking those other three weeks as soon as you get home.

This itinerary concentrates on the capital Reykjavík, the southwest area of the island, and a good chunk of the south coast. It assumes that you fly into Keflavík the day before, make your way to Reykjavík, and stay overnight in the city. After your five days touring, you'll then fly out of Keflavík again, making it a seven-day round trip for North Americans residents. The schedule is jam-packed to make the most of your time, but you can skip activities as you choose to drop the pace a little. Remember to book all your accommodation well in advance.

DAY ONE: REYKJAVÍK

Start your first full day in Reykjavík at **Hallgrímskirkja**, a church high on the city's central hill and easily its most distinctive landmark. Spend a reflective moment inside before heading up the tower for spectacular views of Reyjkavík's rooftops and the mountains beyond. Then stroll down the hill to **Sólfarið** (The Sun Voyager), a steel sculpture of a boat that overlooks the bay. A short waterside walk then takes you to the concert hall

complex of **Harpa**, the remarkable glass architecture that needs to be appreciated from both outside and in. Since you're then close to both **the old town** and the city's famous **Laugavegur** shopping street, you can take your pick of lunch locations.

Afterwards either stroll around **Tjörnin**, the town's picturesque duck/goose/swan pond, or hire an electric scooter and ride south to the **Perlan** exhibition center on top of **Öskjuhlíð** hill. Leave your scooter and walk up the slope through gorgeous Icelandic forest: a rare treat in a country with few trees. That evening consult the listings in local free paper the *Reykjavík Grapevine* to find out what's happening in town, and enjoy your second night in the world's most liveable capital city.

LOGISTICS

Visitors to Iceland typically fly into Keflakvík Airport, located about 45 minutes from Reykjavík by car or bus. The easiest and least expensive way to get into the city from the airport is by hopping on a Flybus, which runs regularly between the airport and Reykjavík's bus terminal. You can also take a cab, which will cost more than the bus.

DAY TWO: GOLDEN CIRCLE

Pick up your pre-booked rental car from **Blue Car Rental,** which has offices in both downtown Reykjavík and Keflavík Airport (where you will eventually drop it off), then hit the legendary Route 1 north out of the city. You're heading for **Þingvellir National Park** to take a gentle stroll around **Þingvallavatn** lake, the **Öxarárfoss** waterfall, and some stunning geological features. Afterwards a short drive delivers you to the historic cave house at **Laugarvatnshellir** for a cup of tea

ATLANTIC
OCEAN

and a tour, before pressing on to **Geysir,** the mainstay of the Golden Circle. Once you've caught its chief attraction **Strokkur** shooting steam and spray high into the air, it might be time for lunch at the **Geysir Centre.** The waterfalls at **Gullfoss** will be your next stop, before heading for a relaxing dip in the **Secret Lagoon,** a natural thermal pool at **Flúðir.** Post-dip, head for **Skálholt** for a look at its historic cathedral and modern replica of a turf house. Round off your day with a short hike around the rim of **Kerið,** a nearby volcanic crater, before retiring to one of the Golden Circle's many cozy Airbnb cottages.

LOGISTICS

It's impossible to see all the major stops on the Golden Circle without a car. You could also join one of the many tour buses that stop along the major sights of the route, but a car will give you much more freedom. Just be sure to check the weather before you leave as Icelandic road conditions can change dramatically, especially in the winter.

DAY THREE: THE SOUTH COAST

Rejoin Route 1 and hit the south coast, your first stop being the remarkable **Seljalandsfoss** waterfall which you can actually walk behind. A short way farther along the road you'll encounter the impressive falls of **Skógafoss** and the **Skogar Open Air Museum,** a collection of historical buildings demonstrating Icelandic life in past times. Continue to **Vík** for lunch and then backtrack a little to the **Dyrhólaey Peninsula**—the most southerly point on the Icelandic mainland—for its lighthouse, dramatic views, and the possibility of puffin sighting. A short hop back east along the coast then takes you to the legendary **Reynisfjara Beach,** with its amazing black sand, basalt column cliffs, and sea stacks. Continuing east on the Ring Road for just over an hour you'll find **Fjaðrárgljúfur,** a stunning canyon with sheer rock walls reaching deep down to the **Fjaðrá River.** Take a hike along the top for breathtaking views. End your day with an overnight stay at the cozy **Fosshotel Núpar,** a godsend in a part of the country with surprisingly little accommodation.

Great Itineraries

DAY FOUR: SKAFTAFELL NATIONAL PARK AND VÍK

Making an early start, head eastward on Route 1 to **Skaftafell National Park** and 40 minutes in, you'll see a turnoff for the park's visitor center. From there you can hike 30 minutes to see **Svartifoss**, which means "black waterfall" and refers to the impressive hexagonal columns of volcanic rock over which the water tumbles. The park is also home to the **Skaftafellsjökull glacier,** where Icelandic Mountain Guides offer half-day expeditions onto the ice. You'll find their base by the visitor's center, but to be sure of availability, book online in advance. Bringing a picnic lunch might be a smart move as you'll drive straight from your glacier walk to the glacier lake of **Jökulsárlón**. You can take boat tours to get up close to the floating icebergs or just admire them from the shore. Adjacent to the lagoon is **Breiðamerkursandur**, or **Diamond Beach,** where huge sparkling chunks of clear blue ice from Jökulsárlón wash up on the black sand. Leave enough time at the end of the day for the two-and-a-half hour drive back to **Vík**, where you'll spend the night.

DAY FIVE: REYKJANES PENINSULA AND THE BLUE LAGOON

In the morning, head west from **Vík** towards the recently-active volcanic region of the **Reykjanes Peninsula**. It's a two-and-a-half hour drive so do leave in good time, but break the journey with a stopover in **Selfoss** to buy a picnic lunch and snacks for your volcano hike. Even though it hasn't erupted since August 2022, the **Fagradalsfjall volcano** is still an awe-inspiring place: its lava entirely filled a valley with black stone, which smoked and steamed for months afterwards. The hike is somewhat demanding, so if that's not for you then visit the nearby **Krýsuvík geothermal area** instead, including taking a stroll around the pools of steaming hot mud at Seltún. Then after a long day of driving and hiking, stop at the legendary **Blue Lagoon** for a relaxing soak in its silica-infused, geothermally-heated waters. And when you're done chilling, the adjacent town of **Grindavík** offers several dinner options before you retire to your hotel in town, leaving you well-located for your trip to the airport the next day. In summer months the Blue Lagoon is open late, so you could even make it an evening activity on your last night in Iceland.

LOGISTICS

The Blue Lagoon is located about halfway between Reykjavík and Keflakvík airport. Flybus makes stops at the Blue Lagoon and taxis often wait here as well. It will only take about 20 minutes to get to the airport from the Blue Lagoon.

Best Tours in Iceland

FOOD TOURS

Reykjavik Food Walk. Stroll the city streets with a knowledgeable local foodie, sampling Icelandic cuisine at some of the city's hidden-gem restaurants. This tour steers away from cliché—no rotten shark or testicles on the table here—and towards national dishes that you'll actually want to eat, such as lamb, fresh fish, and ice cream. ⊠ *Klapparstígur 25, Reykjavík* ⊕ *www.thereykjavikfoodwalk.com.*

GLACIER TOURS

Amazing Tours. These seasoned explorers of Langjökull, the closest glacier to Reykjavík, run all sorts of hikes, snowmobile excursions, and eight-wheel monster truck trips into the icy wilderness. But their top attraction is a journey to the Amazing Crystal Ice Cave, a huge natural cavern that was created in 2021. Nature will eventually take the cave back again, so get there while you can. ⊠ *Eldshöfði 12, Reykjavík* ☎ *517–4455* ⊕ *www.amazingtours.is.*

Icelandic Mountain Guides. Sticking out of the southwest edge of Vatnajökull—Iceland's biggest glacier—is an outlet glacier called Skaftafell. There you'll find Icelandic Mountain Guides who, for nearly three decades, have been getting visitors to strap on crampons and join them for a hike on the ice. Either book online or pull off Route 1 and find them near the Vatnajökull National Park visitors center. ⊠ *Klettagarðar 12, Reykjavík* ☎ *587–9999* ⊕ *www.mountainguides.is.*

GUIDED TOURS

Classic Journeys. This U.S.-based tour operator offers an all-inclusive tour to scratch all your Icelandic itches over six days. You can walk in a national park, snorkel between tectonic plates, ride a horse on a sheep farm, see icebergs close-up, hike on a glacier, and soak in geothermal waters. ☎ *858/454–5004* ⊕ *www.classicjourneys.com.*

Private Hire Iceland. If being part of the tourist crowd isn't your thing, an individualized approach with Private Hire Iceland may be the way to go. This is a great option for those wanting a quieter experience of the country in their own car, driven by a personal guide. ☎ *539–3990* ⊕ *www.privatehire.is.*

West Tours. The Westfjords are an under-explored part of Iceland for good reason: it's not easy to get around and see everything. West Tours makes it possible by leading hikes, organizing horseback rides, and even bringing people out to Hornstrandir Nature Reserve, the best place to catch a glimpse of an arctic fox. ⊠ *Aðalstræti 7, Ísafjörður* ☎ *456–5111* ⊕ *www.westtours.is.*

HORSEBACK RIDING TOURS

Eldhestar. This company offers the largest variety of riding options in south Iceland, with rides as short as a half day or as long as eight days. Eldhestar's horses make magnificent companions for a tour of the Icelandic countryside in summer or winter, and the staff are knowledgeable and helpful. ⊠ *Vellir, 816 Ölfus, Hveragerði* ☎ *480–4800* ⊕ *www.eldhestar.is.*

Best Tours in Iceland

SNORKELING AND SCUBA DIVING TOURS

Dive.is. Some of Iceland's most stunning landscapes are hidden underwater. Explore glacial lagoons where underwater ravines plunge deep into the earth, enabling divers to touch two continents at once. Iceland's premier scuba diving company runs snorkeling trips near Reykjavík that require no previous training and dive trips all around the country for qualified scuba divers. And if you're not qualified, they can train and certify you as well. ⊠ *Hólmaslóð 2, Reykjavík* ☎ *578–6200* ⊕ *www.dive.is*.

VOLCANO TOURS

Reykjavik Excursions. The Reykjanes peninsula is a hotbed of seismic activity and was the site of the famous 2021 Geldingadalsgos "tourist volcano" eruption. You can experience the various geothermal attractions of the region, including the boiling mud pools at Seltún and the Gunnuhver hot springs, by taking the Volcanic Wonders of Reykjanes Geopark tour. The highlight is a guided hike around the fresh lava fields created by the recent eruption, which regularly threatens to resume. ⊠ *BSÍ Bus Terminal, Reykjavík* ☎ *580–5400* ⊕ *www.re.is*.

WHALE WATCHING AND SAILING TOURS

Elding Adventure at Sea. Reykjavík's original whale-watching company started over two decades ago and offers year-round trips with an emphasis on an environmentally sustainable approach. They have expanded into related areas such as puffin watching, and now also operate from a northern base in Akureyri. ⊠ *Ægisgarður 5c* ☎ *519–5000* ⊕ *www.elding.is*.

North Sailing. This highly experienced Húsavík company will cruise you around Skjálfandi Bay looking for whales, and if you're unlucky, they'll offer another trip free of charge. North Sailing also offers whale-watching on a traditional wooden schooner, where hoisting sails and hauling ropes is part of the visitor experience. They even run week-long sailing trips around the fjords of Greenland. ⊠ *Garðarsbraut, Húsavík* ☎ *464–7272* ⊕ *www.northsailing.is*.

On the Calendar

Iceland's busy cultural calendar and vibrant creative communities mean there is bound to be exciting stuff going on, whatever time of year you visit Iceland. Free newspaper the *Reykjavík Grapevine* publishes comprehensive listings of events, but often the best way to discover what's going on in smaller places is just to ask a local.

January

The midwinter feast of **Þorrablót** starts in the middle of January and involves consuming delicacies such as ram's testicles and fermented shark washed down with brennivín, Iceland's signature liquor.

Dark Music Days, Reykjavík's contemporary classical music festival illuminates the city's gloomiest month. ⊕ *www.darkmusicdays.is.*

February

The **Reykjavik Winter Lights Festival** curates a stunning collection of illuminations tbat grace the streets of the capital for four days, giving everyone the perfect excuse for an urban evening stroll. ⊕ *www.visitreykjavik.is/winter-lights-festival.*

Later in the month Reykjavík's **Food and Fun Festival** attracts chefs from all over the world to the city's restaurants, where they compete with each other as they reimagine Icelandic cuisine. ⊕ *www.foodandfun.is.*

March

DesignMarch, which takes place in Reykjavík, is a celebration of the role that design, architecture, and innovation play in Icelandic society. The festival comprises talks, sessions, and exhibitions. ⊕ *designmarch.is.*

April

Ísafjörður, way up north in the Westfjords, is the proud home of rock festival **Aldrei Fór Ég Suður,** (which means "I never went south"—a playful dismissal of Iceland's capital city). This distinctive free-ticketed event is held in a big shed at a shrimp processing plant, and attracts some of the very best Icelandic musicians. ⊕ *www.aldrei.is.*

May

The **Vaka Folk Festival** in Reykjavík celebrates the roots of Icelandic music and the communities around it. Concerts, dance, and the performance of ancient ballads demonstrate the richness of Iceland's cultural history over several days. ⊕ *www.vakareykjavik.is.*

June

At the end of June, the **Reykjavík Fringe Festival** (rvkfringe.is) welcomes all art forms with a grassroots flavor, while earlier in the month nearby Hafnarfjörður plays host to the **Iceland Country Music Festival.**

On the Calendar

Around the longest day of the year, **Secret Solstice**—a three-day outdoor extravaganza where artists play under the midnight sun—takes place in Reykjavík. ⊕ *secretsolstice.is.*

And of course June 17th is **National Day,** a public holiday when Iceland celebrates its independence from Denmark with ceremonies, parades, and festivities.

July

This month you can't throw a hiking boot in Iceland without it hitting a music festival stage, and they're happening all over the country. At Laugarbakki in the northwest, **Norðanpaunk** brings the Icelandic punk community together for a weekend of music with a hardcore DIY ethos. ⊕ *www.nordanpaunk.org.*

And keeping it fast and noisy, to the east of the country in Neskaupstaður, **Eistnaflug** festival provides three days of the best in Icelandic metal. ⊕ *www.eistnaflug.is.*

Also in the east, Seyðisfjörður hosts **LungA,** a progressive arts festival with an eclectic musical line-up. ⊕ *www.lunga.is.*

A little farther up the coast sits the tiny village of Borgarfjörður Eystri which hosts **Bræðslan,** a one-night music festival that has welcomed some of the biggest names on the Icelandic scene. ⊕ *braedslan.is.*

But the music festival that means the most to Icelanders is **Þjóðhátíð** (which means "the national festival"), a massive weekend of live music in the Westman Islands. It can get a little boozy, so be prepared to witness

Icelanders—normally so polite and reserved—really cut loose. ⊕ *dalurinn.is.*

If none of this noisy rock 'n' roll nonsense floats your boat, you may enjoy the biennial **Landsmót**—the National Icelandic Horse Competition—at Hella, in the south. This week-long event showcases the beautiful and legendary Icelandic horse, including riding displays and competitions. ⊕ *www.landsmot.is.*

August

Front and center in Reykjavík's August event calendar is **Pride**: a week of parties, parades, and educational programs where the inclusive nature of Icelandic society means that the whole city joins in. ⊕ *visitreykjavik.is/reykjavik-pride.*

Also grooving in the capital this month is the **Reykjavík Jazz Festival,** six days during which the finest domestic and international musicians in the genre convene in jazz joints across the city. ⊕ *reykjavikjazz.is.*

September

Réttir, the traditional bringing home of sheep after they have spent a summer wandering the hills, takes place in hundreds of Icelandic communities throughout the month of September. Tourists who are handy on a horse can even take part, if they organize it in advance.

But if playing the cowboy (or sheep-person) doesn't appeal, the **Reykjavík International Film Festival** offers a great roundup of groundbreaking independent cinema. ⊕ *www.riff.is.*

October

As Iceland again enters the darker months, the downtempo mood is matched and celebrated by the **Extreme Chill Festival**. Intimate Reykjavík venues play host to the best local and international electronic musicians and their experimental sounds. ⊕ *www. extremechill.org.*

November

Iceland Airwaves is the best known Icelandic music festival internationally, and brings together emerging talent and established artists from Iceland and beyond. The festival takes place across a range of Reykjavík venues, with wristband access allowing you to move around to catch your artists of choice. ⊕ *icelandairwaves.is.*

The **Reykjavík Dance Festival** brings contemporary dance to the city every year, using performance and interactive events to get everybody moving. ⊕ *www.reykja-vikdancefestival.com.*

December

The Icelandic focus in December is on Christmas and the New Year, and it's a magical time to visit. Iceland contributes some unique elements to the festive season such as **Þorláksmessa** on the 23rd, when families eat fermented shark and decorate their tree. **Christmas** itself starts promptly at 6 pm on the evening of the 24th, with presents—often books—exchanged that evening.

And Icelanders go crazy for fireworks on **New Year's Eve.** There are no official displays, but people buy huge amounts of them to set off themselves, a tradition called *sprengja út árið*, or "blowing out the year."

2

Travel Smart ON THE CALENDAR

Contacts

Air

AIRPORTS Akureyri Airport (AEY). ✉ Urðargil 15, Akureyri ☎ 424–4000 ⊕ www.isavia.is/en/akureyri-airport. **Egilsstaðir Airport (EGS).** ✉ Miðvangur 2, Egilsstaðir ☎ 424–4000 ⊕ www.isavia.is/en/egilsstadir-airport. **Keflavík Airport (KEF).** ✉ Keflavíkurflugvöllur, Keflavík, Reykjanesbær ☎ 424–4000 ⊕ www.isavia.is/en/keflavik-airport. **Reykjavík Airport (RVK).** ✉ Vatnsmýri, Reykjavík ☎ 424–4000 ⊕ www.isavia.is/en/reykjavik-airport.

GROUND TRANSPORTATION Airport Direct. ✉ Skógarhlíð 10, Reykjavík ☎ 497–8000 ⊕ www.airportdirect.is. **Flybus.** ✉ BSÍ Bus Terminal, Reykjavík ☎ 580–5400 ⊕ www.re.is/tour/flybus.

🚤 Boat and Ferries

CONTACTS Borea Adventures. ☎ 456–3322 ⊕ www.boreaadventures.com/boat_tours. **Herjólfur.** ☎ 481–2800 ⊕ www.herjolfur.is. **Sæfari Ferry.** ☎ 853–2211 ⊕ en.samskip.is/domestic/

saefari. **Sævar Ferry.** ☎ 695–5544 ⊕ www.hrisey.is/is/thjonusta/hriseyjarferjan-saevar. **Seatours.** ✉ Smiðjustigur 3, Stykkishólmur ☎ 433–2254 ⊕ www.seatours.is. **Smyril Line.** ✉ Kletthals 1, Reykjavík ☎ 470–2803 ⊕ www.smyrilline.is.

🚌 Bus

CONTACTS Strætó. ✉ Hestháls 14, Reykjavík ☎ 540–2700 ⊕ www.straeto.is.

📍 Event and Cultural Information

CONTACTS Reykjavík Grapevine Events. ⊕ events.grapevine.is.

📍 Road and Weather Information

CONTACTS Icelandic Coastal And Road Administration. ☎ 522–1000 ⊕ www.road.is. **Icelandic Meteorological Office.** ✉ Bústaðavegur 7-9, Reykjavík ☎ 522–6000 ⊕ www.vedur.is.

Taxis

CONTACTS BSR. ☎ 561–0000 ⊕ www.taxireykjavik.is. **Hreyfill.** ✉ Reykjavík ☎ 588–5522 ⊕ www.hreyfill.is. **Taxi Iceland.** ☎ 699–6099 ⊕ www.taxi-iceland.com.

📍 Tourist Offices

CONTACTS Akureyri Tourist Information Centre. ✉ Glerárgata 9, Akureyri ☎ 450–1050 ⊕ www.visitakureyri.is. **Egilsstaðastofa Visitor Center.** ✉ Egilsstaðir Camp Site, Kaupvangur 17, Egilsstaðir ☎ 470–0750 ⊕ www.campegilsstadir.is/egilsstadastofa-visitor-center. **Icelandic Tourist Board.** ☎ 535–5500 ⊕ www.inspiredbyiceland.com. **What's On Reykjavík.** ✉ Reykjavík ☎ 551–3600 ⊕ www.whatson.is.

Chapter 3

REYKJAVÍK

3

Updated by
Erika Owen

👁 Sights	🍴 Restaurants	🛏 Hotels	🛍 Shopping	🍸 Nightlife
★★★★☆	★★★★★	★★★★★	★★★★★	★★★★★

WELCOME TO REYKJAVÍK

TOP REASONS TO GO

★ **The thriving restaurant scene:** For a world-class meal, Reykjavík is the place to be.

★ **Nightlife:** Music festivals, an evolving drag scene, and bars with DJs are a defining part of downtown culture; for low-key evenings there are craft beer and cocktail bars.

★ **The harbor:** Feel the wind in your face and take in sea views while you dine or wander in and out of shops.

★ **Regional museums:** Art, history, human anatomy, design—you'll find it all here.

★ **Live music:** Catch a more formal concert at Harpa or head to a local dive bar for an impromptu show.

★ **Iconic sights:** Visit the very top of the gorgeous church, Hallgrímskirkja, far above the city.

For the purposes of this guide, the cultural heart of Reykjavík is divided into City Center East and West, with Lækjargata, a major street that once ran along a stream, as the dividing line.

1 City Center East. To the east of Lækjargata is the extremely recognizable Hallgrímskirkja church, a helpful point from which to orient yourself.

2 City Center West. The western part of the city center encapsulates the Old West Side, Reykjavík's historic quarter.

3 Old Harbor and Vesturbær. Reykjavík Old Harbor is a hub of industrial activity, and home to Harpa, the behemoth concert hall. Vesturbær (the West Town) is home to museums and the revitalized harbor.

4 Greater Reykjavík. Beyond the city center are noteworthy museums like Perlan. Outside the confines of the city is Viðey, the site of Yoko Ono's Imagine Peace Tower. To the far west of Reykjavík is the Seltjarnes peninsula, with large golf courses. At the tip of the peninsula is Grótta Island.

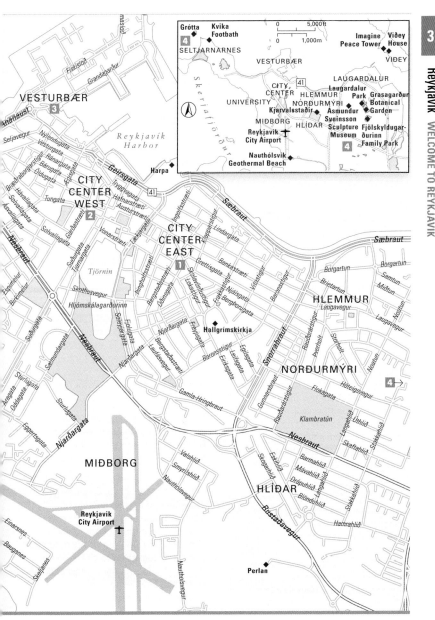

The nation's nerve center and government seat, sprawling Reykjavík is home to half the island's population. On a bay overlooked by proud Mt. Esja (pronounced *eh*-shyuh), with its ever-changing hues, the city is a pleasant sight, its concrete houses painted in light colors and topped by vibrant red, blue, and green roofs. In contrast to the almost treeless countryside, Reykjavík has many tall native birches, rowans, and willows, as well as imported aspen, pines, and spruces.

Reykjavík's name comes from the Icelandic words for smoke (*reykur*) and bay (*vík*). In AD 874, Norseman Ingólfur Arnarson saw Iceland rising out of the misty sea and came ashore at a bay eerily shrouded with plumes of steam from nearby hot springs. Today, most of the houses in Reykjavík are heated by geothermal energy, which avoids air pollution (let alone any "smoke"). You may notice, however, that the hot water brings a slight sulfur smell to faucets.

Reykjavík might be one of the smallest capital cities in the world, but the greater metropolitan area is still big enough to accommodate seven major districts/municipalities, each with its own elected council: Reykjavík, Kópavogur, Garðabær, Hafnarfjörður, Mosfellsbær, Álftanes, and Seltjarnarnes. Most people spend their time in central Reykjavík (district 101), which is also known as "Miðbær"

or "Downtown Reykjavík"; this is where most of the city's cultural attractions and shopping options are located. Other popular areas—especially for tourists—include Vesturbær (West Town), Austurbær (East Town), and Greater Downtown (Seltjarnarnes, in particular).

A city bus can get you anywhere you need to go, but the best way to see Reykjavík is on foot—this helps you get a true sense of the city's past and present.

Prices are relatively on a par with other major European cities. One practical option is to purchase a Reykjavík City Card, available at most of the city's museums and tourist information centers. This card permits unlimited bus travel and admission to city museums, the Fjölskyldugarðurinn Family Park, and any of the city's eight pools, as well as a free ride on the ferry that travels to Viðey island. The cards are valid for one (ISK 4,200), two (ISK 5,850), or three days (ISK 7,200), and they pay for themselves after three or four uses a day. Even without the City Card, admission (ISK 1,950) to one of the city art museums (Hafnarhús, Kjarvalsstaðir, or Ásmundar-safn) gets you free same-day admission to the other two.

Planning

When to Go

There is no bad time to visit Reykjavik, it just depends on how much daylight you'd like to have. During the months of June and July, the Midnight Sun offers near-total daylight around the clock and "summer temperatures" of 55 to 65°F. August also sees extended days. For a more expected amount of sunlight, April, May, September, and October will deliv-er, but the temperatures will be lower outside of Iceland's Arctic summer.

Visit during the wintertime (November, December, January, and February) and expect lots of darkness (in a cozy way), temperatures in the 25 to 35°F range, and constant weather changes. Reykjavik sees a lot of snowfall during this time, but the city's geothermal-heated streets help keep the downtown area walkable. Plus, you can catch the Northern Lights during these colder, darker months. Expect lots of tourists during both sum-mertime and wintertime, but you'll find a reprieve from the crowds during Iceland's shoulder season: February through mid-April and mid-August through mid-November.

Planning Your Time

Although Reykjavík is quite spread out and much less dense than other Nordic capitals, most of the significant landmarks and sights are found in the downtown area. While you can certainly pack a lot of sightseeing into just one day in the city, at least two days will give you time to see major sights as well as more chances to explore the impressive dining and nightlife scenes.

Getting Here and Around

AIR

There are plenty of flights coming into Keflavik Airport, the closest international air travel hub to the capital city. Expect a 45-minute drive once you've left the airport, more if there's significant traffic. You can rent a car to reach Reykjavik or take a shuttle bus straight into the city center. There is also a domestic airport in Reykjavik, should you be traveling on to Akureyri or other local destinations.

AIRPORT TRANSFERS

The Reykjavík FlyBus runs round-trip between Keflavík Airport (from directly outside the terminal building) and the BSÍ Bus Terminal in Reykjavík. From there, you can take one of the connections to larger hotels and guesthouses, or you can take a taxi to your final destination. FlyBuses are scheduled according to flight arrivals and departures. The ride takes around 45 minutes, and the fare is ISK 3,499 per person one-way or ISK 6,499 round-trip.

If you need a quicker transfer from the airport, a taxi may be the most efficient option (as well as the most expensive). The ride from Keflavík Airport to the city center is a little faster than the FlyBus and costs around ISK 15,000 during daytime and more at night. Naturally, larger cars will cost more, and each fee depends on the taxi company or service. There are direct phones to taxi companies in the arrivals hall. From the Reykjavík Airport, a taxi to a hotel in the downtown area costs around ISK 2,000. Municipal Bus 15 also stops in front of the main domestic terminal.

CONTACTS Reykjavík FlyBus. ☎ *580–5400* ⊕ *www.flybus.is.*

BUS

The municipal bus service, affectionately nicknamed "Strætó" (pronounced *stry*-toe), provides extensive, cheap, and reliable service throughout Reykjavík and its surrounding municipalities. Buses are yellow, with an "S" logo on a red circular background. They begin service around 6:30 am, and the last buses of the day tend to depart around 11 pm. Express buses run every 15 minutes during peak times and every half hour during evenings and weekends. Route booklets are available at the main terminals of Hlemmur, Mjódd, and Ártún, as well as at most tourist information centers. A "Strætó bs" app is available for iOS, offering mobile planners, payments, and real-time travel information. The flat fare within the sprawling capital area is ISK 490, payable using the app or to the driver in exact change upon boarding. A single fare allows you to travel any distance in the metro area. Depending on your destination, you may have to change buses; if so, ask for *skiptimiða* (*skiff*-teh-mee-tha), a transfer ticket that you give the second bus driver.

If you plan an extended stay in the Reykjavík area, it may be worthwhile to spend ISK 4,900 on the KLAPP ten, a set of 10 passes or the monthly pass, which costs ISK 8,000. For shorter stays, a practical investment is the Reykjavík City Card, available at most of the city's museums and tourist information centers, which permits unlimited bus usage and admission to any of the capital city's eight pools, the Fjölskyldugarðurinn Family Park, the ferry to Viðey Island, and city-run museums.

CONTACT Strætó. ☎ *540–2700* ⊕ *www.bus.is.*

TAXI

Most taxicabs in Reykjavík are new, fully equipped passenger sedans. They have small "taxi" signs on top and can be hailed anywhere on the street; the "laus" sign indicates that the cab is available. There are taxi stands in a few locations around the city, but it is common to order a taxi by phone—normally you have to wait only a few minutes. Most taxis accept major credit and debit cards. Fares are regulated by meter; rides around Reykjavík run between ISK 2,500 and ISK 5,500. There is no tipping.

CONTACTS BSR Taxi. ✉ *Skógarhlíð 18* ☎ *561–0000* ⊕ *www.bsr.is.* **Hreyfill Taxi.** ✉ *Fellsmúli 26* ☎ *588–5522* ⊕ *www.hreyfill.is.*

Restaurants

The dining scene in Reykjavík has diversified a great deal in the past few years: traditional Icelandic restaurants exist alongside restaurants serving Asian, Italian, Mexican, Indian, and vegetarian fare. You'll also find a number of upscale establishments emphasizing locally grown ingredients and New Nordic cuisine.

Hotels

Lodging ranges from modern, first-class Scandinavian-style hotels to inexpensive guesthouses and B&Bs offering basic amenities at relatively low prices. Iceland's climate makes air-conditioning unnecessary. Most hotel rooms have televisions, though not always cable TV. Lower-price hotels sometimes have a television lounge in lieu of a TV in each room. Ask if your hotel offers complimentary admission to the closest swimming pool.

RESTAURANT AND HOTEL PRICES

Restaurant prices in the reviews are the average cost of a main course at dinner, or if dinner is not served, at lunch. Hotel prices in the reviews are the lowest cost of a standard double room in high season. Restaurant and hotel reviews have been shortened. For full information, visit Fodors.com.

What it Costs in ISK

	$	$$	$$$	$$$$
RESTAURANTS				
	under ISK 2,500	ISK 2,500–4,000	ISK 4,001–5,500	over ISK 5,500
HOTELS				
	under ISK 20,000	ISK 20,000–28,000	ISK 28,001–35,000	over ISK 35,000

Nightlife

Through most of the year, Reykjavík has an active cultural life, which is especially strong in music and the visual arts. The classical performing arts scene tends to quiet down somewhat in summer, though a growing number of rock and jazz concerts—as well as a chamber music festival held in Harpa, called Reykjavík Midsummer Music—have been helping to fill in the gap. The Reykjavík Arts Festival is held annually in May; past festivals have drawn Luciano Pavarotti and David Bowie, among other stars. Check out the *Reykjavík Grapevine* (⊕ grapevine.is) for up-to-date listings; it's biweekly in summer, and monthly in winter.

Nightlife in Reykjavík essentially means two types of establishments: nightclubs with dancing and live music, and pubs. Icelanders tend to dress up for going out, but visitors can get away with being a bit more casual. On weekends, unless you start before 11 pm, be prepared to wait in line, especially if the weather is good. After midnight during the first weekends of summer, it will feel like everyone is out enjoying the additional sunlight. Suffice it to say, Icelanders party en masse.

Shopping

The main shopping downtown is on and around Austurstræti, Aðalstræti, Hafnarstræti, Hverfisgata, Bankastræti, Laugavegur, and Skólavörðustígur.

Tours

Ferðafélag Íslands, or the Iceland Touring Association (ITA), owns and operates numerous mountain huts where hikers and other travelers can get a sleeping-bag accommodation (pre-booking is necessary). The ITA also offers a variety of programs year-round: day tours (hiking, cross-country skiing, or bus tours), weekend tours (Friday evening through Sunday), and longer tours.

Arcanum offers snowmobiling tours, and Dog Sledding Iceland offers dog-sled tours; both companies can take you to see a glacier as well. Icelandic Mountain Guides is the go-to tour company for a wide range of quality adventures and activities, covering everything from superjeep tours, day trips to popular natural wonders, and glacial excursions to memorable multiday or monthlong expeditions. Arctic Rafting specializes in rafting tours, but also offers quad biking, climbing, trekking, biking, and a number of other activities.

Several bus companies, including Reykjavík Excursions and Gray Line, also run bus tours that include museums and art galleries, shopping centers, and the like in around three hours. Reykjavík Excursions also operates a hop-on, hop-off bus service in the city during the summer.

3

Reykjavík PLANNING

Arcanum

ADVENTURE TOURS | One of Iceland's main tour operators, Arcanum specializes in glacier walks, ATV tours, snowmobiling, and jeep tours. Activities take place on or around Sólheimajökull, one of the magnificent glacial tongues of the Mýrdalsjökull ice cap. Most tours include an option for a pick-up in Reykjavík. ⊠ *Sólheimaskála, Ytri Sólheimum 1* ☎ *487–1500* ⊕ *www. arcanum.is.*

Arctic Rafting

ADVENTURE TOURS | This company specializes in river rafting tours, but also offers quad biking, climbing, trekking, biking, and a number of other exciting activities that will get you out of the city. ⊠ *Laugavegur 11* ☎ *564–7000* ⊕ *www. arcticrafting.com.*

DIVE.IS

SPECIAL-INTEREST TOURS | The folks at Dive. is specialize in snorkeling and diving tours of the stunning Silfra Fissure—an area where the American and Eurasian tectonic plates meet, at Þingvellir National Park—as well as a number of other locations in Iceland. ⊠ *Hólmaslóð 2, 101 Reykjavík* ☎ *578–6200* ⊕ *www.dive.is.*

Dog Sledding Iceland

ADVENTURE TOURS | Forty-five-minute mush tours, with real Greenland dogs, are available from this family-run business year-round. Depending on the time of year, the tours with transfer from Reykjavík and cost ISK 44,500 or ISK 47,500. If you have your own transport, you can drive to the basecamp yourself (around two hours from Reykjavík) and take the tour for ISK 29,900 or ISK 32,900 instead. ⊠ *Hólmasel–Gaulverjabæjarhreppi* ☎ *863–6733* ⊕ *www.dogsledding.is.*

Ferðafélag Íslands

(*Iceland Touring Association*)
WALKING TOURS | The Iceland Touring Association, also known as Ferðafélag Íslands, is the best place to sign up for hiking tours, especially for the famous Laugavegur hiking trail. ⊠ *Mörkinni 6* ☎ *568–2533* ⊕ *www.fi.is.*

Gray Line Iceland (*Iceland Excursions*)

BUS TOURS | **FAMILY** | From a *Game of Thrones*–themed bus tour to hunting down the northern lights on an ATV, this operator offers experiences as simple as riding a Highland road from Reykjavík to Akureyri to the more complicated task of hiking Landmannalaugar. Gray Line also offers transfers between Reykjavík and Keflavík International Airport (from ISK 3,400). Day tours—like a hop-on, hop-off city sightseeing experience—start at ISK 7,300. ⊠ *Hafnarstræti 20* ☎ *540–1313* ⊕ *www.grayline.is.*

★ Iceland Adventure Tours

ADVENTURE TOURS | This company offers an impressive array of ways to see the natural environment that Iceland's so famous for. From snorkeling or diving into Silfra Fissure to hiking down into a volcanic crater, the friendly tour guides will be there to make sure you're comfortable every step of the way. An added bonus is that they take photos for you, so all you have to think about is enjoying yourself. ⊠ *Bildshofði 14, Reykjavík* ☎ *519–3777* ⊕ *icelandadventuretours.is.*

Icelandic Mountain Guides

ADVENTURE TOURS | The go-to tour company for a wide range of quality adventures and activities covers everything from glacier walks and super-jeep day tours of popular natural wonders to memorable month-long expeditions. ⊠ *Stórhöfði 33* ☎ *587–9999* ⊕ *www.mountainguides.is.*

★ Íshestar (*Icelandic Riding Tours*)

HORSEBACK RIDING | This company offers horseback rides that range from one to seven hours as well as a variety of half- to multiday tours that include guides and transportation from Reykjavík hotels (it's only a 15-minute drive out of town). The most unique way to spend time in the stunning Icelandic countryside is on horseback; you can experience Icelandic horses' special fifth gait, the *tölt*.

✉ *Sörlaskeiði 26* ☎ *555–7000* ⊕ *www. ishestar.is.*

Reykjavík Excursions
ADVENTURE TOURS | FAMILY | You can join one of many single- or multiday hiking journeys straight from the capital city. Reykjavík Excursions also offers shorter adventures like whale-watching from Reykjavík, northern lights tours, and city sightseeing on a double-decker bus as well as more involved experiences like hiking Þórsmörk. ✉ *BSÍ Bus Terminal, Vatnsmýrarvegi 10* ☎ *580–5400* ⊕ *www. re.is.*

Reykjavík Sailors
BOAT TOURS | Whale-watching, puffin-spotting, northern lights hunting, sea angling—Reykjavík Sailors does it all. You can also request a private tour for any of the company's offerings if you're traveling with a group. ✉ *Hlésgata Vesturbugt F101, Reykjavík* ☎ *571–2222* ⊕ *www. reykjaviksailors.is.*

★ Special Tours
BOAT TOURS | While Special Tours offers all of the regular tours—whale-watching, puffin-watching, and sea angling—don't miss the three-hour northern lights cruise if you're visiting during the wintertime. There's no better way to see the aurora than afloat in the bay. ✉ *Ægisgarður 13, Reykjavík* ☎ *560–8800* ⊕ *www.special-tours.is.*

TukTuk Tours
GUIDED TOURS | Inspired by the auto rickshaws of South Asia, these battery-operated three-wheelers, with trademark yellow-and-black rain covers, can be spotted all over town, taking visitors on a variety of eco-friendly sightseeing tours. It's best to book in advance via phone, but there's always the possibility that you could hop on one at the TukTuk stand in front of Harpa Concert Hall. It's certainly a cheap and cheerful way to discover the city and stock up on a few pearls of local wisdom. Note that seats are low

but nicely heated. ✉ *Harpa Music Hall, Austurbakki 2* ☎ *788–5500.*

Útivist Travel Association
WALKING TOURS | This expert guide service is famous for summer solstice hikes across the Fimmvörðuháls mountain trail, which passes between the ice caps of both Eyjafjallajökull and Mýrdalsjökull. ✉ *Ferðafélagið Útivist, Laugavegur 178* ☎ *562–1000* ⊕ *www.utivist.is.*

Visitor Information

The official tourist information center of Reykjavík is staffed by a team of multilingual personnel offering up-to-date information on all the city's services, lodgings, and tours, as well as the best spots for your preferred dining experience. You can also book tours, exchange currency, and purchase maps, stamps, and the Reykjavík City Card.

CONTACTS Reykjavík Tourist Information Center. ✉ *Tjarnargata 11* ☎ *411–6040* ⊕ *www.visitreykjavik.is.*

City Center East

While you may be able to find quieter moments in the less visited neighborhoods of Reykjavik, City Center East is buzzing with shoppers, diners, partiers, and people-watchers no matter the time of day. It's not rare to find more tourists than locals filling the streets, but even the busiest areas maintain the city's iconic charm. Hallgrimskirkja—the city's tallest church—overlooks the district, with Skólavörðustígur running west and housing some of Reykjavik's most popular shopping spots. Head north to Laugavegur and you'll run into the neighborhood's main artery of restaurants and bars. This street lights up with activity late at night on the weekends, as locals and visitors alike hop from bar to bar.

Hallgrímskirkja is perhaps the most famous church in Iceland.

Don't miss the murals dotting buildings around this neighborhood. From eye-catching branding for local businesses to massive, mystical creatures covering the side of apartment buildings, there's a reason the guided mural tours throughout this area are so popular.

👁 Sights

The Culture House
(*National Cultural House*)
HISTORY MUSEUM | FAMILY | Crests on the facade of the impressive former Landsbókasafnið (Old National Library) name significant Icelandic literary figures; the renovated building now houses interesting cultural displays and art exhibits. Erected between 1906 and 1908, it was primarily a library for most of the 20th century, but its book collection has been moved to the Þjóðarbókhlaðan at the National and University Library of Iceland. A free guided tour in English is offered Tuesday through Sunday at 2 pm, September through May, and weekdays (except Wednesday) between June and August. ✉ *Hverfisgata 15, Miðbær* 🕿 *530–2200* ⊕ *www.culturehouse.is* 💰 *ISK 2,000* ⏱ *Closed Mon. Oct.–Apr.*

★ Hallgrímskirkja (*Hallgrímur's Church*)
CHURCH | FAMILY | Completed in 1986 after more than 40 years of construction, the church is named for the 17th-century hymn writer Hallgrímur Pétursson. It has a stylized concrete facade recalling both organ pipes and the distinctive columnar basalt formations you can see around Iceland. For ISK 1,000, you can climb to the top of the church for incredible views of greater Reykjavík. You may luck into hearing a performance or practice on the church's huge pipe organ. In front of Hallgrímskirkja is a statue of Leif Erikson, the Icelander who discovered America 500 years before Columbus. (Leif's father was Eric the Red, who discovered Greenland.) The statue, by American sculptor Alexander Calder, was presented to Iceland by the United States in 1930 to mark the millennium of the Alþing parliament. ✉ *Hallgrímstorg 1, Miðbær* 🕿 *510–1000* ⊕ *www.hallgrimskirkja.is* 💰 *Tower ISK 1,000.*

Höfði

HISTORIC SIGHT | This historic house stands out for both its architectural and historical importance. It was here, in 1986, that President Ronald Reagan and President Mikhail Gorbachev met and officially marked the end of the Cold War. The house is not open to visitors, but it's worth spending some time exploring the exterior. ✉ *Borgartún 105, Hlíðar* ☎ *552–5375* ⊕ *www.visitreykjavik.is.*

★ Icelandic Punk Museum

OTHER MUSEUM | This tinier-than-tiny museum is crammed into what used to be a set of public bathrooms at the bottom of a stairwell right off a city sidewalk. Somehow it all seems fitting for a museum focused on punk rock. Photos, posters, handbills, equipment, and instruments line the walls and displays at this subterranean memorial to one of the country's favorite music genres. ✉ *Bankastræti 2, Miðbær* ☎ *568–2003* ⊕ *icelandic-punk-museumponksafn-is-lands.business.site* 🖭 *ISK 1,200.*

Ingólfur Arnarson Statue

PUBLIC ART | **FAMILY** | Ingólfur Arnarson is renowned as the first Nordic settler in Iceland. Beyond this statue lies the city's architectural mélange: 18th-century stone houses, small 19th-century wooden houses, and office blocks from the 1930s and '40s. ✉ *Arnarhóll, Miðbær.*

Menntaskólinn í Reykjavík

(*Reykjavík Junior College*)
COLLEGE | Many graduates from the country's oldest educational institution, established in 1846, have gone on to dominate political and social life in Iceland. Former president Vigdís Finnbogadóttir and numerous cabinet ministers, including Iceland's former prime minister, Gunnlaugsson Davið Oddsson, are graduates, as are film producer Hrafn Gunnlaugsson and well-known author Þórarinn Eldjarn. ✉ *Þingholtsstræti 12, corner of Amtmannsstígur and Lækjargata, Miðbær* ☎ *545–1900* ⊕ *www.mr.is.*

The National Gallery of Iceland

ART MUSEUM | With a focus on Icelandic artists, this museum also digs into works of art that help bring the country's folklore and culture to life. This exhibit is pretty small and specific—you can breeze through it in less than an hour—but your ticket fee also grants you admission to two other nearby exhibits: Ásgrím Jónsson's house and the Art Museum of Iceland. ✉ *Fríkirkjuvegur 7, Reykjavík* ☎ *515–9600* ⊕ *www.listasafn. is* 🖭 *ISK 2,000.*

Stjórnarráðshúsið (*Government House*)

GOVERNMENT BUILDING | This low white building, constructed in the 18th century as a prison, today houses the office of the prime minister. ✉ *Lækjartorg Plaza, Stjórnarráðshúsinu við Lækjartorg, Miðbær* ☎ *545–8400* ⊕ *www.for.is* 🕙 *Closed weekends.*

Sun Voyager Sculpture

PUBLIC ART | This steel sculpture resembling a Viking ship is hard to miss as you drive along the water in Reykjavík. If you're traveling on Sæbraut, you'll see it on the water right before you hit the Harpa Concert Hall (when traveling east to west). The Sun Voyager was created by local sculptor Jón Gunnar Árnason. The original intention was to create a dreamlike boat that appears to float off into the sun. If you visit during sunset, you'll feel immediately transported. ✉ *Sæbraut, Miðbær* ☎ *551–5789* ⊕ *www. sunvoyager.is.*

Restaurants

Austur Indíafélagið

$$$ | **INDIAN** | You'll have a tough time choosing your dinner line-up at this Indian restaurant. From the fan-favorite tandoori salmon to the pappadoms, the spices are bold and the flavors are unbeatable when it comes to Indian fare in the city. **Known for:** good vegetarian options; excellent fish curry; beautiful interiors. 🖻 *Average main: ISK4,895*

City Center East

0 — 500 ft
0 — 100 m

Sights ▼

1 The Culture House **C2**
2 Hallgrímskirkja **D6**
3 Höfði **I3**
4 Icelandic Punk Museum **B2**
5 Ingólfur Arnarson Statue **C2**
6 Menntaskólinn í Reykjavík **A3**
7 The National Gallery of Iceland **A4**
8 Stjórnarráðshúsið **B2**
9 Sun Voyager Sculpture **F2**

Restaurants ▼

1 Austur Indiafélagið **E4**
2 Ban Thai Restaurant **I6**
3 Brauð & Co. **E5**
4 Café Loki **D6**
5 Dill Restaurant **F4**
6 Dragon Dim Sum **C3**
7 Gló **D3**
8 Grái Kötturinn **C2**
9 Hlemmur Mathöll **H5**
10 Holt Restaurant **B5**
11 Íslenski Barinn **B2**
12 Jörgensen Kitchen & Bar **I6**
13 Kaffibrennslan **D3**
14 Kol Restaurant **D5**
15 MAT BAR **C3**
16 ÓX **D4**
17 Reykjavík Chips **F5**
18 ROK **D5**
19 Skál! **I5**
20 Snaps Bistro Bar and Restaurant **C5**
21 Solon Bistro & Bar **B3**
22 Sumac **D4**
23 Þrír Frakkar **B6**
24 2Guys **H5**
25 Yuzu Burger **D3**

Quick Bites ▼

1 Café Babalú **C5**
2 Eldur og Ís **B3**
3 Emilie and the Cool Kids **G5**
4 Kaffi Mokka **C3**
5 Kaffifélagið **C3**
6 Kaffitár **B3**
7 Kaktus Espressobar **F5**
8 Reykjavík Roasters **D5**
9 Svarta Kaffið **E4**

Hotels ▼

1 Alda Hotel **F5**
2 Canopy by Hilton Reykjavik City Centre **C3**
3 Center Hotels Laugavegur **H5**
4 Eyja Guldsmeden Hotel **I6**
5 Hótel Holt **B5**
6 Hotel Leifur Eiríksson ... **D6**
7 Hotel Óðinsvé **C4**
8 Hótel VON **F4**
9 Ion City Hotel **D4**
10 Kex **G4**
11 Loft Hostel **B3**
12 Midgardur by Center Hotels **I6**
13 101 Hotel **B2**
14 Room with a View **C3**
15 Sand Hotel **D4**

✉ *Hverfisgata 56, Miðbær* ☎ *552–1630*
🌐 *www.austurindia.is* 🕒 *No lunch.*

Ban Thai Restaurant
$$ | **THAI** | **FAMILY** | When you find yourself tired of Icelandic dishes, check out Ban Thai. Here you'll find traditional Thai dishes with a bit more kick than you might find elsewhere in the city. **Known for:** massive menu; generous portions; quick service. [$] *Average main: ISK2,690* ✉ *Laugavegur 130, Miðbær* ☎ *552–2444* 🌐 *www.banthaiiceland.com* 🕒 *No lunch.*

★ **Brauð & Co**
$ | **BAKERY** | Ágúst Einþórsson is the baker behind this local favorite, with its full displays full of simple yet perfect pastries and other baked goods. It's the kind of unflashy spot you stumble upon and can't get out of your head long after you return home. **Known for:** superfresh cinnamon buns; buttery croissants; early open hours. [$] *Average main: ISK990* ✉ *Frakkastígur 16, Miðbær* ☎ *456–7777* 🌐 *www.braudogco.is* 🕒 *No dinner.*

★ **Café Loki**
$$ | **ICELANDIC** | **FAMILY** | This Icelandic food haven is a must-stop for many people around the world—just take a look at their guest book. Do yourself a favor and visit after taking in the views from the iconic Hallgrímskirkja; you'll feel like you're in the center of a Nordic movie set. **Known for:** location across from Hallgrímskirkja; delicious homemade dishes; friendly service. [$] *Average main: ISK3,100* ✉ *Lokastígur 28, Miðbær* ☎ *466–2828* 🌐 *www.loki.is.*

★ **Dill Restaurant**
$$$$ | **SEAFOOD** | There's only one option at Dill: a tasting menu with a modern spin on traditional Icelandic dishes. In 2017, Dill was the first restaurant in Iceland to be awarded a Michelin star, with chef Gunnar Karl Gíslason at the helm. **Known for:** spectacular tasting menu; careful attention to detail with presentation; downright delicious takes on Icelandic dishes. [$] *Average main: ISK15,900* ✉ *Laugavegur 59, Miðbær* ☎ *552–1522* 🌐 *www.dillrestaurant.is* 🕒 *Closed Sun. and Mon. year-round, Sat. every other week, and Tues. every other week. No lunch.*

Dragon Dim Sum
$ | **ASIAN** | This is the only spot in the city where you can taste a huge variety of dumplings and satay. You'll find it tucked on a quiet street off of Hverfisgata with a few outdoor tables. **Known for:** quick eats; friendly service; best dumplings in the city. [$] *Average main: ISK1,790* ✉ *Bergstaðastræti 4, Reykjavík* ☎ *766–1400* 🌐 *www.dragondimsum.is* 🕒 *Closed Sun.*

Gló
$ | **VEGETARIAN** | The latest brainchild of Solla Eiríks, one of the pioneers of the raw-food movement in Iceland, Gló's menu changes daily and often features imaginative and varied vegetarian dishes such as nut steaks, pies, and delicious coconut curry. The interior has lots of natural light and combines modern furnishings with rustic "log" wallpaper. **Known for:** ample vegetarian and vegan options; the pulled Oumph burger; reasonably priced healthy meals. [$] *Average main: ISK1,900* ✉ *Fákfen 9, Miðbær* ☎ *553–1111* 🌐 *www.glo.is* 🕒 *Closed Sun.*

★ **Grái Kötturinn**
$$ | **CAFÉ** | This plain and simple breakfast spot has won the hearts of many politicians who work nearby—as well as Björk—and it tends to get quite busy. If you feel like taking on a huge meal, give "the Truck" (pancakes, eggs, bacon, fried potatoes, tomatoes, and toast) a go. **Known for:** signature "the Truck" breakfast; frequented by local celebrities; lots of books to read while you wait. [$] *Average main: ISK2,800* ✉ *Hverfisgata 16a, Miðbær* ☎ *551–1544* 🌐 *www.graikotturinn.is* 🕒 *Closed weekends. No dinner.*

★ **Hlemmur Mathöll**

$ | **SCANDINAVIAN** | **FAMILY** | This food hall features eight vendors loved by locals: Brauð & Co., Fuego, SKÁL!, Micro Roast Te & Kaffi, Flatey Pizza, Kröst, Fjárhúsið, and Báhn Mí. It's a great place for groups and kids. **Known for:** local favorites; wide variety of options; kid-friendly atmosphere. [$] *Average main: ISK1,900* ✉ *Laugavegur 107, Miðbær* ☎ *577–6200* 🌐 *www.hlemmurmatholl.is.*

★ **Holt Restaurant**

$$ | **ICELANDIC** | Icelandic art covers the walls of this restaurant in the Hótel Holt, within walking distance of downtown; the cocktail lounge and bar showcase drawings by Jóhannes Kjarval. It has long been at the forefront of Icelandic dining, with impeccable service and mouthwatering wild-game and seafood dishes—favorites include gravlax and reindeer. **Known for:** impressive reserve wine list; welcoming vibe; diverse whiskey selection. [$] *Average main: ISK3,450* ✉ *Hótel Holt, Bergstaðastræti 37, Miðbær* ☎ *552–5700* 🌐 *www.holt.is.*

★ **Íslenski Barinn**

$$ | **SEAFOOD** | From traditional fish pie and meat soup to a spectacular waffle fry, Íslenski Barinn covers a lot of ground on its menu, but the focus is local at this restaurant and bar. You'll also find only beers and spirits made in Iceland—so don't come here looking for imports. **Known for:** delicious fish pie; hyperlocal beer and spirit options; perfect place to mix with the locals. [$] *Average main: ISK2,500* ✉ *Ingólfsstræti 1a, Miðbær* ☎ *517–6767* 🌐 *www.islenskibarinn.is.*

Jörgensen Kitchen & Bar

$$ | **SCANDINAVIAN** | Although Jörgensen Kitchen & Bar has a similar menu to other eateries around the city (burgers, fish-and-chips, cod, catch of the day, etc), what's really intriguing about this restaurant is the private garden area. Dining in this dreamy oasis in the middle of the city's main shopping street is a real pleasure. **Known for:** beautiful garden; Icelandic pancakes; central location. [$] *Average main: ISK3,400* ✉ *Laugavegur 120* ☎ *595–8565* 🌐 *www.jorgensenkitchen.com.*

★ **Kaffibrennslan**

$ | **CAFÉ** | By day, Kaffibrennslan is a cozy café, with a menu full of sandwich and soup options and every coffee drink you could imagine. At night, the scene changes and you're more likely to be taking a shot with the bartender than asking them which sandwich they prefer—no matter what, you're in for a great time. **Known for:** friendly bartenders; cozy seating in the loft; substantial sandwiches. [$] *Average main: ISK1,390* ✉ *Laugavegur, Miðbær* ☎ *511–5888* 🌐 *www.kaffibrennslan101.is.*

★ **Kol Restaurant**

$$$ | **SCANDINAVIAN** | Sipping on a refreshing "Donkey" cocktail will add a spicy warmth to your cheeks while you take in this friendly spot's sights, sounds, and aromas, which intensify as the evening progresses. Each dish is carefully paired with wine and delivered with a detailed narrative by well-informed staff. **Known for:** incredibly cozy interior; "Simply the Best" desserts; inviting and inspired cocktail list. [$] *Average main: ISK4,690* ✉ *Skólavörðustíg 40, Miðbær* ☎ *517–7474* 🌐 *www.kolrestaurant.is.*

★ **MAT BAR**

$$ | **EUROPEAN** | This Nordic-Italian restaurant does the classics very well, but the owner, Guðjón Hauksson, sought out an Italian cheese-maker for the mozzarella; it's best with pickled tomatoes and basil in MAT BAR's take on the traditional Caprese salad. There's an emphasis on seasonal produce, so there's a good chance the menu will be different every time you visit. **Known for:** next-level mozzarella; great cocktail menu; food that's meant to be shared. [$] *Average main: ISK2,990* ✉ *Hverfisgata 26, Miðbær* ☎ *788–3900* 🌐 *www.matbar.is* 🕒 *Closed Sun.*

★ ÓX

$$$$ | **ICELANDIC** | Be prepared to give up all control when you walk into the intimate space that is the 11-seat, Michelin-starred ÓX. The 12-course tasting menu is a surprise, but just give in to the experience and let the chefs introduce you to the freshest Icelandic ingredients you can experience. **Known for:** intimate interiors; superb (and unexpected) tasting menu; next-level service. $ *Average main: ISK42,900* ⊠ *Laugavegur 28, Reykjavík* ☎ ⊕ *www.ox.restaurant* ⊗ *Closed Sun. and Mon. No lunch.*

Reykjavík Chips

$ | **FAST FOOD** | The talented owners here (one of whom is a BAFTA Award–winning musician) are keen to prove that they can make a tasty meal out of the lowly potato. Cooked in the simple Belgian style and offered with a range of tasty sauces and beverages, the "chips" are surprisingly good and certainly worthy of the hype. **Known for:** affordable prices; delicious thick-cut fries; more sauces than you'll know what to do with. $ *Average main: ISK1,050* ⊠ *Vitastígur 10, Miðbær* ☎ *552–2221* ⊕ *www.rvkchips.is.*

★ ROK

$ | **SCANDINAVIAN** | The *plokkfiskur* (fish stew) at this local favorite is the perfect thing to warm you up on a cold night. The restaurant also hosts a Champagne happy hour that includes a bottle of bubbly, licorice, and cantaloupe every day between 4 and 7 pm. **Known for:** traditional Icelandic dishes; Champagne happy hour; extensive cocktail list. $ *Average main: ISK2,390* ⊠ *Frakkastígur 26a, Miðbær* ☎ *544–4443* ⊕ *www.rokrestaurant.is.*

★ Skál!

$ | **SCANDINAVIAN** | Located in the Hlemmur Mathöll food hall, Skál! offers elegant Icelandic platings in a casual setting. The best part is that prices are much more reasonable than you'd see in most restaurants around the city, but you really aren't giving up any quality when it comes to the food. **Known for:** exellent arctic char; reasonable portions; fun food hall location. $ *Average main: ISK2,350* ⊠ *Laugavegur 107, Hlíðar* ☎ *519–6515* ⊕ *www.skalrvk.com.*

★ Snaps Bistro Bar and Restaurant

$$ | **FRENCH FUSION** | Always bustling, this popular bistro bar is famous for its weekend brunch and attracts a lively group of locals, whose musical inflections mingle nicely with the chatter of out-of-towners. Standouts on the French-inspired menu are many, but you can't go wrong with the fish of the day or the beef tenderloin. **Known for:** a full gin and tonic menu; delicious fish of the day specials; fresh oysters. $ *Average main: ISK3,990* ⊠ *Þórsgata 1, Miðbær* ☎ *511–6677* ⊕ *www.snaps.is.*

Solon Bistro & Bar

$$ | **EUROPEAN** | At the artsy Solon Bistro & Bar you can view some modern art, have a meal (try the fish of the day), and enjoy some people-watching through the large windows. You'll find local ingredients alongside Italian staples and fresher-than-fresh seafood dishes on the menu. **Known for:** perfectly prepared seafood; reasonable lunch specials; generous portions. $ *Average main: ISK2,990* ⊠ *Bankastræti 7A, Miðbær* ☎ *562–3232* ⊕ *www.solon.is.*

Sumac

$$ | **MEDITERRANEAN** | Shared plates are the way to go at Sumac, where you're bound to make a few new friends given the lively environment. The menu is set up for tasting a lot of different dishes—perfect when you're with a crew or not quite sure what you're craving. **Known for:** shared plates; lively atmosphere; diverse tasting menu. $ *Average main: ISK3,120* ⊠ *Laugavegur 28, Reykjavík* ☎ *537–9900* ⊕ *www.sumac.is* ⊗ *Closed Sun. and Mon. No lunch.*

Grjótaþorp

Grjótaþorp is a distinctive district in what is believed to be the oldest part of town: its roots trace back to Iceland's earliest settlers. Though its name translates to "rocks' village," the colorful houses in this enchanting quarter of the city are mostly made from wood. Look for a little red house in Garðarstræti named Unúhús, after its one-time owner Una Gísladóttir, whose endeavor to provide young poets, writers, and artists with inexpensive accommodations led to the area becoming known as an important cultural hot spot in the early 20th century—Nobel Prize winner Halldór Laxness was a regular guest there. It begins at Aðalstræti (Main Street).

Þrír Frakkar

$$ | **SEAFOOD** | According to urban legend, it's tradition for Icelanders returning home from abroad to make their first stop at this beloved restaurant, and indulge in chef Úlfar's legendary fish strew. Not just a favorite with the locals, Þrír Frakkar—a curious name that can be interpreted either as "the Three Overcoats" or "the Three Frenchies"—has a number of high-profile celebrity fans, including chef Jamie Oliver, who reportedly dined on guillemot during his visit. **Known for:** great take on classic plokkfiskur; celebrity sightings; traditional dishes like smoked puffin and whale steak. Ⓢ *Average main: ISK3,950* ✉ *Baldursgata 14, at Nönnugata, Miðbær* ☎ *354/552–3939* ⊕ *www.3frakkar.is* ☽ *No lunch weekends.*

2Guys

$$ | **BURGER** | If a smash burger is what you're after, head to this casual spot from Hjalti Vignisson and Robert Aron Magnússon. You'll also find a bar with a set of dart boards for some casual fun. **Known for:** quick service; lots of vegan options; fantastic burgers. Ⓢ *Average main: ISK2,590* ✉ *Laugavegur 105, Reykjavík* ☎ *790–2323* ⊕ *www.2guys.is.*

★ Yuzu Burger

$$ | **BURGER** | **FAMILY** | From the classic cornerstore Sjoppu burger to the BBQ and bacon burger, the menu is far from one-sided at this lunchtime favorite. Plus, there are plenty of vegan options. **Known for:** quick service; Instagram-worthy interiors; unique burger combos. Ⓢ *Average main: ISK2,690* ✉ *Hverfisgata 44, Reykjavík* ☎ *588–8818* ⊕ *www.yuzu.is.*

🍵 Coffee and Quick Bites

Café Babalú

$ | **AMERICAN** | The menu is simple at Café Babalú: choose between crepes, grilled cheese options, or a selection of soups. It's a fantastic spot for a quick lunch near Hallgrimskirkja. **Known for:** friendly service; great value; perfect grilled cheese. Ⓢ *Average main: ISK1,390* ✉ *Skólavörðustígur 22, Reykjavík* ☎ *555–8845* ⊕ *www.babalu.is.*

Eldur og Ís

$ | **ICE CREAM** | **FAMILY** | "Fire and Ice" does two things really well: ice cream and crepes. You can choose from the menu they've put together, or you can make up your own crepe creation. **Known for:** customizable crepes; quick service; great gelato. Ⓢ *Average main: ISK990* ✉ *Skólavörðustígur 2, Miðbær* ☎ *571–2480* ⊕ *www.facebook.com/eldurogis.*

Emilie and the Cool Kids

$ | BAKERY | French-inspired pastries and baked goods are served at this popular coffee shop. There isn't a ton of seating, but you can take the items to go. **Known for:** delectable baked goods; warm service; cozy interior. $ *Average main: ISK999* ✉ *Hverfisgata 98, Reykjavík* ☎ *571–5887* ⊕ *www.emiliescookies. com.*

Kaffi Mokka

$ | CAFÉ | FAMILY | In business since 1958, Iceland's oldest café is a wonderful place to mingle with locals of all kinds. Many consider the waffles at this Reykjavík institution to be the best in town. **Known for:** best waffles in town; great coffees; retro vibe. $ *Average main: ISK1,540* ✉ *Skólavörðustígur 3A, Miðbær* ☎ *552–1174* ⊕ *www.mokka.is* ▬ *No credit cards.*

Kaffifélagið

$ | CAFÉ | This tiny coffee shop has built itself a solid reputation for excellent Italian espresso. Its delightful brand has been dubbed the "best cup of joe to go," and customers gather on the sidewalk, where they sip from paper cups and talk about politics and the weather. **Known for:** quality Italian espresso; friendly service; free Wi-Fi. $ *Average main: ISK1,000* ✉ *Skólavörðustígur 10, Miðbær* ☎ *520–8420* ⊕ *www.kaffifelagid.is.*

Kaffitár

$ | CAFÉ | This is a name you'll see all over Reykjavík—Kaffitár is where Icelanders grab a coffee on their way to work. Some might call it a Nordic Starbucks, but this coffee shop chain is known for paying careful attention to where its beans come from. **Known for:** quick service; consistently good coffee; inventive coffee drinks. $ *Average main: ISK890* ✉ *Bankastræti 8, Miðbær* ☎ *420–2732* ⊕ *www.kaffitar.is.*

★ Kaktus Espressobar

$ | BAKERY | Two friends came together to open this café, which specializes in Italian coffee and baked goods. The interior is airy and lively, the perfect spot to plan your day of adventures. **Known for:** excellent coffee; great value; traditional coffeehouse vibes. $ *Average main: ISK990* ✉ *Vitastígur 12, Reykjavík* ☎ *869–3030* ⊕ *kaktus-espressobar.business.site.*

★ Reykjavík Roasters

$ | CAFÉ | If you're serious about the quality of your cup of joe, then you should feel right at home at Reykjavík Roasters. Owned and operated by some of Iceland's most esteemed, award-winning baristas, Reykjavík Roasters delivers incredibly consistent cups of coffee. **Known for:** carefully selected coffee beans; hip atmosphere; record player where guests are encouraged to play what they want. $ *Average main: ISK1,000* ✉ *Kárastígur 1, Miðbær* ☎ *517–5535* ⊕ *www.reykjavikroasters.is.*

★ Svarta Kaffið

$ | CAFÉ | FAMILY | There are only two options on the menu at Svarta Kaffið: a vegetarian soup and a meat soup. Known locally as the soup spot, this restaurant really has more of a café atmosphere, with a small list of beers and wine on tap too. **Known for:** fantastic soup, including bread bowl option; simple two-item menu; lively atmosphere. $ *Average main: ISK1,500* ✉ *Laugavegur 54, Miðbær* ☎ *551–2999* ⊕ *www.facebook. com/svartakaffid.*

 Hotels

Alda Hotel

$$$$ | HOTEL | At this lovely hotel in the trendy Lighthouse Village area of downtown Reykjavík, guest rooms are decorated in a typical Scandinavian-chic style, with a combination of rich, earthy tones contrasted with fresh, crisp whites and the occasional splash of vibrant color. **Pros:** location in happening neighborhood; high-speed Wi-Fi; great amenities. **Cons:** some rooms do not have great views; communal areas can be quite busy and often loud; lack of storage space in rooms. [$] *Rooms from: ISK40,328* ✉ *Laugavegur 66–68, Miðbær* ☎ *553–9366* 🌐 *www.aldahotel.is* 🛏 *64 rooms* 🍴 *Free Breakfast.*

Canopy by Hilton Reykjavik City Centre

$$$ | **HOTEL** | If being centrally located is your main priority, this hotel is a good option. **Pros:** Wi-Fi included in room rate; central location; free breakfast. **Cons:** location near a nightclub not for everyone; lots of street noise; basic amenities. [$] *Rooms from: ISK33,520* ✉ *Smiðjustígur 4, Reykjavík* ☎ *528–7000* 🌐 *www.hilton.com/en/hotels/rek-capy-canopy-reykjavik-city-centre* 🛏 *112 rooms* 🍴 *Free Breakfast.*

Center Hotels Laugavegur

$ | **HOTEL** | Located right in the center of the buzziest street in downtown Reykjavik, this hotel comes with some serious value. **Pros:** excellent value; great bar and restaurant; central location. **Cons:** no parking; surrounding area can be quite noisy; basic amenities. [$] *Rooms from: ISK19,152* ✉ *Laugavegur 95-99, Reykjavík* ☎ *595–8570* 🌐 *www.centerhotels.com/en/hotel-laugavegur-reykjavik* 🛏 *102 rooms* 🍴 *Free Breakfast.*

Eyja Guldsmeden Hotel

$$ | **HOTEL** | Found right off of Laugavegur, next door to foodhall Hlemmur Mathöll, the location of this hotel could not be better. **Pros:** free breakfast; on-site gym; free parking. **Cons:** surrounding area can be noisy; basic amenities; least expensive rooms on the small side. [$] *Rooms from: ISK26,834* ✉ *Brautarholt 10, Reykjavík* ☎ *519–7300* 🌐 *www.guldsmedenhotels.com/eyja* 🛏 *65 rooms* 🍴 *Free Breakfast.*

★ Hótel Holt

$$$$ | **HOTEL** | This quietly elegant member of the prestigious World Hotels group has impeccable service and free Wi-Fi throughout, making it a favorite among business travelers. **Pros:** free access to gym and swimming pool; excellent restaurant and bar; beautiful art collection. **Cons:** bathrooms can be tiny; slightly formal atmosphere; small rooms. [$] *Rooms from: ISK35,441* ✉ *Bergstaðastræti 37* ☎ *552–5700* 🌐 *www.holt.is* 🛏 *42 rooms* 🍴 *Free Breakfast.*

Hotel Leifur Eiríksson

$ | **HOTEL** | **FAMILY** | Across the street from the hilltop church of Hallgrímskirkja, this hotel is a short walk from most of Reykjavík's major attractions. **Pros:** good location; quiet area; great value. **Cons:** rooms and bathrooms can be small and charmless; no elevator; faded furnishings. [$] *Rooms from: ISK16,621* ✉ *Skólavörðustígur 45, Miðbær* ☎ *562–0800* 🌐 *www.hotelleifur.is* 🛏 *47 rooms* 🍴 *Free Breakfast.*

Hotel Óðinsvé

$$ | **HOTEL** | Five buildings in a calm corner of an older part of town make up this hotel with cheery and efficient guest rooms, some with nice views over Reykjavík's colorful rooftops. **Pros:** central but quiet; good restaurant loved by locals; intimate atmosphere. **Cons:** some rooms lack views; small showers; expensive breakfast options. [$] *Rooms from: ISK22,158* ✉ *Þórsgata 1, Miðbær* ☎ *511–6200* 🌐 *www.hotelodinsve.is* 🛏 *60 rooms* 🍴 *No Meals.*

Hótel VON

$$ | **HOTEL** | Minimal and cozy, the rooms at Hótel VON ride the line between boutique experience and local homestay. **Pros:** good location; gorgeous design; complimentary tea and coffee. **Cons:** basic amenities; no on-site restaurant or bar; no parking. [$] *Rooms from: ISK21,892* ✉ *Laugavegur 55, Reykjavík* ☎ *790–8881* 🌐 *www.hotelvon.is* 🛏 *52 rooms* 🍴 *No Meals.*

★ Ion City Hotel

$$ | **HOTEL** | The Ion City Hotel is the urban counterpart to the original Ion Hotel, near Þingvellir National Park, and the vibe here is certainly luxurious, with a focus on local designers and art throughout. **Pros:** good soundproofing between rooms;

luxurious boutique hotel vibe; great location. **Cons:** no air-conditioning; no room service; small rooms. [$] *Rooms from: ISK25,601* ✉ *Laugavegur 28* ☎ *578–3730* 🌐 *www.ioniceland.is* 🛏 *18 rooms* 🍴 *No Meals.*

★ Kex

$$$ | HOTEL | This spot is technically a hostel, but the private rooms look like they came straight from the pages of an Anthropologie catalog. **Pros:** local hangout; great bar and restaurant; beautiful room decor. **Cons:** can get rowdy on weekends; breakfast not included in room rate; no elevator. [$] *Rooms from: ISK28,627* ✉ *Skúlagata 28, Miðbær* ☎ *561–6060* 🌐 *www.kexhostel.is* 🛏 *32 dorms and rooms* 🍴 *No Meals.*

Loft Hostel

$ | HOTEL | A hostel with private rooms available, Loft is located right off Reykjavík's main shopping streets. **Pros:** local hangout; frequent events; central location. **Cons:** tends to get noisy; small rooms; basic amenities. [$] *Rooms from: ISK19,269* ✉ *Bankastræti 7, Miðbær* ☎ *553–8140* 🌐 *www.lofthostel.is* 🛏 *18 rooms* 🍴 *No Meals.*

Midgardur by Center Hotels

$$$ | HOTEL | The rooms at Midgardur are minimalist and basic, but the service is A+ and won't leave you wanting. **Pros:** on-site gym; great service; outdoor hot tub. **Cons:** services are minimum; no breakfast; basic design. [$] *Rooms from: ISK30,122* ✉ *Laugavegur 120, Reykjavík* ☎ *595–8560* 🌐 *www.centerhotels.com/en/hotel-midgardur-reykjavik* 🛏 *170 rooms* 🍴 *No Meals.*

101 Hotel

$$$$ | HOTEL | At this five-story hotel designed by owner Ingibjörg Pálmadóttir, contemporary works by renowned local artists adorn the walls (the hotel also hosts exhibitions), and large, open-plan rooms are well appointed, with big, comfortable beds, American oak floors, and (in some) freestanding baths. **Pros:** intimate feel; good facilities, including great bar and small pool; large rooms. **Cons:** spa-and-sauna area is small; located in a noisy part of town; lacks a cozy vibe. [$] *Rooms from: ISK48,848* ✉ *Hverfisgata 10* ☎ *580–0101* 🌐 *www.101hotel.is* 🛏 *39 rooms* 🍴 *No Meals.*

Room with a View

$ | APARTMENT | FAMILY | With a number of self-catering apartments in the center of town, this place is for those who prefer to cook their own meals and would like extra space. **Pros:** Jacuzzi and sauna access; full kitchens; independent atmosphere. **Cons:** no on-call staff; no concierge; no lobby or communal waiting area. [$] *Rooms from: ISK19,273* ✉ *Laugavegur 18, Miðbær* ☎ *552–7262* 🌐 *www.roomwithaview.is* 🛏 *46 rooms* 🍴 *No Meals.*

★ Sand Hotel

$$ | HOTEL | Located right in the center of Reykjavík, the Sand is one of the more luxurious hotels in the city. **Pros:** Sóley Organics amenities; beautiful art deco design details; fantastic bakery next door that serves breakfast for guests. **Cons:** rooms along Laugavegur are noisy; very little storage space in rooms; rooms on the small side. [$] *Rooms from: ISK26,423* ✉ *Laugavegur 34, Miðbær* ☎ *519–8090* 🌐 *www.sandhotel.is* 🛏 *67 rooms* 🍴 *No Meals.*

Nightlife

★ Einstök Bar

BARS | Akureyri-based brewery Einstök has opened the brand's first tasting space in the capital city. The interiors are cozy and moody—large groups mingle with solo drinkers enjoying pints of Arctic Pale Ale and other seasonal brews. The outdoor seating is the best on Laugavegur and provides the ultimate people-watching perch. ✉ *Laugavegur 10, Reykjavík* 🌐 *www.einstokbeer.com.*

★ Kaffibarinn

BARS | One of the city's most famous cafés and nightspots—thanks to its associations with local and international celebs, like Damon Albarn from Blur—Kaffibarinn is a relaxed café during the day but it gets hopping on nights and weekends, when DJs show up and play until the wee hours. ✉ *Bergstaðastræti 1, Miðbær* ☎ *551–1588* ⊕ *www.kaffibarinn. is.*

★ Kíkí Queer Bar

DANCE CLUBS | Unofficially Iceland's best gay bar, Kiki Queer Bar is a spirited mix of locals and travelers on any given night. Located in the heart of Reykjavík's nightlife hub, you can dance until the wee hours here. ✉ *Laugavegur 22, Miðbær* ☎ *571–0194* ⊕ *www.kiki.is.*

Kofinn

BARS | This is your basic, no-frills bar serving up drinks and cakes beginning in the afternoon and hosting DJs into the early morning hours. It's located in the main shopping district, making it a great spot to grab a snack and libation in the late afternoon. ✉ *Laugavegur 2, Miðbær* ☎ *551–1855.*

The Lebowski Bar

BARS | Admittedly a tourist attraction, this bar and restaurant is themed after—you guessed it—the Coen Brothers' cult classic *The Big Lebowski*, and has an entire menu dedicated to White Russians. The decor is full of references: the bar is lined with rugs, the barstools look like bowling shoes, and "the Dude" himself can be found on the cocktail napkins. The neon sign out front provides quite the photo op. ✉ *Laugavegur 20a, Miðbær* ☎ *552–2300* ⊕ *www.lebowskibar.is.*

Miami Bar

DANCE CLUBS | Take a trip back in time—specifically, Miami circa the 1980s. The color theme is pastel, the architecture skews brutalist, and the neon lights never stop. Plus, the cocktails hold their own, too. ✉ *Hverfisgata 33, Reykjavík* ☎ *566–7333* ⊕ *www.instagram.com/ miami_hverfisgata.*

Micro Bar

BARS | The best time to visit Micro Bar is between the hours of 3 and 7 pm, when the bar has two beers on special for happy hour. You'll find a solid selection of Icelandic beers and an inviting atmosphere that's perfect for making new local friends. ✉ *Laugarvegur 86, Miðbær* ☎ *865–8389.*

Mikki Refur Coffee & Wine

WINE BARS | During the day, Mikki Refur serves up coffee, but once the sun goes down (or happy hour hits), the wine list becomes the popular choice. There are also small bites to help pace your sips. ✉ *Hverfisgata 18, Reykjavík* ⊕ *www. mikkirefur.is.*

Petersen Svítan

BARS | If you don't feel like heading to the top of Hallgrímskirkja to take in 360-degree views of Reykjavík, check out Petersen Svítan. This rooftop lounge is on the third floor of Gamla Bíó, a historic cinema. In a previous life, the bar was the cinema owner's apartment; today, it's an open-air bar with a bi-level terrace. ✉ *Ingólfsstræti 2a, Miðbær* ☎ *563–4000* ⊕ *www.gamlabio.is.*

★ Prikið

BARS | The line of people waiting to get in to this bar stretches around the block on weekends. And it's totally worth the wait: inside, you'll find some of the city's best DJs, as well as a ton of locals relaxing and mingling. Prikið is open during the day too, when the crowds are much smaller. The burger is a sleeper hit, so try and stop by for lunch if you can. ✉ *Bankastræti 12, Miðbær* ☎ *517–1743* ⊕ *www.prikid.is.*

Stereo

COCKTAIL LOUNGES | Head right this way for the happy hour, which runs from 4 to 7 pm every day. The intimate space often holds exhibit, live music, and DJ sets, so chances are you'll stick around once happy hour ends. ✉ *Skólavörðustígur 8, Reykjavík* ☎ *690–1938* ⊕ *www.stereobar.is.*

★ **Veður**

COCKTAIL LOUNGES | This loud bar's open-floor plan can accommodate groups easily. The best seats are the pillow-topped benches along the window—they were practically made for people-watching. All of the cocktails are great here, but the classics are treated with special care; you can't go wrong with an Old-Fashioned. ✉ *Klapparstígur 33, Miðbær.*

 # Shopping

BEAUTY

Blue Lagoon Shop

SKINCARE | If you didn't make it to the Blue Lagoon—or didn't get a chance to buy their world-renowned products—you can visit this shop in Reykjavík. Here they sell the famous silica mud masks alongside other natural skincare products. ✉ *Laugavegur 15, Miðbær* ☎ *420–8849* ⊕ *www.bluelagoon.com/select-store.*

BOOKS AND RECORDS

★ Lucky Records

MUSIC | This record store, close to Hlemmur bus station, has the largest collection of vintage and contemporary vinyl in Iceland. It also serves as a venue for both underground music artists and up-and-coming alternative bands. ✉ *Rauðarárstígur 10, Hlíðar* ☎ *551–1195* ⊕ *www.luckyrecords.is.*

★ Mál og Menning

BOOKS | Part bookstore, part café, the independent Mál og Menning sells books focusing on all things Iceland. From local authors and photographers to comic book artists with a dark sense of humor, there's something for everyone here. Plus, the café serves up a mean soup-and-bread deal for less than ISK 1,400. ✉ *Laugavegur 18, Miðbær* ☎ *580–5000* ⊕ *www.facebook.com/husmalsogmenningar.*

★ **Smekkleysa** (*Bad Taste*)

MUSIC | This record store with its own label doubles as a gift shop. Smekkleysa is known by locals for releasing music by the Icelandic alt-rock band Sugarcubes, of which Björk was a founding member. Unfortunately the group disbanded in 1992, but you can still buy their music at this shop. ✉ *Hverfisgata 32, Miðbær* ☎ *551–3730* ⊕ *www.smekkleysa.net.*

★ **12 Tónar**

MUSIC | This record shop has its own independent record label, and the staff here can tell you everything about Icelandic music while you sip a great espresso. Some popular local artists at the moment include Ólafur Arnalds, Kaleo, Ásgeir, Agent Fresco, Dikta, Hjaltalín, FM Belfast, GusGus, and the ever-famous Björk. ✉ *Skólavörðustíg 15, Miðbær* ☎ *511–5656* ⊕ *www.12tonar.is.*

CLOTHING

At first glance it's easy for a tourist to view Iceland fashions as a parade of people in sensible weatherproof threads. And Iceland does have four of its own outdoor clothing brands (66°North, Zo-on, Cintamani, and Icewear) to keep you warm in its famously unpredictable weather. But in the trendy downtown area of Reykjavík, you'll discover some of Iceland's most innovative designer and fashion shops. A wander along the city's main shopping streets and back alleys will lead you to some surprising and out-of-the-ordinary designer treasures.

Apotek Atelier

WOMEN'S CLOTHING | What was once a pharmacy is now home to the space where three designers—Ýr Þrastardóttir, Halldóra Sif Guðlaugsdóttir, and Sævar Markús Óskarsson—use to showcase their work. This is the ultimate spot for finding a souvenir others are unlikely to have. ✉ *Laugavegur 16, Reykjavík* ⊕ *www.apotekatelier.com.*

★ Farmers & Friends
WOMEN'S CLOTHING | There's a bit of retro flair to this Iceland-based design brand, which draws inspiration from centuries of local history—specifically music and design. The clothes here are a touch romantic, with just enough pop to become conversation pieces. ⊠ *Laugavegur 37, Miðbær* ☎ *552–1965* ⊕ *www.farmersmarket.is.*

Herrafataverzlun Kormáks og Skjaldar
MEN'S CLOTHING | Here you'll find menswear for all occasions, from casual to formal. They stock upscale international brands like Barbour, Van Gils, and Loake alongside the shop's own label, Kormákur & Skjöldur, at this basement outpost. ⊠ *Lower level, Laugavegur 59, Miðbær* ☎ *511–1817* ⊕ *www.herrafataverslun.is.*

★ Húrra Reykjavík
MIXED CLOTHING | Step inside and you'll be awash in the neutral color palette of this trendy clothing shop. Take some time to dive a bit deeper into the designs on display: they're simple, timeless, and will remind you of your trip for years to come. ⊠ *Hverfisgata 78, Miðbær* ☎ *571–7101* ⊕ *www.hurrareykjavik.is.*

★ Icewear
MIXED CLOTHING | Primarily an outerwear and outdoor gear store, Icewear is a popular local chain that can be found in a number of places around Reykjavík. If you're looking to bring home a wool blanket, this is often the place to find the least expensive options. They may be one of the best deals in the store; prepare to spend the usual (expensive) prices for sweaters, jackets, socks, and shoes. ⊠ *Laugavegur 91, Miðbær* ☎ *585–0503* ⊕ *www.icewear.is.*

★ Kormákur & Skjöldur
MEN'S CLOTHING | This shop offers dapper gentlemen's finery and haircuts. The legacy of Bertie Wooster of London lives proudly on in this store, which, in addition to its own winning brand of threads and cufflinks, sells a fine assemblage of designer goods and star brands such as Harris Tweed and Ben Sherman. Housed in the basement of a budget supermarket on Laugavegur, vintage lighting illuminates a display of antique top hats in one corner while portraits of Iceland's presidents look down on the Stetsons and Borsalinos in another. Every accessory imaginable is available here, with bow ties and pocket watches on display together with beard oil and moustache combs. Late at night, winter shoppers might be treated to a shot of whiskey. ⊠ *Laugavegur 59, Miðbær* ☎ *511–1817* ⊕ *www.herrafataverslun.is.*

KronKron
MIXED CLOTHING | Quirky, colorful, and cool enough to capture a host of celebrity hearts (including Mary J. Blige and the entire cast of *Orange Is the New Black*), KronKron is owned by a lovely Icelandic couple, who have firmly established themselves as extraordinary designers. They specialize in creating unique garments made chiefly from silk, but they are mostly known for their quality "Kron" brand of footwear. Over the years this dedicated duo has created countless shoe styles in every circus-inspired shade imaginable. Designs feature attractive details and are executed by a personally selected team of talented artisans. ⊠ *Laugavegi 63B, Miðbær* ☎ *562–8388* ⊕ *www.kronkron.com.*

Moi Kidz
CHILDREN'S CLOTHING | The name gives it away, but this shop might just have the trendiest outfits you could possibly dress a child in (and that's meant in a very positive, envious way). Deemed an "urban kids fashion brand," Moi Kidz caters to all genders between the ages of 0 and 12. ⊠ *Laugavegur 40, Miðbær* ☎ *436–1144* ⊕ *www.moi-kidz.com.*

★ Nordic Store
MIXED CLOTHING | Walking into the Nordic Store is like stepping into a giant ball of wool. Everywhere you look, you'll find wool sweaters, blankets, socks,

scarves—if you can wear it and it's made from wool, you'll find it here. In addition to clothing, the Nordic Store also has a solid selection of outdoor wear and gear, like running shoes, winter coats, and thermal accessories. ✉ *Laekjargata 2* ☎ *445–8080* ⊕ *www.nordicstore.net.*

★ Reykjavik Raincoats

MIXED CLOTHING | If you ever wonder what kind of outerwear could handle the ever-changing weather patterns of Iceland, this raincoat shop has an answer for you. Aside from being completely functional, the jackets sold at Reykjavik Raincoats are undoubtedly Instagram-worthy as well: classic and minimal (thigh-length and hooded) designs putting bold colors front and center. ✉ *Laugavegur 62, Miðbær* ☎ *571–1177* ⊕ *www.reykjavikraincoats.com.*

Spúútnik

SECOND-HAND | Visiting a secondhand store in another country is always fun— it's a great way to see what the locals are (or were) wearing—and Spúútnik is no exception. This shop is funky, with a focus on clothing and accessories from the 1980s and '90s. ✉ *Laugavegur 28, Miðbær* ☎ *533–2023* ⊕ *www.spuutnikreykjavik.com.*

CRAFTS

Sheepskin rugs and Viking-inspired jewelry are popular souvenirs. An amble along **Skólavörðustígur** from Laugavegur to Hallgrímskirkja church takes you past many tempting woolen, jewelry, and crafts shops, as well as art galleries.

★ The Handknitting Association of Iceland

CRAFTS | The Handknitting Association of Iceland has its own outlet, selling (of course) only hand-knit items of various kinds. The back room is a wonderland of woolen knits and other handmade apparel. ✉ *Skólavörðurstígur 19, Miðbær* ☎ *455–5544* ⊕ *www.handknit.is.*

FOOD AND CANDY

Bónus

FOOD | There are three things that make Bónus more than just a grocery store: first, it has an entire room dedicated to dairy that is basically a giant cooler. Second, the logo is an endearing piggy bank that has somehow managed to keep its smile despite a black eye. And finally, the candy selection is not to be missed. ✉ *Laugavegur 59 Kjörgarður, Miðbær* ☎ *527–9000* ⊕ *www.bonus.is.*

★ Hyalin

FOOD | With a focus on French foods, this delicacy shop imports flavors directly from the City of Lights. From olives and cakes to herbs and truffles, there is something special for every kind of cook here. ✉ *Skólavörðustígur 4a, Reykjavík* ☎ *519–7171* ⊕ *www.hyalin-shop.com.*

★ Vínberið

CANDY | The real draw at this candy shop is the massive selection of local and imported chocolate. If "local candy" is on your souvenir list, this is the place to go. ✉ *Laugavegur 43, Miðbær* ☎ *551–2475* ⊕ *www.vinberid.is.*

GALLERIES

★ Gallerí Fold

ART GALLERIES | Here you'll find a large selection of prints, drawings, paintings, and sculptures by contemporary Icelandic artists, as well as some older Icelandic art. A visit to this space is a crash course in the country's best creators. ✉ *Rauðarárstíg 14, Miðbær* ☎ *551–0400* ⊕ *www.myndlist.is.*

GIFTS AND HOME DECOR

★ Litla Jólabúðin

OTHER SPECIALTY STORE | **FAMILY** | One look at Litla Jólabúðin and you'll know what it's all about: Christmas. The shop is open year-round despite its seasonality, selling ornaments and other wintertime trinkets. Chances are you'll learn a thing or two about Icelandic holiday culture while you're in there. ✉ *Laugavegur 8, Miðbær*

☎ *552–2412* ⊕ *www.facebook.com/little.christmasshop.iceland.*

★ Pastel Blómastúdíó

FLORIST | Dried arrangements are the go-to bouquet at this trendy florist shop, but there's much more than that on offer. You can also take classes or opt into their flower subscription service (a great gift for hosts). ⊠ *Hverfisgata 50, Reykjavík* ☎ *792–3261* ⊕ *www.pastelblomastudio.com.*

★ Rammagerdin

SOUVENIRS | With several storefronts in Reykjavík, plus an outpost in Keflavík airport and another in Perlan and Harpa, Rammagerdin has taken the Icelandic souvenir game to a new level. Almost everything in this shop is handmade locally, and you can't go wrong with anything you pick. ⊠ *Skólavörðustígur 12, Miðbær* ☎ *535–6689* ⊕ *www.rammagerdin.is.*

★ Skúmaskot

CRAFTS | This gallery-slash-store is run by seven local women artists. The items you'll find here are delightfully different from the souvenirs of more pedestrian stores. ⊠ *Skólavörðustígur 21a, Miðbær* ☎ *663–1013* ⊕ *www.facebook.com/skumaskot.art.design.*

★ Ungfrúin Góða

SOUVENIRS | Clothing, housewares, accessories—there's a variety of items you can find at this gift shop. It's certainly less Iceland-focused than other souvenir stops in Reykjavík, but you're bound to see a few locals shopping inside. ⊠ *Hallveigarstígur 10a, Miðbær* ☎ *551–2112* ⊕ *www.ungfruingoda.is.*

★ Woolcano Gift Shop

SOUVENIRS | As the name suggests, there is a whole lot of wool happening at this gift shop. Sweaters, socks, sculptures—you name it, they have it. There are two locations in Reykjavík, and the other is just down the street at Laugavegur 20. ⊠ *Laugavegur 100, Miðbær* ☎ *571–1144.*

JEWELRY

Laugavegur and Skólavörðustígur streets are both filled with jewelry stores that craft unique pieces, often incorporating gold or silver with materials found in Iceland like lava rock, creating a very eye-catching effect.

Anna María Design

JEWELRY & WATCHES | Founded in 1986, this workshop and store sells jewelry for both men and women, made from a variety of materials, including silver, gold, and Icelandic stones. Stepping inside this shop is like walking into an Icelandic daydream. ⊠ *Skólavörðustígur 3, Miðbær* ☎ *551–0036* ⊕ *www.annamariadesign.is.*

★ Aurum by Guðbjörg Jewellery

JEWELRY & WATCHES | This Reykjavík-based jewelry brand is known for creating beautiful pieces with local lava rock. The various collections almost always tie in to Icelandic or Nordic mythology and history. ⊠ *Bankastræti 4, Miðbær* ☎ *551–2770* ⊕ *www.aurum.is.*

★ JS Watch Co

JEWELRY & WATCHES | The official watch of the Icelandic Coast Guard is a favorite among A-list celebrities like Tom Cruise, Katie Couric, Tobey Maguire, and Viggo Mortensen, not to mention His Majesty King Constantine II of Greece. Even if you're not impressed with this "Hall of Fame" list, you still might be tempted to get your hands on one of JS Watch's beautiful timepieces, which are perfectly crafted by a master watchmaker. ⊠ *Laugavegur 62, Miðbær* ☎ *551–4100* ⊕ *www.jswatch.com.*

★ Ofeigur

JEWELRY & WATCHES | This shop sells accessories, jewelry, artwork, and clothing by Icelandic designers. Each piece has a unique tie to the country—either in aesthetic or inspiration—making Ofeigur a unique place to buy a souvenir. ⊠ *Skólavörðustígur 5, Miðbær* ☎ *551–1161* ⊕ *nammi.is.*

★ Orrifin

JEWELRY & WATCHES | Two local jewelry makers, Helga Friðriksdóttir and Orri Finnbogason, own this shop, where they sell the fruits of their labor. All of the jewelry they create is unisex, with a new collection coming out every year. ✉ *Skólavörðustígur 43, Miðbær* ☎ *789–7616* ⊕ *www.orrifinn-jewels.myshopify.com.*

TATTOO PARLORS

★ Icelandic Tattoo Corp

OTHER SPECIALTY STORE | With nine full-time artists, the Icelandic Tattoo Corp is a collective of some of the best talents in Reykjavík. To book time with a specific artist, reach out to them directly via the studio website. ✉ *Ingólfsstræti 3, Miðbær* ☎ *552–7913* ⊕ *www.icelandtattoo.com.*

Irezumi Ink Iceland

OTHER SPECIALTY STORE | This tattoo shop is staffed by a wide range of artists, and there's a good chance you'll find an artist fit for your design. Book in advance as appointments fill up quickly. ✉ *Laugavegur 69, Miðbær* ☎ *760–7821* ⊕ *www.facebook.com/pages/Irezumi-Ink-Iceland/1523203531263774.*

★ Reykjavik Ink

OTHER SPECIALTY STORE | Tattoos make great lifelong souvenirs and Reykjavík Ink is the best-known studio in the city. Make sure to reach out far in advance to schedule time with one of the artists, as walk-ins are rare to snag at this tattoo shop. ✉ *Frakkastígur 7, Miðbær* ☎ *551–7707* ⊕ *www.reykjavikink.is.*

City Center West

One of the most beautiful things Reykjavik has to offer is how walkable it is—and this neighborhood is no exception. You'll find lots of government buildings in the City Center West area, including City Hall and the Parliament House. While they may not warrant the time for a full tour,

Lighthouse Village

Hidden in plain sight, Lighthouse Village is a delightful collaboration between a handful of local designers. Look for the street bollards designed as miniature lighthouses, all painted in bright colors, on Laugavegur. The result of an alliance between a number of local businesses, Lighthouse Village encompasses a few blocks between Barónsstígur and Frakkastígur (also known as Vitahverfi in Icelandic) and extends all the way down to Sæbraut Street, by the coast.

the architecture sets the scene for a beautiful post-lunch stroll. When you're in the mood for museums, head to the Reykjavik Museum of Photography or the Reykjavik Art Museum. But remember that there's plenty of public art to be seen on the streets, as well. Take a walk through the residential bits of this neighborhood; it's not uncommon to see pop-up exhibitions from local galleries and artists peppering the small squares.

There seem to be new bars and restaurants popping up in this area every month, with a focus on modern fusion menus and masterful Scandinavian interiors. The hotels focus on luxury in City Center West, such as Hotel Borg, an accommodation with major Art Deco curb appeal.

◉ Sights

Aðalstræti 10

HISTORY MUSEUM | FAMILY | This museum and exhibition space was put together by the National Museum of Iceland and the Reykjavík City Museum to help celebrate the country's 100th anniversary as a sovereign state. Aðalstræti 10 is the

The Harpa Music Hall and Conference Center is Iceland's most prestigious performance venue.

beginning of a five-location museum that covers Icelandic life through the ages and includes turf houses. ✉ Aðalstræti 10, Miðbær ☎ 411–6375 ⊕ www.reykjavikcit-ymuseum.is 🎫 ISK 1,000.

Alþingishús (Parliament House)
GOVERNMENT BUILDING | Built in 1880–81, this is one of the country's oldest stone buildings. Iceland's Alþingi (Parliament) held its first session in AD 930 and therefore can lay claim to being the oldest representative parliament in the world. You can view its modern-day proceedings from the visitor's gallery here. Depending on the urgency of the agenda, any number of Iceland's 63 members of parliament, from five political parties, may be present. ✉ Austurvöllur Sq., Miðbær ☎ 563–0500 ⊕ www.althingi.is ⊘ Closed weekends.

Dómkirkjan (Lutheran Cathedral)
CHURCH | A place of worship has existed on this site since AD 1200. The current small church, built 1788–96, represents the state religion, Lutheranism. It was here that sovereignty and independence were first blessed and endorsed by the church. It's also where Iceland's national anthem, actually a hymn, was first sung in 1874. Since 1845, members and cabinet ministers of every Alþingi (Parliament) have gathered here for a service before the annual session. Among the treasured items inside is a baptismal font carved and donated by the famous 19th-century master sculptor Bertel Thorvaldsen, who was half Icelandic. ✉ Austurvöllur Sq., Lækjargötu 14a, Miðbær ☎ 520–9700 ⊕ www.domkirkjan.is.

★ Harpa Concert Hall and Conference Center
PERFORMANCE VENUE | The shimmering queen of the country's performing arts scene and home of both the Iceland Symphony Orchestra and the Icelandic Opera, this venue is an amazing modern labyrinth of stunning concert halls, event spaces, and places to dine or purchase designer souvenirs. Many of the city's most popular annual events, such as Air-waves, Sónar, and the Reykjavík Fashion Festival, are now hosted inside these

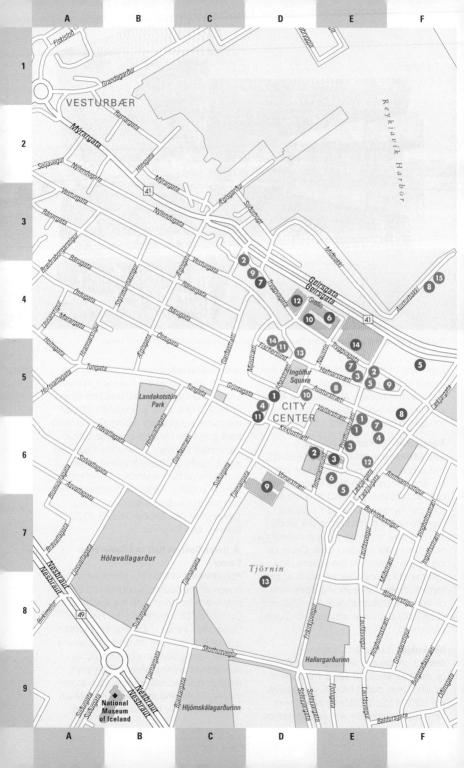

City Center West

KEY	
①	*Exploring Sights*
①	*Restaurants*
①	*Hotels*

0 ———————— 500 ft
0 ———————— 100 m

3

Reykjavík CITY CENTER WEST

Sights ▼

1 Aðalstræti 10 .... D5
2 Alþingishús D6
3 Dómkirkjan E6
4 Harpa Concert Hall
   and Conference Center G4
5 Iceland Phallological Museum.... F5
6 Icelandic Printmakers
   Association E4
7 i8 Gallery D4
8 Lækjartorg F5
9 Ráðhús D6
10 Reykjavík Art Museum D4
11 Reykjavík 871±2:
   The Settlement Exhibition D6
12 Reykjavík Museum
   of Photography D4
13 Tjörnin Pond D8
14 Tollhúsið E5

Restaurants ▼

1 Apotek Restaurant E6
2 Bæjarins Beztu Pylsur E5
3 Brút E5
4 Grillmarkaðurinn E6
5 Hornið E5
6 Hnoss G4
7 Hressó E6
8 Laundromat Café E5
9 Le Kock D4
10 Mandi D5
11 Matarkjallarinn D5
12 Messinn E6
13 Sæta Svínið Gastropub D5
14 Tapas Barinn D5
15 Tides F4

Hotels ▼

1 Apótek Hotel E6
2 Exeter Hotel C3
3 Hótel Borg E6
4 Hótel Reykjavík Centrum D5
5 Hótel Reykjavík Saga E6
6 Kvosin Hotel E6
7 Radisson Blu 1919 Hotel E5
8 The Reykjavik EDITION F4
9 Reykjavik Konsulat Hotel F5

glorious glass-paneled walls. Eldborg, the main hall, is a marvel of visual and acoustic design that wouldn't be out of place in a *Star Wars* movie. ⊠ *Austurbakka 2, Miðbær* ☎ *528–5000* ⊕ *www.harpa.is.*

★ Iceland Phallological Museum

OTHER MUSEUM | This iconic museum could easily be described as the city's most interesting attraction, to say the least; it's exactly what it sounds like: an ode to the male genitalia of mammals from around the world. But don't come just for laughs, as this is truly an educational experience. The museum houses more than 215 specimens from 93 different species. The gift shop is not to be missed. ⊠ *Kalkofnsvegur 2, Miðbær* ☎ *561–6663* ⊕ *www.phallus.is* ⊠ *ISK 2,500.*

★ Icelandic Printmakers Association

ART GALLERY | FAMILY | Established in 1984, there are now more than 100 members creating work in the Icelandic Printmakers Association community. This is their gallery, studio, and event space, which is located inside of the Reykjavik Art Museum and has a bustling calendar of exhibitions, workshops, and studio hours. ⊠ *Tryggvagata 17, Miðbær* ☎ *552–2866* ⊕ *www.islenskgrafik.is* ⊠ *Free* ⊙ *Closed Mon.–Wed.*

i8 Gallery

ART GALLERY | Both Icelandic and international artists display their work at this gallery near the harbor. Exhibitions rotate constantly, and there are often events held at this location featuring local artists. ⊠ *Tryggvagata 16, Miðbær* ☎ *551–3666* ⊕ *www.i8.is* ⊠ *Free* ⊙ *Closed Sun. and Mon.*

Lækjartorg (*Brook Square*)

PLAZA/SQUARE | Now a focal point in Reykjavík's otherwise rambling city center, this square opens onto **Austurstræti,** a semi-pedestrian shopping street. A brook, now underground, drains Tjörnin Pond into the sea (hence the street's name). ⊠ *At Bankastræti and Lækjargata,* *Lækjartorg, Miðbær* ⊕ *www.visitreykjavik.is* ⊠ *Free.*

Ráðhús (*City Hall*)

GOVERNMENT BUILDING | Modern architecture and nature converge at Reykjavík's city hall, a building overlooking Tjörnin Pond. Inside is a visitor information desk and coffee bar with Internet access. A three-dimensional model of Iceland, over 819 square feet in size, is usually on display in the gallery, which often hosts various temporary exhibitions. ⊠ *Bounded by Fríkirkjuvegur, Vonarstræti, and Tjarnargata, Tjarnargata 11, Miðbær* ☎ *411–1000* ⊕ *www.reykjavik.is.*

★ Reykjavík Art Museum

ART MUSEUM | FAMILY | Also known as Hafnarhús, this former warehouse of the Port of Reykjavík now houses the city's main art museum. The six galleries occupy two floors, and there's a courtyard and "multipurpose" space. The museum's permanent collection includes a large number of works donated by the contemporary Icelandic artist Erró. There are also regular temporary exhibitions. Admission is free with the Reykjavík City Card. ⊠ *Tryggvagata 17, Miðbær* ☎ *411–6400* ⊕ *www.listasafnreykjavikur.is* ⊠ *ISK 1,950.*

Reykjavík 871±2: The Settlement Exhibition

HISTORY MUSEUM | FAMILY | The core exhibit here features the remains of a Viking longhouse dating from around 871. Unearthed in 2001 during the construction of the Hotel Centrum, this remarkable find was preserved in situ and now occupies an oval-shaped basement designed specially to frame the excavation site. A large, backlit panoramic image, showing how Reykjavík might have looked during the age of settlement, encircles the longhouse, and an illuminated strip installed in the surrounding walls marks the layer of tephra used to determine the approximate date of the remnants. Sounds and aromas add a multisensory dynamic to the experience, while high-tech media installations provide historical insight into life in Iceland's Saga Age. ✉ *Aðalstræti 16, Miðbær* ☎ *411–6370* 🌐 *reykjavikcitymuseum.is/the-settlement-exhibition* 🎟 *ISK 2,500.*

Reykjavík Museum of Photography
ART MUSEUM | FAMILY | At this museum you can explore thousands of photographs from both amateur and professional photographers, dating back as far as 1860. This is a unique opportunity to explore more than a hundred years of Reykjavík—and Iceland—through a variety of perspectives. ✉ *Tryggvagata 15, Miðbær* ☎ *411–6390* 🌐 *www.borgarsogusafn.is* 🎟 *ISK 1,100.*

Tjörnin Pond
BODY OF WATER | FAMILY | This natural pond by the City Hall is popular among ice-skaters in winter and attracts birds (and bird lovers) year-round. Visitors are discouraged from feeding the birds during nesting season, as it attracts seagulls who like to feast on young waterfowl. ✉ *Between Fríkirkjvegur and Tjarnagata, next to Raðhús (City Hall), Miðbær* 🎟 *Free.*

Tollhúsið
GOVERNMENT BUILDING | The city's Customs House—a bureaucratic necessity, especially for an island nation—is decorated with an impressive mosaic mural. The piece of art depicts scenes from the local harbor and was designed by Gerð Helgadóttir. There isn't a ton to see inside, but the mural is worth a visit in itself. ✉ *Tryggvagata 19, Miðbær* 🌐 *www.tollur.is.*

🍴 Restaurants

Apotek Restaurant
$$$ | SCANDINAVIAN | The menu at Apotek is much the same as those at other upscale spots in Reykjavík—tons of fish, some sort of take on a tasting menu of traditional dishes (often with whale and puffin), and a few turf additions here and there—but the care and attention to detail is obvious here. It's a great splurge for those looking to get in one last memorable meal before heading home. **Known for:** regularly changing tasting menus; vegetarian-friendly dishes; stunning dessert presentation. [$] *Average main: ISK4,290* ✉ *Austurstræti 16, Miðbær* ☎ *551–0011* 🌐 *www.apotekrestaurant.is.*

★ Bæjarins Beztu Pylsur
$ | FAST FOOD | FAMILY | In a parking lot facing the harbor, this tiny yet famous fast-food hut is known for serving the original Icelandic hot dog—and a single person serves about a thousand of them a day from the window. Ask for *eina með öllu* (pronounced "*ayn*-ah med *utl*-lou"), or "one with everything," which gets you mustard, tomato sauce, rémoulade (mayonnaise with finely chopped pickles), and chopped raw and fried onions. **Known for:** quick service; a wide variety of locally loved condiments; incredibly helpful hot dog holders on the nearby tables. [$] *Average main: ISK400* ✉ *Tryggvagata and Pósthússtræti, Austurströnd 3, Miðbær* ☎ *511–1566* 🌐 *www.bbp.is.*

Brút
$$$ | SEAFOOD | Seafood is the spotlight at this restaurant inside the Radisson Blu 1919 Hotel. Do yourself a favor and sign over all control to your server when it comes to the wine—the recommendations are spot on. **Known for:** diverse wine list; heavenly desserts; fresh and impressive seafood. [$] *Average main: ISK4,500* ✉ *Pósthússtræti 2, Reykjavík* ☎ *537–2788* 🌐 *www.brut.is.*

★ Grillmarkaðurinn
$$$$ | EUROPEAN | A collaborative project by well-known culinary innovators Hrefna Rós Sætran (founder and owner of the Fish Market) and Guðlaugur P. Frímannsson, Grillmarkaðurinn serves seasonal, organic, and locally grown ingredients in a beautifully designed interior that's heavy on natural materials such as wood and stone. **Known for:** creative dishes using tried-and-true local ingredients; traditional dishes served with a modern twist; noteworthy tasting menus.

$ *Average main: ISK5,690* ✉ *Lækjargata 2A, Miðbær* ☎ *571–7777* ⊕ *www.grill-markadurinn.is* ▭ *No credit cards.*

★ Hornið

$$ | ITALIAN | FAMILY | This welcoming bistro is light and airy, with lots of natural wood, potted plants, and cast-iron bistro tables. The emphasis is on pizza and pasta, but there's also a selection of meat and fish dishes. **Known for:** large pizza menu; cozy interior; excellent seafood soup. $ *Average main: ISK3,590* ✉ *Hafnarstræti 15, Miðbær* ☎ *551–3340* ⊕ *www.hornid.is.*

Hnoss

$$$ | ICELANDIC | Located inside of Harpa Concert Hall, Hnoss is the newest endeavor from Fanney Dóra, the chef behind local favorite Skál! Naturally this is a great spot for a pre-show meal, but the focus on local ingredients and freshly caught seafood make it worth a trip to Harpa on its own. **Known for:** local seafood; beautiful harbor views; pre-show eats. $ *Average main: ISK4,900* ✉ *Austurbakki 2, Reykjavík* ☎ *655–5500* ⊕ *www.hnossrestaurant.is.*

Hressó

$$ | PIZZA | FAMILY | Fire-baked sourdough pizzas are the thing to get at Hressó, where the atmosphere is casual and the toppings are truly local. If you've ever wanted to try a pizza with shrimp on top, this is the place to do it. **Known for:** sourdough pizza; unique toppings, including shrimp; relaxed atmosphere. $ *Average main: ISK2,590* ✉ *Austurstræti 20, Miðbær* ☎ *561–2240* ⊕ *www.facebook. com/hressingarskalinn.*

Laundromat Café

$$ | AMERICAN | FAMILY | Reminiscent of an American-style diner, Laundromat Café makes two promises: a meal and a place to wash your clothes—and it delivers. The latter can be found in the basement, but you'll find no frills meals, lots of books, and neverending coffee refills in the restaurant. **Known for:** classic American diner food; friendly ambience; great all-you-can-drink coffee. $ *Average main: ISK2,999* ✉ *Austurstræti 9, Reykjavík* ☎ *771–9660* ⊕ *www.thelaundromatcafe. is.*

★ Le Kock

$ | AMERICAN | This restaurant is clearly inspired by American cuisine, from chicken wings to burgers. The potato options are downright creative, especially the Greek potatoes with feta spread, ranch dressing, red grapes, peanuts, and spring onions. **Known for:** creative burger options; American-inspired cuisine; quick service. $ *Average main: ISK2,200* ✉ *Tryggvagata 14, Miðbær* ☎ *571–1555* ⊕ *www.lekock.is.*

Mandi

$ | MIDDLE EASTERN | If you're short on time and you need a snack—or some quick fuel for your next museum visit—Mandi has you covered. The Middle-Eastern dishes span kebab and hummus to shawarma and falafel, but there are a few outliers as well, like burgers and fries. **Known for:** quick service; great falafel; inexpensive prices. $ *Average main: ISK2,100* ✉ *Veltusund 3b, Reykjavík* ☎ *571–1444* ⊕ *www.mandi.is.*

Matarkjallarinn

$$ | SCANDINAVIAN | The atmosphere is the real crowd-pleaser here—especially if you're looking for a romantic restaurant with low lighting for date night or a hip dinner with perfectly fine food. As the name suggests, the surroundings skew toward stone and offer the cozy kind of vibes only a cellar can provide. **Known for:** sceney vibe; friendly bartenders; good for group dinners. $ *Average main: ISK3,990* ✉ *Aðalstræti 2, Miðbær* ☎ *558–0000* ⊕ *www.matarkjallarinn.is.*

★ Messinn

$$ | SEAFOOD | This small restaurant in the heart of the city is famous for its fish pans: the sizzling catch of the day accompanied by butter-fried potatoes and seasonal vegetables. It's a basic dish, but it really can't be beaten. **Known for:** iconic fish pans; generous portions; sharable dishes. [$] *Average main: ISK3,890* ✉ *Lækjargata 6, Miðbær* ☎ *546–0095* 🌐 *www.messinn.com.*

Sæta Svínið Gastropub

$$ | **SCANDINAVIAN** | If your ideal dinner consists of eating on a patio with a good beer in hand, you won't be disappointed by this lively pub. You can even mingle with the locals for a rousing game of bingo on Sunday night. **Known for:** inventive burgers of the month; outdoor seating great for people-watching in the square; lamb sandwich with waffle fries. [$] *Average main: ISK3,990* ✉ *Hafnarstræti, Miðbær* ☎ *555–2900* 🌐 *www.saetasvinid.is.*

Tapas Barinn

$$$ | **SCANDINAVIAN** | If you're interested in trying some of the more traditional dishes of Iceland (think puffin or whale), pay Tapas Barinn a visit. Here you can pass small plates among your group or opt for the more substantial Icelandic Gourmet Feast, which includes smoked puffin, minke whale, and a shot of Brennivín. **Known for:** fantastic tasting menu with Icelandic classics; lively crowd; traditional Iceland ingredients in tapas form. [$] *Average main: ISK5,400* ✉ *Vesturgata 3b, Miðbær* ☎ *551–2344* 🌐 *www.tapas.is.*

★ **Tides**

$$$$ | **ICELANDIC** | Led by Michelin-starred chef Gunnar Karl Gíslason, this cozy restaurant nestled inside the Reykjavik EDITION Hotel is a fantastic spot for a celebration dinner. There is a set menu available, but the friendly staff will also help you choose from the many à la carte seafood dishes, cocktails, and wines on offer. **Known for:** some of the city's best seafood; impressive chef's menu; tasty cocktails and mocktails. [$] *Average main: ISK5,800* ✉ *Austurbakki 2, Reykjavík* ☎ *582–0002* 🌐 *www.tidesrestaurant.is.*

Hotels

Apótek Hotel

$$$ | **HOTEL** | The Art Deco architecture here adds some serious curb appeal to this hotel. **Pros:** great location; free Wi-Fi; lovely Art Deco design. **Cons:** open shower design not for everyone; small rooms; surrounding neighborhood a bit loud. [$] *Rooms from: ISK33,998* ✉ *Austurstræti 16, Reykjavík* ☎ *512–9000* 🌐 *www.keahotels.is/apotek-hotel* 🛏 *45 rooms* 🍴 *No Meals.*

★ **Exeter Hotel**

$$ | **HOTEL** | With a sauna, gym, bakery, and restaurant, there's a lot to love about the Exeter Hotel. **Pros:** walkable distance to the harbor; great restaurant and bakery onsite; hip yet welcoming atmosphere. **Cons:** small rooms; breakfast not included; no parking. [$] *Rooms from: ISK23,994* ✉ *12 Tryggvagata, Reykjavík* ☎ *519–8000* 🌐 *www.exeterhotel.is* 🛏 *106 rooms* 🍴 *No Meals.*

★ **Hótel Borg**

$$$ | **HOTEL** | In contrast to the ultramodern glass-and-chrome architecture around Reykjavík, the city's oldest hotel is pure 1930s Art Deco—from the black marble statues in the entryway to the brass-and-wood railing on the stairs to the square little coffee cups in the rooms. **Pros:** perfect location; lovely Art Deco design; good restaurant. **Cons:** street noise can be an issue on lower floors; some visitors find the beds too firm; no a/c. [$] *Rooms from: ISK31,330* ✉ *Pósthússtræti 11, Miðbær* ☎ *551–1440* 🌐 *www.hotelborg.is* 🛏 *107 rooms* 🍴 *No Meals.*

Hótel Reykjavík Centrum

$ | **HOTEL** | **FAMILY** | Situated downtown, this hotel has rooms decorated in pastel colors, and common areas with lots of natural light thanks to the glass ceiling over the lobby. **Pros:** central location; good value; historical building. **Cons:** small bathrooms; no free parking; room decor lacks personality. [$] *Rooms from: ISK20,841* ✉ *Aðalstræti 16, Miðbær* ☎ *514–6000* 🌐 *www.hotelcentrum.is* 🛏 *89 rooms* 🍴 *Free Breakfast.*

Hótel Reykjavík Saga

$$ | **HOTEL** | **FAMILY** | Located right next to Lake Tjörnin on one of the city's main streets, this hotel features intimate, design-forward rooms and plenty of communal spaces. **Pros:** less expensive than other similar options; good gym and spa onsite; gorgeous design. **Cons:** bathtubs only available in some rooms; no room service; slight business vibe. [$] *Rooms from: ISK27,476* ✉ *Lækjargata 12, Reykjavík* ☎ *562–4000* 🌐 *www.islandshotel.is/hotels-in-iceland/hotel-reykjavik-saga* 🛏 *130 rooms* 🍴 *No Meals.*

Kvosin Hotel

$$$$ | **HOTEL** | **FAMILY** | If you want to stay somewhere that offers a bit more privacy and freedom (including your own kitchen area), this hotel, located in the heart of Reykjavík next to the Dómkirkjan, should be on your radar. **Pros:** large rooms; great for families; all rooms have kitchen facilities. **Cons:** thin walls; basic amenities; service can be less than stellar. [$] *Rooms from: ISK35,471* ✉ *Kirkjutorg, Miðbær* ☎ *415–2400* 🌐 *www.kvosinhotel.is* 🛏 *24 rooms* 🍴 *No Meals.*

Radisson BLU 1919 Hotel

$$$ | **HOTEL** | Located downtown in one of Reykjavík's oldest and most famous buildings, this hotel's exterior is reminiscent of 1919 (the year the building was constructed) but the interior is very sleek and modern, and great attention has been paid to everything from the light fixtures in the foyer to the artwork in the rooms. **Pros:** smart and modern atmosphere; popular on-site restaurant and lounge; great location. **Cons:** slightly sterile atmosphere; excess street noise at night; breakfast not included. [$] *Rooms from: ISK31,468* ✉ *Pósthússtræti 2, Miðbær* ☎ *599–1000* 🌐 *www.radissonblu.com* 🛏 *88 rooms* 🍴 *No Meals.*

★ **The Reykjavik EDITION**

$$$$ | **HOTEL** | From the moment you step into this hotel, you'll know you're somewhere special: the staff is friendly and alert, the on-site spa is worth a visit, and the rooms showcase the best of Scandinavian design taste. **Pros:** next-level service; stunning interiors; incredible on-site restaurant. **Cons:** some rooms feel a bit small; quite expensive; a bit of a walk to the downtown neighborhood. [$] *Rooms from: ISK102,527* ✉ *Austurbakki 2, Reykjavík* ☎ *582–0000* 🌐 *www.marriott.com* 🛏 *253 rooms* 🍴 *Free Breakfast.*

Reykjavik Konsulat Hotel

$$$ | **HOTEL** | Past guests have praised the beyond attentive staff and central location of this hotel. **Pros:** comfortable beds; great service; central location. **Cons:** reports of nearby construction noise; no parking; small rooms. [$] *Rooms from: ISK32,020* ✉ *Hafnarstraeti 17-19, Reykjavík* ☎ *514–6800* 🌐 *www.hilton.com/en/hotels/rekcuqq-reykjavik-konsulat-hotel* 🛏 *50 rooms* 🍴 *Free Breakfast.*

🍸 Nightlife

AUTO

DANCE CLUBS | Right below the Hard Rock Cafe, you'll find this lively nightclub making the most of its near-windowless basement location. According to the owners—Sindri Snær Jensson and Jón Davíð Davíðsson, the duo behind Flatey Pizza and Yuzu Burger—that's the point: to create a space where you'll lose all sense of time. ✉ *Lækjargata 2a, Reykjavík* ☎ *862–2886* 🌐 *www.autoclub.is.*

The Dubliner

BREWPUBS | As one of the few bars in Reykjavík with more TVs than you can count on one hand, the Dubliner is often busiest during televised matches and games. For a pleasant surprise, ask the bartender to make you something special. ✉ *Tryggvagata 22, Miðbær* ☎ *527–3232.*

Húrra

LIVE MUSIC | This venue has hosted live music for as long as most locals can remember, welcoming those who wish to dance into the very late hours of the night. ✉ *Tryggvagata 22, Reykjavík* ⊕ *www.facebook.com/hurra.is.*

Jungle Cocktail Bar

COCKTAIL LOUNGES | A green oasis right in the middle of town, the plant-filled space might make you think you're elsewhere, but you'll be brought right back to reality once you try one of the bar's inventive cocktails. Adventurous drinkers won't want to miss the Cereal Killer, which is made with Bacardi carta blanca, strawberries, cornflakes, oranges, and almonds. ✉ *Austurstræti 9, Reykjavík* ☎ *792–6969* ⊕ *www.jungle.is.*

Lemmy

BARS | Located in one of the oldest houses in Reykjavik, Lemmy is far from just a bar: you can also order a hearty breakfast here. But this spot is at its best when the drinks are flowing and the picnic tables are filled with locals and visitors alike. ✉ *Austurstræti 20, Reykjavík* ☎ *568–2003* ⊕ *www.lemmy.is.*

★ Lola Flórens

COCKTAIL LOUNGES | This space is part vintage shop and part cocktail bar and the interiors play the part. Romantic vibes surround each table, where display cases of crystals and curated vintage clothing set the scene. ✉ *Garðastræti 6, Reykjavík* ☎ *571–9970* ⊕ *www.florens.is.*

Pablo Discobar

DANCE CLUBS | Technically a nightclub, Pablo Discobar also serves food and some notable cocktails. Since the bar is open until 5 am on Friday and Saturday, you'll often find people making this their last stop after a night on the town. There is a bit of a dress code on weekends (think stylish over formal). You can also catch some great drag shows here, if you're lucky. ✉ *Veltusund 1, Miðbær* ☎ *552–7333* ⊕ *www.pablodiscobar.is.*

★ Skúli Craft Bar

BARS | You can't go wrong with any of the craft beers on tap here. This bar is certainly a bit more refined than other beer-focused watering holes in Reykjavík, and prices reflect that. If you're on a budget, opt for smaller pours. ✉ *Aðalstræti 9, Miðbær* ☎ *519–6455* ⊕ *www.facebook.com/skulicraft.*

Tölt Cocktail Bar

COCKTAIL LOUNGES | Located in a cozy nook of the Reykjavik EDITION Hotel, Tölt Cocktail Bar is named after a special gait only used by Icelandic horses. Cocktails are the way to go: the Dark Horse makes a great nightcap with its combination of cognac, pomegranate, chai vermouth, lime, and bitters. ✉ *Bryggjugata 6, Reykjavík* ⊕ *www.editionhotels.com/ reykjavik/restaurants-and-bars.*

 **Performing Arts**

MUSIC

Íslenska Óperan

MUSIC | **FAMILY** | The Icelandic Opera, a resident company, performs during the winter at its home in the Harpa Concert Hall. ✉ *Harpa, Austurbakka 2, Miðbær* ☎ *528–5050* ⊕ *www.opera.is.*

Sinfóníuhljómsveit Íslands

MUSIC | **FAMILY** | The Iceland Symphony Orchestra has bloomed beautifully, winning fine reviews for its tour appearances at Carnegie Hall and the Kennedy Center. Regular performances are held throughout the year at the eye-catching Harpa Concert Hall. ✉ *Harpa, Austurbakki 2, Miðbær* ☎ *545–2500* ⊕ *www.sinfonia.is.*

 Shopping

BEAUTY

★ Fischer

PERFUME | Owned by Jónsi, vocalist for the Icelandic post-rock band Sigur Rós, this might be the most unique shopping experience in Reykjavík. Draped in a dark color palette, Fischer is a whole mood

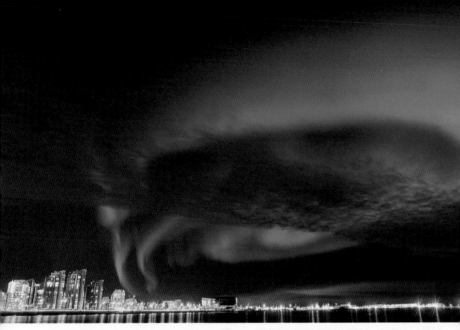

Yes, it is possible to see the northern lights in downtown Reykjavík, depending on the time of year.

from the moment you walk through its doors. Every moment in Fischer is a kind of lesson, from the scents of the room sprays, candles, and perfumes to the story behind the jewelry pieces. Take a moment to climb the ladder in the corner too: there's a special peephole at the top with a delightful little visual waiting to be seen. ⊠ *Fischersund 3, Miðbær* ⊕ *www. fischersund.com.*

★ Madison Ilmhús

COSMETICS | The goal here is all about finding the best products for your own personal style and skin type. Madison Ilmhús specializes in bespoke perfumes and scents, so take some time to peruse everything they have to offer. ⊠ *Aðalstræti 9, Miðbær* ⊕ *www.madison.is.*

BOOKS

★ Penninn Eymundsson Austurstræti

BOOKS | If you're on the hunt for a book, chances are Penninn Eymundsson Austurstræti has what you need. As Iceland's oldest bookstore (established in 1872) it has a tried-and-true reputation for well-stocked shelves. ⊠ *Austurstræti 18, Miðbær* ☎ *540–2130* ⊕ *www.penninn.is.*

CLOTHING

Gyllti Kötturinn

SECOND-HAND | This secondhand shop is immediately recognizable by its logo: a cat surrounded in glitter. It's fun to stop in and browse; there's always something new to see and try on. ⊠ *Austurstræti 8–10, Miðbær* ☎ *534–0005* ⊕ *www. gylltikotturinn.is.*

Kolaportið Flea Market

SECOND-HAND | During the weekend, this lively and colorful flea market is open in an old ground-floor warehouse by the harbor (look for the big banner). Here you'll find treasures from local vendors, as well as handmade crafts. ⊠ *Tryggvagötu 19, Miðbær* ☎ *562–5030* ⊕ *www. kolaportid.is.*

Lækjartorg

MARKET | FAMILY | In summertime Lækjartorg sometimes fills with the stands of outdoor merchants offering everything from woolen items, records, and books to vegetables, fruit, and bread. During evenings and weekends, the food wagons set up shop to sell their wares. Be on the look-out for the waffle vendors in the yellow and blue van—their waffles, topped with jam and cream, are addictive. ⊠ *Hafnarstræti 18, Miðbær* ⊕ *www.visitreykjavik.is.*

FOOD AND WINE

Vínbúðin

WINE/SPIRITS | Alcohol is not widely sold in grocery stores in Iceland—you have to visit government-run liquor stores. They're usually open no later than 8 pm on weekends, and that's where the planning comes in. There are a number of locations around Reykjavík and throughout the country. Just be warned: alcohol in Iceland is not cheap. ⊠ *Austurstræti 10a, Miðbær* ☏ *560–7700* ⊕ *www.vinbudin.is.*

GALLERIES

Kirsuberjatréð

CRAFTS | The Cherry Tree is a collective of 10 women selling their own creations. From music boxes and fishskin purses to pottery and housewares, you never know what you're going to find in this shop. ⊠ *Vesturgata 4, Miðbær* ☏ *562–8990* ⊕ *www.kirs.is.*

★ Kogga Ceramic Gallery & Studio

CERAMICS | This ceramic gallery and studio showcases the work of Kolbrún Björgólfsdóttir, an artist who has been creating pottery since the mid-1970s. Her work is characterized by small drawings etched into the vessels and other forms. ⊠ *Vesturgata 5, Miðbær* ☏ *899–2772* ⊕ *www.kogga.is.*

GIFTS

The VIKING

SOUVENIRS | **FAMILY** | This kitchsy yet fun souvenir shop is perfect if you're looking for a fluffy sheep keychain, *Game of Thrones* mug, or punny Iceland T-shirt. ⊠ *Hafnarstræti, Miðbær* ☏ *551–1250* ⊕ *www.theviking.is.*

Old Harbor and Vesturbær

With its busy slipway and throng of multi-color boats, the Reykjavík Old Harbor is an important part of the city center and a vibrant hub of industrial activity. Over the past few years, the area has also become a hotbed of cultural and culinary activity. It's also where you'll find many of the city center's restaurants, cafés, and small businesses, offering everything from whale-watching tours to Segway rides—you just might discover the city's best lobster soup and crab cakes here, too.

The cultural activity of the Old Harbor has thoroughly spilled over into the neighboring Grandi Harbor area, where you can now explore a new generation of trendy shops, cafés, and attractions, as well as some prime views of the bay. A short walk from the city center, the 107 district of Reykjavík is known as Vesturbær, which translates as "West Town." Home to the University of Iceland and its extensive facilities and institutions, it attracts a concentration of Saga Age literati and other intellectuals.

 Sights

Aurora Reykjavík

OTHER MUSEUM | **FAMILY** | An absolute must-see for northern lights seekers, here visitors get to play with technology simulating the intensity and color spectrum of the auroras while panels explain the physical variations. A high-definition movie of the extraordinary lights in action over Iceland is the highlight of the exhibition, but perhaps even more useful is the practice booth where you can (with the help of detailed instructions) learn the exact settings required to successfully photograph the northern lights. ⊠ *Grandagarður 2* ☏ *780–4500* ⊕ *www.aurorareykjavik.is* ✈ *ISK 2,000.*

92

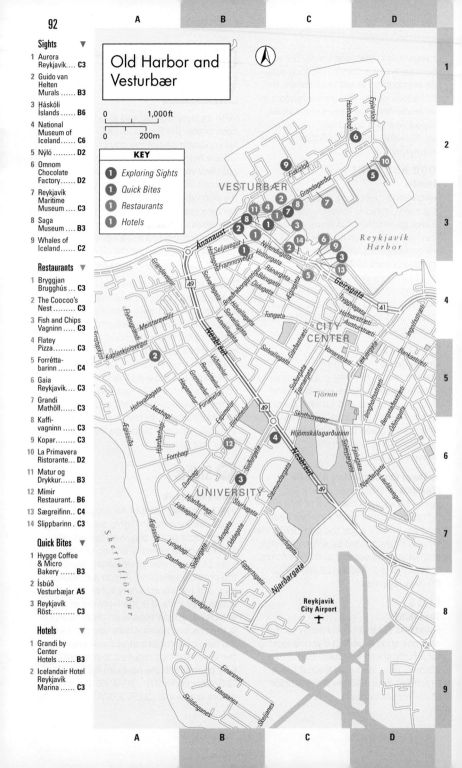

Old Harbor and Vesturbær

0   1,000ft
0   200m

KEY

❶ *Exploring Sights*
❶ *Quick Bites*
❶ *Restaurants*
❶ *Hotels*

★ **Guido van Helten Murals**

PUBLIC ART | The most impressive murals in Reykjavík are the work of Australia-born artist Guido van Helten, who carried out a series of commissions on buildings throughout Iceland between 2013 and 2014. His most noted works are those painted on the walls of an old theater building in the hip Grandi Harbor area of the city, featuring characters from a 1961 staging of Sartre's *No Exit*. Guido frequently uses old photographs to guide his work; those used for this epic mural were sourced from the Reykjavík Museum of Photography. ⊠ *Seljavegur 2, Vesturbær* ⊕ *www.guidovanhelten.com.*

Háskóli Íslands (*University of Iceland*)

COLLEGE | The University of Iceland is the country's oldest and largest institution of higher education. The campus is known for a statue of Sæmundur Fróði, a symbol of learning. Legend has it that after studying abroad, Sæmundur made a pact with the devil to get himself home, promising his soul if he arrived without getting wet. The devil changed into a seal to carry him home. Just as they arrived, Sæmundur hit the seal on the head with his Psalter, got his coattails wet, and escaped with soul intact. ⊠ *Sæmundargötu 2, across from Hringbraut and diagonally southwest from the park lake, Vesturbær* ☎ *525–4000* ⊕ *www.hi.is* ⊠ *Free.*

★ **National Museum of Iceland**

HISTORY MUSEUM | Viking treasures and artifacts, silverwork, wood carvings, and some unusual whalebone carvings are on display here, as well as maritime objects, historical textiles, jewelry, and crafts. There is also a coffee shop. ⊠ *Suðurgata 41, Vesturbær* ☎ *530–2200* ⊕ *www.thjodminjasafn.is* ⊠ *ISK 2,500.*

Nýló

ART MUSEUM | **FAMILY** | Also known as the Living Art Museum, Nýló is located inside the Marshall House and displays some of the more experimental works by local artists. Media range from paint and plant-flavored ice cream to video and sculpture. ⊠ *Grandagarður 20, Vesturbær* ☎ *551–4350* ⊕ *www.nylo.is* ⊠ *Free* ☺ *Closed Mon. and Tues.*

★ **Omnom Chocolate Factory**

FACTORY | You can't walk into a store in Reykjavík without spotting the colorful and artfully designed packaging of an Omnom chocolate bar. The company's factory is located here in town and houses a beloved ice-cream shop featuring the brand's sweet treats. ⊠ *Hólmaslóð 4* ☎ *519–5959* ⊕ *www.omnomchocolate.com.*

Reykjavík Maritime Museum

HISTORY MUSEUM | **FAMILY** | Housed in an old fish freezing plant with great views of the harbor, the city's maritime museum has exhibits on Icelandic fisheries and trading vessels. There's also a whole Coast Guard vessel that can be explored. ⊠ *Grandagarður 8, Vesturbær* ☎ *411–6300* ⊕ *reykjavikcitymuseum.is/reykjavik-maritime-museum* ⊠ *ISK 1,950.*

★ **Saga Museum**

HISTORY MUSEUM | **FAMILY** | In addition to exhibits that explore important moments throughout Iceland's history, this museum also lets you try on clothing from Viking times. The wax models illustrating events of the Sagas are oddly endearing. ⊠ *Grandagarður 2, Vesturbær* ☎ *511–1517* ⊕ *www.sagamuseum.is* ⊠ *ISK 3,000.*

Whales of Iceland

SCIENCE MUSEUM | **FAMILY** | Blue whales, fin whales, humpbacks, and belugas are just some of the 23 different species featured in this great pod of life-size models at the Whales of Iceland exhibition. Located in an old industrial area close to Grandi Harbor—an area undergoing revitalization by an influx of thriving culture—this family-friendly exhibition, which claims to be "the largest whale exhibition in Europe and perhaps even the world," is designed to both educate and foster support of whale tourism, as opposed to whale hunting. ⊠ *Fiskislóð*

23–25, Vesturbær ☎ 571–0077 🌐 www.whalesoficeland.is 🎟 ISK 3,400.

🍴 Restaurants

Bryggjan Brugghús
$$$ | **SEAFOOD** | Toss out any expectations of bar food at this microbrewery hot spot—the menu here will surprise you. From the Lobster Feast to the Beer Piri-Piri Chicken, there's more to Bryggjan Brugghús than its taps. **Known for:** brewery tours; great patio for beer drinking; surprisingly sophisticated menu. [$] *Average main: ISK4,490 ✉ Grandagarður 8, Vesturbær ☎ 456–4040 🌐 www.bryggjanbrugghus.is.*

★ **The Coocoo's Nest**
$$ | **MODERN AMERICAN** | For an affordable treat, environmentally conscious locals flock to this excellent eatery in the Grandi Harbor area to indulge in good, hearty food made with mostly organic ingredients. Apart from its weekend brunch (the perfect hangover cure), the Coocoo's Nest is also famous for exceptional sourdough pizza. **Known for:** delicious sourdough pizza; cozy and trendy interiors; fresh, refreshing juices. [$] *Average main: ISK2,500 ✉ Grandagardur 23, Vesturbær ☎ 522–5454 🌐 www.coocoosnest.is ⏲ Closed Mon.*

Fish and Chips Vagninn
$ | **SEAFOOD** | The owners of this food cart trained intensively in the United Kingdom to perfect British-style fish-and-chips before importing their skills to Iceland. With the excellent quality of fresh Icelandic fish thrown into a hearty mix of mushy peas and chips, which you can drown in malt vinegar, this street food option has become very popular with locals, who still get a kick out of the knowledge that Iceland won "the cod war." **Known for:** traditional British fish-and-chips with mushy peas; great views of the harbor; wide variety of sauces. [$] *Average main: ISK1,990 ✥ This stall is located in the westernmost point of Reykjavík's main harbor, just off the shipyard. ☎ 840–4100 🌐 www.fishandchipsvagninn.is.*

★ **Flatey Pizza**
$ | **PIZZA** | **FAMILY** | This spot serves up Neapolitan-style pies with slow-rising sourdough made on-site. Most of the menu stays relatively traditional when it comes to toppings, but the Pizza of the Week tends to be a bit more creative. **Known for:** unusual pizza of the week toppings (like dates); home-fermented pizza dough; flavorful tomato sauce. [$] *Average main: ISK2,450 ✉ Grandagarður 11 ☎ 588–2666 🌐 www.flateypizza.is.*

Forréttabarinn
$$ | **SEAFOOD** | Located by the harbor, Forettabarinn serves up dishes from around the world along with local beers from the breweries that dot Iceland's coast. The small plates make it a great place to start the night, but the set menus also offer welcoming options for a full meal. **Known for:** beautiful harbor views; good-value prix-fixe meals; diverse menu items from around the globe. [$] *Average main: ISK3,050 ✉ Nýlendugata 14, Vesturbær ☎ 517–1800 🌐 www.forrettabarinn.is.*

Gaia Reykjavík
$$ | **JAPANESE** | Fans of sushi will find a welcoming seat near the harbor at Gaia. The menu ranges from small plates—great for little tastes and sharing with a loved one—to a full six-course tasting menu. **Known for:** inventive cocktails; gorgeous harbor views; tasting plates. [$] *Average main: ISK2,900 ✉ Ægisgarður 2, Reykjavík ☎ 512–8181 🌐 www.gaiareykjavik.is ⏲ Closed. Sun. and Mon.*

★ **Grandi Mathöll**
$ | **ECLECTIC** | This beautifully designed food hall may not be that big, housing just seven food stations, but it brings together some of the most exciting spots to eat in the city. Come here to check out Garlic, the Gastro Truck, Kore Grandi, Grandi's Pasta Shop, Annapurna

Asian Spices, The Sheepfold, The Cold Store, and Fjárhúsið. **Known for:** variety of options; design-forward space; some of Reykjavík's best vendors in one space. ⓢ *Average main: ISK1,400* ✉ *Grandagarði 16, Vesturbær* ☎ *787–6200* ⊕ *www.grandimatholl.is.*

★ Kaffivagninn
ⓢ | ICELANDIC | Way back before the Grandi area was cool, this value restaurant with exceptional harbor views served up good, old-fashioned, hearty Icelandic food for a league of local fishermen. Although it's still mainly patronized by marine-industry natives, an increasing number of tourists now venture through its humble doors to enjoy the quality fish balls and other tasty dishes. **Known for:** fresh seafood stew; vegetarian friendly options; standout fish-and-chips. ⓢ *Average main: ISK2,390* ✉ *Grandagarði 10* ☎ *551–5932* ⊕ *www.kaffivagninn.is.*

Kopar
ⓢ | ICELANDIC | With a name that means "copper" in Icelandic, Kopar is known for its harborside location and intriguing cocktail menu that brings locals and travelers alike to its bar and tables. Try the Stand by Me if you're looking for a delicious cocktail made with Iceland's favorite schnapps (Brennivin). **Known for:** cocktail of the day; fresh ingredients; innovative seafood dishes. ⓢ *Average main: ISK2,390* ✉ *Geirsgata 3, Vesturbær* ☎ *567–2700* ⊕ *www.koparrestaurant.is* ⊗ *Closed Sun.*

★ La Primavera Ristorante
ⓢⓢⓢ | ITALIAN | Nestled on the first floor of the art-centric Marshall House, La Primavera's impressive interiors give you a taste of what's to come on the upper floors. If you never thought you'd find Italian dishes in Iceland to rival those you'd find in Italy, think again. **Known for:** authentic Italian cuisine; impressive interior design; excellent wine menu. ⓢ *Average main: ISK4,990* ✉ *Grandagarði 20, Vesturbær* ☎ *519–7766* ⊕ *www.laprimavera.is* ⊗ *Closed Sun. and Mon.*

Matur og Drykkur
ⓢⓢⓢⓢ | SCANDINAVIAN | It's hard to tell what stands out more at Matur og Drykkur: the accommodating staff or the A+ dishes. Located in an old salt fish factory, the views of the harbor overlook the perfect scene for a post-dinner walk. **Known for:** impressive tasting menu (includes a vegetarian option); preserved lemon sorbet; can't-be-missed dessert menu. ⓢ *Average main: ISK12,900* ✉ *Grandagarður 2, Vesturbær* ☎ *571–8877* ⊕ *www.maturogdrykkur.is* ⊗ *Closed Mon. and Tues. No lunch.*

★ Mímir Restaurant
ⓢⓢ | SCANDINAVIAN | This bright and sophisticated eatery caters to guests and locals alike. Owned by the Farmers Association of Iceland, the restaurant works with local fishermen and farmers to bring the freshest ingredients to the table. **Known for:** unforgettable Farmers Trip tasting menu; impeccable service; central location close to the university. ⓢ *Average main: ISK3,900* ✉ *Hagatorg, Vesturbær* ☎ *525–9970.*

★ Sægreifinn
ⓢⓢ | SEAFOOD | The old fish barrels used as seating in this humble harborside fishing shack are kept warm by an increasing number of tourists and the odd celebrity. The trademark lobster soup is just as good as its well-traveled reputation. **Known for:** famous lobster soup; the aptly named Moby Dick on a Stick (a minke whale kebab); fresh seafood right on the harbor. ⓢ *Average main: ISK2,600* ✉ *Geirsgata 8, Vesturbær* ☎ *553–1500.*

★ Slippbarinn
ⓢⓢ | BISTRO | A port in all weather (especially for local professionals and tourists), this hotel bistro-bar—which also hosts the Reykjavík Bar Summit—has played a key role in reviving the heart of the Old Harbor. It's especially popular on weekends when it pumps out a contagious flow of good vibes to go with its filling brunch, legendary cocktails, and highly addictive licorice-flavored popcorn. **Known**

for: Omnom chocolate cake for dessert; sensational seafood platter; inventive cocktails. $ *Average main: ISK3,900* ⊠ *Geirsgata 8, Vesturbær* ☎ *553–1500* ⊕ *www.slippbarinn.is.*

☕ Coffee and Quick Bites

Hygge Coffee & Micro Bakery

$ | **BAKERY** | This coffeehouse delivers on the hygge theme, right down to the handmade dishware. It's the sister café to Héðinn restaurant and offers the best in baked goods: croissants, cookies, and scones (and don't forget about the coffee). **Known for:** cozy hygge vibes; wonderful baked goods; quick and friendly service. $ *Average main: ISK990* ⊠ *Seljavegur 2, Reykjavík* ⊕ *www.facebook.com/hyggecoffeemicrobakery.*

Ísbúð Vesturbæjar

$ | **ICE CREAM** | **FAMILY** | You'll find a line full of locals winding out the door of this ice-cream shop during the summertime. They offer two kinds of ice cream: "old" and "new," both of which describe the recipes used to make the soft serve (the older recipe is creamier). **Known for:** free chocolate syrup topping; creamy and traditional soft serve; lots of topping choices. $ *Average main: ISK999* ⊠ *Hagamelur* ☎ *552–3330.*

Reykjavík Röst

$$ | **CAFÉ** | Head to Reykjavík Röst to enjoy a harborside coffee. If caffeine isn't your thing, opt for the well-loved hot chocolate. **Known for:** popular hot chocolate; charming harbor views; great happy hour. $ *Average main: ISK2,590* ⊠ *Geirsgata 5, Vesturbær* ☎ *552–7777* ⊕ *www.reykjavikrost.is.*

Hotels

Grandi by Center Hotels

$$$ | **HOTEL** | From the bar to the rooms, guests are surrounded by moody, cozy vibes at this hotel. **Pros:** northern lights wake-up call in winter; great bar; fun design. **Cons:** a bit of a walk from the downtown area; on the expensive side for what you get; no parking. $ *Rooms from: ISK28,957* ⊠ *Seljavegur 2, Reykjavík* ☎ *595–8580* ⊕ *www.centerhotels.com/en/hotel-grandi-reykjavik* ⇘ *195 rooms* ¶ *Free Breakfast.*

Icelandair Hotel Reykjavík Marina

$$ | **HOTEL** | Attention to service, detail, and atmosphere define this harborside hotel, which—thanks to its legendary cocktail bar and bistro—also serves as a popular dining and nightlife hot spot for locals. **Pros:** great conference facilities with a 26-seat cinema and presentation space; charming design; beautiful harbor views from even-numbered rooms. **Cons:** excess noise from neighboring bars; rooms are on the small side; inconsistent room temperatures. $ *Rooms from: ISK26,102* ⊠ *Myrargata 2, Vesturbær* ☎ *560–8000* ⊕ *www.icelandairhotels.com* ⇘ *138 rooms* ¶ *No Meals.*

Nightlife

Héðinn

COCKTAIL LOUNGES | The menu of gin and tonics here shouldn't be missed, as it truly showcases the variety of the classic cocktail. There are also seasonal drinks and thoughtful mocktails. While the bar is relaxed and cozy, this space also serves as a restaurant for guests of the Grandi Hotel. ⊠ *Seljavegur 2, Reykjavík* ☎ *419–2020* ⊕ *www.hedinnrestaurant.is.*

Luna Florens
COCKTAIL LOUNGES | Sister bar to the vintage shop and bar Lola Flórens and sister café to the Coocoo's Nest, Luna Florens serves up inventive cocktails and baked goods. More often than not, you'll find ingredients like turmeric and edible flowers mixed into your drinks. ✉ *Grandagarður 25, Reykjavík* ☏ *552–5454* ⊕ *www.instagram.com/luna_florens.*

 Performing Arts

Cinema at Old Harbour Village No 2
FILM | **FAMILY** | At the top of a warehouse in the Old Harbor district, the Cinema at Old Harbour Village No 2 screens documentaries and nature films. There's also a small exhibition of local artifacts. ✉ *Geirsgata 7b, Vesturbær* ☏ *898–6628* ⊕ *www.thecinema.is* 🎟 *ISK 1,200.*

Shopping

CLOTHING
★ Steinunn
WOMEN'S CLOTHING | Housed in an old fishing net repair shop, Steinunn is the studio of Icelandic fashion designer Steinunn Sigurðardóttir. She creates wearable art of various knits, which you can buy in this location. ✉ *Grandagarður 17, Vesturbær* ☏ *588–6649* ⊕ *www.steinunn.com.*

FOOD AND CANDY
★ Kjötkompaní
FOOD | One of the best parts about renting an Airbnb is the option to cook your own meals. If you find yourself in that situation, head to Kjötkompaní—a butcher shop and deli—to buy your ingredients. They carry all local meats and other enticing treats for your meal. ✉ *Grandagarður 29, Vesturbær* ☏ *578–9700* ⊕ *www.kjotkompani.is.*

JEWELRY
Jens Grandagarði
JEWELRY & WATCHES | The main attraction at Jens Grandagarði are pieces made by the brand's designers in the Stigahlíð workshop. You'll also find offerings from international designers as well. ✉ *Grandagarður 31, Vesturbær* ☏ *546–6446* ⊕ *www.jens.is.*

SPORTING GOODS
Ellingsen
SPORTING GOODS | This Icelandic brand offers tents and camping gear, electric bikes, and clothing for men, women, and children. If you're planning on camping, this is an essential stop for any last-minute shopping. ✉ *Fiskislóð, Vesturbær* ☏ *354/580–8500* ⊕ *www.ellingsen.is.*

TATTOO PARLORS
★ Valkyrie Tattoo Studio
OTHER SPECIALTY STORE | One of the most relaxing things you can do while getting a tattoo is gaze out at the nearby coastline and take in views of the waves—exactly the atmosphere you'll find at this seaside studio. The artists here cover a wide range of styles. ✉ *Fiskislóð 22, Vesturbær* ☏ *537–1900* ⊕ *www.valkyrietattoostudio.com.*

Activities

Vesturbæjarlaug
SWIMMING | **FAMILY** | One of the most popular swimming pools in the city, Vesturbæjarlaug has outdoor geothermal swimming pools, a steam room, a sauna, and hot tubs. There is also a pool specifically for kids. ✉ *Hofsvallagata 107, Vesturbær* ☏ *411–5150* ⊕ *reykjavik.is/stadir/vesturbaejarlaug* 🎟 *ISK 1,100.*

Greater Reykjavík

The Greater Reykjavík area is used to describe the sprawling neighborhoods outside of the city's most central districts. In total, there are six municipalities in the area: Reykjavík, Garðabær, Hafnarfjörður, Kópavogur, Seltjarnarnes, and Mosfellsbær. These areas are largely residential, with schools, office buildings, grocery store chains, and locally owned restaurants. And while it would be easy to call them suburbs, each one has its own historic sights and family-friendly activities, the perfect reasons to explore outside of downtown Reykjavik.

Sights

Árbær Open Air Museum
HISTORY MUSEUM | FAMILY | At the Open-Air Municipal Museum, 19th- and 20th-century houses furnished in period style display authentic household utensils and tools for cottage industries and farming. During the summer you can see demonstrations of farm activities and taste piping-hot *lummur* (chewy pancakes) cooked over an old farmhouse stove. To get to the museum, take Bus 12 or 19. ⊠ *Ártúnsblettur, Grandagarði 8, Árbær* ☎ *411–6300* ⊕ *www.borgarsogusafn.is* ⬛ *ISK 1,950.*

Ásmundur Sveinsson Sculpture Museum
ART MUSEUM | FAMILY | Some of Ásmundur Sveinsson's original sculptures, depicting ordinary working people, myths, and folktale episodes, are exhibited in the museum's gallery and studio and in the surrounding garden. It's on the southwest edge of Laugardalur Park, opposite the traffic circle at its entrance. Entrance is free with the Reykjavík City Card. ⊠ *Sigtún 105, Laugardalur* ⬦ *Take Bus 15 or 17 from Hlemmur station (5 mins)* ☎ *411–6430* ⊕ *www.artmuseum.is/ asmundarsafn* ⬛ *ISK 1,950.*

Fjölskyldugarðurinn Family Park
CITY PARK | FAMILY | Adjacent to Laugardalur Park, Fjölskyldugarðurinn has rides and games, such as Crazy Bikes—a driving school complete with miniature traffic lights—and a scale model of a Viking ship. You can also purchase joint admission to both the Farm Animal Park and Family Park. ⊠ *Fjölskyldugarðurinn, Laugardalur* ☎ *411–5900* ⊕ *www.mu.is.*

Grasagarður Botanic Garden
GARDEN | FAMILY | This free botanic garden in Laugardalur Park has an extensive outdoor collection of native and exotic plants. Coffee, cakes, and other snacks are sold at the cozy Flóran Café, which is open only in summer and on weekends in December. ⊠ *Grasagarður Reykjavíkur Laugardal, Laugardalur, Laugardalur* ☎ *411–8650* ⊕ *www.grasagardur.is* ⬛ *Free.*

Grótta
NATURE SIGHT | Located on the tip of Seltjarnarnes Peninsula, this nature reserve is a fantastic destination for lovers of nature, life, and romance. Here you can look beyond the outline of a lighthouse and take in Iceland's seasonal natural wonders: the northern lights and the midnight sun. ⊠ *Grótta, Reykjavík.*

★ Imagine Peace Tower
PUBLIC ART | FAMILY | A powerful light installation on Viðey Island, created by Yoko Ono, the Imagine Peace Tower is dedicated to the vision of world peace the artist passionately shared with her late husband, John Lennon. The artwork features a large stone wishing well with the words "imagine peace" etched into its white, shiny surface in countless languages. Inside the well are 15 powerful beams that merge into a magnificent force of light when switched on. Yoko visits every year on John's birthday (October 9) to lead the lighting ceremony, where about 2,000 people gather to watch and sing along to Lennon's "Imagine." The impressive tower of light illuminates the skyline until the date of John Lennon's

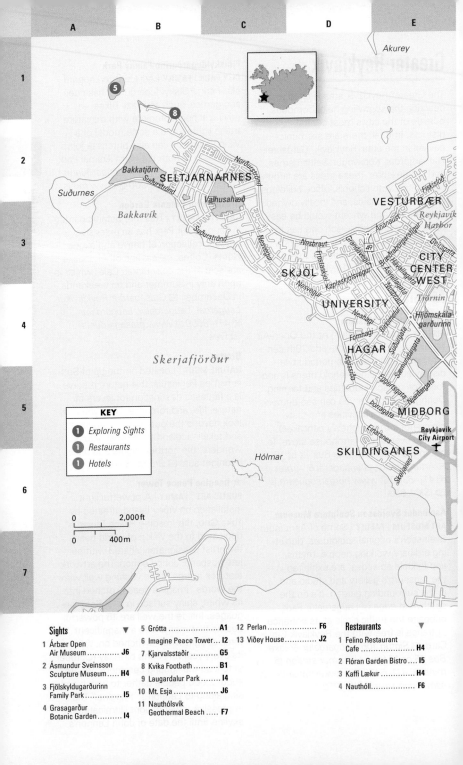

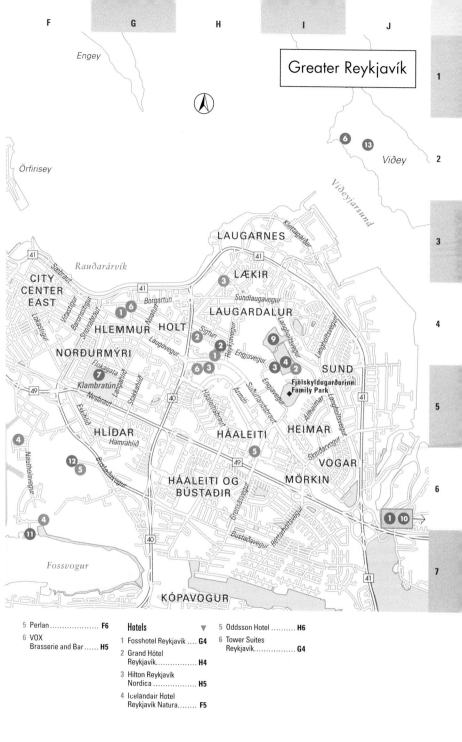

Greater Reykjavík

Engey

Örfirisey

Viðey

Viðeyjarsund

Rauðarárvík

LAUGARNES

CITY CENTER EAST

Sæbraut

LÆKIR

41

41

41

Borgartún

Sundlaugavegur

LAUGARDALUR

HLEMMUR

HOLT

Sigtún

Klettagarðar

Laugavegur

Reykjavegur

Engjavegur

Langholtsvegur

NORÐURMÝRI

Flókagata

Klambratún

Stakkahlíð

Langahlíð

SUND

49

Fjölskyldugarðurinn
Family Park

Suðurlandsbraut

Ármúli

HLÍÐAR

Hamrahlíð

HÁALEITI

HEIMAR

Háaleitisbraut

Skeiðarvogur

Álfheimar

Langholtsvegur

VOGAR

49

HÁALEITI OG
BÚSTAÐIR

MÖRKIN

Grensásvegur

Réttarholtsvegur

40

Bústaðavegur

Fossvogur

40

KÓPAVOGUR

41

Nauthólsvegur

Bústaðavegur

Nesbraut

5 Perlan **F6**
6 VOX
   Brasserie and Bar **H5**

Hotels ▼

1 Fosshotel Reykjavík **G4**
2 Grand Hótel
   Reykjavík **H4**
3 Hilton Reykjavík
   Nordica **H5**
4 Icelandair Hotel
   Reykjavík Natura **F5**

5 Oddsson Hotel **H6**
6 Tower Suites
   Reykjavík **G4**

death on December 8th. Yoko provides a free ferry service for those who wish to attend the annual lighting ceremony. The ferry departs from Skarfabakki pier, less than a 10-minute drive from the city center. ⊠ *Viðey Island* ☎ *533–5055* ⊕ *www.imaginepeacetower.com.*

Kjarvalsstaðir

ART MUSEUM | FAMILY | Inside this modernist building you'll find an impressive permanent exhibit dedicated to the life and works of Jóhannes Sveinsson Kjarval (1885–1972), one of Iceland's most beloved landscape painters. In addition to Kjarval's key works, there's also a rotation of temporary exhibits featuring the works of both local and international artists. Entrance is free with the Reykjavík City Card. ⊠ *Flókagata 24, Hlíðar* ☎ *411–6420* ⊕ *artmuseum.is/kjarvalsstadir* ⊠ *ISK 1,950.*

Kvika Footbath

HOT SPRING | This romantic feature in the district of Seltjarnarnes is located next to the little shark-curing shed down by the sea at Grótta. Designed and installed by Icelandic artist Ólöf Nordal, the hollowed-out dolomite stone is supplied with geothermal water, providing a great place to stop and soak your feet while taking in the views. ⊠ *Grótta, Reykjavík* ⊠ *Free.*

★ Laugardalur Park

CITY PARK | FAMILY | Actually several parks in one large area, Laugardalur Park has one of the best swimming pools in the city as well as a recreational expanse that includes picnic and barbecue areas. There's also an amusement park and a botanic garden with an extensive outdoor collection of native and exotic plants. ⊠ *Laugardalur, Laugardalur* ✛ *Take Bus S2, 5, 14, or 15 east* ☎ *411–8650* ⊕ *www. grasagardur.is* ⊠ *Free.*

Mt. Esja

MOUNTAIN | One of Reykjavík's most recognizable landmarks, Mt. Esja (pronounced *eh*-shyuh) stars in just about every promotional shot or picture postcard of the city. It holds a special place in the hearts of locals, who often take a day trip there to ramble along its network of winding trails. However great it looks from the city, the view from the top of this mountain—not actually a single mountain but a range of many peaks—is even better. Information on transport and trails is available at the tourist information center on Aðalstræti 2 or from Esjustofa, the visitor center and café located at the base of the mountain. ⊠ *Esjustofa–við Mógilsá* ✛ *Bus service to Esjustofa leaves from Hlemmur bus station in Reykjavík city center (Note: you may need to take more than one bus)* ☎ *565–3200* ⊕ *www.visitreykjavik.is/ city-areas/mosfellsbaer/mount-esja.*

Nauthólsvík Geothermal Beach

BEACH | FAMILY | At Reykjavík's geothermal beach at Nauthólsvík, where runoff from the city's hot water supply is used to heat a small lagoon of seawater, temperatures can reach up to 22°C (71.6°F) during the summer. Facilities include changing rooms; showers; hot tubs; a steam room; a barbecue grill; and a small shop selling swimwear, light snacks, and refreshments. Access to the beach and lagoon is free all year round, but the use of the beach facilities is free only between May and September. A small fee (ISK 740) is charged for winter services, with significantly reduced opening hours. Lifeguards are on-site during open hours only. ⊠ *Nauthólsvík Ylströnd* ☎ *511–6630* ⊕ *www.nautholsvik.is* ⊠ *Free.*

★ Perlan

NOTABLE BUILDING | FAMILY | Glittering like the upper hemisphere of a giant disco ball, Perlan (the Pearl) is a grand construction of steel and mirrored glass. Perched atop Öskjuhlíð, the hill overlooking Reykjavík Airport, it's also one of the first landmarks to greet visitors when they arrive to the city. Supported by six massive water tanks and illuminated by 1,900 light bulbs, this impressive building opened in 1991 as a monument to Iceland's invaluable geothermal water supplies. It has since become a major tourist attraction, offering guests a host of amenities beneath its shiny surface, including souvenir shops, a café, an ice cave, a massive exhibition space, and a viewing platform with telescopes. Its crowning glory, though, is its revolving restaurant—it's pricey, but the panoramic views of the city and beyond are second to none. ✉ *Varmahlíð 1, Miðbær* ☎ *566–9000* 🌐 *www.perlan.is* 🎫 *ISK 4,500.*

Viðey House

HISTORIC HOME | The beautiful heart and headquarters of all activities on Viðey Island, Viðey House happens to be the oldest building in Iceland made of stone, and it boasts a restaurant, a bar, and facilities big enough for both intimate concerts and medium-size parties. Downstairs, there's an exhibition of historic items linked to the building's significant past. Across from the house is one of Iceland's oldest churches, from 1774, whose original interior fittings are well preserved. Ferry rides are complimentary to those with a Reykjavík City Card. ✉ *Viðey* ☎ *533–5055* 🌐 *www.videy.com* 🎫 *ISK 1,950.*

🍴 Restaurants

Felino Restaurant Cafe

$$ | ITALIAN | This cafe from Icelandic baker Jóhannes Felixson is a local favorite. You'll often find it packed full of Icelanders catching up over Italian favorites, from pesto chicken to spaghetti bolognese. **Known for:** cozy design; must-try desserts including tiramisu; great pizza. [$] *Average main: ISK2,690* ✉ *Engjateigur 19, Reykjavík* ☎ *517–1919* 🌐 *www.felino.is.*

★ Flóran Garden Bistro

$$ | SCANDINAVIAN | This bistro has a truly unique location inside the botanic gardens of Reykjavík. Of course, much of what you'll find on the menu is grown in the gardens, and you can learn all about the sustainable practices of the kitchen. **Known for:** organic ingredients; truly unique atmosphere; beautiful dish presentation. [$] *Average main: ISK3,400* ✉ *Grasagarðinum Laugarda, Laugardalur* ☎ *553–8872* 🌐 *www.floran.is.*

Kaffi Lækur

$ | SCANDINAVIAN | Attached to a guesthouse offering dorm-style and private rooms, Kaffi Lækur is open to nonguests for breakfast, lunch, and dinner. Don't miss the daily happy hour from 4 to 7 pm and 10 to 11 pm. **Known for:** great happy hour; modern design; part of charming guesthouse. [$] *Average main: ISK2,490* ✉ *Laugarnesvegur 74a, Laugardalur* ☎ *537–6556* 🌐 *www.laekur.is.*

Nauthóll

$$$ | SCANDINAVIAN | FAMILY | Burgers, fish soup, lobster, mussels, deep-fried Camembert, garlic bread—these are just some of the ample nourishment you can find here after a day of swimming at the nearby geothermal beach. This is a also great spot to take a break from walking Ægisíða and its water views. **Known for:** delicious fish soup; good for groups; vegetarian options. [$] *Average main: ISK5,490* ✉ *Nauthólsvegur 106, Miðbær* ☎ *599–6660* 🌐 *www.nautholl.is.*

★ Perlan

$$ | SCANDINAVIAN | FAMILY | This rotating restaurant, atop Reykjavík's geothermal water distribution tanks on Öskjuhlíð Hill, has spectacular panoramic views (one revolution takes about two hours). The international menu emphasizes quick, fresh dishes like salted cod, fish and chips, pizza, and lamb soup. **Known for:** incredible 360-degree views of the city; unique revolving format; varied menu. $ *Average main: ISK2,990* ✉ *Varmahlíð 1, Miðbær* ☎ *566–9000* 🌐 *www.perlan.is.*

VOX Brasserie and Bar

$$$$ | ICELANDIC | The chic restaurant's award-winning chef creates some unique international-themed dishes, and its wine list is one of the city's most impressive. The main menu features items such as arctic char and lamb fillet, and weekend brunch, while less inventive, is generous—and understandably popular. **Known for:** wonderful interior design; notable wine selection; fresh bread and melted brown butter. $ *Average main: ISK6,900* ✉ *The Hilton Reykjavík Nordica, Suðurlandsbraut 2, Háaleiti* ☎ *444–5050* 🌐 *www.vox.is.*

Hotels

Fosshotel Reykjavík

$ | HOTEL | This mammoth hotel in the business district of Reykjavík has spectacular views and huge common areas. **Pros:** very easily accessible; fun happy hour at the Beer Garden; stunning harbor views. **Cons:** parking not included in room rate; some rooms are on the small side; no a/c. $ *Rooms from: ISK18,560* ✉ *Höfðatorg, Þórunnartún 1, Hlíðar* ☎ *531–9000* 🌐 *www.fosshotel.is* 🛏 *327 rooms* 🍴 *Free Breakfast.*

★ Grand Hótel Reykjavík

$$ | HOTEL | Guest rooms here are separated into categories from budget to business class, and the more expensive are naturally more spacious (most are neutral in terms of decor). **Pros:** complimentary shuttle service to downtown every morning; clean and spacious rooms; breakfast included in room rate. **Cons:** slightly businesslike atmosphere; 10- to 15-minute walk or shuttle ride to center of town; less cozy than other hotels. $ *Rooms from: ISK26,029* ✉ *Sigtún 38, Hlíðar* ☎ *514–8000* 🌐 *www.islandshotel.is/hotels-in-iceland/grand-hotel-reykjavik* 🛏 *311 rooms* 🍴 *Free Breakfast.*

Hilton Reykjavík Nordica

$$ | HOTEL | Hilton's first hotel in Iceland is geared primarily toward business travelers, though families are given priority for larger standard rooms. **Pros:** good bar and restaurant; modern furnishings; quiet location. **Cons:** slightly out of city center; very businesslike vibe; service can be slow during peak check-in hours. $ *Rooms from: ISK22,107* ✉ *Suðurlandsbraut 2, Háaleiti* ☎ *444–5000* 🌐 *www.hiltonreykjavik.com* 🛏 *251 rooms* 🍴 *No Meals.*

Icelandair Hotel Reykjavík Natura

$$$$ | HOTEL | Accommodations at this lively airport-side hotel come in a variety of themed rooms, each with its own sentimental dedication to a famous Icelandic artist, poet, or natural wonder. **Pros:** great on-site spa; amazing amenities; close to the geothermal beach and landmark building the Pearl. **Cons:** away from the city center (free bus passes are provided); small rooms; some tour companies don't pick up or drop off at this location. $ *Rooms from: ISK37,873* ✉ *Nauthólsvegur 52, Miðbær* ☎ *444–4500* 🌐 *www.icelandairhotels.com/en/hotels/natura* 🛏 *222 rooms* 🍴 *No Meals.*

★ Oddsson Hotel

$$ | HOTEL | The interior of this hotel would look right at home in a Wes Anderson movie; there's a wide range of room styles to fit groups of different sizes—family suites even include private kitchenettes. **Pros:** beautiful interiors; affordable room options; breakfast included in room rate. **Cons:** can get noisy; self check-in not for everyone; rooms tend to get stuffy. $ *Rooms from: ISK21,500* ✉ *Grensásvegur 16a, Háaleiti* ☎ *419–0200* 🌐 *www.oddsson.is* 🛏 *77 rooms* 🍴 *Free Breakfast.*

Tower Suites Reykjavík

$$$$ | **HOTEL** | If you're after the best views in the city, Tower Suites and its eight accommodations will deliver. **Pros:** luxury interiors; soft beds; panoramic views. **Cons:** limited number of suites; quite expensive; no breakfast included. [$] *Rooms from: ISK59,664* ✉ *Katrínartún 2, Reykjavík* ☎ *416–0000* 🌐 *www.tower-suites.is* 🛏 *8 suites* 🍴 *No Meals.*

Shopping

CLOTHING

66° North Outlet

OUTLET | This respected outerwear brand has been keeping Icelanders warm since 1926. The outlet shop is a good way to save a few dollars without skimping on quality. And what better place to buy your cold-weather gear than a country straddling the Arctic Circle? ✉ *Faxafen 12, Háaleiti* ☎ *535–6678* 🌐 *www.66north.com.*

CRAFTS

★ **Islandia**

SOUVENIRS | If you're on the hunt for a souvenir, Islandia is a great place to spend some time. Inside the shop, you'll find a range of woolens, gifts, and souvenirs. ✉ *Kringlan Mall, Kringlan 4-1, Háaleiti* ☎ *540–2315.*

★ **Storkurinn**

KNITTING | Knitters, listen up: Storkurinn sells locally sourced wool in all colors. The inventory of imported wool is certainly larger, but this is the place if you're looking to find some local yarns for your next project. ✉ *Síðumúli 20, Háaleiti* ☎ *551–8258* 🌐 *www.storkurinn.is.*

HOME DECOR

Myconceptstore

HOUSEWARES | What began as an online shop offering a variety of skincare products and well-made accessories is now a beautiful brick-and-mortar store. It's the perfect spot for design-conscious travelers on the search for a souvenir or two. ✉ *Hjallabrekka 1, Miðbær* ☎ *519–6699* 🌐 *www.myconceptstore.com.*

SHOPPING MALLS

Kringlan Mall

SHOPPING CENTER | **FAMILY** | This mall has a number of charming clothing stores and a movie theater, as well as good places to get souvenirs. It's on the east side of town at the intersection of Miklabraut and Kringlumýrarbraut. Kringlan's free shuttle bus departs from the tourist information center (Aðalstræti 2) at 11 and 2, Monday through Saturday; the return trip departs Kringlan at 1:30 on weekdays. ✉ *Kringlunni 4–12, Háaleiti* ☎ *517–9000* 🌐 *www.kringlan.is.*

Smáralind

SHOPPING CENTER | **FAMILY** | One of Iceland's two major shopping malls, Smáralind (pronounced *smow*-ra-lind), is in Kópavogur, a community neighboring Reykjavík to the south. It's huge—you'll find 90 stores across three floors—and houses, among other stores, British-based Debenhams as well as Iceland's own hypermarket chain, Hagkaup. From Reykjavík, you can take the S2 or 24 bus, but for a bit more than ISK 2,000, you can take a cab and save a lot of precious shopping time. ✉ *Hagasmára 1* ☎ *528–8000* 🌐 *www.smaralind.is.*

SPORTING GOODS

Íslensku Alpanir

SPORTING GOODS | This store has everything you would ever need to brave the Icelandic weather. If you're camping, hiking, or just spending an extended amount of time outside, you'll find something here to make your life easier. ✉ *Faxafen 12, Háaleiti* ☎ *534–2727.*

Rent a Tent

SPORTING GOODS | Those planning to spend a few nights under the stars can skip the tent when packing their bags (more room for souvenirs!) and just rent one here. The professionals at Rent a Tent know exactly what kind of gear you're going to need to face the elements.

✉ *Smiðjuvegur 6, Kópavogur* ☎ *848–5805* ⊕ *www.rentatent.is.*

Útilíf

SPORTING GOODS | If you plan on spending time outdoors, this is a one-stop shop for all the items you'll need. Útilíf carries basic gear and clothing for hiking, climbing, walking, and other outdoor sports. ✉ *Hagasmári 1, Kópavogur* ☎ *545–1500* ⊕ *www.utilif.is.*

Activities

FISHING

The Reykjavik Angling Club

FISHING | Since 1939, the Reykjavik Angling Club has been managing the Elliðaár River, which is chock full of salmon and runs through the middle of Reykjavík. The club can also provide information on fishing in the area. ✉ *Rafstöðvarvegur 14, Árbær* ☎ *568–6050* ⊕ *www.svfr.is.*

Veiðihornið

FISHING | If you find yourself in need of some tackle, head to Veiðihornið, where they stock all of the bait, tackle, gear, and advice you'll need to have a great time. They are known around town for having the most experienced staff and the biggest selection. ✉ *Síðumúli 8, Háaleiti* ☎ *568–8410* ⊕ *www.veidihornid.is.*

GOLF

Golfklúbbur Ness

GOLF | At the southern tip of Seltjarnarnes, the westernmost part of the Reykjavík area, Golfklúbbur Ness has a well-kept 9-hole course. The best part is that you won't find a hole on the course that doesn't have a great view. ✉ *170 Seltjarnarnes* ☎ *561–1930* ⊕ *www.nkgolf. is* 🍴 *ISK 4,500 for nine holes, ISK 9,000 for 18 holes* 🏌 *9 holes, 2,894 yards, par 36* ⊘ *Closed Nov.–Apr.*

Golfklúbbur Reykjavíkur

GOLF | This golf club is the granddaddy of them all, a challenging 18-hole course just east of Reykjavík. The greens fee includes full use of clubhouse facilities. ✉ *Korpúlfstaðir, Grafarholt* ☎ *585–0200* ⊕ *www.grgolf.is* 🍴 *ISK 12,000 for 18 holes* 🏌 *18 holes, 6,590 yards, par 71 (Grafarholt); 18 holes, 6,800 yards, par 72 (Korpa).*

HORSEBACK RIDING

Laxnes Horse Farm

HORSEBACK RIDING | **FAMILY** | Two-hour horseback-riding tours (14,900 ISK) include guides and transportation to and from Reykjavík. There are also combo tours that vary from spending a day learning about life at the Laxnes farm to riding around the Golden Circle. ✉ *271 Mosfellsdalur* ☎ *566–6179* ⊕ *www.laxnes.is.*

Chapter 4

REYKJANES PENINSULA AND THE SOUTH COAST (WITH THE GOLDEN CIRCLE)

4

Updated by
Hannah Jane Cohen

 Sights
★★★★★

 Restaurants
★★★☆☆

Hotels
★★★★☆

 Shopping
★★★☆☆

Nightlife
★★☆☆☆

WELCOME TO REYKJANES PENINSULA AND THE SOUTH COAST (WITH THE GOLDEN CIRCLE)

TOP REASONS TO GO

★ **Blue Lagoon:** One of the most famous hot springs in the world, this bright blue, warm, mineral-filled lake is a bathing spot like no other.

★ **Fagradalsfjall Volcano:** A wasteland of spiky jagged lava, this tuya volcano, which last erupted in August 2022, is still steaming.

★ **Þingvellir National Park:** The oldest national park in Iceland is both culturally and geologically unique. Its many crackling steep cliffs and canyons are a reminder that the ground there is slowly ripping apart as each year the American and Eurasian tectonic plates move farther away from each other.

★ **Gullfoss:** Gullfoss is one of the largest, and most famous, waterfalls in Iceland, and you shouldn't miss the opportunity to see it up close.

★ **Geysir:** The original Geysir all other geysers are named after, Geysir only erupts a few times a year, but the more reliable Strokkur nearby erupts about every five minutes.

1 **Reykjanesbær.** Once home to rugged fishermen and other seafarers, and later the heart of an American military base, this region has two towns with excellent shops and restaurants, not to mention proximity to Iceland's international airport.

2 **Garður.** What was once the most populated village on the Reykjanes Peninsula is now a small, charming town popular with northern lights hunters and bird lovers.

3 **Grindavík.** This important fishing and industrial center is home to the Fagradalsfjall volcano and the world-famous Blue Lagoon.

4 **Hafnarfjörður.** This old fishing town, embedded in the lava of Reykjavík's outskirts, is home to Viking fairs and elves (if you believe the lore) alike.

5 **The Golden Circle.** Originally known as "the Kings Road," this is now the most iconic tourist route in Iceland, comprising three natural wonders: Þingvellir, Geysir, and Gullfoss.

6 **Flúðir.** Flúðir and its small neighboring towns are the vegetable-growing hubs of Iceland.

7 **Hveragerði.** Locals here are known for their love of baked goods and obscenely hot geothermal swimming pools; they have declared their town "the flower capital of the island."

8 **Selfoss.** This busy inland town is located by the huge white-water Ölfusá River.

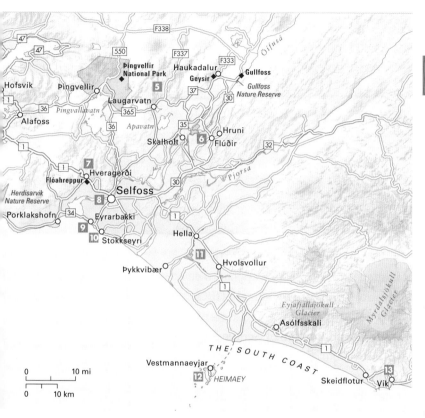

9 Eyrarbakki. This tranquil and tiny fishing village has beautiful black beaches and the friendliest people.

10 Stokkseyri. The ghost town of Iceland, Stokkseyri is a beautiful fishing village by day, but it is rumored that spirits of dead sailors haunt the black sand beaches at night.

11 Hella and Hvolsvöllur. The volcano Hekla watches over Hella; to the east is the small town of Hvolsvöllur.

12 Vestmannaeyjar. Literally the "Western Islands," this archipelago was formed by volcanic eruptions.

13 Vík. The southernmost town in Iceland is defined by its black sea stacks and is one of the few places to buy groceries and alcohol in the area.

WINTER IS HERE TO STAY: ICELAND FOR *GAME OF THRONES* FANS

Þingvellir National Park

Many parts of Iceland, especially the untamed rural landscapes, appear to be fantastical and surreal. Fittingly, HBO's wildly popular fantasy series *Game of Thrones*, an adaptation of George R.R. Martin's *A Song of Ice and Fire* book series, was filmed in the country's most cinematic locales. Iceland is used throughout the series to represent the "far north," aka the "Land Beyond the Wall," which is home to many creatures and characters in the *GoT* universe.

Not surprisingly, J.R.R. Tolkein also took much inspiration from Icelandic landscapes and sights when writing *The Lord of the Rings*, including Mount Hekla in Hella, which served as inspiration for Mount Doom. Additionally, the Star Wars saga films *Rogue One* and *The Force Awakens* were also filmed in Iceland. This goes to show that some of the most imaginative minds see Iceland as one of the most visually phenomenal places on earth.

THEMED TOURS

Game of Thrones-dedicated theme tours are not as popular as they once were, but you can easily devise your own with a little online sleuthing. Gray Line Iceland (⊕ *www.grayline.is*) offers a private day tour to filming locations like the Þjórsárdalur Valley, complete with behind-the-scenes tales. Guide to Iceland (⊕ *guidetoiceland.is*) has a six-day tour in the summer through the Golden Circle, the South Coast, and the Snæfellsnes Peninsula.

ÞINGVELLIR NATIONAL PARK

This UNESCO World Heritage site along the Golden Circle doubled as the Bloody Gate (the passage to the Eyrie), the stronghold of House Arryn, in the show's third season. Look out for the canyon Almannagjá which might look especially familiar to fans.

ÞÓRUFOSS

This waterfall, 18 meters (62 feet) high, found close to the Golden Circle, was the shooting location for the home of the Children of the Forest.

Þórufoss

GRJÓTAGJÁ CAVE

This volcanic cave near Lake Mývatn in North Iceland is perhaps best known for its role in the third season of *Game of Thrones*, where Jon Snow and Ygritte share an intimate moment on screen.

DIMMUBORGIR

Dimmuborgir is a frozen lava field not too far from Lake Mývatn in North Iceland. It's also the site of Mance Rayder's army camp in season three of the show. It's rumored that during filming, the temperature dropped to 12°F.

SVÍNAFELLSJÖKULL IN SKAF-TAFELL NATIONAL PARK

Famously used as a filming location for *Game of Thrones* as well as films like *Interstellar*, *Journey to the Center of the Earth*, *Rogue One*, and *The Force Awakens*, among others, Svínafellsjökull has been nicknamed the "Hollywood Glacier." The glacier in southeast Iceland made an appearance in season two of the show as the landscapes of the region known as Beyond the Wall.

STÖNG

Located on the edge of the Highlands, Stöng is a farmstead in the Þjórsárdalur valley, said to be inhabited up until the year 1300. There are Viking settlement ruins here; Mount Hekla actually erupted in 1104, which caused devastation to the farms in this area, but Stöng remained above-ground. There's a reconstructed Viking turf house to keep an eye out for, and a secret lagoon. On the show, Stöng is the site of Olly's village.

MÝRDALSJÖKULL GLACIER

This glacier in southwest Iceland was featured in season two of the series, as the Fist of the First Men. The nearby Hofðabrekka area represented Northern Westeros.

KIRKJUFELL

Photogenic "Church Mountain" on the Snæfellsnes peninsula is the most photographed peak in Iceland. It had a guest role on the show as Arrowhead Mountain in seasons six and seven.

Grjótagjá Cave

Iceland's southern "left leg" (if looking at the map as a crooked duck) contains both the Golden Circle and the Blue Lagoon—arguably two of the country's most popular and breathtaking attractions—as well as the Reykjanes Peninsula.

The Southwest is also home to some of Iceland's most iconic landscapes—from steep black cliffs, lonely lighthouses, and bubbling mud pots to spouting geysers, dormant volcanoes, and some of the largest white-water cascades in all of Europe. Streams of hot water shoot from geysers up to the skies, while the shopping mall–size Gullfoss waterfall plummets at incredible speed and volume down from the lava-bed highlands towards the unforgiving North Atlantic ocean. And here's the best bit: all of these attractions and more can be accessed comfortably as day trips from Reykjavík.

The lesser-known Reykjanes Peninsula has its own unique natural wonders. It's the only place in the world where the Mid-Atlantic Ridge is visible above sea level, exposing the American and Eurasian tectonic plates as they move ever farther apart from each other. As one of Iceland's most geologically diverse areas, the Reykjanes Peninsula has some spectacular sights. The most famous of these is undoubtedly the Blue Lagoon geothermal spa, but there are also other colorful bubbling geothermal areas, diverse mountains and lakes, and gloomy lava-tube caves, as well as small, lonely wooden churches and charming regional fishing towns slowly adapting to new realities. Of course, the peninsula also plays host to the Fagradalsfjall Volcano, which wowed the world in 2021 and 2022 with its spectacular eruptions. While the volcano has since quieted, it's now a desolate steaming lava field that is luckily just a tree-hour long hike from the main highway.

One of the most scenic routes in all of Europe, the Golden Circle loops for 186 miles, taking in some of the most spectacular sites in the country. The first big stop on the route is where the original settlers of Iceland had their Alþingi, one of the oldest parliamentary institutions in the world. It is both culturally and naturally unique. Next stop is the Geysir hot spring area with the Strokkuur geyser that erupts every few minutes more than 100 feet into the sky. The third and last stop is the most famous waterfall in all of Iceland: Gullfoss, or "Golden Waterfall." White glacial water pours down from the highlands and into a deep canyon at a volume, speed, and power that seems incomprehensible. The Golden Circle trip is offered by many tour operators, but it is also a very enjoyable and quite easy route to explore on your own.

Hundreds of thousands of tourists visit the three famous sights of the Golden Circle each year, which has allowed the neighboring towns to flourish. Numerous restaurants and shops have popped up—each more inventive than the next—all around the area. It is highly recommended to stop in smaller, out-of-the-way places in search of hidden gems.

Planning

When to Go

The Golden Circle can be visited at any time, although you'll find vastly different scenes during each season. Summer brings luscious green moss and other flora to the country roads, making for an enjoyable road trip. Temperatures are mild then and nighttime hours are short, meaning you could stop by attractions late in the evening and still be met with bright sunlight.

That said, there's something otherworldly about the Golden Circle in winter. The bright blue rapids of Gullfoss freeze up, turning into sparkling tides of ice and glacial water. Against the snow and harsh Icelandic wind, the steaming blows of Geysir are only more breathtaking, and there's nothing like a frosty stroll around the winding paths of Þingvellir on a foggy winter afternoon. Plus, a nighttime drive on the highway might even yield a surprise spotting of the Northern Lights.

The Reykjanes Peninsula is equally timeless, though the twisting roads might be a bit dangerous in the winter for drivers without experience in such climates. And the grassy pastures and bright lupine fields of Reykjanes are a true delight in the summer when one can wiggle their bare toes on the rocky beaches of Kleifarvatn or the smooth Sandgerði coastline. The Peninsula is also full of fabulous hikes that are much more enjoyable without the snow, hail, and winds of an Icelandic winter.

It's also important to note that in the winter, road conditions can be perilous, so be sure to visit ⊕ *www.road.is* before you head out.

Getting Here and Around

BUS

Currently, no public buses service the attractions of the Golden Circle, though there are the Icelandic bus company Strætó stops in several surrounding towns, including Laugarvatn, Reykholt, Flúðir, Hveragerði, and more on the 72 and 73 routes. These can be reached by taking the 51 or 52 lines from Reykjavík and switching at the Selfoss stop.

CONTACTS Strætó. ☎ *540–2700* ⊕ *www. bus.is.*

CAR

Driving is the most popular way to see this region. The Golden Circle route should take you seven or eight hours by car, if you make stops at the various sights. At Gullfoss, the farthest point, you're only 115 km (71 miles) from Reykjavík, and most of the drive is along paved main roads.

Restaurants

There are numerous local eateries dotting the roads of the Golden Circle, often filled by the large amounts of travelers that pass through the area daily. Most are designed for casual meals and serve traditional Icelandic fare like meat soup and fried fish along with more American and European-friendly options like burgers and pizza. Prices can be higher than usual, but that is expected of such a highly trafficked area.

For a quick bite, most gas stations or service centers offer the traditional Icelandic *pylsur*—hot dog—a popular roadside snack for Icelanders. For the true experience, ask for "eina með öllu" which will give you the hot dog along with all the toppings, including raw onions, cooked onions, and two unique sauces. While gas station hot dogs might not be popular in other countries, in Iceland they are a delicacy enjoyed by all

4

Reykjanes Peninsula and the South Coast (with the Golden Circle) PLANNING and a satisfying bite guaranteed to tide you over during those long car rides.

Hotels

There is no region in Iceland outside of Reykjavík that has more hotels than the Golden Circle and Reykjanes Peninsula. Due to the ample amounts of tourists, guesthouses and comfortable lodges pepper the highways, most of which offer free breakfast and have an on-site restaurant. While there are a few high-end retreats in the area, most hotels are made for quick one-night stays, allowing you to promptly continue on with your trip. Hotels here also tend to have good relationships with local tour providers, so they often serve as pick-up spots for any sightseeing or adventures you have planned on your way.

RESTAURANT AND HOTEL PRICES
Restaurant prices in the reviews are the average cost of a main course at dinner, or if dinner is not served, at lunch. Hotel prices in the reviews are the lowest cost of a standard double room in high season. Restaurant and hotel reviews have been shortened. For full information, visit Fodors.com.

What it Costs in ISK

$	$$	$$$	$$$$
RESTAURANTS			
under ISK 1,000	ISK 1,000– 2,999	ISK 3,000– 4,000	over ISK 4,000
HOTELS			
under ISK 21,000	ISK 21,000– 30,999	ISK 31,000– 41,000	over ISK 41,000

Tours

★ Arctic Adventures
ADVENTURE TOURS | One of the oldest and most established Icelandic tour operators, Arctic Adventures knows what they're doing. From small tours of the Golden Circle and peaceful snorkeling in the Silfra fissure to exploring sparkling ice caves and guiding rumbling black sand ATV rides, Arctic Adventures has something for all levels of adrenaline junkies. They also have a number of combination tours—so you can even see the Golden Circle and also snowmobile on a glacier on the same day. ⊠ *Skutuvogur 2* ☎ *562–7000* ⊕ *www.adventures.is.*

Base-Camp Iceland
PRIVATE GUIDES | **FAMILY** | If you are looking for a more private and personal experience, Base-Camp Iceland offers smaller custom tours off-the-beaten-track. With years of experience, they will take you in their luxury 4X4 vehicles to both main attractions and more obscure places, their guides sharing neat bits of information along the way. They offer the Golden Circle Private Tour and an active adventure tour to the Reykjanes UNESCO Geopark, along with other personalized journeys. ⊠ *Gasstöðin Hlemmur, Reykjavík* ☎ *777–0708* ⊕ *www.base-campiceland.is.*

Gray Line Iceland
BUS TOURS | **FAMILY** | Operating as a travel agency for over 30 years in Iceland, Gray Line offers traditional sightseeing day tours, private tours, and airport transfers. The Gray Line Bus Terminal is at Klettagarður 4, but they pick up and drop off at a number of bus stops in the Reykjavík city center. Drop by at their city center office at Hafnarstræti 20 for information about their tours. ⊠ *Hafnarstræti 20* ☎ *540–1313* ⊕ *www.grayline.is.*

Reykjavík Excursions

BUS TOURS | One of the largest tour operators in Iceland, Reykjavík Excursions offers a daily eight-hour guided Golden Circle tour. All their coaches are equipped with free Wi-Fi. Reykjavík Excursions also operates the Flybus from Keflavík International Airport. ⊠ *BSÍ Bus Terminal, Vatnsmýrarvegi 10* ☎ *580–5400* ⊕ *www.re.is.*

Tröll Expeditions

ADVENTURE TOURS | This adventure travel company's roster reads like a list of the greatest hits of Icelandic travel: the Golden Circle, the south coast, glacier hikes, snorkeling, and more. Basically, you could just book every tour they offer and trust that you'd have an amazing trip in the country. ⊠ *Fiskislóð 45G* ☎ *519–5544* ⊕ *www.troll.is.*

Reykjanesbær

50 km (31 miles) southwest of Reykjavík.

This town's proximity to the only international airport in Iceland has meant that Reykjanesbær is a rapidly growing and ever-changing area. After years of U.S. military presence, the town has a mix of American pop culture and remnants of an old proud fishing village. It is the first place you will see when you arrive, and the last before you go.

GETTING HERE AND AROUND

Route 41 connects Reykjanesbær to Reykjavík. On weekdays Strætó Bus 55 runs between Keflavík airport and Reykjavík's BSÍ bus terminal, but on weekends it goes only as far as east of Hafnarfjörður. A ticket costs ISK 1,960, and the journey takes about 1 hour, 15 minutes.

FESTIVALS
Ljósanótt

ARTS FESTIVALS | **FAMILY** | In early September, Reykjanesbær puts on its festival of lights. People from all over the country fill the streets and wander among art

openings, vintage car shows, and outdoor concerts. The grand finale is a magnificent fireworks show by the harbor. ⊠ *Reykjanesbær* ☎ *421–6700* ⊕ *www.ljosanott.is* 🎫 *Free.*

VISITOR INFORMATION

Located in the Duus Museum, the Reykjanes Visitor Center serves as an information center for the whole peninsula. Not only can you learn about the various tours around the region, but there's also a small exhibition about the local geology.

CONTACTS Reykjanes Geopark Visitor Center. ⊠ *Duusgata 2–8, Reykjanesbær* ☎ *420–3246* ⊕ *reykjanesgeopark.is.*

Sights

Duus Museum

HISTORY MUSEUM | Located near the Keflavík marina, this artistic and cultural center of Reykjanesbær houses exhibition halls for the Art and Heritage Museums of Reykjanesbær. The museum offers diverse and exciting exhibitions, concerts, and cultural activities throughout the year. One of them is the ongoing exhibition of more than 100 model boats—all built by the skipper Grímur Karlsson. ⊠ *Duusgata 2–8, Reykjanesbær* ☎ *420–3245* ⊕ *www.duusmuseum.is* 🎫 *ISK 1,000.*

Rokksafnið
(The Icelandic Museum of Rock 'n' Roll)

OTHER MUSEUM | In the 1940s, the U.S. army brought rock 'n' roll to Reykjanesbær, and the town has been in love ever since. The Icelandic Museum of Rock 'n' Roll honors the town's love for the genre and invites visitors to walk through the history of Icelandic pop and rock starting in 1930. Among photographs and texts are electric guitars and legendary outfits from various Icelandic rock stars. The experience is heightened by a karaoke booth where visitors can belt out ballads or grab drum sticks and rock out. ⊠ *Hjallavegur 2, Reykjanesbær* ☎ *420–1030* ⊕ *www.rokksafn.is* 🎫 *ISK 1,500.*

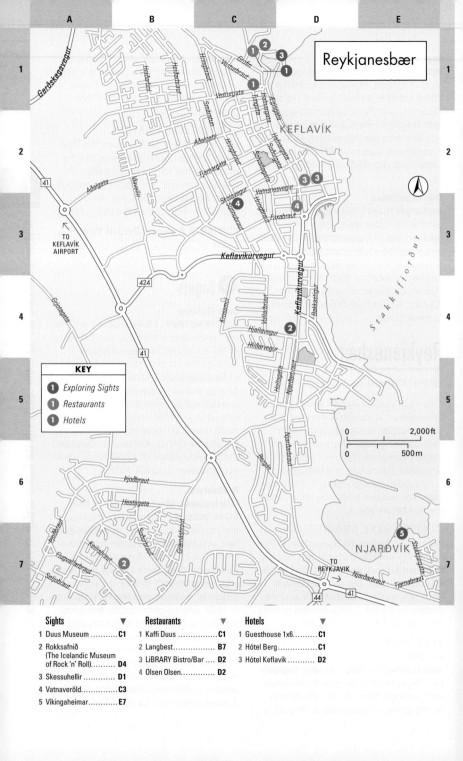

Reykjanesbær

KEFLAVÍK

TO
KEFLAVÍK
AIRPORT

NJARÐVÍK

TO
REYKJAVIK
→

Stakksfjörður

KEY

1 Exploring Sights

1 Restaurants

1 Hotels

0 ———— 2,000 ft

0 ———— 500 m

Sights ▼	Restaurants ▼	Hotels ▼
1 Duus Museum **C1**	1 Kaffi Duus **C1**	1 Guesthouse 1x6.......... **C1**
2 Rokksafnið (The Icelandic Museum of Rock 'n' Roll).......... **D4**	2 Langbest................. **B7**	2 Hótel Berg................. **C1**
3 Skessuhellir **D1**	3 LiBRARY Bistro/Bar **D2**	3 Hótel Keflavík **D2**
4 Vatnaveröld.............. **C3**	4 Olsen Olsen.............. **D2**	
5 Víkingaheimar............ **E7**		

Skessuhellir

PUBLIC ART | FAMILY | At the far end of the marina in Reykjanesbær you will find the dark and mysterious cave of the notorious giantess, Skessan. An incredible art installation based on a character from the books of Herdís Egilsdóttir, the giantess is over five meters high and she even snores and burps, making it an especially fun visit for children. ✉ *Grófin, Bakkavegur 20, Reykjanesbær* ☎ *421–3796* 🌐 *www.skessan.is* 🎫 *Free.*

Vatnaveröld

POOL | FAMILY | If you are traveling with small children, this is the perfect place to escape cold Icelandic winter days or to give babies a break from the strong Nordic sun in summer. Waterworld is an indoor activity pool for the youngest generation, with bucket showers, small slides, and a friendly seal. There is also an outdoor pool, four hot tubs, and steam baths for the older generation. Children up to age 10 can enter free with an adult. ✉ *Sunnubraut 31, Reykjanesbær* ☎ *420–1500* 🎫 *ISK 1,000.*

Víkingaheimar

OTHER ATTRACTION | FAMILY | Here you will find Íslendingur, an exact replica of the Viking Age Gokstad ship, which was a remarkable archaeological find of an almost-completely intact Viking ship. Learn about the Norse settlement and mythology while you sit at the stern and imagine the sea breeze tickling your face. For early risers, they also serve breakfast under the ship starting at 7 am; it's by appointment only, so make sure to contact them in advance. ✉ *Víkingabraut 1* ☎ *422–2000* 🌐 *www.vikingworld.is* 🎫 *ISK 1,500.*

🍴 Restaurants

Kaffi Duus

$$$ | INTERNATIONAL | FAMILY | Overlooking the dark blue waters of Faxaflói Bay, Kaffi Duus has been part of the Keflavík Marina since the 1990s. They offer an extensive seafood menu that features a mix of Icelandic and Indian dishes, guaranteeing that anyone can find something to suit their fancy. **Known for:** bustling marina atmosphere; Duus Museum next-door; seafood lover's paradise. [$] *Average main: ISK3,950* ✉ *Duusgata 10, Reykjanesbær* ☎ *421–7080* 🌐 *www.duus.is.*

Langbest

$$ | PIZZA | FAMILY | For over 20 years, Langbest has fed the citizens of Reykjanesbær to great acclaim. This is a must-stop for some of the region's best pizza, but they also serve hamburgers, steaks, and more. **Known for:** signature béarnaise sauce that locals eat with their pizza; plenty of vegan and vegetarian options; impressive pizza. [$] *Average main: ISK2,750* ✉ *Keilisbraut, Reykjanesbær* ☎ *421–4777* 🌐 *www.langbest.is.*

LiBRARY Bistro/Bar

$$$ | INTERNATIONAL | This lively and elegant hotel bistro is perfect for a refreshing cocktail and a rich meal after a long day of endless lava fields and hot springs. On the weekends they serve brunch. **Known for:** juicy béarnaise burger; dessert cocktails; diverse brunch options. [$] *Average main: ISK3,750* ✉ *Park Inn by Radisson, Hafnargata 57, Reykjanesbær* ☎ *421–5220* 🌐 *www.librarybistro.is.*

Olsen Olsen

$$ | AMERICAN | FAMILY | The people of Keflavík talk about Olsen Olsen like it's a family member—its legend precedes it. Grab a burger and a Coke and get a taste of what it was like when the U.S. Army introduced Icelanders to rock 'n' roll and fast food. **Known for:** affordable burgers; the Olsen Olsen sandwich (bacon and baked beans); location in the heart of Keflavík. [$] *Average main: ISK2,270* ✉ *Hafnargata 62, Reykjanesbær* ☎ *421–4457* 🌐 *www.olsenolsen.is.*

Hotels

Guesthouse 1x6

$ | **B&B/INN** | **FAMILY** | At this unique and artistic guesthouse on a quiet street, each room is special and made out of driftwood and volcanic stone. **Pros:** artsy and attractively eclectic decor; close to the airport and town center; outdoor handmade stone hot tub. **Cons:** expensive breakfast; shared bathrooms; extra fee for aiport pickup. [$] *Rooms from: ISK18,000* ✉ *Vesturbraut 3, Reykjanesbær* ☎ *857–1589* 🌐 *www.1x6.is* 🛏 *6 rooms* 🍴 *No Meals.*

Hótel Berg

$$ | **HOTEL** | **FAMILY** | This modern hotel sits by a peaceful harbor at the northern end of Keflavík in close proximity to the airport. **Pros:** stunning rooftop pool; close proximity to the aiport (and free shuttles); peaceful atmosphere. **Cons:** simple breakfast; guest-room style sometimes seems more important than comfort; walls can be thin. [$] *Rooms from: ISK29,000* ✉ *Bakkavegur 17, Reykjanesbær* ☎ *422–7922* 🌐 *www.hotelberg.is* 🛏 *36 rooms* 🍴 *No Meals.*

Hótel Keflavík

$$$ | **HOTEL** | For over 30 years, Hótel Keflavík has been welcoming visitors beginning or finishing their trip to Iceland. **Pros:** beyond helpful staff; early breakfast buffet; good location (close to the airport, shops, and restaurants). **Cons:** restaurant closes at 9 pm; noise pollution in some rooms; rooms that have not been renovated have outdated decor and furniture. [$] *Rooms from: ISK34,400* ✉ *Vatnnesvegur 12–14, Reykjanesbær* ☎ *420–7000* 🌐 *www.kef.is* 🛏 *70 rooms* 🍴 *Free Breakfast.*

Nightlife

Cafe Petite

PUBS | By day this place is a charming café offering unlimited Wi-Fi, good coffee, and some tasty pastries. By night it turns into a cool little pub that's open till midnight on weekdays with great deals on cocktails, a wide variety of Icelandic beers, and pool tables. ✉ *Framnesvegur 23, Reykjanesbær* ✣ *Behind the tire shop* ☎ *583–5889.*

Paddy's Beach Pub

BARS | People of all ages and walks of life hang out at this Icelandic Irish "beach bar" in the heart of Keflavík. Come for a pint around dinnertime to hear the town stories from the older locals, then sit on the patio and watch as the bar transitions into the liveliest nightclub in town. ✉ *Hafnargata 67, Reykjanesbær* ☎ *421–5100.*

Shopping

Draumaland

SOUVENIRS | In the heart of Reykjanesbær, the friendly Nanna has operated this glamorous gift shop for more than 30 years. Selling fresh flowers and high-quality design items handpicked from all over Scandinavia, you will find popular items like famous Moomin cups and Georg Jensen kitchenware. ✉ *Tjarnagata 3, Reykjanesbær* ☎ *421–3855.*

Activities

KAYAKING

Reykjanes Seakayak

KAYAKING | The Reykjanes Peninsula is known for its beautiful black-sand beaches, magnificent bird life, and charming lighthouses, all of which can be explored on foot. If you are up for an adventure, however, one exciting way to explore them is by sea kayak. Reykjanes Seakayak is family-owned and operated from their farm at Þórustaðir in Vatnleysisströnd, between Reykjanesbær and Hafnarfjörður. They offer two-hour guided tours on kayaks that are considered quite easy and safe. ✉ *Vatnleysisströnd, Þórustaðir, Reykjanesbær* ☎ *892–2618* 🌐 *www.facebook.com/reykjanesseakayak.*

Garður

9 km (5 miles) north of Reykjanesbær.

Garður was once the most populated village on the peninsula, but now it's a quiet town well worth visiting to have a picnic by the black sand beaches while watching birds catch fish.

GETTING HERE AND AROUND

Take a right turn on Route 45 from any of these three places: Reykjanesbær, Highway 41, or Sandgerði, and continue all the way to the end. Bus 89 goes from Keflavík to Garður and Sandgerði daily.

Sights

★ Garðskagaviti
LIGHTHOUSE | **FAMILY** | Two lighthouses can be found on Garðskagi, and Garðskagaviti is the smaller and older of the two. It is also known as "the lighthouse of love": wives of fishermen would take a stone from the black-sand beaches surrounding the town, go to the top of the lighthouse, and walk in circles and pray for their husbands out at sea. Nowadays, you won't find too many women roaming the stairs, but if the northern lights forecast looks good, this beach is a great place to watch them. You also might be rewarded with some prime bird-watching—species like gull-billed tern, American bittern, and purple gallinule can be spotted here. ✉ *Skagabraut, Reykjanesbær* ☎ *893–8909* 🌐 *www.gardskagi.com.*

Garður Swimming Pool
POOL | **FAMILY** | The northernmost swimming pool on the peninsula is a charming little pool with a red color scheme. It contains all the necessities of an Icelandic swimming pool, including a gym, sports hall, two hot tubs, a kiddie pool, and a sauna. ✉ *Garðbraut 94* ☎ *425–3145* 🌐 *www.ig.is* 🎟 *ISK 950.*

Hvalneskirkja
CHURCH | Taking Highway 45 from Garður, you will drive through the colorful little town of Sandgerði, one of Iceland's major fishing communities. About 6 km (4 miles) on from there, you will pass this funky-looking church smiling down on you from a hill. The church at Hvalsnes was consecrated in 1887. It was built with basalt stone retrieved from the surrounding area, and the wood interior was crafted with driftwood from the nearby shores. ✉ *Hvalnes.*

Restaurants

Röstin Restaurant—The Old Lighthouse Café
$$$ | **ICELANDIC** | **FAMILY** | Even if you're not hungry, a stop by Röstin Restaurant is worth it for the sea views alone. Located on the second floor of the Heritage and Maritime Museum of Garðskagi, the eatery offers classic Icelandic meals with a twist. **Known for:** charming old-school atmosphere; beautiful ocean views; stellar fish soup, an Icelandic must. [$] *Average main: ISK3,000* ✉ *Skagabraut 100* ☎ *422–7220* 🌐 *www.facebook.com/RostinRestaurant.*

Hotels

Garður Apartments
$ | **APARTMENT** | In addition to simple, spacious, and well-equipped apartments right by the sea in Garður, this guesthouse features satellite TV and a kitchen. **Pros:** only 100 meters from the coastline; close to Keflavík airport; good place for hunting northern lights in winter. **Cons:** noise travels between apartments; no double rooms in the studio apartments; few dining options in town. [$] *Rooms from: ISK17,200* ✉ *Skagabraut 62a, Reykjanesbær* ☎ *779–0707* 🌐 *www.gardurapartments.is* 🛏 *6 apartments* 🍴 *No Meals.*

Lighthouse Inn

$$ | HOTEL | FAMILY | Located mere steps from the beautiful coastline at Garður and only a 10-minute drive from the Keflavík airport is this log hotel. **Pros:** only a 10-minute drive from the airport; great place for a morning or evening walk; considered a prime spot for northern lights. **Cons:** quiet town with few options for entertainment; rooms are a bit dark; no bathtubs in rooms. [$] *Rooms from: ISK20,000* ✉ *Norðurljósavegur 2, Reykjanesbær* ☎ *433–0000* 🌐 *www.lighthouseinn.is* 🛏 *26 rooms* 🍴 *Free Breakfast.*

Shopping

Kjörbúðin

GENERAL STORE | In case you forgot your toothbrush, there is a small supermarket in town where you will find all necessities. It also has some quick food options like sandwiches, which are handy for a road trip or a small picnic by the scenic beach in Garður. ✉ *Sunnubraut 4* ☎ *422–7122* 🌐 *www.samkaup.is.*

Grindavík

32 km (20 miles) south of Garður.

Life in Grindavík has pretty much revolved around fishing for the past 10 centuries, but over the past few years, it has seen remarkable growth as a tourist destination. After all, it's not only home to the world-famous Blue Lagoon, but it also played host to the 2021 and 2022 eruptions of the Fagradalsfjall volcano, which captivated viewers from all over the world. While the eruption has since quieted, the lava field has continued to remain a popular destination; with its fields and mountains of still-steaming volcanic rock, it's a true natural wonder. And luckily, the eruption site is just a two to three-hour hike from the highway.

GETTING HERE AND AROUND

On Route 41 to Reykjanesbær, take a left turn and take Route 43 to Grindavík. Strætó bus 88 goes from Keflavík to Grindavík daily on weekdays; on weekends it only goes from Grindavík to the crossroads, where you must connect to Bus 55.

VISITOR INFORMATION

At the Saltfisksetur Information Desk, you can pick up maps of hiking trails and get insights into the many natural wonders of the region. There is also a small exhibition on the history of salted cod in Iceland.

CONTACTS Saltfisksetur Information Desk. ✉ *Hafnargata 12a, Grindavík* ☎ *420–1190.*

Sights

★ **Blue Lagoon**

HOT SPRING | This world-renowned therapeutic pool is now a sheltered site where man-made structures blend with natural geologic formations. A reception area includes food concessions and boutique shops where you can buy health products made from the lagoon's mineral-rich ingredients. Bathing suits are available to rent, and high-tech bracelets keep track of your locker code, any purchases, and the length of your visit. The lagoon is only 20 minutes from Keflavík Airport and 50 minutes from Reykjavík by car. Buses run from the BSÍ bus terminal in Reykjavík to the Blue Lagoon frequently. Booking in advance is essential. For a more personalized experience, you can also book a spa treatment at the lagoon's on-site Retreat Hotel, whether or not you're staying at there. This is a little-known way to have your own private lagoon experience. ✉ *Bláa lónið, Norðurljósavegur 9* ☎ *420–8800* 🌐 *www.bluelagoon.com* 🎟 *ISK 11,990.*

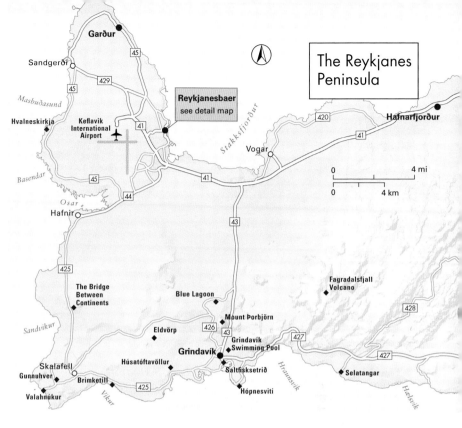

★ The Bridge Between Continents

NATURE SIGHT | Across a wide tension crack that opened due to the divergent movements of the North American and Eurasian plates is a narrow footbridge built as a symbol for the connection between Europe and North America. You can (symbolically) walk from one continent to another in seconds, marveling at the tectonic forces at work on this island; the average rifting of the plates amounts to about 2 cm per year. The bridge is just off Route 425, and there's plenty of information on-site as well as some classic photo ops (many visitors pretend to hold the bridge up). ⊠ *Skógarbraut 945, Reykjanesbær.*

Brimketill

NATURE SIGHT | Five kilometers (3 miles) west of Grindavík, this naturally carved lava tub is constantly filled and drained by ocean surf. Folklore says that the geological pool was the giantess Oddný's favorite spot to bathe. On windy days it's thrilling to watch the incredible force of the sea—just be careful of slippery rocks. ⊠ *Grindavík.*

Eldvörp

NATURE SIGHT | This 10-km-long (6-mile-long) row of craters formed in the Reykjanes Fires, a volcano-tectonic episode in AD 1210–1240. The whole area has a spooky and majestic vibe thanks to the steam escaping the craters as well as a nearby borehole. Eldvörp is a bit hidden, but several well-marked walking trails pass near it, including the Reykjavegur. It's also accessible on foot, by bike, and by car on a dirt track from the Grindavík–Blue Lagoon link road. ⊠ *Grindavík* ⊕ *Take the Grindavík–Blue Lagoon link road, and follow signs.*

The world-famous Blue Lagoon in Grindavík is a therapeutic geological wonder.

★ Fagradalsfjall Volcano

VOLCANO | The Fagradalsfjall volcano eruption site—which began erupting once again in August 2022 after a year-long hiatus —is a must-visit in Iceland. Where else can you stand but feet away from newly-made continental crust? There are a few different paths to explore here, all varying in difficulty from easy to advanced, but hiking boots are strongly recommended no matter which path you take. Expect to spend around four to five hours actually hiking. The site itself is just an hour's drive from Reykjavík—take Highway 41 towards Keflavík and turn onto Highway 43 towards Grindavík, then follow Highway 427 until you see a plethora of parking lots. There are also numerous tour operators that offer various trips to the volcano via guided hikes, helicopter, or airplane, but don't be afraid to just go yourself and have a long picnic there. You'll want to stay for a while. Just note that if your visit coincides with an active period of the volcano, be sure to check in advance that the current hiking conditions are safe. ⊠ *Grindavík* ✛ *Highway 427 from Grindavík, marked parking lots will be obvious* 🖻 *ISK 1,000 parking fee.*

Gunnuhver

HOT SPRING | This geothermal field is named for Guðrún Önundardóttir's ghost, who sought revenge after being mistreated by a lawyer. After several deaths connected to Guðrún (also called Gunna), a sorcerer was sent to put her to rest in the hot spring. The walk over the historical bridge is well worth the wet clothes and the strong smell of sulfur. ⊠ *Gunnuhver hot springs, Grindavík* ✛ *East by the Reykjanes lighthouse.*

Hópnesviti

LIGHTHOUSE | Walk or drive from the town of Grindavík to Hópsnes, and you will find old shipwrecks that washed ashore in the 20th century. At the end of the path is the lighthouse, Hópnesviti, which on clear days has views of the Eldey Island bird colony. The walk should take about two hours, with various stops along the way. ⊠ *Hópsnes, Grindavík.*

The Icelandic Saltfish Museum

HISTORY MUSEUM | Once regarded as Iceland's most valuable export, Saltfiskur (a dried and salted fish) has its own museum in Grindavík. Saltfisk production has a long and important history, which is told with great care in this museum. ✉ *Hafnargata 12a, Grindavík* ☎ *420–1190* 🎟 *Free.*

Mount Þorbjörn

MOUNTAIN | The petite but stunning mountain Þorbjörn is set between Grindavík and the Blue Lagoon. The mountain is only about 200 meters high, but it offers a spectacular 360-degree view of the surrounding area—including endless lava fields, mossy hills, the Atlantic Ocean, and the milky Blue Lagoon. The top of the mountain is split in two with a tight canyon in the middle called "the Thieves Gap." The peak is easily accessible by marked hiking trails, and near the foot of the mountain on the north side is a small forest and a wooden playground. ✉ *Þorbjarnarfell, Grindavík.*

Selatangar

OTHER ATTRACTION | About 8 km (5 miles) east of Grindavík, just off the main road, you will see an information board about this historical site. Drive about 1 km (½ mile) along a rocky dirt road (ideally in a 4X4 vehicle), and at the end of road you will see a parking spot. From there a scenic 15-minute walk (with views of the wild ocean crashing into the black shores) takes you to the ruins of a former fishing station constructed from lava rocks. The stone is believed to date back to AD 1150, but the station was maintained from the Middle Ages until 1885. ✉ *Selatangar, Grindavík.*

★ **Valahnúkur**

NATURE SIGHT | This mountain was formed in a single geologic event, and while exploring this magical stretch of coastline, you can see evidence of the different phases of the eruption. Tuff forms during an explosive eruption, and pillow lava forms when lava flows underwater. Out on the sea, you can see majestic black cliffs that serve as castles for birds. A bit farther out you can see the famous Eldey Island, where the great auk (a now-extinct species of bird) used to live. The auks survived the longest in Iceland, but the last great auk was killed on June 3, 1844 for a Danish natural history collector. Eldey is now a bird sanctuary. To reach Valhnúkur, take the road that leads off Route 425 through lava fields. Turn right (the turn is marked, "Reykjanesviti"), at the T-intersection, and then go 900 meters on an unpaved road, past the impressive Reykjanesviti lighthouse. On the way back, take the left branch at the T-intersection, and in 500 meters you'll reach Gunnuhver, Iceland's biggest mud pool. ✉ *Valahnúkur, Efstahraun 9, Grindavík.*

🍴 Restaurants

Bryggjan

$$ | **CAFÉ** | **FAMILY** | This little café in an old netting factory by the harbor is famous for lobster soup and homemade cakes. Loved by locals and tourists alike, Bryggjan is adorned with flying buoys and framed photos from the town's older days. **Known for:** delicious lobster soup; very creamy cakes; fishing village feel. [$] *Average main: ISK2,400* ✉ *Miðgarður 2, Grindavík* ☎ *426–7100* 🌐 *www.bryggjan.com.*

Hjá Höllu

$$ | **MODERN EUROPEAN** | **FAMILY** | This breakfast-and-lunch spot in Grindavík started in Halla's kitchen at home. Her specialty is fresh, healthy daily to-go bags, which are filled with snacks, fresh juices, a hot lunch, and something sweet—perfect for a long day of sightseeing. **Known for:** chic Scandinavian-style café; weekly changing menu; fantastic steak sandwich. [$] *Average main: ISK2,900* ✉ *Víkurbraut 62, Grindavík* ☎ *896–5316* 🌐 *www.hjahollu.is* 🕓 *Closed Sun. No dinner.*

★ **Lava Restaurant**

$$$$ | **ICELANDIC** | Eating world-class food at a restaurant built into a lava cliff with views of the milky Blue Lagoon is a once-in-a-lifetime opportunity you will never forget. The set menu offers a gourmet meal for pescatarians, vegetarians, and carnivores at a reasonable price (by Icelandic standards). **Known for:** combines fine dining with the wild spirit of Icelandic nature; the perfect dine-in-your-robe post-spa meal; stunning lava rock wall. $ *Average main: ISK6,000 ⊠ Blue Lagoon, Norðurljosavegur 9, Grindavík ☎ 420–8800 ⊕ www.bluelagoon.is.*

★ Moss Restaurant

$$$$ | SCANDINAVIAN | A stellar experience for the senses, the set menus at Moss Restaurant take diners on an Iceland-inspired food journey. Situated at the highest point of the Blue Lagoon, guests gaze through floor-to-ceiling windows upon the moonlike surroundings while enjoying delicious and diverse dishes made from seasonal produce gathered from the mountains, the rivers, the mossy fields, and the sea. **Known for:** unforgettable setting; chef's table menu; outstanding vegetarian and vegan options. $ *Average main: ISK19,900 ⊠ Norðurljósavegur 11, Grindavík ☎ 420–8700 ⊕ www.bluelagoon.is ⊙ Closed Mon. and Tues.*

 ## Hotels

★ Retreat Hotel

$$$$ | HOTEL | This beautifully minimalist yet warm hotel is right on-site at the Blue Lagoon and is known for its spa treatment, which allows you to have a private experience of the lagoon itself. **Pros:** views of the lagoon and volcanic horizon; luxury suites, some with their own personal lagoon; modern decor. **Cons:** incredibly expensive; gets booked up quickly; large variation in prices. $ *Rooms from: ISK189,000 ⊠ Norðurljósavegur 11, Grindavík ☎ 420–8700 ⊕ www.bluelagoon. com ⤳ 62 suites ⦿ Free Breakfast.*

Silica Hotel

$$$$ | HOTEL | If you have always dreamed of having your very own private Blue Lagoon for a day you should stay at the

extravagant Silica Hotel. **Pros:** all rooms have private verandas with views of the lagoon; award-winning design; excellent service. **Cons:** on the higher end of the price range; no steam room; strong sulfur smell might be hard to get used to for those who just arrived in Iceland. $ *Rooms from: ISK82,900 ⊠ Norðurljósavegur 7, Grindavík ✦ 10-min walk from Blue Lagoon ☎ 420–8900 ⊕ www.bluelagoon.com ⤳ 35 rooms ⦿ Free Breakfast.*

 ## Nightlife

Papa's Restaurant

PUBS | If you're craving a pub-like atmosphere, stop by Papa's for refreshing Icelandic beer on tap, a burger, or crispy fish-and-chips. They show sporting events like fights and soccer matches on a flat-screen TVs. Papa's is also locals' go-to spot for take-away pizza. ⊠ *Hafnargata 7a, Grindavík ☎ 426–9955 ⊕ www.papas.is.*

 ## Shopping

Palóma

WOMEN'S CLOTHING | The constantly changing Icelandic weather might suddenly leave you needing a fashionable raincoat or a cute summer dress, and this women's wear store is here for you. One of the few clothing stores in the area, Palóma is stocked with beautiful jackets, dresses, jeans, and even jewelry adorned with Icelandic quotes. ⊠ *Víkurbraut 62, Grindavík ☎ 426–8711 ⊕ www.paloma.is.*

Vínbúðin

WINE/SPIRITS | The only stores allowed to sell alcohol in Iceland are government-owned alcohol stores called Vínbúðin, usually found in larger towns. If you are visiting Grindavík on your way out to small towns or remote areas, remember to stop at Vínbúðin for any beer, wine, or hard liquor you'd like to take with you. ⊠ *Víkurbraut 62, Grindavík ☎ 426–8787 ⊕ www.vinbudin.is.*

🏃 Activities

4x4 Adventures Iceland

FOUR-WHEELING | Exploring the seemingly endless lava fields of the Reykjanes Peninsula with its surprising natural wonders while riding an ATV is a popular and thrilling activity for many visitors. This family-run company offers various tours on ATVs and buggies ranging in duration from one to seven hours. They offer pickup for an extra fee. ⊠ *Þorkötlustaðir 3, Grindavík* ☎ *857–3001* ⊕ *www.4x4adventuresiceland.is.*

Grindavík Swimming Pool

SWIMMING | **FAMILY** | This classic Icelandic swimming pool was built in the 1990s and has a nice outdoor pool, cold pot, children's pool with a mushroom that rains, and a big waterslide. It also has two hot tubs. ⊠ *Austurvegur 1, Grindavík* ☎ *426–7555* ⊠ *ISK 980.*

Húsatóftavöllur

GOLF | Just 4 km (2½ miles) from the Blue Lagoon is this scenic 18-hole golf course marked by lava fields. The first five holes take you along the Reykjanes coastline where you will feel the power of the ocean, and the other 13 holes are above the highways and surrounded by red and green mossy lava. ⊠ *Grindavík Golf Course, Húsatóftum, Grindavík* ☎ *426–8720* ⊕ *www.gggolf.is* ⊠ *ISK 8,000, cart rental ISK 1,000* 🏌 *18 holes, par 70.*

Hafnarfjörður

40 km (25 miles) northeast of Grindavík, 18 km (11 miles) south of Reykjavík.

Embedded in the lava at the outskirts of Reykjavík, this old fishing town is the third largest town in the capital area. Hafnarfjörður is home to Viking fairs and is also a notorious hotspot for the elves, or as Icelanders call them, the *huldufólk* or hidden people. In fact, you'll see many of the streets here wind precariously around large rock formations. These are elf rocks (aka their homes), and if you believe the legends, you'll give them a wide girth—or else. If you want to enjoy the small cafés, craft beer bars, restaurants, and harbor town atmosphere of Reykjavík in a less crowded, slower-paced environment, Hafnarfjörður is the place for you.

GETTING HERE AND AROUND

Route 55 goes through Hafnarfjörður from Keflavík Airport all the way to Reykjavík. Strætó Bus 1 runs to Hafnarfjörður from the center of Reykjavík and takes only about 20 minutes. While that route travels down to the city center, it continues on to the southern reaches of the town. Within the city, Buses 21 and 19 will get you to all the nooks and crannies of the area.

FESTIVALS
Viking Festival Hafnarfjörður

CULTURAL FESTIVALS | **FAMILY** | Hafnarfjörður holds a Viking festival every June. Over the course of a weekend, the historical reenactment group Rimmugýgur has thrilling sword fights in traditional Viking clothing, tells tales of the Old Icelandic Vikings to children and adults alike, and teaches their guests how to make jewelry out of bones and stones. There's also a fun market where one can pick up leatherwear, swords, drinking horns, and other Viking necessities. ⊠ *Víðistaðatún, Hjallabraut 51, Hafnarfjörður* ✛ *Víðistaðatún is a park that can be accessed through various sides* ⊕ *www.facebook.com/rimmugygur* ⊠ *Free.*

TOURS
★ Hidden Worlds Tour

CULTURAL TOURS | **FAMILY** | A walking tour is often a great way to get to know a city and its residents, and when some of them are believed to be living in certain rocks and the towering lava cliffs, a knowledgeable tour guide can be a real asset. This tour company hands you a map of the hidden people of Hafnarfjörður and asks you to follow along to some of the most beautiful sights in

Hafnarfjörður while you hear wonderful stories of Icelandic elves. It operates twice a week on Tuesdays and Fridays during the summer or on request at other times. ⊠ *Strandgata 6, Hafnarfjörður* ☎ *695–9558* ⊕ *www.alfar.is* ⌷ *ISK 5,300.*

VISITOR INFORMATION

CONTACTS Hafnarfjörður Tourist Information Center. ⊠ *Town Hall, Strandgata 6, Hafnarfjörður* ☎ *585–5500* ⊕ *www. hafnarfjordur.is.*

◉ Sights

Hafnarborg Center of Culture and Fine Art
ART MUSEUM | Founded in 1983, Hafnarfjörður's first art museum holds 10 to 12 exhibitions each year, focusing not only on the work of prominent Icelandic artists but also on experimental work by up-and-coming creators. In addition, they often host artist talks and other cultural events. On one side of the ground floor is a small museum shop that sells Icelandic design souvenirs, and on the other side is Krydd, a restaurant that offers some particularly spectacular pizza. ⊠ *Strandgata 34* ☎ *585–5790* ⊕ *www.hafnarborg.is* ⌷ *Free* ⊙ *Closed Tues.*

★ Hellisgerði

CITY PARK | FAMILY | Tucked away from the main street in Hafnarfjörður, this local park is the perfect place to get lost. There, pathways wind between lava formations, a playground is hidden by towering spruces, and a mystical pond beckons you to stop and listen to the melodious birdsong. Hellisgerði is notoriously the home of *huldufólk,* or "hidden people"—if you stay long enough, maybe you'll meet one. The Hidden Worlds group stops here on its tour. ⊠ *Hellisgata 3, Hafnarfjörður* ⊹ *Corner of Hellisgata and Reykjavíkurvegur* ☎ *664–5674* ⊕ *www.facebook.com/hellisgerdiofficial.*

Kleifarvatn

BODY OF WATER | While driving the Krýsuvíkur road (Route 42) from Hafnarfjörður to the south coast of the peninsula, you will see the mystical Kleifarvatn, the largest lake in Reykjanes and the setting for *The Draining Lake,* a crime novel by the famous Icelandic author Arnaldur Indriðason. Around the lake are secret caves and places where you can find complete silence. ⊠ *Krýsuvík, Krýsuvíkur.*

★ Seltún

HOT SPRING | This colorful geothermal area, with raw bubbling mud pots and steam and hot little rivers emerging from the earth, is one of the gems of the Reykjanes peninsula. Located on the scenic Krýsuvík road (Route 42)—which passes volcanic sandstone cliffs, lakes with black-sand beaches, and outlandish lava formations—this stop is a must along the interesting drive. The minerals spewed from the ground at unbelievable temperatures stain the rocks in blood reds, deep blues, beige yellows, and neon greens. The nicely restored walking paths and spacious parking lot make it easily accessible for most visitors. There are also bathrooms available. ⊠ *Krýsuvík, Seltún, Hafnarfjörður.*

Suðurbæjarlaug

POOL | FAMILY | Hafnarfjörður has three swimming pools, but Suðurbæjarlaug has a late-1980s charm and is the only one with an outdoor pool. There are indoor and outdoor changing rooms, two waterslides, a steam bath, and a nice little path that twists around the pool ideal for cooling off between dips in the numerous hot tubs. ⊠ *Hringbraut 77, Hafnarfjörður* ☎ *565–3080* ⊕ *www.hafnarfjordur.is* ⌷ *ISK 850.*

🍴 Restaurants

Brikk

$ | BAKERY | FAMILY | At this great modern bakery-café by the harbor, you can enjoy delicious sourdough bread with tasty, original salads and mouthwatering pastries, either to eat there or to take with you on a road trip. In a city with as fierce a bakery scene as Hafnarfjörður, this spot is a true stand-out, and you'd be hard-pressed to find a local who isn't obsessed with their cheese and tuna spreads. **Known for:** reasonable prices; famous cinnamon buns with salted caramel topping; dangerously good cheesy salad. ⓢ *Average main: ISK800* ✉ *Norður-bakki 1b, Hafnarfjörður* ☎ *565–1665* ⊕ *www.brikk.is.*

Fjörukráin

$$$$ | **ICELANDIC** | **FAMILY** | Located in the second oldest building in Hafnarfjörður and shaped like a Norwegian Stave church, you will travel in time and land in a dark, wooden scene filled with Viking-inspired art. Fjörukráin serves traditional Icelandic meals on Viking-style trays carried by waiters dressed in Viking clothes. **Known for:** Viking-themed entertainment bordering on the kitschy; live music; fun history lesson. ⓢ *Average main: ISK4,290* ✉ *Viking Village, Strandgata 55, Hafnarfjörður* ☎ *565–1213* ⊕ *www.fjorukrain.is* ⊘ *No lunch.*

Ísbúð Vesturbæjar

$$ | **ICE CREAM** | **FAMILY** | In any weather—even the most brutal snowstorm—Icelanders will meet their friends for an ice cream. Ísbúð Vesturbæjar is a famous family-owned ice-cream parlor with one of the best Bragðarefur (blended mix of crushed-up candy and vanilla soft-serve) in all of Iceland. **Known for:** old-fashioned ice cream (creamier than other Icelandic ice cream); large portions; must-try Bragðarefur flavor. ⓢ *Average main: ISK1,300* ✉ *Fjarðargata 19, Hafnarfjörður* ☎ *552–3390* ⊕ *www.isbudvesturbaejar.is.*

★ Pallett

$$ | **CAFÉ** | Tucked away in the sleepy fishing town of Hafnarfjörður, Pallett looks at times like an ad from a 1970s issue of *Vogue* with its jungle of houseplants, a rotary telephone at the counter, and cassette player blaring in the background. But this is more than just a hipster hangout: the food is hearty, wholesome, and inherently British (think freshly baked scones with homemade jam) and

the coffee is made from award-winning beans. **Known for:** heaven for coffee nerds; part of the slow living movement; only place in Iceland that does mince pies. ⓢ *Average main: ISK1,000* ✉ *Strandgata 75* ☎ *571–4144* ⊕ *www.pallett.is* ⊟ *No credit cards.*

★ Von Mathús

$$$$ | **INTERNATIONAL** | **FAMILY** | This restaurant celebrates the history of Hafnarfjörður with old fishing gear strung between the tables and chandeliers made from old buoys. Dive into seasonally focused Icelandic dishes with a twist while watching the boats huddle together in the harbour. **Known for:** delightful fresh fish; exciting vegan options; well-curated set menus. ⓢ *Average main: ISK4,300* ✉ *Strandgata 75, Hafnarfjörður* ☎ *583–6000* ⊕ *www.vonmathus.is* ⊘ *Closed Sun. and Mon.*

 ## Hotels

Hótel Vellir

$ | **HOTEL** | While not in the most charming neighborhood, Hótel Vellir is convenient to both the Reykjavík city center and Keflavík Airport, close to the biggest indoor geothermal pool in Iceland, and only a 10-minute walk to restaurants and shops in downtown Hafnarfjörður. **Pros:** airport transfers and tour reservations at the front desk; new and modern rooms; good gym on-site. **Cons:** the view and the surrounding area are not very exciting; hard to reach if you don't have a car; noise pollution if your room faces the highway. ⓢ *Rooms from: ISK20,000* ✉ *Tjarnarvellir 3, Hafnarfjörður* ☎ *420–0080* ⊕ *www.hotelvellir.com* ⇱ *68 rooms* ⓞ *No Meals.*

Hotel Viking

$$ | **HOTEL** | **FAMILY** | This delightfully cheesy hotel—which along with the restaurant Fjörukráin makes up a building referred to as the Viking Village—is a paradise for anyone that wants a themed experience with modern amenities. **Pros:**

lively restaurant; kitschy but fun design; great for families (especially ones that like fantasy). **Cons:** lots of children; theme borders on cheesy at times; basic rooms are small. $ *Rooms from: ISK22,000* ✉ *Viking Village, Strandgata 55, Hafnarfjörður* ☎ *565–1213* ⊕ *www.fjorukrain. is* ➪ *55 rooms* ⦵ *Free Breakfast.*

Nightlife

Ölhúsið Hafnarfirði
BARS | If you are looking to watch the game, play some darts, or catch some live music on a late Friday night in Hafnarfjörður, then Ölhúsið is the place to be. It offers a late-night hangout on the weekends, happy hour from 3 till 7, and a consistently great selection of beers. ✉ *Reykjavíkurvegur 60, Hafnarfjörður* ☎ *555–0022* ⊕ *www.olhusid.is.*

Shopping

AndreA
WOMEN'S CLOTHING | Icelandic designer Andrea Magnúsdóttir runs this bright and welcoming boutique by the harbor. Her selection of beautiful dresses and sleek jewelry make it tough to leave empty-handed. ✉ *Norðurbakki 1, Hafnarfjörður* ☎ *551–3900* ⊕ *www.andrea.is.*

Litla Hönnunar Búðin
SOUVENIRS | What used to be a charming and tiny design boutique is now a beautiful and spacious store located in the heart of Hafnarfjörður. They carry a wide selection of gifts by trendy Icelandic and Scandinavian designers, including posters, ceramics, jewelry, and much more. ✉ *Strandgata 19, Hafnarfjörður* ☎ *555–7010* ⊕ *www.litlahonnunarbudin.is.*

Sigga and Timo
JEWELRY & WATCHES | One of the most beloved jewelry stores in Iceland was founded by a Finnish-Icelandic couple, who are known for their romantic yet timeless designs that you can wear for a lifetime. Their expertise in working with precious metals and stones makes their engagement rings very popular with couples from all over the world. ✉ *Linnetsstígur 2, Hafnarfjörður* ☎ *863–7333* ⊕ *www.siggaogtimo.is.*

Activities

Urriðavöllur Golf Course
GOLF | Located only 10 minutes from central Hafnafjörður, this course is known for being more playful than competitive. The local landscape features prominently in its design: one hole stretches across a lava field, and another plays 100 meters above sea level. The clubhouse is stylish, with a popular on-site restaurant. And if you're interested, midnight golf is available upon request. ✉ *Urriðavöllur, Hafnarfjörður* ☎ *565–9092* ⊕ *www.oddur. is* 🏌 *18 holes, par 71* ⊙ *Closed May–Oct.* ➪ *Greens fee ISK 14,000; cart rental ISK 7,000.*

The Golden Circle

The Golden Circle is a famous tourist route comprising three famous natural sights: Þingvellir National Park, Geysir, and Gullfoss. As a result of its popularity, the route is often crowded with tourists, but few dare to skip it—seeing these natural wonders is a once-in-a-lifetime experience. While you can visit the sights in any order, visitors typically come from the direction of Reykjavík and therefore start at Þingvellir National Park, then Geysir (close to the town of Haukadalur), and end with Gullfoss.

All three sights can be visited in one day (whether on a guided tour or with your own rental car), but you can also make sure you get the most out of your visit by extending the trip to a couple of days and staying overnight in one of the smaller towns that surround the natural wonders.

Þingvellir

About 50 km (31 miles) northeast of Reykjavík, 56 km (35 miles) northeast of Hafnafjörður.

After not quite an hour's drive from Reykjavík along Route 36, across the Mosfellsheiði heath, the broad lava plain of Þingvellir National Park suddenly opens up in front of you. This has been the nation's most hallowed place since AD 930, when the settler Grímur Geitskör chose it as the first site for what is often called the world's oldest parliament, the Icelandic Alþingi (General Assembly). In July of each year delegates from all over the country camp at Þingvellir for two weeks, meeting to pass laws and render judicial sentences. Iceland remained a nation-state ruled solely by the people without a central government until 1262, when it came under the Norwegian crown. Even then—and although it had lost its lawmaking powers—the Alþingi continued to meet at Þingvellir until 1798.

The natural beauty of Þingvellir is a wonder of its own. With vivid flora and fauna spreading across the lava fields and a deep, clear blue lake with species of fish found nowhere else on earth, it is possibly the best place in the world to see and feel the continental divide between the North American and Eurasian tectonic plates. Steep cliffs and deep canyons are the visible signs that the earth itself is being torn apart right there in Iceland's oldest national park; the biggest cliffs on the east side are the start of Europe, and the wall of Lögberg on the west side marks the start of North America. The valley between them—with its lake, rivers, and small waterfalls—geographically belongs to no continent at all. Volcanoes surround the valley on every side, and across the park are hiking trails and easy walking paths in this unimaginable postcard of a place.

GETTING HERE AND AROUND

The easiest way to get to Þingvellir is with a rental car. Take the Ring Road about 11½ km just past the town of Mosfellsbær; turn right on Route 36, Þingvallavegur. Parking per vehicle costs ISK 750 for a passenger car. No buses currently stop here, but Þingvellir is a stop on almost every tour of the Golden Circle.

VISITOR INFORMATION

At the top of the Almannagjá rift is the Þingvellir Visitor Centre with information about the ecology and geology of the park as well as its extensive history. There's also a small cafeteria, a souvenir shop, and an interactive exhibit about the park. In front of the center are parking lots (ISK 750) and toilets.

CONTACTS Þingvellir Visitor Centre. ⊠ *Þingvellir* ☎ *482–2660* ⊕ *www.thingvellir.is.*

Sights

Drekkingarhylur

HISTORIC SIGHT | "The Drowning Pool" is where, for a couple of hundred years, women were drowned—most of them sentenced to death for incest, having children out of wedlock, or other alleged sex-related crimes. Þórdís Halldórsdóttir was the first woman to be drowned in Drekkingarhylur in AD 1590; her crime was perjury, for swearing she was a virgin when indeed she was pregnant. ⊠ *Þingvellir* ⊕ *www.thingvellir.is.*

Lögberg

HISTORIC SIGHT | A path down into Almannagjá from the top of the gorge overlooking Þingvellir leads to the high rock wall of Lögberg (Law Rock). At the time of the Icelandic Commonwealth Period, from AD 930 until 1262, Lögberg was the hub of the annual Alþingi meeting. The Lögsögumaður (law speaker) recited a third of the existing laws, which he had memorized, to the assembled parliament each year. After that recitation, anyone could step forward at Lögberg and give a speech or relay news. When Icelanders took allegiance to the Norwegian king in 1262, the authority of Lögberg disappeared. ⊠ *Thingvellir National Park, Þingvellir* ⊕ *www.thingvellir.is.*

Nikulásargjá

NATURE SIGHT | FAMILY | Reached by a footbridge, this gorge is better known these days as Peningagjá (Money Gorge) because it's customary to fling a coin into the gorge's ice-cold water and make a wish. Don't even dream about climbing down to wade here—it might look shallow, but it's more than 30 feet deep. ⊕ *www.thingvellir.is.*

★ Silfra

NATURE SIGHT | Most people visit Þingvellir for its historical and geological significance, but in this same place another perspective awaits those who don't mind trading their walking boots and windbreaker for a dry suit and flippers. Named one of the top three freshwater dives on the planet, at Silfra you can snorkel on the surface of crystal clear water or dive to depths up to 30 meters. Exploring these underwater cracks is like entering another world: the silence is striking—a perfect companion to the vision of muted blues, bejeweled with silver globules of gas mushrooming to the surface from the divers below. An adventure in this underwater wonderland between the continents of North America and Europe leaves you with vivid images but no words. For tours with knowledgeable instructors, book with dive.is, Tröll Expeditions, or Arctic Adventures. ⊠ *National Park Þingvellir, Þingvellir.*

Þingvallabærinn

GOVERNMENT BUILDING | Across the plain from Lögberg stands the church and the gabled manor house of Þingvallabærinn, where the government of Iceland often hosts visiting heads of state. Þingvallakirkja, the quaint church of Þingvellir, is nearby. Free one-hour tours of the area are offered every day in summer, leaving from the church at 10 am. Note that the

house of Þingvallabærinn is the official summer residence of the prime minister of Iceland and can only be admired from the outside. ☎ *482–2660* ⊕ *www. thingvellir.is.*

★ Þingvellir National Park

NATIONAL PARK | FAMILY | Located at the northern end of Þingvallavatn—Iceland's largest lake—Þingvellir National Park is a powerful symbol of Icelandic heritage. Many national celebrations are held here, and it was named a UNESCO World Heritage Site in 2004. Besides its historical interest, Þingvellir holds a special appeal for naturalists: it is the geologic meeting point of two continents. At Almannagjá, on the west side of the plain, is the easternmost edge of the North American tectonic plate, otherwise submerged in the Atlantic Ocean. Over on the plain's east side, at the Heiðargjá Gorge, you are at the westernmost edge of the Eurasian plate.

A path down into Almannagjá from the top of the gorge overlooking Þingvellir leads straight to the high rock wall of Lögberg (Law Rock), where the person once chosen as guardian of the Icelandic laws would recite them from memory. At the far end of the gorge is the Öxarárfoss (Öxará Waterfall); beautiful, peaceful picnic spots sit just beyond it. Behind Lögberg the river cascades down and forms the forbidding Drekkingarhylur pool. ☎ *482–2660* ⊕ *www.thingvellir.is* ⌗ *Free; parking ISK 750.*

Hotels

Hótel Grímsborgir

$$$$ | HOTEL | This classic American-style country hotel guarantees luxury on every account: it's secluded, peaceful, and only a 15-minute drive from Selfoss, and 20 kilometers (12 miles) from Þingvellir National Park. **Pros:** excellent restaurant on-site; ideal location to spot the Northern Lights; multiple outdoor hot tubs. **Cons:** dated compared to the other luxury hotels in the area; pricey; not much within walking

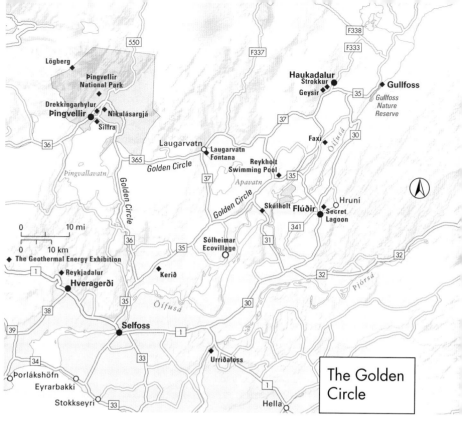

The Golden Circle

distance. $\boxed{\$}$ *Rooms from: ISK52,400*
$\boxtimes$ *Árborgir 30, Selfoss* $\textcircled{a}$ *555–7878*
$\oplus$ *www.grimsborgir.com* $\rightleftarrows$ *64 rooms*
$\lceil\bigcirc\rceil$ *Free Breakfast.*

★ ION Adventure Hotel

$$$$ | HOTEL | Clean, green, and emerging
from the landscape, the ION Hotel is a
striking sight in the primordial surrounds
of Nesjavellir, a geothermal area close to
Þingvellir National Park. **Pros:** well serviced
by tour operators providing a range of outdoor activities; striking design in an unusual landscape; luxury spa with an oudoor
hot tub and bar. **Cons:** culturally speaking,
it's completely off-piste (no nearby shops,
bars, or restaurants); proven difficult for
some cars to reach in winter; right next to
a geothermal power plant. $\boxed{\$}$ *Rooms from:*
ISK63,000 $\boxtimes$ *Nesjavöllum við Þingvallar-*
vatn $\textcircled{a}$ *578–3720* $\oplus$ *www.ioniceland.is*
$\rightleftarrows$ *46 rooms* $\lceil\bigcirc\rceil$ *No Meals.*

Haukadalur

60 km (37 miles) east of Þingvellir.

The geothermal field in Haukadalur is
one of Iceland's classic tourist spots.
The famous Geysir hot spring (the literal
origin of the term *geyser*) erupts only a
few times a year, but the more reliable
Strokkur spouts boiling water as high
as 100 feet at five-minute intervals. In
the same area, there are small natural
vents from which steam rises as well
as beautiful exotic-color pools. Don't
crowd Strokkur, and always be careful
when approaching hot springs or mud
pots—the ground may be treacherous,
suddenly giving way beneath you. Stay
on formal paths or established tracks.

GETTING HERE AND AROUND

From Þingvellir, continue east on Route 36, turn left on Route 365, and left again on Route 37; drive until you see Laugarvatn. Bus 73 runs to Laugarvatn from Selfoss daily and takes 1 hour, 15 minutes.

From Laugarvatn, take Route 37 northeast for 30 km (18 miles) to the junction with Route 35, which you'll take 10 km (6 miles) northeast to get to Geysir. (From Lake Laugarvatn you can take the short spur Route 364 southwest to Route 37.)

TOURS

The Cave People

CULTURAL TOURS | On this guided tour it feels like you've been transported back 100 years, to a time when certain Icelanders still lived in caves. Laugarvatnshellar are two man-made caves near Laugarvatn; no one has yet determined exactly when they were made or by whom. In the beginning of the 20th century two separate couples moved into the caves and lived there for a couple of years. Their "house" in the caves has now been redone, and these charismatic guides will lead you on a journey and tell you interesting stories of the cave people. Afterwards you are offered coffee or tea and some Icelandic pastries. ⊠ *Laugarvatnshellir, Háholt 2c, Haukadalur ⊹ Off main road between Þingvellir and Laugarvatn* ☎ *888–1922* ⊕ *www.thecavepeople.is* ⊠ *ISK 2,100.*

 Sights

Faxi

WATERFALL | This stunning waterfall doesn't come close to the famous Gullfoss in size, but it makes up for it with less crowding and an abundance of salmon. Faxi is located about 12 km (7½ miles) south of Gullfoss, and visitors are able to explore the waterfall from different viewpoints by following the path. ⊠ *Biskupstungubraut, Haukadalur* ⊠ *ISK 700.*

★ Geysir

NATURE SIGHT | The world-famous Geysir (from which all other geysers get their name), shoots boiling water and steam 100 feet in the air when it erupts every few months. From Þingvellir, the first stop in the Golden Circle, continue east on Route 36, turn left on Route 365, and turn left again on Route 37 at Laugarvatn. At the end of Route 37, turn left and take Route 35 northeast to Hótel Geysir, which is next to the hot springs. ⊠ *Haukadalur.*

Laugarvatn Fontana

HOT SPRING | **FAMILY** | Swimming in a cold, refreshing lake for a few minutes and then running back to the hot tub or sauna is a unique healing exercise that rewards you with a rush of endorphins. If you think it's too cold on this island for that, Fontana offers a relaxing warm soak in the tub. They also have a lovely geothermal bakery, which they offer tours of twice a day. ⊠ *Laugarvatn, Hverabraut 1, Haukadalur ⊹ Right by the lake* ☎ *486–1400* ⊕ *www.fontana.is* ⊠ *ISK 4,500.*

Laugarvatn Sundlaug

POOL | **FAMILY** | For families with children who want to play and be loud, or for those who would rather not splurge on the Fontana spa, the swimming pool at Laugarvatn is a great choice. Located right by the shallow lake, there is a spacious 25-meter pool with three hot tubs and a sauna. ⊠ *Hverabraut 2, Haukadalur* ☎ *480–3041* ⊠ *ISK 1,050.*

★ Strokkur

NATURE SIGHT | This highly popular active geyser is located in the Geysir Geothermal area, and is also along the Golden Circle. Though not as powerful as the Great Geysir, it does erupt much more frequently. ⊠ *Haukadalur.*

Restaurants

★ Efstidalur II

$$$ | BURGER | This family farm serves amazingly fresh dishes at their restaurant, Hlöðuloftið, including stuffed trout from the nearby lake and hamburgers from their own meat. But their downstairs ice-cream bar truly takes farm-to-table to another level with the delicious homemade ice cream you can enjoy while watching the dairy cows through a big glass window. **Known for:** truly sublime ice cream; the Skyr burger; family-run ethos. ⓢ *Average main: ISK3,500* ✉ *Efstidalur, Haukadalur* ☎ *486–1186* ⊕ *www.efstidalur.is.*

Geysir Glíma

$$ | INTERNATIONAL | FAMILY | This popular lunch spot serves traditional Icelandic hot dishes, like fish and lamb stews, just a few meters from its namesake Golden Circle sight. They also offer pastries, pizza, and sandwiches, so the whole family should be able to find something to their taste. **Known for:** hot-spring bread; traditional Icelandic fish stew; high-end canteen vibe. ⓢ *Average main: ISK2,890* ✉ *Geysir Center, Biskupstungubraut, Haukadalur* ☎ *481–3003* ⊕ *www.geysirglima.is* ⊙ *No dinner.*

Restaurant Mika

$$$ | PIZZA | FAMILY | A kind Polish family runs this restaurant on the Golden Circle route. Don't let the humble exterior fool you: inside you will find some of Iceland's best pizzas and handmade chocolates. **Known for:** delectable chocolate; great place to stop for food on the Golden Circle; langoustine, lamb, and lots of pizza. ⓢ *Average main: ISK3,900* ✉ *Skólabraut 4, Selfoss* ☎ *486–1110* ⊕ *www.mika.is.*

Skjól

$$ | INTERNATIONAL | FAMILY | This laid-back and charming restaurant at a campground near Geysir serves excellent pizzas and burgers. They also have a selection of beer, as well as nachos—together they make the perfect ending to a long day of sightseeing. **Known for:** occasional live music nights; excellent vegan burger; tasty waffles. ⓢ *Average main: ISK2,900* ✉ *Kjóastaðir 1, Biskupstungnabraut, Haukadalur* ☎ *899–4541* ⊕ *www.skjolcamping.com.*

Við Faxa

$$ | SCANDINAVIAN | FAMILY | This charming low-key country restaurant and café is a nice pit stop on the Golden Circle, with a deck overlooking the beautiful Faxi waterfall. Stop by for coffee and homemade dessert or stay for a lovely piece of fish. **Known for:** signature soup and bread perfect for a cold day; Golden Circle lunch spot; patio seating. ⓢ *Average main: ISK2,100* ✉ *Faxi waterfall, Biskupstunga, Haukadalur* ☎ *774–7440* ⊙ *Closed winter.*

Hotels

Geysir Hestar

$ | HOTEL | This guesthouse is located on a horse farm within close driving distance to both Gullfoss and Geysir and provides both rooms and wooden cottages for rent. **Pros:** great for animal lovers; gorgeous location along the Golden Circle route; very friendly owners. **Cons:** main guesthouse has shared bathrooms and kitchen; no breakfast or dinner service; small rooms. ⓢ *Rooms from: ISK16,000* ✉ *Kjóastaðir 2, Haukadalur* ☎ *847–1046* ⊕ *www.geysirhestar.com* ⇥ *11 rooms* �“OI *No Meals.*

★ Hótel Geysir

$$$ | HOTEL | Experience Nordic style at its best at this surprisingly chic hotel next to the famous Geysir and Strokkur springs. **Pros:** beautiful Nordic decor; restaurant with excellent cuisine and hot spring views; good base for exploring the area. **Cons:** pricey compared to nearby accommodations; far from grocery stores or nightlife; no hot pools to soak in. ⓢ *Rooms from: ISK37,500* ✉ *Haukadalur* ☎ *480–6800* ⊕ *www.hotelgeysir.is* ⇥ *83 rooms* ⊚OI *Free Breakfast.*

134

Shopping

Galleri Laugarvatn

SOUVENIRS | FAMILY | A funky little art gallery founded by an Icelandic couple in search of new life in the countryside, Galleri Laugarvatn has a wide variety of Iceland handcrafts from well-known Icelandic designers and local artists. Next door they have a cafe where you can get light meals for a reasonable price; the homemade waffles are especially lovely. ⊠ Laugarvatn, Háholt 1, Haukadalur ☎ 868–7781 ⊕ www.gallerilaugarvatn.is.

Geysir Center

SHOPPING CENTER | FAMILY | In front of a parking lot, close to Geysir, is this large shopping complex where you'll find established Icelandic outdoor and fashion brands, a souvenir shop with Viking-theme key chains, and a soup and fast-food canteen. ⊠ Haukadalur 35, Haukadalur ☎ 480–6800 ⊕ www.hotelgeysir.is.

Krambúð

GENERAL STORE | This classic countryside supermarket offers all the necessities for locals, including some fantastic burgers. It makes a smart pit stop before heading farther east or west, as supermarkets tend to be far apart. ⊠ Dalbraut 6, Haukadalur ☎ 486–1126 ⊕ www.kram-budin.is.

Activities

GOLF

Haukadalsvöllur

GOLF | The sun hangs low, the air smells of birch, and every 10 minutes or so a geyser erupts—and you take a swing. The beautiful and challenging 9-hole course in Haukadalur has two rivers, Beiná and Almenningsá, that play a big role in its design. You can rent clubs on-site and get refreshments at a small café with great views. ⊠ Geysir Golf Course, Haukadalur 3, Haukadalur ☎ 790–6800 ⊕ www.geysirgolf.is 🏌 9 holes, par 72 ⚲ Club rental: ISK 2,500; Greens fees: ISK 7,000.

HORSEBACK RIDING

Geysir Hestar

HORSEBACK RIDING | FAMILY | This Icelandic horse farm is only 4 km (2½ miles) east of the famous Geysir. They manage over 100 horses and offer various riding experiences for the whole family—special rides around the farm for small children, day trips through the magnificent Hvítá River and up the canyon to Gullfoss, and even week-long trips. ⊠ Kjóastaðir 2, Haukadalur ☎ 847–1046 ⊕ www.geysirhestar.com.

Gullfoss

10 km (6 miles) east of Haukadalur.

The typical last stop along the Golden Circle route is the thundering 105-foot-high Gullfoss (Golden Falls), a double cascade in the river Hvítá that turns at right angles mid-drop into a dramatic chasm. It's the largest volume falls in Europe and a majestic sight any time of year, but during the cold winter, the outer layers of the waterfall can freeze, creating a dramatic effect. Watch your step and stick to the path.

GETTING HERE AND AROUND

From Þingvellir, continue east on Route 36, turn left on route 365, and turn left again on Route 37 at Laugarvatn. When Route 37 ends, turn left and take Route 35 northeast to Hótel Geysir, next to the hot springs; from there it's another 10 minutes on to the falls. Gullfoss can also be reached by private bus. Reykjavík Excursions' "Iceland On Your Own" service runs between Reykjavík and Akureyri, stopping at Geysir and Gullfoss en route. In summer, that bus leaves daily at 8 am from BSÍ Bus Terminal in Reykjavík. The trip takes about 2½ hours, since the bus stops at major sites for 30 minutes to give passengers time to explore.

TOURS

Arctic Rafting

ADVENTURE TOURS | FAMILY | Rafting in the canyon just below the majestic Gullfoss while being sprayed by the Hvítá River, which runs all the way from Langjökull glacier, is an incredible and exhilarating experience. For almost 40 years, adrenaline junkies have been whitewater rafting from the Drumbó River base and it now serves as the home for Arctic Rafting, a tour company that will give you a hearty dose of excitement on your trip to Iceland—and maybe some rapids. After the tour you'll be greeted by a hot sauna, with the option of a refreshing beer or dinner. You can arrange a pickup in Reykjavík or meet them on location in Drumboddstaðir. ✉ *Drumboddstaðir, Haukadalur* ☎ *486–8990* 🌐 *www.arcticrafting.com* 🎟 *ISK 14,990* 🕒 *Closed Sept.–May.*

Sights

★ Gullfoss

WATERFALL | FAMILY | Iceland's most famous waterfall is a truly spectacular scene. There used to be a modest visitor center named in memory of Sigríður Tómasdóttir, who fought against a hydroelectric reservoir scheme that would have flooded the falls in the early 20th century. Today it's a tour-booking center, a small shop, and a restaurant that prides itself on a warm and filling Icelandic meat soup. The center's bathrooms are free to use. ✉ *Biskaupstungubraut* ☎ *486–6500.*

Hotels

Hótel Gullfoss

$$ | HOTEL | FAMILY | Family-run for more than 20 years, this hotel sits in a valley just five minutes from the magnificent Gullfoss. **Pros:** great location; country-style cooking at the hotel restaurant; spacious and modern rooms. **Cons:** no hot tub; quite busy; no entertainment in the area. $ *Rooms from: ISK24,600* ✉ *Brattholt* ☎ *486–8979* 🌐 *www.hotelgullfoss.is* 🛏 *35 rooms* 🍴 *Free Breakfast.*

Flúðir

31 km (19 miles) south of Gullfoss.

Flúðir and its small neighboring towns are the vegetable-growing hubs of Iceland due to geothermal heating and fertile white-water rivers. Before the tourist boom in Iceland, Flúðir was mostly known for mushrooms and pleasant weather, but now it is a growing community focused on innovative and sustainable tourism.

GETTING HERE AND AROUND

If you're completing the Golden Circle at Gullfoss, the route back to the Ring Road at Selfoss has a lot of exciting stops and sights on the way. Most people follow Route 35, which passes through Reykholt, but it's also possible to take a little detour and visit Flúðir. Strætó Buses 72 and 73 also serve Flúðir via Selfoss daily.

Sights

Flúðir Swimming Pool

POOL | FAMILY | Those who don't want to splurge on a ticket to the Secret Lagoon may wish to check out the local swimming pool at Flúðir, which also has two nice hot tubs and a natural sauna. ✉ *Flúðalaug, Túngata, Haukadalur* ☎ *480–6625* 🎟 *ISK 1,000.*

Reykholt Swimming Pool

POOL | FAMILY | In the beautiful but unexciting village of Reykholt (not to be confused with the historical town in West Iceland) is a nice swimming pool for relaxing and stretching out. For those who need to blow off some steam, there is also a small gym and sports hall in the building. ✉ *Reykholt, Biskupstungur, Selfoss* ☎ *480–3040* 🎟 *ISK 1,050* 🕒 *Closed Sun. late Aug.–May.*

Land of Fire and Ice

Iceland is nicknamed the "Land of Fire and Ice" due to its volcanic activity and massive glaciers. Previously covered completely in ice, the island was born out of volcanic eruptions over millions of years. Today volcanic ash mixes with the bright blue of glaciers to form Iceland's distinct and mesmerizing landscape. Revisiting the history of some of the most well-known volcanoes and volcanic eruptions can help a visitor get a sense of the country's temperamental yet magical topography.

Eyjafjallajökull

A volcano covered with an ice cap in the southern region of Iceland, Eyjafjallajökull last erupted on February 26, 2010, with 3,000 earthquakes detected at its epicenter. This world-famous volcano can be spotted in films like *The Secret Life of Walter Mitty* and is referenced in various songs.

Eldhraun

The pillowlike moss along the Ring Road, right before Kirkjubæjarklaustur, was actually created by a devastating volcanic eruption in the 1700s. In fact, it was the third largest lava flow on earth, occurring during the Laki eruption. It's also where Apollo 11 came to train for the moon landing. If you feel so inclined, pull off to the side of the road to feel for yourself just how soft the landscape is, but be respectful as the moss is fragile.

Fagradalsfjall

The eruption of the Fagradalsfjall volcano in the Reykjanes Peninsula was Iceland's most recent volcanic eruption. Lasting from March 19, 2021 all the way until September 18, 2021 (with another minor eruption in August 2022), it's become an important site for scientists who are using the newly-cooled lava to study the Earth's deep mantle.

Mount Hekla

The ominous Mount Hekla, visible from places like Hella in the South, was the inspiration for J.R.R. Tolkien's Mount Doom in the fantasy epic *The Lord of the Rings*. Nicknamed the "Gateway to Hell," Hekla is in an active volcanic zone, but hasn't erupted since the year 2000. Volcanic eruptions in Iceland have never killed or harmed anyone, though geologists keep a close eye on Hekla nonetheless. Though it can erupt without warning, some even ski around its rim in the spring or hike to the summit.

⭐ **Secret Lagoon**

HOT SPRING | Taking a dip in a natural hot spring surrounded by green fields and a tiny geyser sounds great, but when you add in showers and cold drinks, it's almost too good to be true. Locals have left this lagoon largely untouched but have set up new facilities. It's even more magical during winter when people sit in the warm water with steam rising all around them. If you're lucky, the northern lights will put on a show across the sky while you're there. ✉ *Hvammsvegur* ☎ *555–3351* ⊕ *www.secretlagoon.is* 🎫 *ISK 3,000.*

Skálholt

CHURCH | The historic settlement of Skálholt is the location of one of two former episcopal seats in Iceland, and for over 700 years it was the national center of culture, politics, and education. The cathedral has been restored many times, most recently in 1963. A 1954 archaeological excavation turned up a

A major site in the Golden Circle, the Geysir shoots boiling water and steam 100 feet in the air.

sarcophagus that is believed to contain the bones of one of Skálholt's most powerful bishops, Páll Jónsson; it is now on display in the basement of the church along with other relics. The cathedral is still a center for music and culture, and it hosts an annual concert series over five weekends in July and August, featuring composers and musicians from all over the world. ⊠ Skálholt, Selfoss ☎ 486–8801 ⊕ www.skalholt.is.

🍴 Restaurants

Fish and Chips
$$ | BRITISH | FAMILY | Just outside the Secret Lagoon you will find a small shed serving delicious fish-and-chips. You can take them to go, sit out front at a picnic table if the weather is nice, or escape the Icelandic wind and cold and eat standing up in the warm and cozy shed. **Known for:** crispy fish-and-chips with four dipping sauces; rugged exterior; erratic hours (check Facebook before you go). $ *Average main: ISK1,890* ⊠ *Hvammsvegur,* *Flúðir* ☎ *848–5811* ⊕ *www.facebook.* *com/fiskikofinn.*

★ Flúðasveppir Farmers Bistro
$$$ | ECLECTIC | FAMILY | The only mushroom farmers in Iceland invite you to feast on pâté, spreads, sauces, and ice cream—all made out of mushrooms. There's an emphasis on slow cooking, and their herbs, meat, and vegetables come from neighboring farms. **Known for:** "Georg the Great" carrot cocktail named after the founder; charming setting; gourmet buffet. $ *Average main: ISK3,200* ⊠ *Garðarstígur 8* ☎ *519–0808* ⊕ *www.* *farmersbistro.is.*

Minilik Resturant
$$ | ETHIOPIAN | FAMILY | In an unassuming summer cottage at the town limits of Flúðir, you will find traditional Ethiopian specialties cooked and served by an Ethiopian-Icelandic couple. Eating spicy food with your hands surrounded by Ethiopian art is a real treat after a full day of sightseeing in the intense Icelandic terrain. **Known for:** plenty of vegetarian options; ceremonial Ethiopian coffee;

The stunning Secret Lagoon in Flúðir is enclosed by green fields.

only Ethiopian restaurant in Iceland. $ *Average main: ISK2,800* ✉ *Skeiða- og Hrunamannavegur, Selfoss* ☎ *846–9798* ⊕ *www.minilik.is* ⊗ *Closed Mon.*

Hotels

Blue Hotel Fagrilundur
$ | **HOTEL** | Hidden in the trees in Reykholt is this charming wooden cottage with cozy rooms. **Pros:** welcoming host who offers local tips to travelers; very satisfying breakfast; close to main sights on the Golden Circle route yet still secluded. **Cons:** some rooms have a shared bathroom; very little to do in town at night; rooms a bit small. $ *Rooms from: ISK17,000* ✉ *Reykholt, Skólabraut 1, Selfoss* ☎ *772–6869* ⊕ *www.bluevacations. is* ⊋ *40 rooms* ❤️ *Free Breakfast.*

★ Torfhús Retreat
$$$$ | **HOTEL** | Despite being in a simple turf house, the Torfhús Retreat is one of the most luxurious hotels in all of Iceland. **Pros:** so peaceful, you'll feel far away from the modern world; prix-fixe dinner that'll wow you; houses are true architectural marvels. **Cons:** not as many amenities as you'd expect for the price; extremely expensive; far away from restaurants, stores, and shops. $ *Rooms from: ISK100,000* ✉ *Dalsholt, Selfoss* ☎ *788–8868* ⊕ *www.torfhus.is* ⊋ *25 suites* ❤️ *Free Breakfast.*

Shopping

Bragginn Studio
CRAFTS | An old army barrack that was once used for storing potatoes is now a multifunctional art space. Although some of their exciting workshops and courses must be booked ahead of time, you can also stop by to meet the artists Bjarni and Erna and pick up beautiful ceramics in addition to some lovely local stories. Hours vary depending on artist availability. ✉ *Birtingaholt 3, Haukadalur* ☎ *897–9923* ⊕ *www.bragginnstudio.is.*

Krambúðin

FOOD | This is the only supermarket in the area, so if you are in need of any necessities or want to grab a snack for the late-night munchies, energy drinks for hikes, or have a romantic picnic by the river, make a pit stop here. ☒ *Skeiða- og Hrunamannsvegur, Selfoss* ☏ *486–6633* ⊕ *www.krambudin.is.*

Kurl Project Iceland

WOMEN'S CLOTHING | If you walk about 100 meters farther than the Secret Lagoon, you will find a small boutique tucked away behind a big greenhouse. This is the storefront and workshop of the Icelandic clothing brand Kurl Project, which is all designed and produced in Iceland by tailor and owner Erna Óðinsdóttir. ☒ *Garðyrkjustöðin Hvammur, Hvammsvegur* ☏ *899–8423* ⊕ *www.kurlproject.com.*

Activities

Selsvöllur

GOLF | Flúðir is known for being on the good side of the weather gods, so golfing is a popular activity around here. The 18-hole Efra-Sel course is one of two in the area and is known for being quite challenging. On-site you will also find a nice restaurant serving burgers and pizza. ☒ *Efri-sel* ☏ *354/486–6454* ⊕ *www. kaffisel.is* ⚲ *18 holes, par 70* ⛳ *Greens fees ISK 5,000 on weekdays, ISK 6,000 on weekends; ISK 6,500 for cart.*

Hveragerði

60 km (37 miles) southwest of Flúðir.

This town is built on a hot spring field and since the 1920s, people have harnessed the active geothermal energy to support greenhouses for vegetables, flowers, and fruits. Locals are also known for their love of baked goods and obscenely hot geothermal swimming pools, and they have declared their town the flower capital of the island.

GETTING HERE AND AROUND

Hveragerði is along the Ring Road, aka Highway 1. There are frequent daily buses from the Mjódd Terminal in Reykjavík; Strætó Buses 51 and 52 stop at the petrol station by the main road in Hveragerði.

VISITOR INFORMATION

Right off the Ring Road, located in the Sunnumörk shopping center, you will find a tourist center. It has a good selection of maps, brochures, and souvenirs as well as free Wi-Fi.

CONTACTS Regional Information Center.
☒ *Sunnumörk 2–4, Hveragerði* ☏ *483–4601* ⊕ *www.hveragerdi.is.*

Sights

The Geothermal Energy Exhibition

OTHER ATTRACTION | All of Iceland's electricity comes from renewable sources and 90% of Icelandic homes use geothermal water for heat. If you are interested in seeing how this sustainable energy system works, you should visit the Geothermal Energy Exhibition at the Hellisheiði Power Plant, the largest single-site geothermal unit in the world. People of all ages can learn about geothermal utilization via interactive installations and displays. Afterward, you can check out the gift shop and take in the moonlike landscape while enjoying some treats at the on-site café. ☒ *Hellisheiðavirkjun, Hveragerði* ✛ *Located off the Ring Rd. about 20 mins from Reykjavík, before you arrive at Hveragerði* ☏ *591–2880* ⊕ *www.geothermalexhibition.com* ☒ *ISK 1,990.*

NLFÍ - Health Clinic and Spa

HOT SPRING | **FAMILY** | This clinic is where Icelanders come to regain their health and peace of mind. Spa treatments like deep-heat mud baths and massages are available to both visitors and prescription-bearing patients. Before and after treatments you are welcome to use the hot tub, sauna, or swimming pool. There is also an on-site restaurant that offers healthy dishes made mostly from local ingredients. ✉ *Grænumörk 10, Hveragerði* ☎ *483–0300* 🌐 *www.heilsustofnun.is* 🎫 *Mud bath: ISK 6,400.*

The Quake 2008

HISTORY MUSEUM | FAMILY | In May 2008 a massive earthquake (6.3 magnitude) struck the southern part of Iceland. The epicenter of the quake was about 2 km (1 mile) southeast of Hveragerði, so many buildings in this area suffered severe damage. This exhibition, located in the Sunnumörk shopping center, relates personal accounts of the earthquake and displays photographs and surveillance camera footage. Visible through the floor of the building is an earthquake crack that is thought to be around 5,000 years old. At the exhibition there is also an earthquake simulator, so visitors can experience for themselves what a powerful earthquake feels like. ✉ *Sunnumörk 2, Hveragerði* ☎ *483–4601* 🌐 *www.hveragerdi.is* 🎫 *Free (small fee for earthquake simulator).*

Reykjadalur

TRAIL | A beautiful hiking trail leads from Hveragerði to Reykjadalur (Steam Valley). The colorful hills, waterfall, and natural hot springs make it very popular with tourists and locals alike. At the end of the trail, you can bathe in a geothermal river surrounded by green hills and the occasional roaming lambs. The hike takes about an hour and a half. ✉ *Reykjadalur, Hveragerði* ✣ *Trail starts about 1 km (1/2 mile) from Ring Rd.*

Sundlaugin Laugaskarði

POOL | FAMILY | The charming little geothermal swimming pool in Hveragerði was once the biggest in Iceland. Although that's no longer the case, it still has a special characteristic: as a "constant stream" pool—heated with steam coming directly from the ground—the water is considered by many to have health benefits. The setting around the pool is green and lovely, and it has one of the best natural saunas in the country. ✉ *Laugaskarð, Reyjamörk, Hveragerði* ☎ *483–4113* 🌐 *www.facebook.com/laugaskard* 🎫 *ISK 1,050.*

🍴 Restaurants

Almar Bakarí

$ | BAKERY | Stop at this local bakery for a taste of Icelandic pastries—be sure to try *ástarpungar* (deep-fried sweet bread with raisins), *snúður* (Icelandic cinnamon buns), or *kókoskúla* (sweet bread mixed with cocoa). They also serve fresh sandwiches, salads, and soups with sourdough bread. **Known for:** indoor and outdoor seating; cakes for special occasions; sweet Icelandic treats. [$] *Average main: ISK700* ✉ *Sunnumörk 2, Hveragerði* ☎ *483–1919* 🌐 *www.almarbakari.is.*

Mathöll Suðurlands

$$ | ECLECTIC | High-end food halls are a big trend in Iceland—and Mathöll Suðurlands is right up there with the best of them. Part of the Greenhouse hotel and shopping center, it offers a number of established and up-and-coming eateries. **Known for:** Yuzu's kimchi-smothered chicken burgers; cocktails at the Nýlendubarinn; option to have Asian-style fried noodles, fresh ice cream, and a few tacos for dinner. [$] *Average main: ISK2,800* ✉ *Austurmörk 6, Hveragerði* ☎ *464–7336* 🌐 *www.thegreenhouse.is.*

★ Ölverk Pizza and Brewery

$$ | PIZZA | FAMILY | Tucked away in this small town is a local brewery that uses geothermal energy to make quirky and tasty beers and eclectic and delicious wood-fired pizzas. The selection of draft beers changes depending on what concoction these master brewers made that week, but expect to find very creative ingredients—many of which are local. **Known for:** the Ölverk beer flight; pretzel with beer cheese dip; lots of unique pizza toppings (if you're adventurous, try the one with bananas). [$] *Average main:*

ISK2,950 ✉ *Breiðumörk 2, Hveragerði* ☎ *483–3030* 🌐 *www.olverk.is.*

★ Varma Restaurant

$$$$ | **SCANDINAVIAN** | This elegant restaurant is set in a glass solarium with panoramic views of the river Varmá and a beautiful green valley. It honors the Icelandic geothermal cooking technique where hot springs are used to cook delicacies from local, seasonal ingredients. **Known for:** lamb fillet cooked 12 hours in the hot spring; incredible hot spring–cooked chocolate cake; chef's specialty includes an array of Icelandic dishes. [$] *Average main: ISK5,620* ✉ *Hverhamrar, Hveragerði* ☎ *483–4959* 🌐 *www.frostandfire.is* ⏲ *No lunch.*

Hotels

Frost and Fire Hotel

$$$ | **HOTEL** | **FAMILY** | Sitting proudly alongside the Varmá River, the Frost and Fire hotel offers proximity to nature while just a short walk from shops and restaurants. **Pros:** sizzling sauna and hot tubs fed by the hotel's private borehole; terrific views of the countryside; breakfast sourced from local farms. **Cons:** small guest rooms; rooms could use an update; views from rooms vary based on price. [$] *Rooms from: ISK37,000* ✉ *Hverhamar, Hveragerði* ☎ *483–4959* 🌐 *www.frostandfire.is* 🛏 *22 rooms* 🍴 *Free Breakfast.*

The Greenhouse Hotel

$$ | **HOTEL** | This leafy locale feels distinctly upscale, with lots of plants, high-end design, cozy rooms, and a trendy clientele. **Pros:** gorgeous roof terrace; fantastic food options; trendy design and atmosphere with an eco-friendly ethos. **Cons:** weekend nights can get noisy outside; food hall gets extremely busy; rooms are small. [$] *Rooms from: ISK22,400* ✉ *Austurmörk 6, Hveragerði* ☎ *464–7336* 🌐 *www.thegreenhouse.is* 🛏 *49 rooms* 🍴 *No Meals.*

Hotel Eldhestar

$ | **HOTEL** | **FAMILY** | This charming country hotel dedicated to the Icelandic horse is located right off the Ring Road, only a few minutes' drive from Hveragerði. **Pros:** eco-friendly hotel; spacious farm-to-table restaurant on-site; horse stables nearby. **Cons:** outdoor areas can sometimes smell a little horsey; basic breakfast; noise from hot tub and common areas sometimes travels to rooms. [$] *Rooms from: ISK19,000* ✉ *Eldhestar Hotel, Suðurlandsvegur, Hveragerði* ☎ *480–4800* 🌐 *www.hoteleldhestar.is* 🛏 *37 rooms* 🍴 *Free Breakfast.*

Shopping

Vínbúðin

WINE/SPIRITS | In Iceland you can only buy beverages stronger than 2.25% ABV in state-owned liquor stores called Vínbúðin. In Hveragerði you will find Víbúðin inside Sunnumörk, the shopping center facing the Ring Road. ✉ *Sunnumörk 2, Hveragerði* ☎ *481–3932* 🌐 *www.vinbudin.is.*

Activities

★ Eldhestar

HORSEBACK RIDING | **FAMILY** | Since the 10th century, it has been forbidden to import horses to Iceland, which has resulted in a unique horse breed that Icelanders take pride in. One special characteristic of the Icelandic horse is that it has five different gaits: in addition to the normal walk, trot, and gallop, there is also *tölt* and *skeið* (flying pace). If you fancy meeting these majestic creatures and exploring Icelandic nature in a new way, you should stop by Eldhestar, right outside of Hveragerði. One of the most well-established riding companies in Iceland, they offer a wide variety of tours—from short tours for beginners to multiday tours that include accommodations and meals. One of their more popular day tours is the "Horses and Hot Springs" day tour, where the group stops for a dip in a steaming natural pool. ⊠ *Suðurlandsvegur, Hveragerði* ☎ *480–4800* ⊕ *www.eldhestar.is.*

Selfoss

14 km (9 miles) southeast of Hveragerði.

Located by the rapid river Ölfusá, Selfoss is an important trade hub and the largest town in South Iceland, with around 7,000 residents. The Ring Road runs right through town, so it's home to a wide variety of excellent restaurants and small local stores.

GETTING HERE AND AROUND
The Ring Road (Route 1) is the main street through Selfoss. Most buses from Reykjavík to Höfn, including those from Reykjavík Excursions, stop at the N1 gas station in Selfoss. Strætó Buses 51 and 52 both stop in Selfoss on their way from Reykjavík. To continue on your journey, Strætó buses 72, 73, and 75 all go from Selfoss further east.

TOURIST INFORMATION
You will find the tourist information office Located within the Penninn Eymundson bookstore in the center of Selfoss. There you can access free maps of the region as well as service lists and free Wi-Fi.

CONTACTS Selfoss Area Information Office. ⊠ *Penninn Eymundson, Brúarstræti 6, Selfoss* ☎ *540–2316* ⊕ *www.south.is.*

 Sights

Bobby Fischer Center
HISTORY MUSEUM | FAMILY | In a beautiful old white house is this biographical museum with memorabilia from the 11th World Chess Champion, Bobby Fischer. The American earned the title when he defeated the Soviet chess grandmaster and reigning World Champion Boris Spassky in Reykjavík in the summer of 1972. Taking place at the height of the Cold War, it is considered by many to be the match of the 20th century. On display are items from the event and curios related to Fischer's time in Iceland from 2005 to 2008. Fischer is buried a few hundred meters away at the Laugardælir cemetery. ⊠ *Austurvegur 21, Selfoss* ☎ *894–1275* ⊕ *www.fischersetur.is* 🖭 *ISK 1,000* ⊙ *Closed Sept.–May.*

Íslenski Bærinn Turf House
HISTORIC HOME | Until the modern era, Icelanders lived primarily in turf houses, dwellings covered with a grassy roof for insulation against extreme weather. While most have been lost to time, a few have been meticulously preserved, including this gem just outside of Selfoss. Stop by to admire the architecture and learn about the old days of the island at their tiny museum. They also occasionally offer classes and workshops on traditional Icelandic tools and handicrafts—check their Facebook page to see the latest updates. ⊠ *Austur Meðalholt, Selfoss* ☎ *694–8108* ⊕ *www.islenskibaerinn.is* 🖭 *ISK 1,600* ⊙ *Closed Sept.–May.*

Kerið
NATURE SIGHT | This 3,000-year-old volcanic crater makes for a scenic stop on the Golden Circle route. In the middle of the crater is a striking blue lake that you can walk around and explore. ⊠ *Kerið, Selfoss* ✛ *15 km (9 miles) north of Selfoss, right off Rte. 35* 🖭 *ISK 400.*

Sólheimar Ecovillage
TOWN | FAMILY | Possibly the oldest eco-village in the world, Sólheimar was established 80 years ago. Around 100 people of different backgrounds and abilities live in the sunny village. Together they sustainably run six creative art workshops, an organic bakery, and a café. They also practice forestry and horticulture. Vala, the market and art gallery, sells exquisite woodcrafts, handmade candles, face masks, and more. ⊠ *Sólheimar, Selfoss* ☎ *422–6000* ⊕ *www.solheimar.is.*

Sundhöll Selfoss

POOL | **FAMILY** | Right in the heart of Selfoss you will find one of the biggest swimming pools in the south of Iceland. Sundhöllin has both indoor and outdoor swimming, a children's pool, sauna, ice baths, and hot tubs. They also offer indoor and outdoor changing rooms and wheelchair access. It's open late on weekdays (until 9:30 pm), which makes it a perfect stop after dinner. ⊠ *Tryggvagata 15, Selfoss* ☎ *480–1960* ⊕ *www.facebook.com/sundhollselfoss* ☐ *ISK 1,100.*

Tré og list

ART GALLERY | **FAMILY** | In an old converted cowshed on the banks of the beautiful Þjórsár, you will find a peculiar gallery founded by the couple Ólafur Sigurjónsso and Bergþóra Guðbergsdóttir. Inside is an old church organ that was deemed beyond repair after the volcanic eruption in Vestmanneyjar, as well as exquisite woodcraft pieces from local artist Sigga á Grund and old farming tools from the municipality. ⊠ *Forsæti í Flóa, Forsæti 5, Selfoss* ☎ *894–4835* ⊕ *www.treoglist.is.*

Urriðafoss

WATERFALL | This might not be the biggest waterfall in Iceland, but it's one of the most powerful, boasting the highest average water flow of any Icelandic waterfall, and the second in all of Europe. There is a small parking area and visitor's center. ⊠ *Urriðafossvegur, Selfoss.*

🍴 Restaurants

Bókakaffið

$ | **CAFÉ** | **FAMILY** | There is something so soothing about being surrounded by stacks of books. This bookstore-café right in the center of Selfoss offers coffee, lovely pastries, a selection of books in English, and a piano that is always in tune. **Known for:** local hangout; accommodating to vegans and those with food allergies; hot chocolate to warm you up in winter. $ *Average main: ISK600*

⊠ *Austurvegur 22, Selfoss* ☎ *482–3079* ⊕ *www.bokakaffid.is* ⊙ *Closed Sun.*

★ Friðheimar

$$ | **CAFÉ** | Iceland might not be a place you'd normally associate with the production of delicious tomatoes, but thanks to the abundance of geothermal energy, hothouses like those at Friðheimar can produce more than 300 tons of them a year. At its greenhouse café—a popular stop with those traveling on the Golden Circle route—its juicy variety of tomato is the star ingredient of every dish on the menu, including the superlative soup, the bizarrely good tomato ice cream, and perhaps the best Bloody Mary you'll ever have. **Known for:** focaccia with deliciously creative toppings; truly spectacular tomatoes in a variety of forms; advance reservations needed. $ *Average main: ISK1,300* ⊠ *Friðheimar* ☎ *486–8894* ⊕ *www.fridheimar.is.*

Græna Kannan

$ | **CAFÉ** | **FAMILY** | Located inside a high-ceilinged greenhouse, this organic café only serves products made from organically cultivated foodstuffs, with most of its pastries coming from the bakery in town. Experience the unique, positive atmosphere in Sólheimar while enjoying food and drink made with love. **Known for:** reservations required in winter; great place to mingle with locals; various events held here during summer. $ *Average main: ISK800* ⊠ *Sólheimar, Selfoss* ☎ *422–6070* ⊕ *www.solheimar.is.*

Ísbúð Huppu

$ | **ICE CREAM** | **FAMILY** | If there are two things Icelanders love, it's swimming pools and ice cream. This charming ice-cream parlor offers delicious flavors, including Icelandic favorites like Bragarefur as well as the Icelandic version of gelato. **Known for:** classic ice cream done perfectly; bragðarefur, an old-time favorite amongst Icelanders; huppu shake. $ *Average main: ISK850* ⊠ *Eyrarvegur 2, Selfoss* ☎ *482–1311* ⊕ *www.isbudhuppu.is.*

Kaffi Krús

$$ | **INTERNATIONAL** | **FAMILY** | Located in a bright yellow historic house right by the river, Kaffi Krús has fed locals and tourists alike for over 25 years. In its charming setting, which is furnished with a mix of modern and antique pieces, they offer a variety of great pizzas, burgers, and cakes. **Known for:** 16 varieties of homemade cakes; truly satisfying salads; the perfect late-night combo farmers' brie and Bóndi Icelandic beer. [$] *Average main: ISK2,990* ✉ *Austurvegur 7, Selfoss* ☎ *482–1266* 🌐 *www.kaffikrus.is.*

Tommi's Burger Joint

$$ | **BURGER** | **FAMILY** | If you just want a tasty, well-priced burger, some fries, and no fuss, stop by Tommi's famous burger joint in Selfoss. They serve simple, juicy burgers (both beef and vegetarian) in a space full of American and Icelandic pop culture references. **Known for:** great burgers at a good price; delicious milkshakes; extra béarnaise sauce to dip your fries in. [$] *Average main: ISK2,390* ✉ *Eyrarvegur 32, Selfoss* ☎ *571–8288* 🌐 *www.tommis.is.*

★ Tryggvaskáli Restaurant

$$$$ | **SCANDINAVIAN** | Located in the oldest house in Selfoss, Tryggvaskáli takes you back a century to the sitting room of an upper-class family. Allow yourself to feel like the honorary guest at a dinner party; your hosts will offer excellent Icelandic and international farm-to-table dishes. **Known for:** signature dish of slow-cooked salmon; traditional Icelandic desserts; mismatched antiques that give a cozy but elegant vibe. [$] *Average main: ISK4,550* ✉ *Austurvegur 2, Selfoss* ☎ *482–1390* 🌐 *www.tryggvaskali.is.*

Hotels

★ Camp Boutique

$$ | **HOTEL** | Imagine getting to experience the Icelandic wilderness firsthand, except with high-end furniture, cozy carpets, and a heated mattress—enter Camp Boutique, Iceland's prime destination for glamping. **Pros:** unforgettable and unique experience; stylish decor; private black-sand beach is but a walk away. **Cons:** far away from restaurants, stores, and other necessities; experience is largely dependent on weather; shared kitchen facilities and bathroom. [$] *Rooms from: ISK24,500* ✉ *Loftsstaðir – Vestri, Selfoss* ☎ *848–5805* 🌐 *www.campboutique.is* 🛏 *12 tents* 🍴 *No Meals.*

Bubble Hotel Iceland

$$$ | **HOTEL** | For a once in a lifetime experience, sleep under the Midnight Sun or the northern lights in a luxurious bubble, with unforgettable nighttime vistas. **Pros:** peaceful and quiet; comfortable and warm beds; insane views if the weather is good. **Cons:** experience is largely dependent on weather; shared bathrooms and showers; bubbles are somewhat close together. [$] *Rooms from: ISK34,900* ✉ *Ölvisholt, Selfoss* ☎ *773–4444* 🌐 *www.buubble.com* 🕒 *Closed Sept.–May* 🛏 *5 bubbles* 🍴 *No Meals.*

Guesthouse Bitra

$$ | **B&B/INN** | **FAMILY** | Located in the beautiful Flóahrepp countryside, right along Route 1 near Selfoss and Hveragerði, this guesthouse with views over the mountain Hekla was initially built as a women's prison (though those plans were never realized). **Pros:** delicious breakfast buffet; great location for activites like hiking, horseback riding, and fishing; views of mountain Hekla. **Cons:** basement rooms tend to run colder than others; rooms are basic if spacious; 17 rooms share two bathrooms. [$] *Rooms from: ISK24,000* ✉ *Suðurlandsvegur, Bitruvegur, Selfoss* ☎ *480–0700* 🌐 *www.guesthousebitra.is* 🛏 *17 rooms* 🍴 *Free Breakfast.*

Hótel Selfoss

$$ | **HOTEL** | **FAMILY** | Sitting on the banks of the grand river Ölfusá with views of the nearby mountain, Hótel Selfoss offers tranquility just a few minutes' walk to the town center, with all its restaurants and

shops. **Pros:** hotel spa offers massage services and various beauty treatments; bar with happy hour specials; close to the Ring Road, river, and town center. **Cons:** design and furniture are a bit dated in the old wing; breakfast is only adequate; noise travels from room to room. [$] *Rooms from: ISK30,000* ✉ *Eyrarvegur 2, Selfoss* ☎ *480–2500* 🌐 *www.hotelselfoss.is* 🛏 *139 rooms* 🍴 *Free Breakfast.*

Julia's Guesthouse

$ | B&B/INN | FAMILY | The sweet Julia from Switzerland runs a charming country guesthouse that is home to cats, birds, and even a bunny. **Pros:** great location both for the Golden Circle and for getting back to Reykjavík; reasonable rates; ideal for animal lovers. **Cons:** not suitable for those allergic to cats; shared bathrooms and showers (the triple room has its own bathroom); credit cards not accepted. [$] *Rooms from: ISK10,000* ✉ *Hnaus, Selfoss* ☎ *856–4788* 🌐 *www.julias-guesthouse.com* 💳 *No credit cards* 🛏 *3 rooms* 🍴 *Free Breakfast.*

Shopping

Gallery Flói

CRAFTS | Behind a green door, right off the main road that leads through Selfoss, is a collection of beautiful curios waiting to be discovered. Gallery Flói is the pride of Fanndís Hulda, a local artist who makes glass beads, ceramics, handmade soaps in the shape of lambs, and much more, all of which are popular gift items with locals and tourists alike. ✉ *Þingborg 1, Selfoss* ☎ *868–7486* 🌐 *www.galleryfloi.com.*

Hannyrðabúðin

OTHER SPECIALTY STORE | While traveling through Iceland, you will come across beautiful handknit sweaters in all kinds of colors and patterns. If you already know how to knit or you want to learn, this store offers kits with everything you need to make a traditional Icelandic sweater that will last you a lifetime. ✉ *Eyravegur 23, Selfoss* ☎ *555–1314* 🌐 *www.hannyrd-abudin.is.*

Selfoss Centre

SHOPPING CENTER | Featuring 10 restaurants and a selection of shops, the Selfoss Centre is a must-visit. Art lovers can pick up some local pieces at the Listasel Gallery co-op while fashionistas can drool over the clothes and jewelry at Kalli Úr and Motive. And no visit is complete without a bouquet of fresh flowers from 1905 Blómahús. ✉ *Eyravegur 1, Selfoss* ☎ *454–0800* 🌐 *www.selfoss.com.*

Sveitabúðin Sóley

SOUVENIRS | Stop by this charming little gift shop, located 7 km (4½ miles) east of Stokkseyri and 14 km (8½ miles) south of Selfoss, and have a look at the wide variety of beautiful Icelandic- and European-designed items on display. If you're lucky, the staff will offer you some coffee on the house and a map of South Iceland filled with local insight. Shop hours vary; check the website or give them a call. ✉ *Tunga, Selfoss* ☎ *699–1961* 🌐 *www.tunga.is.*

Þingborg

OTHER SPECIALTY STORE | This nonprofit wool workshop is housed in an old white house by the Ring Road. Since the 1990s, local women have been knitting here and selling their wares, including *lopapeysa* (the iconic Icelandic wool sweater that has kept Icelanders warm for centuries). They also sell yarn and knitting needles, so visitors can learn how to make their own sweaters. ✉ *Gamla Þingborg, Selfoss* ✥ *Near the Ring Rd.* ☎ *482–1027* 🌐 *www.thingborg.is.*

Activities

Sólhestar

HORSEBACK RIDING | FAMILY | This family-run company of almost 10 years offers hour-long tours where beginners and children get to know the friendly and petite Icelandic horse. They also have exciting day-long and multi-day tours for

Raufarhólshellir is the fourth-largest lava cave to be discovered in Iceland.

more experienced riders. Located only 10 minutes from Selfoss and 30 minutes from Reykjavík, riding tours take place by the majestic Ölfusá river and the feet of the beautiful Ingólfsfjall mountain. ⊠ *Borgargerði, Selfoss* ☎ *892–3066* ⊕ *www. solhestar.is.*

Eyrarbakki

12 km (7 miles) southwest of Selfoss.

Eyrarbakki and its neighbor fishing village Stokkseyri, 6 km (4 miles) apart, are often regarded as sibling towns because of their history and proximity. The two towns are backed by the beautiful, black seaside, with colorful houses and friendly inhabitants. The towns are both located between two glacial rivers, Ölfusá and Þjórsá.

GETTING HERE AND AROUND

From Selfoss, both Eyrarbakki and Stokkseyri can be reached in about 10 minutes by car. Stokkseyri and Eyrarbakki can also be accessed through the less traveled but beautiful South Coast Road. From Grindavík take Route 42 (the South Coast Road) that will lead you through the town of Þorlákshöfn. When you exit Þorlákshöfn, take Route 38 and take a right turn at Route 34.

 Sights

Konubókastofa

LIBRARY | The Women's Book Room celebrates Icelandic female authors. Rannveig Anna Jónsdóttir conceived this small nonprofit entity after realizing that many books written by Icelandic women were out of print, obscure, or difficult to obtain. More than 3,000 books written by some 600 authors are now on display in two rooms of the historical Blátún building at Eyrarbakki. It shares the building with the local public library, which is housed on the second floor. ⊠ *Túngata 40, Eyrarbakki* ☎ *862–0110* ⊕ *www.konubokastofa.is* 🗗 *Free* ⊙ *Usually closed Mon.–Sat. but opening hours vary.*

★ **Raufarhólshellir**

CAVE | At 1,360 meters, the Lava Tunnel is the fourth-longest lava cave discovered in Iceland. The cave is remarkably spacious—from 10 to 30 meters wide and up to 10 meters tall—making it quite easy and accessible for most people. Walking along the lava's 5,200-year-old path is a humbling experience in itself, and the views of the geological formations and spectacular colors are extraordinary. In winter, big crystal-like ice sculptures form inside the cave entrance. The standard Lava Tunnel tour takes about an hour. ✉ *Þorlákshafnarvegur, Eyrarbakki* ☎ *760–1000* 🌐 *www.thelavatunnel.is* 🎫 *ISK 7,400.*

Strandarkirkja

CHURCH | "The miracle church," as it often called by locals, was built in the 12th century. The southern coast of Iceland is known for its severe weather, rough coast, and hidden reefs. Legend has it that a group of sailors were negotiating with God while trying to get back to harbor in a bad storm and promised to build a new church wherever the ship landed. Suddenly a light appeared in the sky and guided the sailors to shore. The sailors kept their promise, and the bay nearby was named Engilsvík (Angel's Bay). Since then, Icelanders have donated to Strandarkirkja when their family is going through rough times in hopes that their prayers will be answered. ✉ *Selvogi, Eyrarbakki* ☎ *483–3771.*

Restaurants

Hafið Bláa

$$$ | **SEAFOOD** | **FAMILY** | Three kilometers west of Eyrarbakki, this seafood restaurant sits almost right on the ocean—surprisingly uncommon in Iceland. Hafið bláa serves fresh seafood and very sweet Icelandic desserts. **Known for:** must-try fish soup; fantastic views; quite a scenic spot to see the northern lights. [$] *Average main: ISK3,850* ✉ *Óseyri, Eyrarbakki* ☎ *483–1000* 🌐 *www.hafidblaa.is* 🕒 *Closed Mon. and Tues.*

Rauða Húsið

$$$$ | **SEAFOOD** | Eyrarbakki's only restaurant can be found in a stately red house facing the town church. Thankfully, it happens to serve one of the best lobster soups in the south of Iceland. **Known for:** perfect chocolate lava cake; creamy lobster soup; Icelandic country romance. [$] *Average main: ISK5,500* ✉ *Búðarstígur 4* ☎ *483–3330* 🌐 *www.raudahusid.is.*

Hotels

Seaside Cottages

$$ | **B&B/INN** | These modest yet beautiful country-inspired cottages are located just a few steps from the North Atlantic Ocean. **Pros:** quiet atmosphere; scenic and romantic location; clean and well equipped. **Cons:** only one of the cottages has a washing machine; the smaller cottage may be too small for more than two people; poor cell phone reception. [$] *Rooms from: ISK25,000* ✉ *Eyrargata 37a, Eyrarbakki* ☎ *898–1197* 🌐 *www.seasidecottages.is* 🛏 *2 cottages* 🍴 *No Meals.*

Shopping

Laugabúð

SOUVENIRS | In this charming little corrugated iron house you will find traditional sweets, handmade soaps, and postcards depicting views of Eyrarbakki. Stepping into the shop feels like entering a small museum; it is styled after a convenience store managed by the legendary Guðlaugar Pálsson from 1919 until his death in 1993. Be aware that it's only open on weekends. ✉ *Eyrargata 46, Eyrarbakki* ☎ *483–1443.*

Stokkseyri

6 km (3½ miles) south of Eyrarbakki.

Stokkseyri is an unusual fishing village with a mystical air about it. With activities like kayaking, museum hopping, and ghost hunting, this town has something for everyone.

GETTING HERE AND AROUND

From Selfoss, both Route 34 and Route 33 will lead you to Stokkseyri. Route 34 leads you through Eyrarbakki on your way to Stokkseyri. Stokkseyri can also be reached from the town of Þorlákshöfn; take Route 38 until you reach Route 34, and turn right.

Sights

Draugasetrið (*Ghost Center of Iceland*)

OTHER ATTRACTION | **FAMILY** | Get to know some of the most notorious ghosts of Icelandic history while being guided through a 1,000-square-meter maze at the Menningarverstöðin (cultural center) in Stokkseyri. The Ghost Center can be found on the third floor, and on the first floor, you will find the Icelandic Wonders Museum, which is dedicated to elves and the northern lights. According to Icelandic legend, ghosts can appear in all shapes or forms, and some of them may still roam the halls today. ⊠ *Menningarverstöðin, Hafnargata 9, Stokkseyri* 🕾 *895–0020* ⊕ *www.draugasetrid.is* 🎫 *ISK 2,000* ☉ *Closed Sun.–Fri. in fall and winter.*

Sundlaugin Stokkseyri

POOL | **FAMILY** | On a slow day, you might just find yourself alone at this casual little swimming pool in the center of town. The hot tubs are a great place to meet locals, so don't be afraid to say hello. ⊠ *Stjörnusteinar 1a, Stokkseyri* 🕾 *480–3260* 🎫 *ISK 1,100.*

Þuríðarbúð

MUSEUM VILLAGE | If you would like to see where the brave fisherman that battled the North Atlantic Sea slept and ate during their days ashore in the 18th and 19th centuries, check out this restored turf house. It once belonged to Þuríður Einarsdóttir, one of the few female boat captains in Iceland. ⊠ *Strandgata, Stokkseyri* 🕾 *483–1504.*

Restaurants

Fjöruborðið

$$$$ | **SEAFOOD** | **FAMILY** | The highlight of Fjöruborðið is the incredible lobster tail. Pay a bit more for the side order of veggies with couscous, and you're on your way to culinary delirium. **Known for:** langoustine soup worth the hour drive; advanced reservations needed; incredible, food coma-inducing three-course menu. $ *Average main: ISK6,350* ⊠ *Eyrarbraut 3a* 🕾 *483–1550* ⊕ *www.fjorubordid.is.*

Hotels

Guesthouse Heba

$ | **B&B/INN** | **FAMILY** | The lovely Heba and her husband run this four-room bed and breakfast in a beautiful dark green house facing the ocean. **Pros:** delicious home-made breakfasts; great view of the North Atlantic Ocean; quiet and comfortable. **Cons:** quite small; far from amenities; quarters may be too close for some. $ *Rooms from: ISK18,000* ⊠ *Íragerði 12, Stokkseyri* 🕾 *565–0354* ⊕ *www.guesthouseheba.com* 🛏 *4 rooms* 🍴 *Free Breakfast.*

Kvöldstjarnan Guesthouse

$$$ | **B&B/INN** | **FAMILY** | In a modern yet cozy guesthouse in Stokkseyri are two bright apartments—one that sleeps up to five people and the other seven. **Pros:** great for families; big hot tub outside; friendly owners. **Cons:** no single rooms; two-night minimum; few options for dinner in this small village. $ *Rooms from: ISK39,000* ⊠ *Stjörnusteinn 7, Stokkseyri* 🕾 *483–1800* ⊕ *www.kvoldstjarnan.is* 🛏 *2 apartments* 🍴 *Free Breakfast.*

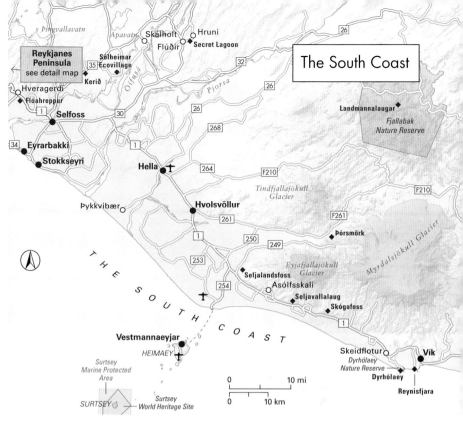

The South Coast

Activities

Kayakferðir Stokkseyri

KAYAKING | FAMILY | Explore the nature and bird life around Stokkseyri with this kayak tour operator, founded in 1995. The area consists of small and large ponds connected by narrow canals that are visited by wild birds and seals. At times all you see is high grass, which is a refreshing change from endless lava fields and moss. The tours are also an incredible value compared to many other kayaking tours in Iceland—a two-hour tour will only set you back ISK 5,500. ⊠ *Heiðarbrún 12a, Stokkseyri* ✚ *Right next to the swimming pool* ☎ *695–2058* ⊕ *www.kajak.is* ✆ *Closed Oct.–May.*

Hella and Hvolsvöllur

Hella is 51 km (32 miles) east of Stokkseyri, Hvolsvöllur is 14 km (9 miles) southeast of Hella.

Hella is a small agricultural community that sits on the banks of the river Ytri-Ranga. Home to the world's largest Icelandic horse show, it's one of Iceland's most important horse-breeding areas. On good weather days, you can see the volcano Hekla watching over the town.

The Ring Road runs through the small town of Hvolsvölllur, east of Hella. The towns surrounding this area feature prominently in "Njáls Saga," one of the most famous old Icelandic sagas. Today the town provides services for the surrounding farms and the area's ever-growing tourism industry.

You're likely to see a rainbow at Skógafoss, a waterfall that is 60 meters high.

GETTING HERE AND AROUND

The Ring Road passes through Hella on its way east. Frequent buses stop at the Olís Petrol Staion in Hella, including Reykjavík Excursions. Likewise, Strætó Bus 51 stops at Hella daily on its way from Reykjavík to Höfn as does Bus 52.

VISITOR INFORMATION

Located right off the Ring Road, the staff here will provide you with maps as well as information about the region and guided tours.

CONTACTS Árhús Information Center Hella. ✉ *Rangárbakkar 6, Hella* ☎ *487–5577* ⊕ *www.arhus.is.*

 Sights

Caves Of Hella

CAVE | **FAMILY** | Ancient crosses, wall carvings, and carved seats decorate twelve mysterious caves outside of Hella. Filled with historical remains, they have only recently begun to be excavated—and researchers already think they might predate the Vikings. Four are currently open to the public, but take note that you're only allowed to see the caves on guided tours, which are offered in English every day at 12 and 4 pm. ✉ *Ægissíða 4, Hella* ☎ *620–6100* ⊕ *www.cavesofhella.is* 🎟 *ISK 3,900.*

Landmannalaugar

NATURE PRESERVE | Accessible only during summer, Landmannalaugar is a vast area of stunning natural beauty located in the remote southern highlands. It sits about 600 meters above sea level in the Fjallabak Nature Reserve, between a glacial river and lava field that was formed in the 15th century. With its dazzling multicolored rhyolite mountains, a blue lake inside a red crater, and bubbling geothermal areas, it becomes a popular hang-out in the summer. The spot is also the starting point for the famed Laugavegur hike, an advanced multi-day trek that connects Landmannalaugar and Þórsmörk. From June to September, buses run daily from Reykjavík to Landmannalaugar and back by Reykjavík Excursions. And don't forget to take a soak in the hot springs while here. ✉ *Hella ⚓ Hrauneyjar via Route F208 from Hvolsvöllur (182 km from Reykjavík).*

LAVA Centre

SCIENCE MUSEUM | FAMILY | In the town of Hvolsvöllur, take an educational break and learn about how this volcanic island was shaped by countless eruptions. At the LAVA Centre you are introduced to the 32 volcanic systems in Iceland. There is an interactive scene that reveals the wonders of volcanic activity, a film about local volcanoes, and a balcony that offers you a panoramic view of four dormant volcanoes. ✉ *Austurvegur 14, Hvolsvöllur* ☎ *415–5200* ⊕ *www.lavacentre.is* 🎟 *ISK 3,990.*

The Saga Centre and Valhalla Restaurant

HISTORY MUSEUM | FAMILY | Njáls Saga— the most famous of the medieval Sagas of Icelanders—is told through a lively exhibition here at the Saga Centre. Only a 10-minute drive from Hella lies Hvolsvöllur, the town where it took place over a thousand years ago. Set in the settlement age, you will learn the stories of war heroes, family feuds, and Icelandic politics. To satisfy your hunger after immersing yourself in the saga, Valhalla Restaurant is located on-site; they serve beer and pub food like pulled pork, burgers, and fries. ✉ *Hlíðarvegur 14, Hvolsvöllur* ☎ *487–8781.*

★ Seljalandsfoss

WATERFALL | This waterfall is situated right off the ring road, so anyone who drives by can't help but marvel at its majesty. Seljalandsfoss is 65 meters tall and its special trait is that you can walk behind it. Be ready to be heavily drizzled by the fresh mountain water but be careful because the steps can be slippery. Bathroom facilities and a small coffee shop can be found by the parking lot. There are also lots of beautiful short walking paths all around the waterfall that can easily add to this unique experience. ✉ *Þorsmerkurvegur, Hvolsvöllur.*

Seljavallalaug

HOT SPRING | In a narrow valley beneath the now world-famous Eyjafjallajökull is one of the more authentic geothermal baths around, with the hot springs from the mountain running straight into the pool. The 25-meter pool was built in 1923 and is considered semi-abandoned and therefore is free of charge. There are changing rooms next to the pool— though they are basic and often dirty. Granted, Seljavallalaug might not be the hottest hot spring around—it's more often than not a tepid warm—but the peaceful atmosphere more than makes up for it. ✉ *Seljavallalaug, Hvolsvöllur* ⚓ *From Rte. 1 take Rte. 242 to Seljavellir, and then it is a 15-minute walk from the parking lot.*

★ Skógafoss

WATERFALL | Farther east, about 25 minutes away from Seljalandsfoss, you will find another falling beauty, framed in by green hills in the summer and ice during winter. The waterfall Skógafoss is located at Skógar, a small Icelandic village, south of the volcano Eyjafjallajökull. Skógafoss is around 60 meters high, 25 meters wide, and is square in shape. A steep staircase leads up to the top of the hill above the falls, and on the way up you will often see a rainbow. ✉ *Hvolsvöllur.*

★ Þórsmörk

NATURE PRESERVE | Sheltered between three towering glaciers (Tindfjallajökull, Eyjafjallajökull, and Mýrdalsjökull) and surrounded by three rivers (Krossá, Þröngá, and Markarfljót), is the Þórsmörk nature reserve. Named after the hammer-wielding Norse god Þór, it is among the most popular hiking destinations in Iceland. At Þórsmörk you will find snow-capped mountain ridges, twisted gorges, moss-covered caves, and hidden waterfalls. The area has scenic surprises around every corner, making it a true hiker's paradise. The views are especially dramatic in the fall when the whole valley turns into a spectacle of colors, from oranges, yellows, and reds to the ever-present lava black of the rock beneath. It can be hard to get to—effectively unreachable during winter—but it is worth the hassle. Þórsmörk cannot be reached in a regular car or even regular 4WDs. You will need to take an amphibious bus or travel with a guide in a Superjeep to cross the unpredictable and dangerous rivers that close off the valley to the south. ⊠ Hvolsvöllur ✛ 158 km from Reykjavík ⊕ www.volcanotrails.com.

Restaurants

★ Hotel Rangá Restaurant

$$$$ | SCANDINAVIAN | The large windows of this luxury country-lodge restaurant frame an engaging pastoral scene starring the bountiful Rangá (one of Iceland's best fishing rivers) with Hekla (a famous sleeping volcano known as "the Gateway to Hell") in the background. Here guests dine on a variety of locally sourced seasonal produce, and are often given the full VIP treatment from enthusiastic owner Friðrík, who takes great pride in everything from the presentation of the food to the minutiae of its preparation. **Known for:** sous vide salmon served with a labor-intensive dill vinaigrette; Christmas buffet in December; seasonal gourmet menu at reasonable prices. ⓢ Average main: ISK5,200 ⊠ Suðurlandsvegur ☎ 487–5700 ⊕ www.hotelranga.is.

HYGGE

$$$ | INTERNATIONAL | Housed in one of the oldest buildings in South Iceland, this restaurant offers a panoramic view of the golf course below and the four volcanoes that guard the beautiful area. They serve fusion dishes that combine local, seasonal ingredients with South American techniques. **Known for:** baked brie on garlic bread paired with Viking White Ale; chance to meet and chat with Icelandic golfers; fresh and filling Thai trout. ⓢ Average main: ISK3,550 ⊠ Strandarvöllur, Strönd, Hella ☎ 772–2247 ⊕ www.hyggeiceland.com.

Kanslarinn

$$ | AMERICAN | FAMILY | Simply put, Kanslarinn is like a classic American roadside diner with an Icelandic country twist. The space itself is not intended to impress, but their classic diner dishes and Icelandic favorites consistently deliver. **Known for:** meat soup the way Icelanders like it; free Wi-Fi; local delicacy of pepper steak from horsemeat. ⓢ Average main: ISK2,950 ⊠ Dynskálar 10c, Hella ☎ 487–5100.

Stracta Bistro

$$$ | INTERNATIONAL | FAMILY | A great option after a long day of traveling, this hotel restaurant offers an elegant but casual place to sit down and have a well-rounded Icelandic meal. They have an à la carte menu but also offer take-out box lunches for traveling guests. **Known for:** traditional Icelandic fish gratin; terrific vegan options; upscale atmosphere. ⓢ Average main: ISK3,200 ⊠ Rangárflatir 4, Hella ☎ 531–8010 ⊕ www.stractahotels.is.

🛏 Hotels

Hótel Anna

$$ | B&B/INN | A small, family-run hotel located between the two greatest waterfalls of the South, this romantic, old-fashioned spot serves excellent meals made from local ingredients in their restaurant. **Pros:** scenic hiking trails close to hotel; excellent lamb and steak served in restaurant; Jacuzzi and sauna open late. **Cons:** restaurant closes rather early; no amenities or restaurants nearby; few vegan options at restaurant. ⓢ Rooms from: ISK26,000 ⊠ Moldnúpur, Hvolsvöllur ☎ 487–8950 ⊕ www.hotelanna.is ⇄ 7 rooms ⓄⒾ Free Breakfast.

Hotel Rangá

$$$$ | HOTEL | This rustic four-star hotel with uniquely decorated themed rooms and outdoor Jacuzzis is located in the countryside just east of Hella. **Pros:** stunning location; excellent restaurant

(modern Nordic cuisine with French and Italian influences); celebrity hot spot. **Cons:** very hyped; decor is more "country" than "luxury"; few entertainment options at night. $ *Rooms from: ISK45,000* 🖾 *487–5700* ⊕ *www.hotelranga.is* 🛏 *51 rooms* ⏐○⏐ *Free Breakfast.*

★ Skálakot Manor Hotel
$$$$ | **B&B/INN** | Right by the root of a mountain lies this horse farm that has been in the same family for seven generations and their meticulously built, incredibly cozy yet luxurious manor. **Pros:** guided horseback rides to Seljalandsfoss from the hotel; luxurious guestrooms with cozy bathrobes and lovely selection of soaps; candlelit farm-to-table dinners in the dining room. **Cons:** standard breakfast; sauna and hot tub access costs extra; expensive. $ *Rooms from: ISK60,000* 🖾 *Skálakoti, Hvolsvöllur* 🖾 *487–8953* ⊕ *www.skalakot.is* 🛏 *14 rooms* ⏐○⏐ *Free Breakfast.*

Stracta Hotel
$$ | **HOTEL** | **FAMILY** | This hotel right off the Ring Road offers various types of accommodations, from self-catering apartments to deluxe suites—all in the same luxurious Nordic style. **Pros:** restaurant has great views of surrounding volcanoes; two wooden-barrel saunas outside are very charming and open for all guests; wake-up calls for departures and northern lights. **Cons:** no toiletries in rooms; rooms are quite small; noise travels between rooms. $ *Rooms from: ISK25,500* 🖾 *Rangárflatir 4, Hella* 🖾 *354/531–8010* ⊕ *www.stractahotels.is* 🛏 *166 rooms* ⏐○⏐ *Free Breakfast.*

Volcano Huts
$$ | **HOTEL** | Located in Þórsmörk and accessible via the Reykjavík Excursions Highlands bus—or the Fimmvörðuháls or Laugavegur hikes—accommodations here include mountain huts, cabins, and luxury camping facilities with ready to use tents. **Pros:** only lodging option in Þórsmörk; hearty buffet dinner; social atmosphere and friendly clientele. **Cons:**

far walk from many hiking trails; remote location; public showers. $ *Rooms from: ISK26,000* 🖾 *Þórsmerkurvegur Þórsmörk via road F249, Hvolsvöllur* 🖾 *419–4000* ⊕ *www.volcanotrails.com* 🛏 *14 rooms, 2 mountain huts, 1 cottage* ⏐○⏐ *No Meals.*

Shopping

Vínbúðin
WINE/SPIRITS | In Iceland you can only buy beverages stronger than 2.25% ABV in state-owned liquor stores called Vínbúðin. They can only be found in some of the bigger towns, so make sure to make a pit stop when you see one. 🖾 *Suðurlandsvegur 1, Hella* 🖾 *487–8487* ⊕ *www.vinbudin.is.*

Activities

Hella Swimming Pool
SWIMMING | **FAMILY** | This colorful swimming pool is very family-friendly, with a children's pool and three waterslides. For the parents there are two hot tubs and a Jacuzzi outside to ease those muscles and let all worries drift away with the steam. 🖾 *Útskálar 4, Hella* 🖾 *488–7040* 🖾 *ISK 1,100.*

Strandarvöllur
GOLF | **FAMILY** | At Strönd at Rangárvellur, just 7 km (4 miles) outside of Hella, is an 18-hole course run by the Hella Golf Club. You can rent golf clubs and carts and, after countless swings, enjoy a lovely meal or a refreshing beer at the restaurant on-site. The course has spectacular mountain views, and you can spot four volcanoes: Hekla, Tindfjallajökul, Eyjafjallajökull, and Mýrdalsjökull. In the summertime, you can pay a little extra to golf at midnight in what feels like endless Icelandic sunshine. 🖾 *Hella Golf Club, Strandarvöllur, Hella* 🖾 *487–8208* ⊕ *www.ghr.is* 🏌 *18 holes, 70 par* ☞ *Greens fee ISK 7,500; cart rental ISK 7,000.*

Vestmannaeyjar

58 km (36 miles) south of Hella.

Moving in and out of sight as you drive along the south coast is a cluster of islands called Vestmannaeyjar. The archipelago was mostly formed over 11,000 years ago by underwater volcanic eruptions, the exception being the very young island Surtsey, which was formed in 1963. The main island is still a dormant volcano, and by the mountainside, the ground is still warm from the last eruption roughly 40 years ago.

Heimaey, the largest and the only inhabited island of Vestmannaeyjar, is only a 30-minute ferry ride away from the Landeyjahöfn. While sailing into the charming town of Heimaey, you will be greeted by grass-covered, towering white cliffs heavily populated by numerous bird species. Next, you will see the colorful houses of the small town, filled with a wide variety of exciting restaurants, shops, and bars.

On the first weekend of August, the island is overcrowded with Icelanders from the mainland partying at the biggest summer festival of the year, Þjóðhátíð. On that weekend the usually calm island transforms into one giant party.

GETTING HERE AND AROUND

A day trip to Vestmannaeyjar by boat is well worth the trip, but it is also very enjoyable to stay overnight and explore in depth what the island has to offer. Vestmannaeyjar can be reached only by boat or plane; Vestmannaeyjar has a tiny airport, but no airlines currently fly there.

The ferry—currently the only way to reach Heimaey—departs from Landeyjahöfn, a harbor not too far from Hvolsvöllur, up to seven times a day in the summertime. To reach Landeyjahöfn, turn off the Ring Road to route 254. Strætó buses also have scheduled trips to Landeyjarhöfn from the Mjódd bus terminal.

TOURS

★ Ribsafari Boat Tours

ADVENTURE TOURS | If you're up for a bumpy ride, Ribsafari tours offer a fun way to spot puffins and marvel at and explore the hidden sea caves under the islands as well as learn about the history and nature of the islands. They offer one- and two-hour boat trips that are sure to get your adrenaline going. ☒ *Tangagata 7* ☎ *661–1810* ⊕ *www.ribsafari.is* ☒ *From ISK 14,900 for one hour.*

Sights

★ Eldheimar

OTHER MUSEUM | In 1973, in the middle of the night, the Eldfell volcano on Vestmannaeyjar suddenly exploded, causing the immediate evacuation of more than 5,000 people. At this tech museum—built around the ruins of two houses that were buried by the lava—you can learn about the eruption. To call the museum entertaining would be an understatement as it's filled with video footage and interactive displays that truly underscore the awe-inspiring and destructive power of the earth. ☒ *Gerðisbraut 10* ☎ *488–2700* ⊕ *www.eldheimar.is* ☒ *ISK 2,900.*

★ Sea Life Trust Beluga Whale Sanctuary

WILDLIFE REFUGE | **FAMILY** | Little White and Little Grey are two of the cutest residents of Iceland. Originally from a Shanghai water park, the belugas found sanctuary in 2019 at this specially built facility, which helps the marine mammals reacclimatize to a more natural environment and also works as a puffin rehabilitation center. The sanctuary offers daily tours of their facilities, where you can learn more about the whales and get up-close-and-personal with some puffins. They also offer boat tours of the bay where Little White and Little Grey will live out their lives. ☒ *Ægisgata 2* ☎ *620–2724* ⊕ *belugasanctuary.sealifetrust.org* ☒ *Admission ISK 3,050; boat tour ISK 16,900* ⊗ *Closed Nov.–May.*

The cliffs at Reynisfjara black sand beach are home to many puffins in the summer.

Restaurants

Gott Restaurant

$$$ | SEAFOOD | FAMILY | An honest family bistro run by a renowned and highly decorated chef is only a few minutes' walk from the harbor. Opt for the fish of the day; it is always fresh and delicious. **Known for:** fish of the day; freshly baked bread; upscale but inviting atmosphere. $ *Average main: ISK3,300* ⊠ *Bárustígur 11* ☎ *481–3060* ⊕ *www.gott.is.*

★ Slippurinn

$$$$ | ICELANDIC | For those looking to try authentic Icelandic food, look no further than this beloved family-run eatery. Specializing in fresh fish, their ethos is all about sustainability and slow food. **Known for:** bright and welcoming interior; seven-course set menu that covers the best of Icelandic cuisine; pan-fried fish that you'll later dream about. $ *Average main: ISK5,000* ⊠ *Strandvegur 76* ☎ *481–1515* ⊕ *www.slippurinn.com* ☺ *Closed Sun.–Tues. and late Sept.-May.*

Hotels

Hótel Vestmannaeyjar

$$ | HOTEL | This hotel right in the heart of Vestmannaeyjar offers every luxury one needs for a great night's stay, namely an excellent restaurant, a romantic lounge where cocktails can be enjoyed, a spa to relax in after a long day of exploring, and scenic views from rooms. **Pros:** modern Scandinavian decor; excellent restaurant for cocktails; nice spa area that includes hot tubs, showers, and a sauna. **Cons:** not all rooms have great views; rooms are small; noise from street. $ *Rooms from: ISK28,350* ⊠ *Vestmannabraut 28* ☎ *481–2900* ⊕ *www.hotelvestmannaey-jar.is* ⇥ *43 rooms* ❑ *Free Breakfast.*

ⓨ Nightlife

The Brothers Brewery

BREWPUBS | Owned by best friends (not brothers), this local brewery is guaranteed to put a smile on your face and some warmth in your belly. The brews are top notch and if you have the time, make sure to take their beer tour. ✉ *Bárustígur 7* ☎ *659–7500* 🌐 *www.tbb.is.*

Vík

93 km (58 miles) from Hella.

A layer of mist seems to cling to the little town of Vík all year long, giving it a bewitching atmosphere. This southernmost town in Iceland is known for its dramatic black sea stacks, called Reynisdrangar, rising out of the ocean. Surrounded by some of the most scenic glacial views imaginable on the north side and black sand, puffin-populated beaches on either side of the Ring Road, Vík is an excellent base of operations when exploring the south coast. You'll also find several restaurants, a liquor store, and a grocery store.

👁 Sights

Dyrhólaey

NATURE SIGHT | Not far from Vin is a small island (connected to the main body of Iceland) with a shallow inland lagoon filled with sea birds and a massive sea archway, 120 meters high, stretching out into the sea. At Dyrahólaey you will also find a spectacular white lighthouse, the southernmost tip of Iceland. ✉ *Dyrhólaey, Vík* ☎ *487–1480* 🌐 *www.south.is.*

★ **Reynisfjara**

BEACH | Take route 215 for 5 km (3 miles) to reach the popular black sand beach, Reynisfjara, located on the western side of Reynisfjall. The surrounding cliffs are the home to thousands of puffins in the summer, as well as arctic terns and fulmars. The dramatic splattering of the explosive waves on the obsidian black beach is a thrill to watch, but for safety reasons visitors must stay far from the edge of the water. The waves off Reynisfjara can rise quickly, sweeping people up in seconds, which has resulted in many accidents and even deaths. Offshore are the towering basalt sea stacks, Reynisdrangar. Their silhouette is seen from both Vík and Reynisfara. ✉ *Route 215, Vík.*

🍴 Restaurants

Smiðjan Brugghús

$$ | **BURGER** | After a long day of exploring the south coast, a burger and beer from Vík's Smiðjan Brugghús is just what the doctor ordered. This brewery serves up its own luxurious craft beer brewed on the premises along with a selection of comfort food including wings, chicken and waffles, BBQ ribs, and, of course, loaded burgers. **Known for:** lively and fun atmosphere; delicious craft beer; awesome chicken and cauliflower wings. [$] *Average main: ISK2,700* ✉ *Sunnubraut 15, Vík* ☎ *571–8870* 🌐 *www.smidjan-brugghus.is.*

Suður-Vík Restaurant

$$$ | **ECLECTIC** | In an old beautiful house overlooking the mountains, Suður-Vík offers a wide variety of dishes, ranging from wild game to artisanal pizza. In the basement they have a bar that stays open late. **Known for:** five-cheese pizza and Icelandic beer on tap; great place for a nightcap; local favorite. [$] *Average main: ISK3,000* ✉ *Suðurvíkurvegur 1, Vík* ☎ *487–1515* 🌐 *www.facebook.com/Sudurvik.*

🛏 Hotels

Hótel Kría

$$$$ | **HOTEL** | At this luxurious hotel within walking distance of the famous black-sand beaches of Vík, rooms are sleek and modern, and Drangar, the in-hotel restaurant, serves gourmet Icelandic cuisine with breathtaking views of the mountains. **Pros:** convenient location; delicious restaurant; breathtaking views. **Cons:** some noise from road; somewhat expensive compared to other similar hotels; more commercial than other nearby accommodations. [$] *Rooms from: ISK46,000* ✉ *Slét-tuvegur, Vík* ☎ *416–2100* 🌐 *www.hotelkria.is* 🛏 *73 rooms* 🍴 *Free Breakfast.*

WEST ICELAND AND SNÆFELLSNES PENINSULA

Updated by
Erika Owen

 Sights
★★★☆☆

 Restaurants
★★☆☆☆

 Hotels
★★☆☆☆

 Shopping
★★☆☆☆

 Nightlife
★☆☆☆☆

158

WELCOME TO WEST ICELAND AND SNÆFELLSNES PENINSULA

TOP REASONS TO GO

★ **Snæfellsjökull National Park:** One of Iceland's natural highlights, you can see volcanoes, glaciers, craters, lava tube caves, lava fields, and cliffsides all on the same day here.

★ **History:** Iceland's most famous poet and historian, Snorri Sturluson, lived in Reykholt in the 13th century; you can still visit his home next to Snorralaug, possibly the oldest hot spring in Iceland.

★ **Flatey Island:** This remote settlement, only accessible in the summer, is perhaps the quietest place in the whole country.

★ **Quaint fishing villages:** Ólafsvík and Stykkishólmur and their old-school charm will grace your dreams for weeks after you return home.

★ **Library of Water:** This museum is a one-of-a-kind look at the country's main natural resource.

1 Akranes. One of the larger towns in the area and a great place to stock up on groceries, coffee, and baked goods.

2 Borgarnes. A cozy fishing town on the Borgarfjörður, a fjord with ocean views in every direction.

3 Reykholt. Home to one of Iceland's oldest structures, along with several waterfalls and hot springs.

4 Húsafell. A small town with excellent hiking trails

5 Snæfellsjökull National Park. A park with every natural formation you could think of all in one place.

6 Hellissandur. A village dating back to the 16th century (don't miss the charming maritime museum).

7 Ólafsvík. A scenic town that used to be a major port for trade with Denmark.

8 Grundarfjörður. An unassuming town that is home to Kirkjufell, or "Church Mountain."

9 Stykkishólmur. A fishing town filled with historic homes and a volcano museum.

10 Flatey. A one-hotel island with less than 10 permanent residents.

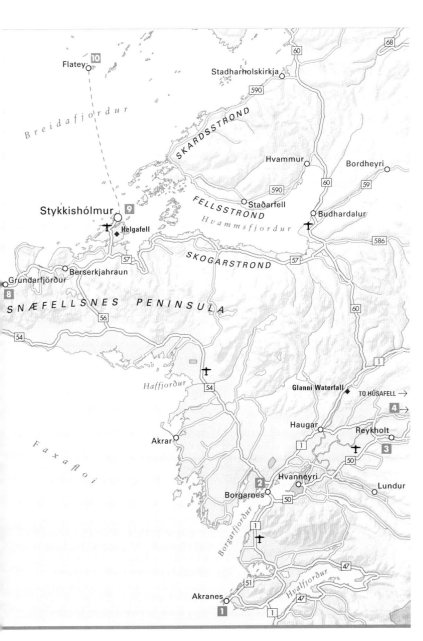

If you're traveling to Iceland and have only a few days in the country, West Iceland is the perfect region to explore. Many of the photos and stories from people who have been to the island come from outside Rekjavík's city limits, and it's one of a dwindling number of places in the world where you can put yourself in the middle of nature without any distractions.

You'll get only a small taste of what the country has to offer in Reykjavík, but the good news is that you can drive about an hour west and find yourself surrounded by lava fields, volcanic craters, and fjords even prettier than you could imagine.

In addition to a handful of towns (Borgarnes, Akranes, and Ólafsvík, to name a few) West Iceland includes the Snæfellsnes Peninsula in its western-most corner. This area is a wonderland of natural sights, from Saxholl Crater to Snæfellsjökull. You can whip through the peninsula in a day or so, but dedicate at least two days to really take in everything it has to offer. Snæfellsnes National Park can be seen in an afternoon (if you aren't doing any serious hiking) and will wow you with its stark differences in terrain. In a span of hours, you'll see moss-covered fields of lava rock, bird-covered cliffs, rolling hills of Arctic lupine (if you're visiting during the summer), and the bluest water you've ever seen.

This region is also important to the country's history. So many of the sights and attractions played a role in the Sagas,

a series of stories that tell the country's beginnings. If you're looking to do some pre-trip reading on the history of West Iceland, look to the Landnámabók, a book breaking down the settlement of Iceland in the 9th and 10th centuries. Gunnlaug's Saga, Hordur's Saga, Laxdæla Saga, Egil's Saga, and Eyrbyggja Saga all take place in West Iceland.

The area was also home to Iceland's most famous poet and historian, Snorri Sturluson, who lived between 1179 and 1241. Visiting his home and the hot spring he used to frequent is worth a trip to West Iceland in itself, especially if you fancy yourself a history buff.

Most towns you'll encounter in this region are small and scarcely populated. There are only 10 towns that have more than 50 residents, with Akranes being the most bustling with a population of a whopping 6,500. Despite this, keep in mind this is still one of the busier regions of Iceland—once you get up north, you'll find yourself driving through even more remote areas. If Reykjavík is the only place on your Iceland itinerary, do yourself a favor and find some time to drive out of the city and into the west.

Planning

When to Go

Like most regions in Iceland, winter can be a tough season for traveling outside of Reykjavík. Huge snowstorms often cause road closures and it's likely you'll get stuck in the more remote areas for uncertain amounts of time. And even though Snaefellsnes Peninsula is relatively close in mileage to the capital city, winter is not the time to visit.

To really experience the splendor of this area's fishing towns, visit during the late spring through late summer (May through early September). This is when the energy of the region really shines through.

Getting Here and Around

BOAT

The Ferry Baldur is convenient for travelers looking to take in views of the entire region. This particular ferry carries cars and people across the Breiðafjörður Bay—from Stykkishólmur to Flatey Island and then on to the Westfjords region.

CONTACTS Ferry Baldur. ☎ *433–2254* ⊕ *www.seatours.is/our-ferries/baldur.*

BUS

The same bus system that runs in Reykjavík has routes throughout West Iceland and the Snæfellsnes Peninsula. Strætó has seven lines servicing Borgarnes, Akranes, Stykkishólmur, Hellisandur, and Grundarfjörður as well as other smaller towns in the area.

CONTACTS Strætó Bus Service. ✉ *Hestháls 14, Reykjavík* ☎ *540–2700* ⊕ *www. straeto.is/en.*

CAR

Exploring western Iceland and the Snæfellsnes Peninsula by car is the easiest and most convenient way to take in the sights. In fact, renting a car is the only way you can really spend some time in the region. There are bus tours that travel here from Reykjavík, but renting a car takes you off the tourist path and gives you the freedom to make your own schedule. Driving from Reykjavík is simple and will only take you an hour to reach the southernmost point of the region. The views keep getting more scenic as you go.

Main roads in West Iceland are paved and relatively well maintained. Keep in mind that you may encounter some serious potholes if you're driving early in the spring after a major snowfall. The roads within Snæfellsjökull National Park are very well maintained and have proper signposting for various natural attractions.

One thing to keep in mind is that the police force in Iceland takes speeding very seriously. Tickets in Iceland are very expensive, so mind the speed limit.

Restaurants

Most restaurants in remote regions of Iceland (aka anywhere that isn't Akureyri or Reykjavík) are associated with hostels, hotels, and guesthouses. Most of the time, you can count on there being an eatery attached to the place where you're spending the night. Restaurant hours vary, so make sure to double-check how late things are open if you want to ensure a hot meal. It can be easy to lose track of time, especially during the warmer months when the sun barely sets.

Do not sleep on the fresh seafood in this area. The catch of the day will always rival (or top) the best fish you've ever had. Fish and chips is another trustworthy option. If you're looking to try a little bit of everything the region has to offer, the food trucks in the Stykkishólmur harbor is a great place to start.

Hotels

There are plenty of guesthouses, homestays, hotels, and camping opportunities around West Iceland and the Snæfellsnes Peninsula—in fact, it may seem that all you see are hotels as you drive through the region. There isn't a ton in the way of nightlife, restaurants, and shops, which can make the lodging-to-activity balance seem a little off. Although you can find larger hotel chains (Fosshotel, Icelandair) in this part of the country, there are far more guesthouses. Opt for the latter if you're looking for a cozy experience that will get you closest to feeling like a local. More often than not, they're owned by families who will also give you the great advice on what to see in the area.

You'll find the most hotels and guesthouses in Stykkishólmur and Borgarnes, the largest towns in the area. Elsewhere, the options get a bit more scarce, though they do exist. To be safe, it's best to plan out your traveling schedule at least a day in advance so you don't get stuck somewhere without accommodations (and no camping gear).

Camping is a little trickier in West Iceland since there isn't a hard-and-fast "no camping outside of campgrounds" rule like there is in the South. As a general rule, always check with any property owner before you set up camp in an area that isn't a campground. If you don't get the landowner's blessing, move on.

RESTAURANT AND HOTEL PRICES
Restaurant prices in the reviews are the average cost of a main course at dinner, or if dinner is not served, at lunch. Hotel prices in the reviews are the lowest cost of a standard double room in high season. Restaurant and hotel reviews have been shortened. For full information, visit Fodors.com.

What it Costs in ISK			
$	$$	$$$	$$$$
RESTAURANTS			
Under ISK 1,500	ISK 1,500– 2,999	ISK 3,000– 4,000	Over ISK 4,000
HOTELS			
Under ISK 20,000	ISK 20,000– 30,000	ISK 30,001– 45,000	Over ISK 45,000

Safety

Iceland is one of the safest places in the world, but there are still some things to keep in mind. The natural beauty of West Iceland and the Snæfellsnes Peninsula—the volcanic craters, the mountain valleys, the hot springs—require careful attention. Make sure to steer clear of mountain and cliff edges, and do your exploring with a friend—or at least let someone know where you're going to be.

Another thing to keep in mind is Icelandic weather. It can change with a moment's notice, and you don't want to get stuck 10 miles into a remote hike without rain gear or an extra pair of socks. Keep a close eye on the radar and always pack an extra insulated, waterproof layer on your person.

Tours

There are plenty of tours to check out while you're in West Iceland. In fact, it's sometimes the safest (and at times, only) option when you're exploring places like Vatnshellir Cave and hiking Snæfellsjökull. Most tour companies offer guided experiences to the peak of Snæfellsjökull, while supplementing with bus and hiking tours along other parts of the region.

Glacier Paradise

PRIVATE GUIDES | **FAMILY** | This tour operator focuses on getting you up close and personal to one of the island's most well-known glaciers, Snæfellsjökull. There are two options for visitors: a snow-cat tour, available between April and August, and a midnight sun tour, available in June and July. Both last approximately three hours and gives guests the experience of navigating some of Iceland's iconic F-roads before catching sight of the summit. Whether you go in the winter or summer, there are no bad views of the glacier that inspired Jules Verne's *Journey to the Center of the Earth.* ⊠ *Samkomuhúsið á Stapa* ☎ *861–2844* ⊕ *www.glacierparadise.is.*

★ Glacier Tours Snæfellsjökull

ADVENTURE TOURS | **FAMILY** | If you're looking to head to the top of Snæfellsjökull, Glacier Tours Snæfellsjökull can help. This tour company offers snowcat tours between May and August and snowmobile tours in May and June. It's a truly unique way to see this rugged area of the peninsula. Plus, the views at the top are incredible. ⊠ *Stóri-Kambur* ☎ *865–0061* ⊕ *www.theglacier.is.*

★ Go West

ADVENTURE TOURS | **FAMILY** | With its focus on sustainable tourism, Go West lets you take in the many sights of West Iceland while leaving only footprints. The family-run operator makes a special effort to neutralize carbon emissions and travel without compromising nature, while also highlighting local history. They also offer hiking and glacier tours. ⊠ *Arnarstapavegur* ☎ *695–9995* ⊕ *www.gowest.is.*

Visitor Information

CONTACTS Borgarnes Regional Information Centre. ⊠ *Hyrnan at Brúartorg* ☎ *437–2214* ⊕ *www.west.is.* **Snæfellsnes Tourist information Centre.** ⊠ *Grundargata 30* ☎ *354/848-6272* ⊕ *www.snaefellsnes.is.*

Akranes

48 km (30 miles) north of Reykjavík.

A quick trip up north from Reykjavík, Akranes is the largest community in the western corner of the country, and it's a great place to stock up on necessities. If you plan on camping in West Iceland or up in the Westfjords, take advantage of the grocery stores and outerwear shops you'll find here.

GETTING HERE AND AROUND

Akranes is less than an hour from Reykjavík, making it the perfect location for an afternoon trip out of the capital city. It's best to rent a car and explore on your own, but you can ride the local bus, Strætó, between Reykjavík and Akranes too. Once you're there, the town is easily walkable.

Sights

Akranes Folk Museum

HISTORY MUSEUM | **FAMILY** | For a history lesson on Akranes and the surrounding region, make a visit to this museum, where you'll learn about the working life of the locals and the living conditions of the first settlers. The museum has exhibits on fishing, farming, social life, and housekeeping—you'll even find a rowboat with a full fishing rig that dates back to 1874. Three of the museum's buildings are homes fully furnished as they would have been when the area's first settlers called Akranes home. If you're lucky, you'll catch the forge in action; the museum staff get it up and running for visitors on occasion. ⊠ *Garðaholt 3, 300 Akranes* ☎ *433–1150* ⊕ *www.museum.is* ▱ *ISK 1,000* ☉ *Closed mid-Sept. 16–mid-May (unless by appt.).*

Glymur Waterfall

WATERFALL | The best thing about Glymur Waterfall is that you have to take a nice, long hike to see it. Along the way, you'll walk through a cave, cross a river, and

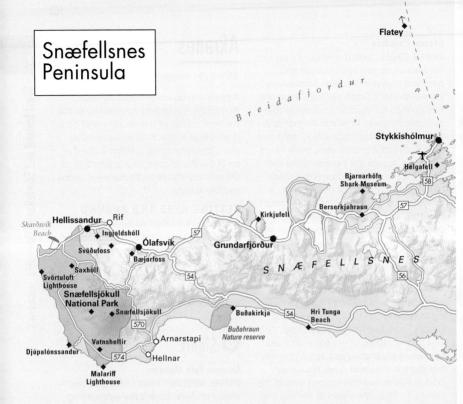

Snæfellsnes
Peninsula

Flatey

Breidafjordur

Stykkishólmur

Helgafell

Bjarnarhöfn
Shark Museum

58

Berserkjahraun

57

Skarðsvík   Hellissandur   Rif
Beach

Kirkjufell

Ingjaldshóll

Svöðufoss   Ólafsvik   57

Saxhóll   Bæjarfoss   Grundarfjörður

S N Æ F E L L S N E S

Svörtuloft
Lighthouse   54   56

Snæfellsjökull
National Park

Snæfellsjökull   Buðakirkja   54   Hri Tunga
Beach

570

Buðahraun
Vatnshellir   Arnarstapi   Nature reserve

Djúpalónssandur   574   Hellnar

Malariff
Lighthouse

F a x a f l o i

0   5 mi

0   5 km

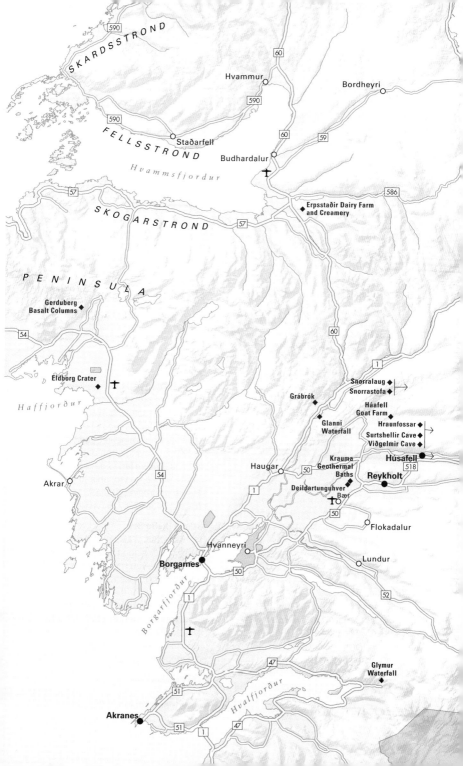

head into a stunning mountain valley. The south side of the waterfall is said to have better views, so keep that in mind as you get closer. Expect to spend between 3–3½ hours round-trip. ✉ *Arkanes* ✥ *Driving northwest on Road 1, turn right onto Road 47. In 6½ km (4 miles) you will see a sign for the falls. Make a turn at the sign onto a dirt road and you will find a parking lot from which you can begin your hike.*

★ Guðlaug Baths
HOT SPRING | On Langisandur Beach, you'll be greeted by the Guðlaug Baths. The manmade springs are located in a natural rock garden and have a stunning view of Reykjavík across the bay. There's a small fee to enjoy these public hot springs, and they can get quite crowded on especially sunny days (the pool itself isn't very large). ✉ *Langisandur, Arkanes* 🌐 *www.skagalif.is/is/visit-akranes/gudlaug-gudlaug-baths* 🎫 *ISK 500.*

Old Akranes Lighthouse and Shipwreck
NAUTICAL SIGHT | There are actually two lighthouses in Akranes situated right next to each other. The much larger and picturesque lighthouse joined its smaller neighbor in 1947, and is still in operation and open to the public. Many visitors get their photographs of the Northern Lights here. Along the harbor, you can see the wreck of the old herring ship *Höfrungur* (meaning "Dolphin"), built in 1955 and abandoned after sinking at an unknown point in time.

Beaches

Ytri Tunga Beach
BEACH | **FAMILY** | This area next to a farm of the same name is well known for its nearby "Seal Beach," where harbor seals and grey seals spend the summer months basking in the near-constant sunlight on rocks just offshore. You're likely to see them in the area year-round, but you're more likely to catch the eye of a friendly seal swimming by in the warmer months. **Amenities:** none. **Best for:** solitude, wildlife-watching. ✉ *Arnarstapi* ✥ *From Guesthouse Hof, drive a few minutes west on Snæfellsnesvegur before taking the first available right turn toward the beach.*

Restaurants

Café Kaja
$$ | **VEGETARIAN** | If you thought finding a café that could accommodate dietary preferences like vegan and gluten-free would be difficult, you'll be pleasantly surprised by Café Kaja. Here you'll find meals prepared with raw and organic veggies, plant-based milks for your coffee, and vegetarian options galore. **Known for:** expansive vegetarian and vegan options; great soups; friendly service. [$] *Average main: ISK1,990* ✉ *Stillholt 23* ☎ *840–1665* 🌐 *www.kajaorganic.com.*

Galito
$$$ | **SEAFOOD** | **FAMILY** | You'll get the best of land and sea at Galito, from burgers and cod to sushi and even pizza. There's something for everyone here, which is especially tempting in a region that isn't known for having a ton of restaurant options. **Known for:** wide-ranging menu; great service; reasonable lunch specials. [$] *Average main: ISK3,890* ✉ *Stillholt 16–18* ☎ *430–6767* 🌐 *www.galito.is.*

Grjótið Bistro Bar
$$ | **ICELANDIC** | **FAMILY** | The menu is always changing at this locally owned restaurant—you might find anything from Thai favorites to hearty burgers. It's a great place for the family, given the friendly atmosphere. **Known for:** lively atmosphere; friendly staff; ever-changing menu. [$] *Average main: ISK2,490* ✉ *Kirkjubraut 10, Akranes* ☎ *792–9222* 🌐 *www.facebook.com/grjotid.*

★ Lesbókin Café
$ | **CAFÉ** | Exactly what you would imagine a cozy, small-town coffee shop to be, Lesbókin Café is the perfect place to hole

up and dig into your day's itinerary with a latte. If you're lucky, you'll find a special piece of milk-foam art waiting for you. **Known for:** cozy interiors; quality coffee; delicious waffles. [$] *Average main: ISK1,200* ✉ *Kirkjubraut 2* ☎ *863–5793.*

Hotels

Gallery Guesthouse

$ | **HOTEL** | Located a 40-minute drive from Reykjavik, Gallery Guesthouse is a basic accommodation for those on their way into the Icelandic wilderness. **Pros:** luggage storage available; free parking; central location. **Cons:** outdated design; basic amenities; small rooms. [$] *Rooms from: ISK10,880* ✉ *Merkigerði 7, Akranes* ☎ *868–3332* 🌐 *staywest.is/galleryguesthouse* 🛏 *9 rooms* 🍴 *Free Breakfast.*

Hotel Glymur

$$ | **B&B/INN** | At Hotel Glymur, each room comes with a fantastic view of the fjord or the surrounding mountain range. **Pros:** massage bathtubs in suites; stunning views from every room; friendly service. **Cons:** don't expect the best meal of your life; tiny rooms; restaurant smells permeate some rooms. [$] *Rooms from: ISK29,261* ✉ *Hvalfjardarsveit, 301 Saurbaer, Arkanes* ☎ *430–3100* 🌐 *www.hotelglymur.is* 🛏 *22 rooms* 🍴 *No Meals.*

Hotel Laxarbakki

$ | **B&B/INN** | **FAMILY** | You've got options at Hotel Laxarbakki: there are single, double, twin, and family rooms as well as a charming cottage. **Pros:** hot tub and sauna; free Wi-Fi; variety of accommodations. **Cons:** food could be improved; basic amenities; outdated design. [$] *Rooms from: ISK16,048* ✉ *Hvalfjarðarsveit, Akranes* ☎ *551–2783* 🌐 *www.laxarbakki.is* 🛏 *21 rooms* 🍴 *No Meals.*

Moar Guesthouse

$ | **B&B/INN** | Located at the foot of Akrafjall Mountain, there are no bad views at this guesthouse. **Pros:** stunning views of the mountain; great value; lots of hiking trails nearby. **Cons:** outdated design; basic accomodations; shared kitchen facility. [$] *Rooms from: ISK9,790* ✉ *Kalmansbraut, Innri Akraneshreppur, Akranes* ☎ *655–0506* 🌐 *www.traveltomoar.com* 🛏 *6 rooms* 🍴 *No Meals.*

Borgarnes

39 km (24 miles) north of Akranes.

Located right on the bay, Borgarnes is a scenic fishing town on the western coast. The Settlement Center is certainly worth a visit, and the local pool is a popular place for tourists and locals alike, perfect if you're looking for a spot to relax after a long day of sightseeing. This is a great place to spend the night or grab a bite to eat, given its many restaurant and hotel options—far more than you'll find in other towns in West Iceland.

GETTING HERE AND AROUND

If you don't rent a car, you can take the Strætó bus to Borgarnes. Bus 57, Bus 58, Bus 81, and Bus 82 all make stops.

Sights

★ **Bjössaróló Playground**

OTHER ATTRACTION | **FAMILY** | This brightly colored oasis is for kids and adults alike looking to have a bit of fun. Getting here is an adventure in itself—intentionally so, as designed by the creator of this wonderland. Spend some time playing on the slides, teeter-totters, climbing dome, and swings. Everything in the playground was made from salvaged discarded materials, which somehow makes it all a little more delightful. ✉ *Skúlagata 23, Borgarnes.*

Eldborg Crater

NATURE SIGHT | If you're looking for a more challenging hike, check out Eldborg Crater. After walking 2½ hours, you'll find a 196-foot crater sweeping up from the lava fields. You can walk around as well as up the crater.

The Eldborg Crater is surrounded by lava fields.

Gerduberg Basalt Columns

NATURE SIGHT | At the edge of the Hnappadalur Valley, north of Borgarnes, you'll find the Gerduberg Basalt Columns, which form an immense wall of striking geometric patterns. You won't be able to see the hundreds of columns from the road, which only adds to the sense of mystery. ✉ *Borgarnes.*

★ The Settlement Center

HISTORY MUSEUM | **FAMILY** | There are two main exhibits at the Settlement Center: a breakdown of the Saga of the Settlement of Iceland and a display of Egill Skallagrímsson, both Iceland´s most famous viking and the country's first poet. It's a fantastic place to stop early on in your trip, so you can bring the knowledge with you on the rest of your travels. ✉ *Brákarbraut 13–15* ☎ *354/437–1600* 🌐 *www.landnam.is* 🎟 *ISK 3,000.*

🍴 Restaurants

Englendingavík

$$ | **SCANDINAVIAN** | From lamb shanks to spaghetti, you never quite know what's going to show up on the menu at Englendingavík. The historic building is surrounded by equally aged architecture; it's almost like stepping back in time—a much cozier time. **Known for:** lovely patio space; charming and informative staff; hygge vibes. [$] *Average main: ISK2,800* ✉ *Skúlagata 17, Borgarnes* ☎ *896–8926* 🌐 *www.englendingavik.is.*

Geirabakari Kaffihus

$ | **BAKERY** | If all-you-can-eat soup and bread is your idea of the perfect lunch, get yourself to Geirabakari Kaffihus. You can also enjoy pastries, baked goods, coffee, or soup, all with a great view of the mountains. **Known for:** gorgeous mountain views; all-you-can-eat soup and bread; tasty baked goods. [$] *Average main: ISK800* ✉ *Digranesgata 6* ☎ *437–1920.*

Grillhúsið

$$ | **AMERICAN** | **FAMILY** | The mood at Grillhúsið is very casual, and the open layout—it almost feels like a diner—is great for containing children with some energy to burn. You'll find burgers, wraps, sandwiches, and the random Tex-Mex item on the menu. **Known for:** wide-ranging menu; kid-friendly atmosphere; reasonable prices. $ *Average main: ISK2190* ✉ *Brúartorg 6* ☎ *437–1282* ⊕ *www.grillhusid.is.*

La Colina Pizzeria

$$ | **PIZZA** | **FAMILY** | Wood-fired pizza is the main appeal here, and there are plenty of options to choose from. Don't sleep on the homemade garlic oil the restaurant offers on the side—it will take your pizza to a whole new level. **Known for:** cozy and quiet atmosphere; wide variety of pizza options; homemade garlic oil. $ *Average main: ISK2,700* ✉ *Hrafnaklettur 1b* ☎ *437–0110* ⊕ *www.facebook.com/lacolinapizzeria.*

Snorri's Kitchen & Bar

$$ | **GERMAN** | The menu at Snorri's Kitchen & Bar is a true trip around the world—think German-inspired schnitzel, classic American chicken nuggets, and fish and chips featuring the local catch, to just name a few. All dishes are presented with the artistic attention to detail Icelandic restaurants are known for. **Known for:** friendly atmosphere; memorable three-course tasting menus; great seafood dishes. $ *Average main: ISK2,359* ✉ *Borgarbraut 59* ☎ *419–5959* ⊕ *www.b59hotel.is/dining.*

Hotels

Bjarg Borgarnes

$ | **B&B/INN** | **FAMILY** | On the outskirts of Borgarnes, you'll find this guesthouse, which manages to give you the convenience of being near town yet the quiet of being in the middle of nowhere at the same time. **Pros:** great views from every room; historical elements integrated into decor; charcoal grill on the property

that guests can use. **Cons:** very small rooms; basic amenities; thin walls make all conversations public. $ *Rooms from: ISK19,211* ✉ *Bjarg* ☎ *437–1925* ⊕ *www.heyiceland.is/accommodation/detail/680/bjarg* ↪ *4 rooms, 1 private home rental* ⦿ *Free Breakfast.*

Blómasetrið Guesthouse

$ | **B&B/INN** | **FAMILY** | For a more authentic local experience, you can do a homestay at Blómasetrið, which also has a café and gift shop on-site; or, for a little more privacy, you can stay in one of the apartments. **Pros:** great mountain views in each room; gift shop and café on-site; good variety of room options. **Cons:** not a lot of privacy; small common areas in the main home; shared bathrooms. $ *Rooms from: ISK17,522* ✉ *Skúlagata 13* ☎ *437–1878* ⊕ *www.blomasetrid.is* ↪ *3 rooms, 1 apartments* ⦿ *No Meals.*

★ Englendingavík

$ | **B&B/INN** | **FAMILY** | The loudest noise you'll hear at this beautiful 1890 house is birdsong, and although luxury amenities are not the focus, there's no substitute for the coziness of staying at this family's home. **Pros:** good on-site restaurant; family-run with a very welcoming environment; prime location near Borgarnes. **Cons:** communal living is stressed over privacy; breakfast not included; no luxury amenities. $ *Rooms from: ISK19,373* ✉ *Skúlagata 17, Borgarnes* ☎ *896–8926* ⊕ *www.englendingavik.is* ↪ *5 rooms* ⦿ *No Meals.*

Ensku Húsin

$$ | **B&B/INN** | **FAMILY** | Before opening its doors to guests in 1998, Ensku Húsin had been a popular spot for fishermen since 1884. **Pros:** great fishing opportunities; delicious communal dinners; tons of hiking trails. **Cons:** thin walls; breakfast not included in rate; small rooms. $ *Rooms from: ISK23,580* ✉ *By Langá* ☎ *437–1826* ↪ *10 rooms* ⦿ *No Meals.*

★ **Helgugata Guesthouse**
$ | **B&B/INN** | This beyond charming guesthouse has five rooms, two communal sitting areas, a library, and a big garden with views of the nearby fjord. **Pros:** free coffee and tea; great garden views of the fjord; impressive breakfast spread. **Cons:** don't expect too much privacy; no a/c; lack of nightlife in the area. [$] *Rooms from: ISK19,375* ✉ *Helgugata 5* ☎ *690–5857* 🌐 *helgugata.inn.fan* 🛏 *5 rooms* 🍴 *Free Breakfast.*

Hótel Bifröst
$$ | **HOTEL** | **FAMILY** | This hotel manages a good balance of business amenities and cozy and comfortable rooms. **Pros:** on-site hot tub; breakfast is included in room rate; fantastic location for hikers. **Cons:** check-in can be slow; located on a university campus so can get noisy; basic amenities. [$] *Rooms from: ISK28,390* ✉ *Bifröst* ☎ *433–3030* 🌐 *www.hotelbifrost.is* 🛏 *52 rooms* 🍴 *Free Breakfast.*

Hótel Borgarnes
$$ | **HOTEL** | With more of a business focus than other options in the area, Hótel Borgarnes has ample conference rooms and meeting facilities. **Pros:** free parking; helpful hotel staff; free Wi-Fi for guests. **Cons:** businesslike vibe; dated decor and interior design; small rooms. [$] *Rooms from: ISK27,920* ✉ *Egilsgata 16* ☎ *437–1119* 🌐 *www.hotelborgarnes.is* 🛏 *75 rooms* 🍴 *No Meals.*

Hotel Hafnarfjall
$$ | **B&B/INN** | **FAMILY** | The striking views are the main attraction here, but the simply decorated guest rooms are a comfortable place to lay your head after a day of hiking the nearby mountain or fishing at the harbor. **Pros:** great location in a forest and near the mountains; private rooms and facilities available; on-site restaurant. **Cons:** breakfast not included in room rate; very standard decor and interior design; basic amenities and some shared bathrooms. [$] *Rooms from: ISK23,847* ✉ *Hafnarskogur* ☎ *437–2345* 🌐 *www.hotelhafnarfjall.is* 🛏 *16 rooms, 5 bungalows* 🍴 *No Meals.*

★ **Hotel Rjúkandi**
$$ | **HOTEL** | Pull up a mental image of a red-roof home nestled in a valley between mountain ranges, and chances are Hotel Rjúkandi comes pretty close. **Pros:** picture-perfect building; incredibly remote location; eco-friendly focus. **Cons:** location might be too remote for some; rooms book up quickly; can be hard to adjust the temperature in rooms. [$] *Rooms from: ISK21,758* ✉ *Snæfellsnesvegur 311* ☎ *788–9100* 🌐 *www.rjukandi.com* 🛏 *14 rooms* 🍴 *Free Breakfast.*

Icelandair Hotel Hamar
$$ | **HOTEL** | **FAMILY** | One of the largest accommodations in Western Iceland, this 54-room hotel is located on an 18-hole golf course, but you'll also find a bar, restaurant, outdoor hot tubs, and unmatched mountain views here. **Pros:** Northern Lights wake-up call; incredible mountain views; ISK 2,500 credit to spend on food and drink included in room rate. **Cons:** small bathrooms in some rooms; hot tubs close at night; breakfast not included. [$] *Rooms from: ISK27,000* ✉ *Hamarsvöllur 310* ☎ *433–6600* 🌐 *www.hotelhamar.is* 🛏 *54 rooms* 🍴 *No Meals.*

Kría Cottages
$ | **B&B/INN** | **FAMILY** | Drive 10 minutes from the center of Borgarnes and you'll find yourself at the cozy Kria Cottages, three accommodations owned by a local family. **Pros:** close location to shops and restaurants; waterfront views; private hot tub for guests. **Cons:** decor lacks personality; shared bathroom; small rooms. [$] *Rooms from: ISK18,600* ✉ *Kveldúlfsgata 27* ☎ *437–1159* 🌐 *www.kriaguesthouse.is* 🛏 *3 cabins* 🍴 *No Meals.*

Lambalækur Guesthouse
$ | **B&B/INN** | **FAMILY** | This rustic Norwegian wood house has eleven bedrooms with a handful that share bathrooms. **Pros:** central location to many sights; self-serve

breakfast; wool sweaters available to borrow. **Cons:** some rooms have shared bathrooms; late-night check-ins have to pick keys up from another property; steep stairs. [$] *Rooms from: ISK16,743* ✉ *By Langá river* ☎ *865–3899* 🛏 *11 rooms* 🍴 *Free Breakfast.*

Shopping

★ Ljómalind Local Market
MARKET | Nearly 70 local artisans and farmers sell their goods at the Ljómalind Local Market. A group of women started the market in 2013, and it has since become a local favorite for grabbing dinner ingredients as well as a beloved stop for tourists looking for a souvenir. ✉ *Brúartorg 4, Borgarnes* ☎ *437–1400* 🌐 *www.ljomalind.is/en.*

★ Ullarselið Wool Centre
CRAFTS | **FAMILY** | The locals of Hvanneyri (about a 17-minute drive from Borgarnes) banded together to set up a shop selling their handmade wares. If you're looking for something knitted, spun, woven, or combed, Ullarselið has you covered and then some. ✉ *Hvanneyrarkirkj, Hvanneyri, Borgarnes* ☎ *437–0077* 🌐 *www.ull.is.*

Activities

Borgarnes Swimming Pool
SWIMMING | **FAMILY** | This stadium houses an outdoor and indoor pool as well as a steam bath and hot tubs. Expect to run into many locals at this community hot spot. If you have kids in tow, you're in luck: there are three waterslides, as well as a dedicated children's pool. There is also a gym on-site for those looking to get a work-out in. ✉ *Þorsteinsgötu 1, Borgarnes* ☎ *433–7140* 🌐 *www.sundlaugar.is.*

Reykholt

41 km (25 miles) northeast of Borgarnes.

It's impossible to leave Reykholt without a history lesson of sorts. Sure, the city is surrounded by gorgeous sights and natural attractions, but it's also the home of medieval writer Snorri Sturluson, who was responsible for two of Iceland's most important pieces of writing: the Prose Edda and the Heimskringla. It was in Reykholt that most of his writing was completed. Aside from reading up on the life and times of Sturluson, you can visit glaciers, waterfalls, the strongest hot spring in Europe, and other natural wonders in this area.

GETTING HERE AND AROUND

Reykholt is located off of Route 518, about a 30-minute drive from Borgarnes. There is no direct public bus line between Reykjavík and Reykholt, but you can get to this area via bus from Borgarnes: take Strætó Bus 58 from Reykjavík to Borgarnes, and then hop on Bus 81 to Reykholt. If you rent a car, getting to and from the cities in West Iceland is simple and—more often than not—quick.

Sights

★ Deildartunguhver
HOT SPRING | Europe's most powerful hot spring, Deildartunguhver produces enough geothermal energy to heat two nearby cities: Akranes and Borgarnes. Every second, 380 pints of boiling hot water churns through the spring. You have to see it in person in order to comprehend its power. ✉ *Road 50, Reykholt* ✣ *Off of Borgarfjarðarbraut, right before it intersects with Hálsasveitavegur.*

Erpsstaðir Dairy Farm and Creamery
FARM/RANCH | FAMILY | People flock here for the award-winning ice cream, but it's the educational side of the visit that will keep you coming back. Located in a valley in the rolling mountain ranges of West Iceland, Erpsstaðir might just be the most scenic farm you'll ever see. Ask for a tour and, depending on when you're there, you may see calves being fed or get a quick lesson on how the couple who own the small farm make their delicious ice cream. ☎ *868–0357* 🌐 *www.erpsstadir.is.*

★ **Háafell Goat Farm**
FARM/RANCH | FAMILY | The main goal here is to give locals and visitors a peek at the lives of a farmer and farm animals. Háafell mainly cares for Icelandic goats, which are endangered, but they also keep sheep, chickens, horses, dogs, and cats. You can visit the farm on a tour or just browse the shop for products made on-site. ✉ *Hvítársíðuvegur, 320 Borgarnes* ☎ *845–2331* 🌐 *www.geitur.is* 🎟 *ISK 1,500.*

★ **Krauma Geothermal Baths**
HOT SPRING | This man-made hot spring gets its geothermal water from Deildartunguhver, the most powerful hot spring in Europe. Here you can relax in any of the six different baths (one cold, five hot), two steambaths, or the relaxation room. There is also a restaurant on-site. ✉ *Deildartunguhver, 320 Reykholt* ☎ *555–6066* 🌐 *www.krauma.is/en* 🎟 *ISK 4,900.*

Snorralaug
HOT SPRING | What may well be the oldest hot spring in Iceland was first mentioned in the writings of medieval Icelandic historian and poet Snorri Sturluson, who used to bathe here. The water is often far too hot for a dip, so visit the nearby Snorrastofa instead to learn about Sturluson himself. ✉ *Snorrastofa.*

★ **Snorrastofa**
HISTORIC HOME | FAMILY | Next to the Snorralaug hot spring, you'll find Snorrastofa, the main residence of medieval writer Snorri Sturluson. It's known as the location where some of the country's most treasured pieces of literature were written. There's also a shop on-site where you can pick up souvenirs, local handmade items, and books on Icelandic history and culture. ✉ *320 Reykholt* ☎ *354/433–8000* 🌐 *www.snorrastofa.is/en* 🎟 *ISK 1200.*

★ **Víðgelmir Cave**
CAVE | Although the rooftop of Víðgelmir, the country's largest lava tube cave, has collapsed, you can still experience its intriguing rock formations and incredible colors. Operators like Into the Glacier lead tours of the cave. They will pick you up in Húsafell and bring you straight to Víðgelmir—it's a quick 15-minute drive. You can explore the cave on your own, but a group tour is better; guides provide all necessary safety gear and tell you everything you need to know about what you're seeing. 🌐 *www.intotheglacier.is* 🎟 *ISK 7,000.*

🍴 Restaurants

★ **Friðheimar**
$$ | VEGETARIAN | FAMILY | When you eat at Friðheimar, you're in for an experience. The restaurant is located in a tomato greenhouse and every single thing on the menu uses tomatoes in some shape or form. **Known for:** perfect tomato soup; fun atmosphere; unique green-tomato-and-apple pie. [$] *Average main: ISK2,800* ✉ *Bláskógabyggð* ☎ *486–8894* 🌐 *www.fridheimar.is.*

★ **Restaurant Mika**
$$$$ | PIZZA | FAMILY | A mix of Scandinavian fare and inventive pizzas grace the menu at this roadside restaurant. Located right as you enter Reykholt, Mika is a local hotspot with a few outdoor seating options—perfect for taking in the extended sunlight. **Known for:** good vegan options; great pizza; scenic outdoor seating. [$] *Average main: ISK4,390*

Deildartunguhver is Europe's most powerful hot spring.

✉ *Skólabraut, Reykholt* ☎ *486–1110* 🌐 *www.mika.is/matsedill-nytt.*

🛏 Hotels

Fossatún Country Hotel

$ | **B&B/INN** | **FAMILY** | You have three options at Fossatún Country Hotel: booking a room in the main hotel, staying in the communal guesthouse, or renting a camping pod. **Pros:** beautiful waterfall views; fun self-guided walks with a folklore focus; wide variety of accommodation options. **Cons:** very remote location in the countryside; small rooms; not all rooms offer privacy. [$] *Rooms from: ISK11,300* ✉ *Fossatúni* ☎ *433–5800* 🌐 *www.fossatun.is* 🛏 *12 rooms* 🍴 *Free Breakfast.*

Hverinn

$ | **HOTEL** | **FAMILY** | You'll find a little bit of everything at Hverinn: a guesthouse, a private apartment for rent, a campground, a restaurant, and a hot tub. **Pros:** wide variety of accommodation options; private hot tub; friendly staff. **Cons:** can get loud during camping high season; small hotel rooms; dated decor. [$] *Rooms from: ISK11,630* ✉ *Björk Kleppjárnsreykjir* ☎ *863–0090* 🌐 *www.hverinn.is* 🛏 *4 rooms, 1 apartment, 100 campsites* 🍴 *No Meals.*

Húsafell

25 km (15 miles) east of Reykholt.

First things first: Húsafell is tiny. But if you're looking to set up camp in a remote village in Iceland, this is the place to do it. Its relatively close proximity to Reykjavík makes it a good place to spend a night under the stars if you've got only a short time in the country. There are a handful of sights to see while you're here as well, including the mighty Húsafell Stone, which has been used to show off feats of strength for generations.

GETTING HERE AND AROUND

Húsafell is easiest to get to by car, but there is a bus to and from Reykjanesbær (Bus 88). Once you're in Húsafell, the town itself is walkable but some out-of-town sights require a car.

Sights

Hraunfossar

WATERFALL | As opposed to stronger, more intimidating waterfalls like Dettifoss, Hraunfossar (Lava Waterfalls) is a series of delicately flowing rivulets over the Hallmundarhraun lava field. Located about an hour's drive north of Reykjavík, this is a great (and less crowded) alternative to the waterfalls you'll find along the Golden Circle. Don't miss the nearby Barnafoss, another waterfall, which is located a quick walk down the Hvitá River.

The Húsafell Stone

HISTORIC SIGHT | Weighing in around 410 pounds, the Húsafell Stone was once used as a measure of strength by men hoping to score a job on nearby working ships. Even before that, it functioned as a gate for a sheep pen built by Snorri Björnsson in the 18th century. Today, you can try and lift it for fun (and bragging rights). ⌧ *Hwy 518, Húsafell.*

Kaldidalsvegur–Route 550

SCENIC DRIVE | Iceland's Central Highlands are a tricky terrain reserved for experienced drivers, but most drivers could feel comfortable taking a drive on Kaldidalsvegur, also known as the Highlands for beginners. Take a drive along Route 550 and you'll get a taste of the valleys, massive rocks, rivers, and mountains that the Central Highlands have to offer. To get to this road, drive east out of Húsafell and turn right on Route 550. Driving south along Kaldidalsvegur will eventually bring you to a fork, where you can head east on Route 338 toward the Central Highlands (make sure you have the proper car for this trip) or hop on Route 52 to the west.

★ Sturlureykir Horse Farm

FARM/RANCH | Horseback riding is a popular activity all across Iceland, and the family-run Sturlureykir Horse Farm will let you take in the sights with help from one of their friendly steeds. The farm offers horse rentals as well as guided tours. You can also pay a visit to the stable, where one of the family members will walk you through what it's like to work and live at a horse farm in Iceland's countryside. ⌧ *Sturlureykir Horse Farm, 320 Reykholt* ☎ *691–0280* ⊕ *www.sturlureykirhorses.is* 🎫 *ISK 8,500.*

Surtshellir Cave

CAVE | Measuring one mile in length, Surtshellir is the longest lava cave in the country. The innermost section is known as "the Ice Cave" and houses—you guessed it—massive ice columns. A ladder descends from the cave opening. Make sure to bring the proper safety gear if you plan on doing any extensive exploring: A map or guidebook, a hard helmet with a lamp, and warm clothing are all essential. Multiple companies offer excursions into the cave with a trained guide. ⌧ *Off Rte. 578* ⊗ *Closed fall, winter, and spring.*

 Restaurants

Húsafell Bistró

$$ | **CAFÉ** | **FAMILY** | The soup bar is the main draw at this bistro attached to Hotel Húsafell. There are vegetarian options on the menu, making it an easy stop for groups with various dietary needs. **Known for:** excellent soup bar; quick bites; good variety of pizzas. $ *Average main: ISK2,390* ⌧ *Húsafell* ☎ *435–1550* ⊕ *www.husafell.com.*

Hotels

★ Hotel Húsafell

$$$$ | **HOTEL** | There are few hotel options here, but Hotel Hísafell has everything you need for a solid home base while exploring the region. **Pros:** beautiful design; great location for outdoor activities; access to geothermal pools and float gear. **Cons:** rooms can get quite hot;

lackluster buffet breakfast; basic amenities given room rate. $ *Rooms from: ISK45,900* ✉ *Stórarjóður* ☎ *435–1551* ⊕ *www.hotelhusafell.com* ⤳ *48 rooms* ⏍ *Free Breakfast.*

Snæfellsjökull National Park

209 km (130 miles) northwest of Reykjavík, 186 km (115 miles) west of Húsafell.

A national park since June 2001, Snæfellsjökull is a treasure chest of Icelandic natural attractions and jaw-dropping scenery you can't see in many other places around the world. It stretches all the way from the summit of its namesake volcano to the coastline of the Atlantic Ocean. Measuring in at nearly 66 square miles, the park is home to a number of must-see sights: Djúpalónssandur beach, the Lóndrangar basalt fortress, and the Vatnshellir lava tube cave, to name a few. This park is a paradise of hiking and photo opportunities and showcases some of the country's most dramatic landscapes.

The national park can be seen in a single day—or even an afternoon if you really push it—but it's nice to spend a few days in the area so you can take full advantage of local hiking opportunities. The main draw of the park is its namesake glacier, which you can summit with the help of local guides and tour operators. If you're looking for some added perspective, watch the original film adaptation of Jules Verne's *Journey to the Center of the Earth*—some of the 1959 film takes place in the area and the 2008 remake was filmed here.

GETTING HERE AND AROUND

Plenty of tour buses take people between Snæfellsjökull National Park and Reykjavík, but if you're looking to build your own itinerary, renting a car is

your best bet. The drive from Reykjavík on a clear day is a real treat. Once you're inside the park, there are plenty of signs directing you to the area's most popular viewpoints and attractions. Roads are relatively well maintained but do keep an eye on the weather as a heavy bout of rain can turn this area into a bit of a mud pit.

Sights

Búðakirkja

CHURCH | It's no surprise Búðakirkja is one of the most photographed churches in Iceland given its stark color against the mountains and ocean. Originally built in 1703, the church was eventually torn down due to lack of use and reconstructed in 1987. The real draw may be how remote this church is—the only other thing in the village of Búðir is the adjacent hotel. Behind the church toward the ocean, there is a series of paths for hikers and walkers. After taking your photos of the church and its cemetery, escape the small crowd of tourists and walk along the water for a bit of solitude. If you're there during the summertime, it'll be just you and the roaming sheep. ✉ *Garðsbrún 6* ✛ *Off of Rte. 54, close to Búðavegur* 🎫 *Free.*

Djúpalónssandur

BEACH | Known to locals as the Black Lava Pearl Beach, Djúpalónssandur makes for a breathtaking walk. Start down Nautastígur, or the Path of the Bull (you can see it from the parking lot), which winds around massive lava rock formations. Behind the path, you'll spot two freshwater lagoons, known collectively as Djúpulón. Head to the beach to find pieces of the *Epine* GY7 wreckage, a British trawler that met its end east of Dritvík cove in March 1948.

Malarrif Lighthouse

LIGHTHOUSE | Compared to the other, brightly colored lighthouses you'll find around the coast, the Malarrif Lighthouse is a somewhat brutal-looking construction. It has great views of the Atlantic Ocean and Snæfellsjökull volcano though and sits just a short walk from the park's information center.

Saxhóll

NATURE SIGHT | If you want to explore a volcanic crater without hiking too far, Saxhóll is the place. The most interesting views are from the top, where you can take in the whole scene at the center of the crater. Getting up is easier than you would think; man-made steps lead visitors up to the crest, and you'll be up at the top before you know it. Make sure to spend time walking around the peak, but watch your step.

★ Snæfellsjökull

NATURE SIGHT | On a clear day, you can see this 700,000-year-old glacier from Reykjavík. Book with local tour outfitters to hike the glacier or even ride a special terrain-specific bike on it. This is the place that inspired Jules Verne's novel *Journey to the Center of the Earth.*

Svöðufoss

WATERFALL | If you're looking to beat the crowds and find a waterfall to call your own, head to Svöðufoss (pronounced "*svuew*-thoo-foss"). This 32-foot waterfall spills over a set of basalt columns, and on particularly clear days, you can see Snæfellsjökul glacier behind them.

Svörtuloft Lighthouse

LIGHTHOUSE | If you're visiting during the summertime, head to the Svörtuloft Lighthouse at low tide. The surrounding cliffs, which are made up of dramatic black lava, are a sight to see against the bright-orange lighthouse.

★ Vatnshellir

CAVE | This cave leads to close-up views of an ancient lava tube that last flowed 8,000 years ago. There's a small building at the cave opening in Snæfellsbær where you can buy tickets for the tour; hard hats are provided. ✉ *Gufuskalar, 360 Snaefellsbaer* ☎ *787–0001* 🌐 *www.summitguides.is/vatnshellir-cave-op1r6* 🎟 *ISK 4,500.*

Hotels

★ Hotel Búdir

$$$$ | **HOTEL** | After you see the iconic Búðakirkja church, you'll dream of nights of peaceful slumber under the stars surrounded by fields, and the Hotel Búdir is the closest you'll come to that. **Pros:** fantastic restaurant; prime location in Snæfellsjökull National Park; perhaps the quietest hotel you'll ever stay in. **Cons:** expensive; breakfast not included with room rate; not much to do in the area if you're not into the outdoors. [$] *Rooms from: ISK47,430* ✉ *356 Snæfellsbær* ☎ *435–6700* 🌐 *www.hotelbudir.is* 🛏 *28 rooms* 🍴 *No Meals.*

Hellissandur

18 km (11 miles) north of Snæfellsjökull National Park.

This village on the northwestern tip of Snæfellsnes Peninsula may be small—don't expect a bustling scene here—but there are sights that make it worth a stop on your trip. Given the lack of hotels in the area, it's best to find another locale to lay your head and reserve Hellissandur for a stop on your tour of the west coast.

GETTING HERE AND AROUND

Driving here from Reykjavík is simple and obstacle-free (as long as the weather is good) with beautiful scenery. Route 54 will take you along the coast all the way up from Borgarnes. If you're trying to get here by bus, it's a bit trickier. Take Bus 57 from Reykjavík to Borgarnes, and then grab a seat on Bus 58 from Borgarnes to Stykkishólmur. From there, take Bus 82 to Hellissandur (the last stop on that route). Once you're in Hellissandur, the city is walkable, though you'll want a car to explore some of the more remote sights.

Sights

★ Fishermen's Park and Maritime Museum

HISTORY MUSEUM | FAMILY | Located in one of the oldest fishing villages in Iceland, the Fishermen's Park and Maritime Museum has a number of traditional turf houses you can explore while learning all about the industry that has long supported this community. Part of the museum is the back garden (free), where you'll find large whalebones from the nearby shore. If you're feeling strong, you can try to lift one of the Steintök, or lifting stones, that local people used to showcase their strength years ago. There are four total that range in weight from 50 to 339 pounds. ⊠ *Utnesvegur* 🕾 *844–5969* ⊕ *themaritimemuseumhellissandi.business.site* 🎫 *ISK 1,300.*

Ingjaldshóll

HISTORIC SIGHT | One of the more historic sites in West Iceland, Ingjaldshóll was once home to important government officials, including the Sturlunga Clan, who ruled West Iceland throughout the 12th and 13th centuries. Today, you'll find the oldest concrete church in the world, as well as a fun split-rock illustration, carved by famed sculptor Páll Guðmundsson, depicting Eggert Ólafsson and Ingibjörg Guðmundsdóttir (his wife). ⊠ *Ingjaldshólskirkja, Hellissandur.*

Svöðufoss

WATERFALL | FAMILY | The Laxa River falls 131 feet at Svöðufoss. A four-minute drive outside of Hellissandur, it's the perfect place to bring a picnic lunch on a nice day. To get to these falls, drive along Route 54 and turn off toward Sveinnstadir. Continue past the farm to a house called Foss. From there, Svöðufoss is an 800-meter walk from the road. If you're in the mood for more waterfall scenes, continue walking to Kerlingarfoss. ⊠ *Hellissandur.*

Restaurants

Gilbakki

$$ | ICELANDIC | FAMILY | This spot is all about homemade cakes, fish soup, and small plates. While there may not be many options on the menu, it offers up snacks and meals for all appetites. **Known for:** good coffee; perfect fish soup; delicious baked goods. 💲 *Average main: ISK2,200* ⊠ *Hellissandur* 🕾 *436–1001* ⊕ *www.facebook.com/gilbakki.*

★ Viðvík

$$$$ | SEAFOOD | If you want the best meal you can get in Hellissandur—and possibly the entire region—head to Viðvík. The catch of the day is always a good bet in Iceland, but treat yourself to the three-course chef's menu here—you won't be disappointed. **Known for:** fabulous three-course tasting menu; next-level service; family-owned vibe. 💲 *Average main: ISK5,200* ⊠ *360 Hellissandur* 🕾 *436–1026* ⊕ *www.facebook.com/vidvikrestaurant* 🕓 *Closed Mon. and Tues.*

Hotels

Welcome Hotel Hellissandur

$ | HOTEL | This is a great option if you plan on spending most of your time exploring nearby Snæfellsjökull National Park and just need a place to rest between hikes. **Pros:** incredibly quiet; unbeatable location; breakfast included in the room rate. **Cons:** very basic decor; few amenities; interior design lacks personality. 💲 *Rooms from: ISK16,758* ⊠ *Klettsbúð 9* 🕾 *487–1212* ⊕ *hellissandur.welcome.is* 🛏 *20 rooms* 🍴 *Free Breakfast.*

Ólafsvík

9 km (6 miles) east of Hellissandur.

Ólafsvík was once an important port between Denmark and Iceland in the 17th and 18th centuries. Today, it's a quiet fishing village with incredible curb appeal. Bird-watching and hiking are beloved activities in this area, and it's the perfect town to use as a base for exploring nearby Snæfellsjökull National Park.

GETTING HERE AND AROUND
Ólafsvík is located right on Route 54, making it an easy drive up the western coast. If you're trying to get here via public transportation, you can do so by way of Stykkishólmur. Hop on Strætó Bus 57 from Reykjavík and get off at Borgarnes. From there, take Bus 58 to Stykkishólmur. You can get to Ólafsvík from Stykkishólmur on Bus 82 (it'll be the last stop). Getting around Ólafsvík is simple, and the city can be easily explored on foot. You will need a car to see some of the more remote sights.

 Sights

Bæjarfoss
WATERFALL | The waterfall Bæjarfoss (pronounced "*bye*-yar-foss") is within walking distance from town. It's an easy hike on a somewhat hidden path—walk toward the back of town from Hotel Ólafsvík. You can also pick up the trail at the edge of town, but you will have to scramble over some fenced areas. The waterfall is small but incredibly scenic, and you won't find the crowds that you will at some of Iceland's larger falls. ⊠ *Ólafsvík.*

Pakkhús Museum
HISTORY MUSEUM | FAMILY | Learn about the history of Ólafsvík in this converted trading store. Afterward, grab a cup of coffee or a snack in the on-site café. ⊠ *Ólafsbraut 12, Ólafsvík* ☎ *433–6930.*

 Beaches

Skarðsvík Beach
BEACH | FAMILY | Iceland may be known for its black-sand beaches, but this golden-sand beach is secluded and far less crowded than Reynisfjara near Vík. **Amenities:** parking (free). **Best for:** solitude; sunrise; swimming. ⊠ *Ólafsvík.*

 **Restaurants**

★ **Kaldilækur**
$ | CAFÉ | Take a break from your tour of the west coast for a slice of cake at this quaint coffee shop. They also have solid coffee and a great selection of baked goods—everything you need to keep you going while sightseeing. **Known for:** tasty date cake; friendly service; really cold beer. $ *Average main: ISK1,000* ⊠ *Mýrarholt 2, Ólafsvík* ☎ *846–6619* ⊕ *www.facebook.com/kaldilaekur.*

Reks
$$$ | BURGER | With burgers, salads, and seafood, the menu covers a lot of ground at this fjord-adjacent restaurant. Given its central locale, this is a popular place for locals and visitors settling down from a long day of whale-watching tours, so book ahead if possible. **Known for:** great service; delicious lamb burger; great views of the fjord. $ *Average main: ISK3,490* ⊠ *Grundarbraut 2, Ólafsvík* ☎ *436–6625* ⊕ *www.skerrestaurant.is/is/menu.*

★ **Sker**
$$$ | SEAFOOD | As with any restaurant in a coastal town—and Sker is located right on the sea—fish is the way to go here. Travelers also come (and come back) to this restaurant for its broad menu, which ranges from seafood and pizza to vegan options. **Known for:** fresh seafood; plenty of vegan and vegetarian options; beautiful views of the bay. $ *Average main: ISK3,750* ⊠ *Ólafsbraut 19, Ólafsvík* ☎ *436–6625* ⊕ *www.skerrestaurant.is.*

 Hotels

Við Hafið Guesthouse
$ | HOTEL | FAMILY | The location right near the bay makes a room at this hotel worth three times its rate. **Pros:** great location for whale watching; central location for outdoor activities; friendly service. **Cons:** basic amenities; very little decor and interior design; small rooms. $ *Rooms from:*

The peculiar mountain of Kirkjufell stands guard over the town of Grundarfjörður.

ISK18,230 ⊠ Ólafsbraut 55, Ólafsvík
🖼 436–1166 ⤴ 44 beds, 15 private rooms
⦿ Free Breakfast.

Shopping

Gallerí Jökull
CRAFTS | If you're looking for something special and locally handmade, head to Gallerí Jökull. There are plenty of jewelry and accessory options, but you'll also find yourself wondering whether there's room in your suitcase for that wool sweater or hat. ⊠ Norðurtangi 3, Ólafsvík 🖼 865–0451 ⊕ www.instagram.com/galleri_jokull.

Grundarfjörður

26 km (16 miles) west of Ólafsvík.

Grundarfjörður is known for being home to Kirkjufell, a mountain just outside of town with a strangely shaped peak. The town itself doesn't have much to speak of, but it delivers the essentials: a

grocery store, gas station, hostel, and a few restaurants. Don't miss the waterfalls just past the mountain—if you get there early enough, you'll have the entire area to yourself.

GETTING HERE AND AROUND
If you're driving, you can reach Grundarfjörður by continuing along Route 54 out of Ólafsvík. By bus, you can take Strætó Bus 57 from Reykjavík to Borgarnes, then Bus 58 to Stykkishólmur, and finally Bus 82 to Grundarfjörður. This is the same route to Ólafsvík, though you'll be getting off a stop sooner (if traveling from Reykjavík).

Sights

Kirkjufell
MOUNTAIN | It's possible to climb "Church Mountain," but you might want to enlist the help of a local guide to get to the top. At the peak, you'll find fossils and other remnants from years past. Don't miss the nearby waterfall, Kirkjufellsfoss, which is

especially striking early in the morning. ✉ *Grundarfjörður.*

Saga Centre

OTHER MUSEUM | FAMILY | There's an interesting array of exhibits at this museum and visitor center. Inside the Saga Centre, you'll find a full-size fishing boat and tons of fishing gear, as well as a children's toy collection. You can also pick up local hiking maps, as well as use the on-site Wi-Fi and grab a snack at the café. ✉ *Grundargata 35* ☎ *438–1881.*

🍴 Restaurants

Bjargarsteinn Mathús

$$$$ | SCANDINAVIAN | The menu may be small and handwritten, but dining here is an experience. Stepping inside the family-run restaurant feels like walking into, well, a family home. **Known for:** excellent seafood; cozy interiors; beautiful views of the water. [$] *Average main: ISK4,390* ✉ *Sólvellir, Grundarfjörður* ☎ *438–6770* 🌐 *bjargarsteinn.business.site* 🕓 *Closed Mon. and Tues. No lunch.*

59 Bistro Bar

$$ | BURGER | FAMILY | Whether you're catching a soccer game or grabbing a much-needed meal after climbing nearby Kirkjufell Mountain, this space delivers. The beer on tap is local, the meals are hearty, and the locals are friendly. **Known for:** top-notch burgers; lively atmosphere; views of Kirkjufell. [$] *Average main: ISK2,290* ✉ *Grundargata 59, Grundarfjörður* ☎ *438–6446* 🌐 *www.facebook.com/kaffi59* 🕓 *No lunch Sun.*

Harbour Cafe

$$ | PIZZA | For a quick bite, settle into a pizza or panini at this waterside café. It's casual and quick, so don't expect a special presentation or intricate ingredients. **Known for:** lunchtime paninis; twelve different pizza options; great value. [$] *Average main: ISK2,495* ✉ *Nesvegur, Grundarfjörður* ☎ *562–6533.*

Meistarinn

$ | HOT DOG | FAMILY | This hot dog food truck has an intriguing naming system when it comes to its menu: each item is named after a member of the Danish Royal Family. The Icelandic hot dogs here are tasty, affordable, and filling. **Known for:** quirky menu item names; quick service; great views of the harbor. [$] *Average main: ISK590* ✉ *Grundargata 33* ☎ *848–0153.*

🛏 Hotels

Kirkjufell Hotel

$$ | HOTEL | FAMILY | This practical hotel has basic amenities but offers fantastic views of the fjord. **Pros:** great views; breakfast included with room rate; private rooms and bathrooms. **Cons:** outdated decor; located in an industrial part of town; no elevator. [$] *Rooms from: ISK28,511* ✉ *Nesvegur 8* ☎ *438–6893* 🌐 *www.kirkjufellhotel.is* 🛏 *29 rooms* 🍴 *Free Breakfast.*

The Old Post Office Guesthouse

$ | HOTEL | As the name suggests, this guesthouse was once a mail hub, shuttling correspondence to the locals of this remote town. **Pros:** wonderful views of Krikjufell; shared kitchen facilities; great value. **Cons:** small rooms; basic amenities; not all rooms have private bathrooms. [$] *Rooms from: ISK14,953* ✉ *Grundargata, Grundarfjörður* ☎ *430–8043* 🌐 *www.topo.is* 🛏 *7 rooms* 🍴 *No Meals.*

Stykkishólmur

39 km (24 miles) northeast of Grundarfjörður.

You can't really get a bad view from any of the towns in West Iceland, but the Stykkishólmur harbor—surrounded by tiny islands—is truly special. Once you tire of the ocean views, take a walk through town. Stykkishólmur is known for its historic homes, which have been carefully renovated over time. There are enough museums, restaurants, and hotels that you can easily spend an entire day (or two) in this area.

GETTING HERE AND AROUND

For drivers, take Route 54 out of Grundarfjörður until you hit the end in Stykkishólmur. You can also access this town by Strætó via Borgarnes. Take Bus 57 from Reykjavík to Borgarnes and then take a seat on Bus 58, which will bring you to Stykkishólmur. The city is walkable, but a car is recommended if you plan on exploring outside the city limits.

Sights

Berserkjahraun

HISTORIC SIGHT | The real highlight of this spot is its history: Berserkjahraun is an area mentioned in the Eyrbyggja Saga telling the tale of two Swedish berserkers, Halli and Leiknir. A farmer named Styr the Slayer took the berserkers off of his brother's hands, and Halli quickly fell in love with Styr's daughter. He posed a challenge to the pair: before he would allow Halli to marry his daughter, the berserkers had to build a road through the seemingly impassable lava field. Halli and Leiknir succeeded, only to meet their demise in a special sauna designed by Styr to kill them, and their supposed burial site can still be visited today. It may be grim, but you can't say it's not an exciting tale. To get here, head west on Snæfellsnesvegur where it splits from Helgafellssveitarvegur, and follow the gravel road on the left before you hit a bridge taking you over the water. ⊠ *Stykkishólmur.*

Bjarnarhöfn Shark Museum

OTHER MUSEUM | **FAMILY** | Located in the town of Bjarnarhöfn right outside of Stykkishólmur, this museum is the place to go if you want to learn all about the wonderous shark. You can even give Iceland's traditional fermented shark dish a taste here. ⊠ *Bjarnarhofn, Stykkishólmur* ☎ *438–1581* ⊕ *www.bjarnarhofn.is* ⌦ *ISK 1,400.*

Glanni Waterfall

WATERFALL | You'll find the Glanni Waterfall after hiking from a parking lot near a golf course. At the end of your walk, you'll also see Paradise Hollow, the perfect place for a picnic breakfast or lunch. ⊠ *Stykkishólmur.*

Grábrók

NATURE SIGHT | Walk the 560 feet to the top of this volcanic crater to take in the sights of the Borgarfjörður region and the stunning Lake Hreðarvatn. Grábrók was formed by a fissure eruption 3,000 years ago. ⊠ *Stykkishólmur.*

Helgafell

MOUNTAIN | "Holy Mountain" has surely earned its name. The church built here honors Þórólfr Mostrarskegg, the first settler of the area. This sacred location makes an appearance in the Icelandic Sagas, and local folklore says that if you hike to the top without looking back once or saying a word, you will have three wishes fulfilled. ⊠ *Stykkishólmur.*

★ Library of Water

ART GALLERY | **FAMILY** | Iceland has no shortage of thought-provoking art exhibits and museums, but the Library of Water is one of its most unique. The main exhibit, *Water, Selected,* presents 24 glass columns filled with melted ice collected from glaciers around the country. When light hits the glass columns, beams are reflected onto a rubber floor embossed with both Icelandic and English words pertaining to the weather. ⊠ *Bókhlöðustígur 19, Stykkishólmur* ☎ *865–4516* ⊕ *www.libraryofwater.is.*

Restaurants

★ Narfeyrarstofa

$$$$ | **SEAFOOD** | This restaurant is located in the oldest section of Stykkishólmur inside a bright, airy building. The menu is full of local seafood, as well as lamb from the region. **Known for:** first-rate seafood; quaint interior design; blue mussels from the bay. $ *Average main: ISK4,900*

Did You Know?

The church at Helgafell ("Holy Mountain") honors the area's first settler. Local folklore has it that if you hike to the top of Holy Mountain without looking back, you'll be granted three wishes.

✉ *Aðalgata 3, Stykkishólmur* ☎ *533–1119* 🌐 *www.narfeyrarstofa.is.*

★ **Sjávarpakkhúsið**
$$$ | **SEAFOOD** | The fresh catch of the day, sourced from local fishermen, is a crowd pleaser at Sjávarpakkhúsið. Come early for a meal at this popular spot; dinnertime can get crowded with locals enjoying the view of Stykkishólmur harbor. **Known for:** great harbor views; fresh catch of the day; local favorite. [$] *Average main: ISK3,790* ✉ *Hafnargata 2, Stykkishólmur* ☎ *438–1800* 🌐 *www.sjavarpakkhusid.is.*

Hotels

Fosshotel Stykkishólmur
$$$ | **HOTEL** | **FAMILY** | The Fosshotel chain is known for trendy interior design and friendly service, and the Stykkishólmur location is no exception. **Pros:** delicious restaurant on-site with gorgeous views; private rooms and bathrooms; friendly service. **Cons:** chain-hotel vibe; not as cozy as local guesthouses; breakfast not included. [$] *Rooms from: ISK32,564* ✉ *Borgarbraut 8, Stykkishólmur* ☎ *354/430–2100* 🌐 *www.islandshotel.is* 🛏 *87 rooms* 🍴 *No Meals.*

Harbour Hostel
$ | **HOTEL** | This charming hostel offers shared and private rooms with simple decor. **Pros:** bike rentals for guests; prime location next to the harbor; private rooms available. **Cons:** no shoes on past the front door; shared facilities in the dorms; few outlets in the shared bunk rooms. [$] *Rooms from: ISK9,900* ✉ *Hafnargata 4, Stykkishólmur* ☎ *517–5353* 🌐 *www.harbourhostel.is* 🛏 *10 rooms* 🍴 *No Meals.*

★ **Höfðagata Gisting**
$ | **B&B/INN** | Holding the title of the oldest bed and breakfast in Stykkishólmur, Höfðagata Gisting is centrally located to all of the city's best offerings, including the harbor, community pool, museums, and restaurants. **Pros:** great central location; cozy interior design; friendly hosts and service. **Cons:** shared bathrooms with some rooms; small rooms; not much privacy. [$] *Rooms from: ISK18,668* ✉ *Höfðagata 11* ☎ *831–1806* 🛏 *6 rooms, 1 apartment.*

★ **Hotel Breidafjördur**
$$ | **B&B/INN** | The family-run Hotel Breidafjördur, which was the first schoolhouse in the village in 1897 and later a bakery, offers both private rooms and hostel-style accommodations. **Pros:** unique history; breakfast included in room rate; free parking. **Cons:** basic amenities; some road noise; outdated decor. [$] *Rooms from: ISK21,475* ✉ *Aðalgata 8, Stykkishólmur* ☎ *433–2200* 🌐 *www.hotelbreidafjordur.is* 🛏 *11 rooms* 🍴 *Free Breakfast.*

★ **Hótel Egilsen**
$$ | **HOTEL** | This design-forward hotel's one goal is to make you feel as cozy as humanly possible. **Pros:** Instagram-worthy building; L'Occitane amenities; beautiful interior restoration of a historic home. **Cons:** breakfast not included in room rate; tiny rooms; be ready to carry your luggage upstairs. [$] *Rooms from: ISK26,575* ✉ *Aðalgata 2, Stykkishólmur* ☎ *554–7700* 🌐 *www.egilsen.is* 🛏 *10 rooms* 🍴 *No Meals.*

Hotel Fransiskus
$$$ | **HOTEL** | **FAMILY** | In the 1930s, a group of Catholic nuns traveled to Stykkishólmur to start a community, building a chapel, monastery, and hospital; today, the chapel still serves as a place for travelers to rest as Hotel Fransiskus. **Pros:** breakfast is included in room rate; each floor has its own communal lounge; interesting history. **Cons:** some rooms have less-than-ideal views; close proximity to hospital can get noisy; converted hospital-room accommodations can be off-putting. [$] *Rooms from: ISK31,715* ✉ *Austurgata 7, Stykkishólmur* ☎ *422–1101* 🌐 *www.fransiskus.is* 🛏 *21 rooms* 🍴 *Free Breakfast.*

Hotel Stundarfridur
$ | **HOTEL** | **FAMILY** | Each room at Hotel Stundarfridur is equipped with a flat-screen TV, Wi-Fi, and a private bathroom.

Pros: as quiet as it gets; spacious rooms; great northern lights location. **Cons:** can be hard to find; a bit of a drive from Stykkishólmur (12 km); breakfast not included. $ *Rooms from: ISK16,118* ⊠ *Birkilundi 43* ☎ *856–2463* ⊕ *www.stundarfridurehf.is* ➟ *7 rooms* ¶⊙¶ *No Meals.*

Sýsló Guesthouse

$$ | B&B/INN | FAMILY | Located smack-dab in the center of town, Sýsló Guesthouse has great hilltop views of nearby Breiðafjörður Bay. With close access to the town's museums, restaurants, bars, and historic homes, you can't go wrong embarking on a stroll through the winding streets. **Pros:** great central location; spot-on interior design; free coffee and tea. **Cons:** breakfast not included in room rate; check-in is in another building; small rooms. $ *Rooms from: ISK24,271* ⊠ *Aðalgata 7, Stykkishólmur* ☎ *831–1806* ⊕ *www.syslo.is* ➟ *7 rooms* ¶⊙¶ *No Meals.*

Shopping

★ Bókaverzlun Breiðafjarðar

SOUVENIRS | You'll find a little bit of everything in this store, from books and locally made soaps to yarn and macabre skull-themed decor. If you're on the hunt for a souvenir, there's a good chance you're going to find it at Bókaverzlun Breiðafjarðar. ⊠ *Borgarbraut 1, Aðalgata, Stykkishólmur* ☎ *438–1121.*

Flatey

34 km (21 miles) north off the coast of Stykkishólmur.

Visit Flatey Island and you'll feel that you've been cast adrift in time. It was once a busy fishing community, but today only six residents live on the island year-round—which makes sense, given that it's accessible only during the warm summer months. There's only one hotel on the island, so make sure to plan ahead for this truly unique experience; it might just be the quietest place in the country, with only occasional birdsong breaking the silence.

GETTING HERE AND AROUND

There's only one way on and off the island: by Seatours ferry from Stykkishólmur or Brjánslækur in the Westfjords, which runs less frequently in the winter. Tickets from Stykkishólmur cost ISK 3,060 in winter and ISK 3,920 in summer. Seatours have teamed up with the Hotel Flatey, which offers a discounted room rate with the purchase of a round-trip ferry ticket. The hotel is open only during the summer, so you can't spend the night any other time of year.

The island is small—a little over a mile long and about half a mile wide—and that's a good thing since no cars are allowed on the island and you have to get around on foot. The hotel tends to fill up quickly during prime summer months.

CONTACTS Seatours. ⊠ *Smiðjustígur 3, Flatey* ☎ *433–2254* ⊕ *www.seatours.is.*

Hotels

★ Hotel Flatey

$$$ | B&B/INN | It's the only accommodation on the entire island, but luckily Hotel Flatey is a beautiful property with a lot of charm. **Pros:** incredibly serene and quiet; very unique experience; cozy rooms and communal spaces. **Cons:** getting here is a commitment; not open during the winter months; no nearby nightlife. $ *Rooms from: ISK35,342* ⊠ *Flatey* ☎ *422–7610* ⊕ *www.hotelflatey.is* ➟ *11 rooms* ¶⊙¶ *Free Breakfast.*

WESTFJORDS

Updated by
Erika Owen

◉ Sights	🍴 Restaurants	🛏 Hotels	🛍 Shopping	🍸 Nightlife
★★★☆☆	★★☆☆☆	★★☆☆☆	★☆☆☆☆	★☆☆☆☆

WELCOME TO WESTFJORDS

TOP REASONS TO GO

★ **Hornstrandir Nature Reserve:** Witness a secluded community of arctic foxes and other local wildlife.

★ **Dynjandi:** The region's most stunning water-fall draws people from all over the world.

★ **Dreamy drives:** In summer, drive along the stunning coastline of the peninsula and see some of the country's most impressive landscapes.

★ **Solitude:** Though there's been an uptick in tourism, fewer tour buses come to the Westfjords than other parts of Iceland, meaning you'll have more space to yourself.

1 Ísafjörður. This town in the northern region of the Westfjords wraps around a bay and can be recognized by its 18th- and 19th-century wooden homes. It's also the gateway to the stunning Hornstrandir Nature Reserve.

2 Flateyri. There's an interesting and devastating history of avalanches in this area.

3 Þingeyri. Located on scenic Dýrafjörður, Þingeyri is a good spot to fill up on gas, groceries, and views—it enjoys the natural wonders of smaller communities, plus many amenities they lack.

4 Patreksfjörður. The largest town in the Southern Westfjords was once a major force in the country's fishing industry, and commercial fishing and processing continue to be the area's main industries.

5 Hólmavík. Visit Hólmavík and you're sure to leave with tales of the region's history of witchcraft.

6 Drangsnes. You can catch the ferry to Grimsey Island here.

NORWEGIAN SEA

Horn

Hornstrandir
Nature Reserve

Latrar

HORNSTRANDIR

Smidhjuvik

Jökulfirðir

Furufjordhur

Minnibakki

Sudereyri

Drangajökull

Ísafjardardjúp

Unadhsdalur

Saebol

2

1

Ísafjörður

Flateyri

Ulsfa

Hamar

60

Arnes

61

635

61

643

Þingeyri

3

Arngerdhareyi

60

Dynjandi
Nat'l Monument

61

Kaldranes

Bildudalur

Vatnsdalsvatn
Nature Reserve

Hólmavík

5

6

63

608

Drangsnes

60

68

60

61

Fjardharhorn

62

60

607

68

Reykhólar

Stadharholskirkja

0   10 mi

0   10 km

60

Head to the Westfjords for mountains, waterfalls, pink-sand beaches, hot springs, and bird-watching cliffs. Despite its natural beauty, it happens to be one of the least-traveled regions of the country. But perhaps that should come as no surprise as the Westfjords occupy one-third of the Icelandic coastline, so getting from place to place takes a lot of driving, plus it's so far from other must-see Icelandic destinations that a trip here demands its own itinerary.

The Westfjords are really accessible only during the summer months (late May—if you're lucky—through August). The area receives a massive amount of snowfall every year, and roads are often closed in winter for safety reasons. The only way to get around the region is by car, so it can be nearly impossible to drive as early as September through April. When you're traveling to the Westfjords, it's important to keep a close eye on the weather to anticipate any road closures or obstacles. Even in summer, expect quick changes in weather—rain, sleet, hail, sunshine, sometimes even snow. Pack extra layers and always make sure you check in on the weather radar frequently, especially if you're venturing out on a multiday hike or camping trip—trails and fields can get windy, and you don't want to be unprepared.

This region is famous around the world for its numerous hiking trails. Plenty of tour operators will guide you on multiday hikes, but there are also trails spanning a few hours to a full day that you can take on your own. The best way to find the perfect hiking trail for you is to visit one of the regional information centers and tell a staff member what you're looking for. They can direct you to a local hike that fits all of your qualifications.

Hotels can be few and far between, so many visitors choose to camp while exploring the Westfjords. Many agree that this is the best way to experience the region, and there is no shortage of campgrounds all across the area.

The small towns of Iceland may be short on restaurants, bars, and hotels, but you'll find plenty of museums in communities along the Westfjords. They may sound niche but are worth the visit, even if you're just curious. These communities take a lot of pride in their local industries, and you'll be glad you stopped in.

Planning

When to Go

Given the quick-changing weather patterns during the winter months, the only time you can really experience the Westfjords is during the summer. Snowstorms as early as September can shut down roads for the season, so it's best to get your trip in between late May and late August. You'll be doing yourself a big favor: you have to rent a car to visit this region of Iceland and you don't want to get stuck in any unexpected squalls.

When planning your trip, make sure to factor in enough time for the possibility of bad weather—even in the warmest months, snow can make an appearance.

Getting Here and Around

AIR

There are a number of ways to reach the Westfjords by plane. The most common is to fly into Keflavík International Airport and rent a car (the scenery makes the driving time worth it). Visitors can also choose to fly into Reykjavík International Airport and take a short flight to Ísafjörður on Air Iceland Connect, which has two daily 40-minute flights.

CONTACTS Air Iceland Connect. ☎ 570–3030 ⊕ www.airicelandconnect.com.

BOAT

Taking a ferry is not only one of the prettiest ways to travel between West Iceland and the Westfjords, but also one of the quickest. Ferry Baldur has daily trips crossing Breidafjörður Bay. You can hop on at Stykkishólmur on the Snæfellsnes Peninsula, as well as Brjánslækur in the north of Iceland.

CONTACTS Ferry Baldur. ⊠ Brjánslækur ☎ 433–2254 ⊕ www.seatours.is.

BUS

There are a number of ways to access the Westfjords by bus. If you're coming from Reykjavík, you can take Strætó, the public bus system, to Hólmavík year-round. During the summertime, there's a Strætó route that travels between Hólmavík and Ísafjörður. You can also take a bus via Westfjords Adventures between Brjánslækur and Patreksfjörður in the summer. There are also local buses between Patreksfjörður, Tálknafjörður, and Bíldudalur.

CONTACTS Strætó. ⊠ Höfðagata ☎ 540–2700 ⊕ www.straeto.is. **Westfjords Adventures.** ☎ 456–5006 ⊕ www.westfjordsadventures.com.

CAR

Renting your own car gives you the greatest freedom on a visit to the Westfjords. The sights in this area can be miles away from one another, and public bus routes are severely limited. If you want to get away from the small crowds of tour buses, rent a car and be on your way. The roads are relatively well maintained during the summertime, but don't take them on during the winter months—more often than not, you'll find foul weather shutting down roads all over the place.

Restaurants

There are restaurants and cafés located in most of the towns and villages in the Westfjords, but don't expect a breadth of diverse options. If you plan on cooking for yourself, it's a good idea to bring a cooler and visit a grocery store whenever you pass one. Many of the guesthouses, campsites, and hostels in the area have shared kitchen access, so you can whip up your own meals when needed.

Hotels

There are plenty of lodging options scattered among the scenery in the Westfjords. Accommodations in this region are often family-run properties, which adds a cozy dose of hospitality when you arrive. Don't expect the check-in process to be as simple as you would in a bustling city like Reykjavík though. Many hotels and guesthouses don't have 24-hour reception, so you may have to call the owners when you arrive—it's best to acquaint yourself with the check-in process before you get there. The Westfjords region is filled with stunning sights and rugged beauty so many travelers choose to camp. The weather is unpredictable, however, and at times it's too windy to set up a tent, so it's a good practice to have a backup hotel or guesthouse in mind just in case.

RESTAURANT AND HOTEL PRICES

Restaurant prices in the reviews are the average cost of a main course at dinner, or if dinner is not served, at lunch. Hotel prices in the reviews are the lowest cost of a standard double room in high season. Restaurant and hotel reviews have been shortened. For full information, visit Fodors.com.

What it Costs in ISK			
$	$$	$$$	$$$$
RESTAURANTS			
under ISK 1,500	ISK 1,500–2,999	ISK 3,000–4,000	over ISK 4,000
HOTELS			
under ISK 20,000	ISK 20,000–29,999	ISK 30,000–40,000	over ISK 40,000

Safety

Iceland is consistently ranked one of the safest places on Earth, but the country's natural volcanism and the rugged terrain of the Westfjords can be dangerous. When you're in areas with high geothermal activity—say, geysers or boiling mud baths—be careful where you're stepping. And the same goes for the lava fields, which may be pretty, but where it's really easy to twist an ankle if you're not paying attention. When hiking, take all of the usual precautions: don't get too close to the edges of mountains and cliffs; hike with a friend or let someone know where you plan on going; and make sure to dress in layers. Getting stuck in bad weather can be one of the most dangerous situations in Iceland. Also—and it should go without saying—make sure to respect the local ecology: leave only footprints, and pick up after yourself.

Tours

Seatours

BOAT TOURS | The main ferry operator between Flatey, Brjánslækur, and Stykkishólmur, Seatours also offers one of the most unique experiences you can have in Iceland: the Viking Sushi Adventure Voyage, where guests can eat freshly dredged seafood (like scallops and sea urchin) while gliding through Breiðafjörður. ⊠ *Smiðjustígur 3* ☎ *433–2254* ⊕ *www.seatours.is.*

West Tours

ADVENTURE TOURS | **FAMILY** | In addition to the usual offerings—whale- and bird-watching, boating, hiking, kayaking, and sea angling—West Tours offers some pretty enticing adventures. Check out the day trip to Hesteyri, an abandoned village in the Hornstrandir Nature Preserve that can only be reached by boat. If you're looking to relax, check out the kayaking in Ísafjörður. ⊠ *Aðalstræti 7* ☎ *456–5111* ⊕ *www.westtours.is.*

Wild Westfjords
ADVENTURE TOURS | **FAMILY** | Offering both single- and multiday tours of this remote region of Iceland, Wild Westfjords will show you the best the area has to offer when it comes to skiing, hiking, bird-watching, and village visits. They may be best known for bringing travelers along to participate in the Fossavatns-gangan, a mid-April ski marathon dating back to 1935. ⊠ *Pollgata 4* ☎ *456–3300* ⊕ *www.wildwestfjords.com.*

Visitor Information

CONTACTS Hólmavík District Information Office. ⊠ *Höfðagata 8–10* ☎ *451–3111* ⊕ *www.holmavik.is/info.* **Westfjords Regional Information Center.** ⊠ *Neðsti-kaupstaður 400, Ísafjörður* ☎ *450–8060* ⊕ *www.westfjords.is.* **Westfjords Tourist Information Office.** ⊠ *Aðalstræti 7* ☎ *456–5444* ⊕ *www.edinborg.is.*

Ísafjörður

544 km (338 miles) north of Reykjavík.

You'll find Ísafjörður nestled in a fjord—as its name suggests—in the northwest section of the Westfjords, south of and across the bay from the Hornstrandir Nature Reserve. From the moment you drive into town, you'll be wowed by the area's dramatic landscapes. The city's location alone, surrounded by the fjord, gives your time here a fairytale vibe. Ísafjörður is a town with a lot of history, which is palpable as you walk through the city's oldest section, with its wooden homes. This town has been and still is a fishing community, and you can learn all about its history at the Westfjords Herit-age Museum, which houses a collection of old fishing boats and gear.

GETTING HERE AND AROUND
During the summer months, there are three Westfjords Adventures buses every week between Patreksfjörður and Ísafjörður. There are also two daily flights from Reykjavík into Ísafjörður on Air Iceland Connect. Once you're in town, you'll find it's quite walkable, but it's best to rent a car to take in the nearby natural sights.

TOURS
★ Aurora Arktika
BOAT TOURS | Although custom itineraries are available, a handful of tours from this company are designed to showcase the best of what the Westfjords have to offer. Experiences focus on multiday journeys to different parts of the Westfjords; all of the sailboat tours depart from the harbor in Ísafjörður. The six-day Iceland Sailboat Skiing tour will show you some of the best skiing in the country by way of sailboat. A sailboat will also be your home base for Sail and Run in Iceland, which features guided runs along some of the most stunning landscapes in the Westfjords. ⊠ *Ísafjörður harbor, Ísafjörður* ☎ *899–3817* ⊕ *www.aurora-arktika.com.*

Sights

Arctic Fox Center
WILDLIFE REFUGE | **FAMILY** | Iceland isn't known for its abundance of wildlife, but it is home to the adorable and elusive arctic fox. You can find these animals in the wild—and if you do, watch them from afar and let them be—but you're sure to see them at the Arctic Fox Center in Súðavík, a quick drive from Ísafjörður. At this wildlife refuge and research center, guests are invited to learn all about these curious little mammals. The arctic fox population has been dwindling for years, and the center also puts forth efforts to maintain it. ⊠ *Eyrardalur, 420 Súðavík, Ísafjörður* ☎ *456–4922* ⊕ *www.arcticfox-centre.com* 🎫 *ISK 1,500.*

Edinborg Cultural Center
VISITOR CENTER | **FAMILY** | The main tourist information center is also an archive of all things Ísafjörður. The ground floor serves as the town's library, while the second

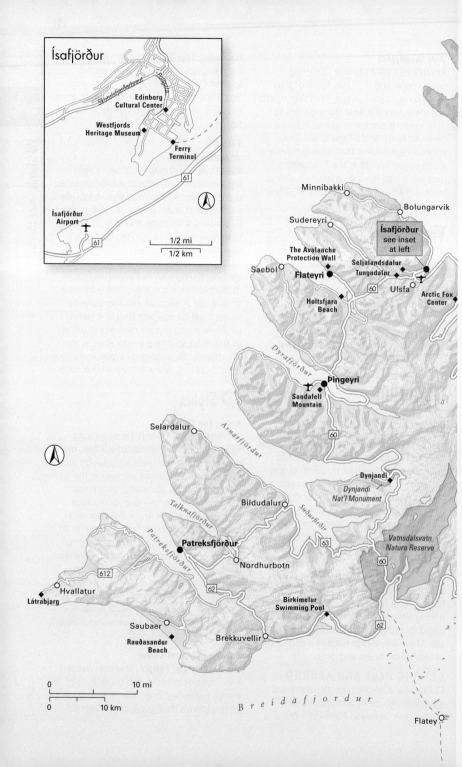

Ísafjörður

Skutulsfjarðarbraut

Edinborg
Cultural Center

Westfjords
Heritage Museum

Ferry
Terminal

Ísafjörður
Airport

61

61

1/2 mi
1/2 km

Minnibakki

Bolungarvik

Sudereyri

Ísafjörður
see inset
at left

The Avalanche
Protection Wall

Seljalandsdalur
Tungudalur

Saebol

Flateyri

Ulsfa

60

Arctic Fox
Center

Holtsfjara
Beach

Dyrafjörður

Þingeyri

Sandafell
Mountain

Selardalur

Arnarfjörður

60

Dynjandi

Dynjandi
Nat'l Monument

Bildudalur

Talknafjörður

Suðurfjörður

Vatnsdalsvatn
Nature Reserve

Patreksfjörður

Patreksfjörður

63

Nordhurbotn

60

Hvallatur

612

Látrabjarg

62

Birkimelur
Swimming Pool

Saubaer

62

**Rauðasandur
Beach**

Brekkuvellir

0   10 mi
0   10 km

B r e i d a f j o r d u r

Flatey

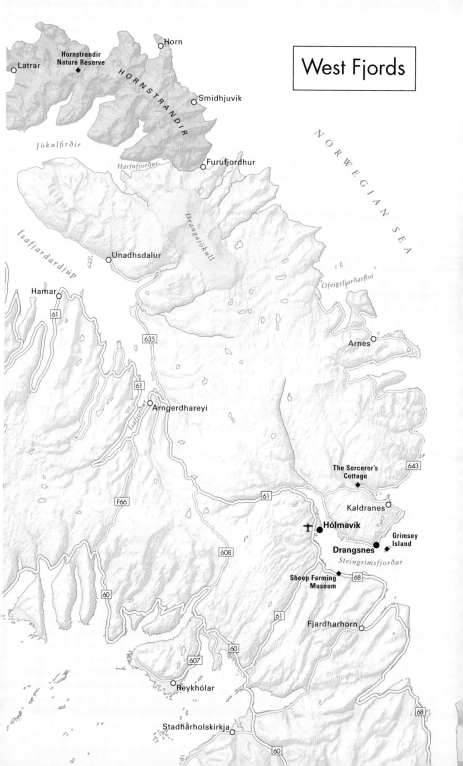

West Fjords

Horn

Latrar

Hornstrandir
Nature Reserve

H O R N S T R A N D I R

Smidhjuvik

Jökulfirðir

Harfnfjorður

Furufjordhur

N O R W E G I A N   S E A

Drangajökull

Unadhsdalur

Ofeigsfjarðarfloi

Ísafjarðardjúp

Hamar

61

635

Arnes

61

Ísafjörður

Arngerdhareyi

The Sorceror's
Cottage

643

F66

61

Kaldranes

Hólmavík

Grimsey
Island

Drangsnes

Steingrimsfjorður

608

Sheep Farming
Museum

68

60

Fjardharhorn

61

60

607

Reykhólar

68

Stadharholskirkja

60

A fishing town nestled into a fjord, the views in Ísafjörður are remarkable.

floor houses a number of exhibits covering life in the Westfjords through the ages. ⊠ *Eyrartún* ☎ *450–8220* ⊕ *www. safnis.is* ✆ *Closed Sun.*

★ Hornstrandir Nature Reserve

NATURE PRESERVE | Ísafjörður is the place to catch a ferry to the Hornstrandir Nature Reserve. Two companies offer regular service to the area in the summer: Borea and Sjóferðir. Tickets can be pricey, but it's worth the investment. There is a wide range of hiking trails, and it's common to see arctic foxes, as this region boasts one of the largest communities of them in the country. Getting here in winter is often impossible due to severe weather. ⊠ *Aðalstræti 10* ☎ *591–2000.*

Tungudalur

FOREST | **FAMILY** | If you've got a short amount of time in the area, head to Tungudalur for some natural sights. Here you'll find a small but beautiful waterfall, a modest forest, the town's skiing center, and a full golf course. There's plenty to do, but take some extra time around

the waterfall and forest; you won't find many of the latter around the country. ⊠ *Ísafjörður.*

★ Westfjords Heritage Museum

OTHER MUSEUM | **FAMILY** | Learn about the rich history of the local fishing industry and how it's helped regional growth at the Westfjords Heritage Museum. It takes a deep dive into the lives of the fishermen that built this community and what it was like to live in the area when it was first settled. Note that some resources refer to this museum as the Maritime Museum. ⊠ *Neðstikaupstaður, Ísafjörður* ☎ *456–3291* ⊕ *www.nedsti.is* ✉ *ISK 1,500* ✆ *Closed mid-Sept.–mid-May.*

🍴 Restaurants

Einarshusid

$$ | **PIZZA** | Located inside the hotel of the same name, this spot is beloved for its pizza. You'll love the friendly service and cozy furniture—there are sofas in place of more traditional chairs. **Known**

for: great pizza; cozy atmosphere; great service. $ *Average main: ISK1,900* ✉ *415 Bolungarvík* ☎ *456–7901* ⊕ *www. einarshusid.is.*

Husið

$$ | **EUROPEAN** | **FAMILY** | Head to Old Town to dine at Husið, which offers a wide variety of menu options from burgers to seafood. They also offer brunch, which is not often found in the more remote areas of Iceland. **Known for:** large beer selection; vegetarian options; good kids' menu. $ *Average main: ISK2,690* ✉ *Hrannargata 2, Ísafjörður* ☎ *456–5555* ⋔ *Casual.*

★ Tjöruhúsið

$$$ | **SEAFOOD** | **FAMILY** | You never know exactly what the menu will be at the family-owned Tjöruhúsið, and for good reason: it all depends on what the local fishermen catch. You have your pick of two dinner seatings, at 7 pm and 9 pm (so don't be late), and three menu options—soup only, fish only, or fish and soup. **Known for:** super fresh catch of the day; delicious soups; strict dinner seatings and small menu. $ *Average main: ISK3,200* ✉ *Nedsti kaupstadur* ☎ *456–4419* ⊘ *Closed Mon.*

Hotels

Hótel Ísafjörður Torg

$$ | **HOTEL** | **FAMILY** | Located in the heart of the city, Hótel Ísafjörður is a great base for exploring the museums and restaurants in the area. **Pros:** central location; friendly service; breakfast included in the room rate. **Cons:** can get noisy; basic amenities; small rooms. $ *Rooms from: ISK27,000* ✉ *Silfurtorgi 2* ☎ *456–4111* ⊕ *www.hotelisafjordur.is* ⤵ *35 rooms* ⋔⊙⫶ *Free Breakfast.*

Nightlife

Dokkan Brugghús

BARS | This microbrewery is the only one in the region and for this alone it's worth a stop. It only helps that the

brews—Fossawatn, Skarfur Stout, Dynjandi IPA—are delicious and often named after local sights. ✉ *Sindragata 14* ☎ *788–1980* ⊕ *www.dokkanbrugghus.is.*

Edinborg Bistro

LIVE MUSIC | By day, Edinborg Bistro is a restaurant—and a quite good one at that—but at night, it welcomes musicians in to perform for locals and those just passing through. ✉ *Aðalstræti 7, Ísafjörður* ☎ *456–8335* ⊕ *www.facebook. com/edinborgbistro.*

Shopping

Penninn Eymundsson Ísafirði

BOOKS | **FAMILY** | You'll find yourself surrounded by books (both Icelandic and English) in Penninn Eymundsson Ísafirði. There's also a café inside, in case you want a cup of coffee while reading your new book. ✉ *Hafnarstræti 2, Ísafjörður* ☎ *456–3123* ⊕ *www.penninn.is.*

Flateyri

21 km (13 miles) west of Ísafjörður.

Flateyri was in its prime in the 19th century, when it was a trading post and—somewhat unfortunately—a hub for whaling and shark hunting. Today, it's a popular spot for those looking to try their hand at sea angling. Plan on spending an afternoon here, as there are plenty of museums and historic spots, plus a beach to explore. Fun fact: the area hosts what just may be the northernmost sand-castle-building competition in the world.

Flateyri has also had its fair share of avalanches, and these days it's equipped with special protection, which you can see when you visit. The village bookshop has been transformed into a museum that goes over this tragic history.

The village of Flateyri was a trading post in the 19th century.

GETTING HERE AND AROUND

Driving to Flateyri is certainly the easiest way to get there, but there are local buses that connect Þingeyri, Flateyri, and Ísafjörður. This bus route runs three to four times daily on weekdays (depending on the weather).

 ## Sights

The Avalanche Protection Wall

OTHER ATTRACTION | Flateyri has an unfortunate history of frequent (and frequently lethal) avalanches, and a protective wall has been built to better protect the town and its residents. Located directly above the city, you can see it from most spots in town. A relatively easy route leads up to the wall where there are some spectacular views. ⊠ *Flateyri* ✛ *The wall encompasses the back end of the town—you can't miss it.*

Holtsfjara Beach

BEACH | **FAMILY** | Every July, crowds flock to Holtsfjara Beach for the annual sandcastle-building competition. The white-sand beach—a rare sight in Iceland—is a local favorite for those warm-blooded enough to jump in the chilly water. ⊠ *Flateyri.*

Seljalandsdalur

NATURE SIGHT | **FAMILY** | This nearby valley is great for walking or, when there's snow on the ground, skiing. If you're traveling on Seljalandsvegur and pass Fosshestar on your right, you'll find that the road splits, so you can follow Seljalandsvegur or head left on Skutuls-fjarðarbraut. Stay on Seljalandsvegur for a third of a mile before taking a slight right onto a gravel road. From here, there is a parking lot where you can leave your car and head into Seljalandsdalur. ⊠ *Flateyri.*

Restaurants

★ Vagninn

$$$ | **SEAFOOD** | The first thing to know about this small-town, middle-of-nowhere restaurant is that you can get an amazing lamb burger. The second thing to know is that the best time to go is on weekends, when there's live music playing late into the night. **Known for:** live music on weekends; delicious lamb burger; great views of the surrounding bay. $ Average main: ISK3,800 ⊠ Hafnar-stræti 19 ☎ 456–7751.

Hotels

Fisherman Hotel
$$ | **HOTEL** | Hotels can be far and few between in this region of Iceland and often follow an "all-in-one" mentality; this spot is no exception with its role as a restaurant, hotel, bar, and gathering space. **Pros:** delicious seafood restaurant on-site; free breakfast; free parking. **Cons:** noise can carry between rooms; basic amenities; small rooms. $ Rooms from: ISK20,382 ⊠ Aðalgata 14-16, Suðureyri ☎ 450–9000 ⊕ www.fisherman.is ⊅ 18 rooms ⦿ Free Breakfast.

Korpudalur
$ | **HOTEL** | The best part about Korpudalur may be how far removed you are from civilization and how close you are to Iceland's biggest attraction: nature. **Pros:** beautiful remote setting; incredibly quiet; private rooms available. **Cons:** few rooms so it can book up quickly; some shared bathrooms; basic amenities. $ Rooms from: ISK14,000 ⊠ Kirkjubol Korpudal ☎ 456–7808 ⊕ www.hostel.is ⦾ Closed mid-Sept.–mid-May ⊅ 6 rooms.

Shopping

★ The Old Bookstore
BOOKS | **FAMILY** | This is exactly what it sounds like: a historic spot to buy a new read. The Old Bookstore has been owned by the same family since 1914, and everything you find inside—aside from the books—has remained relatively unchanged since then. Beyond the books, however, you'll also find an exhibit that tells the history of the town. ⊠ Hafnarstraeti 3 ☎ 840–0600 ⊕ www.flateyribookstore.com.

Þingeyri

39km (24 miles) south of Flateyri.

Located on the stunning Dýrafjörður fjord, Þingeyri is a small village and the home of the oldest functioning black-smith workshop (now a museum) in the country. Small, random facts like this will keep you entertained on your visit here, since there isn't much in the way of nightlife, shopping, or dining. That's not necessarily a bad thing, however; in Þingeyri, you get to experience a small fishing community as it's meant to be experienced—without distraction. This area is often referred to as "the Alps of the Westfjords."

GETTING HERE AND AROUND
It's possible to drive from Reykjavík to Þingeyri. The total trip is 408 km (253 miles), and the road is paved. Otherwise, there are local buses that connect Þingeyri and Flateyri.

Sights

★ Dynjandi
WATERFALL | **FAMILY** | One of the most famous waterfalls in the Westfjords, Dynjandi is a 45-minute drive from Þingeyri. Some refer to this waterfall as "the bridal veil," given its stairwell formation. It actually comprises seven waterfalls in total, all feeding one another in the most graceful way. Expect a crowd if you go in the middle of the day as this waterfall draws a lot of visitors to the area. ⊠ Þingeyri ⊹ Take the gravel road toward the waterfall off of Vestfjarðavegur; then follow signs.

★ Old Blacksmith's Workshop
HISTORY MUSEUM | Opened in 1913, this blacksmith shop was run by Guðmundur J. Sigurðsson after learning the trade in Denmark. Today, it's a living museum that still has all of the old machines, and you can learn about blacksmithing as it was done more than 100 years ago. This is the

perfect activity for a family with kids of various ages. ✉ *Smiðjustígur 2, Þingeyri.*

Sandafell Mountain

MOUNTAIN | Hikers shouldn't miss this mountain right outside of Þingeyri. Whether you hike it or take a 4X4 vehicle to the top, the views are absolutely incredible. ✉ *Þingeyri* ✥ *Follow Aðalstræti into the town of Þingeyri; Sandafell is located directly behind the town.*

🍴 Restaurants

★ Simbahöllin

$$ | **CAFÉ** | Built in 1915, this former general store is now a restaurant loved by locals and visitors alike. Go for Belgian waffles in the morning or afternoon, and visit again at night for the local catch of the day and lamb tagine. **Known for:** superb Belgian waffles; soup of the day; local institution. [$] *Average main: ISK1,600* ✉ *Fjarðargata 5* ☎ *899–6659* 🌐 *www.simbahollin.is.*

🛏 Hotels

Hotel Sandafell

$$ | **HOTEL** | **FAMILY** | There aren't many options when it comes to lodging in Þingeyri, but Hotel Sandafell checks all the boxes. **Pros:** breakfast included in the room rate; beautiful views from all rooms; friendly service. **Cons:** interior design could use some love; basic amenities; shared bathrooms. [$] *Rooms from: ISK16,500* ✉ *7 Hafnarstræti, Þingeyri* ☎ *456–1600* 🌐 *www.hotelsandafell.com* 🕓 *Clsoed mid-Sept.–mid-May* 🛏 *21 rooms* 🍴 *Free Breakfast.*

Patreksfjörður

130 km (81 miles) southwest of Þingeyri.

Throughout the 20th century, Patreksfjörður was a major Icelandic fishing center, and it continues to play a large part in commercial fishing today. One of the larger cities you'll encounter in the Westfjords, it has plenty of lodging and dining options as well as a community pool where you can mingle with the locals. Don't miss the biggest draw of this town: its proximity to Látrabjarg, a massive sea bird colony on the westernmost tip of the Westfjords.

GETTING HERE AND AROUND

There are six flights a week from Bíldudalur. You can also reach this city by bus, but it will be a journey: hop on Strætó in Reykjavík and ride it to Stykkishólmur, then take the ferry from Baldur to Brjánslækur, and finally a bus to Patreksfjörður. As you can imagine, it's easier to drive yourself. Keep in mind that many tourist-oriented businesses shut down in winter on account of the weather.

VISITOR INFORMATION

CONTACTS Patreksfjörður Tourist Information Center. ✉ *Þórsgata 8a* ☎ *456–5006.*

👁 Sights

Birkimelur Swimming Pool

POOL | **FAMILY** | Pools are central to Icelandic communities and the Birkimelur Swimming Pool is no exception. Relax among the locals in this man-made pool, which is heated with geothermal water. There are changing rooms on-site, as well as a sauna. ✉ *Barðastrandarvegur, Patreksfjörður* ☎ *456–2040* 🌐 *www.westfjords.is/en/service/birkimelur-swimming-pool* 🕓 *Closed mid-Aug.–May.*

Hnjótur Museum

HISTORY MUSEUM | **FAMILY** | The exhibits at the Hnjótur Museum speak for themselves—there are no flashy additions, gadgets, or A.I. Learn all about the region's history through traditional garments, reenactments of British trawler rescues, and a full-size plane that's open to explore. ✉ *Örlygshöfn* ☎ *456–1511* 🌐 *www.hnjotur.is* 🎟 *ISK 1,250* 🕓 *Closed Oct.–Apr.*

★ **Látrabjarg**

NATURE SIGHT | The cliffs at Látrabjarg are home to millions of birds—the main reason people from around the world flock to this region—and to answer your burning question: yes, you can see adorable puffins here. You'll also catch sight of razorbills, fulmars, and guillemot in the clouds of birds that surround this area; in fact, no fewer than 10 sea bird species call these cliffs home. Látrabjarg is actually just one of four sections of cliffs in this area: the Keflavíkurbjarg, Bæjarbjarg, Breiðavíkurbjarg, and Látrabjarg cliffs. All have slightly different viewpoints with one thing in common: a whole lot of birds. There's also a scenic lighthouse on-site, which happens to be the westernmost lighthouse in Europe. To get here, drive along Route 612 until you can't anymore; this is the westernmost point of the Westfjords.

★ **Rauðasandur Beach**

BEACH | **FAMILY** | Although black-sand beaches may get the most attention in Iceland, the red sand of Rauðasandur Beach is something that needs to be seen in person. What makes it that golden red color? Pulverized scallop shells. Depending on the day, the beach can appear more yellow, red, or black. To get here from Patreksfjörður, take Route 62 and follow the signs for Route 614, then take Route 612. Note that the road leading to this beach is not unpaved and is often quite rough—and it's a windy road, so take it slow. ✉ *Patreksfjörður.*

🍴 Restaurants

★ **Cafe Dunhagi**

$$$ | **ICELANDIC** | **FAMILY** | This spot sources many of its ingredients from the surrounding fjord, offering an authentic taste of local life. This spot is often busy so call to book a table ahead of time. **Known for:** lively atmosphere; local ingredients; stunning scenery. [$] *Average main: ISK3,200* ✉ *Sveinseyri, Tálknafjörður* ☎ *662–0463* 🌐 *www.cafedunhagi.is* 🕒 *Closed Mon.*

Hópið

$$ | **EUROPEAN** | **FAMILY** | The menu at this casual restaurant favors burgers, pizza, seafood, and salads. The town of Tálknafjörður is a quick trip from Patreksfjörður and offers up stunning scenery—the best kind of side dish for your meal. **Known for:** good variety on menu for picky eaters; great value; friendly service. [$] *Average main: ISK2,690* ✉ *Hrafnadalsvegur, Tálknafjörður* ☎ *456–2777* 🕒 *No lunch weekends.*

★ **Stúkuhúsið**

$$ | **SEAFOOD** | **FAMILY** | If you want to do yourself a favor, grab an outdoor table at Stúkuhúsið (assuming the weather is cooperating), order dinner, take in the views, and finish up with a slice of rhubarb pie. The food here is fresh and delicious, the service is friendly, and the desserts are the perfect ending to your day. **Known for:** always tasty catch of the day; outdoor dining; vegetarian options. [$] *Average main: ISK2,400* ✉ *Aðalstræti 50, Patreksfjörður* ☎ *456–1404* 🌐 *www.stukuhusid.is.*

🛏 Hotels

Fosshotel Westfjords

$$$ | **HOTEL** | **FAMILY** | Despite its business-like vibe, this outpost from the Fosshotel chain is a solid choice for your stay in Patreksfjörður, and you'll get the trusted service this brand is so well known for. **Pros:** central location; friendly service; trusted brand. **Cons:** breakfast not included in room rate; somewhat sterile decor and interior design; can get noisy. [$] *Rooms from: ISK35,995* ✉ *Aðalstræti 100* ☎ *456–2004* 🌐 *www.islandshotel.is* 🛏 *40 rooms* 🍽 *No Meals.*

Hotel Breidavik Guesthouse

$ | **HOTEL** | **FAMILY** | This guesthouse offers up rooms with private bathrooms, shared facilities, and campground spots, making it a great spot to meet fellow travelers. **Pros:** free breakfast; washing machine access; close to Latrabjarg. **Cons:** not

The Drangses Hot Tubs are hot springs overlooking the ocean that are free to the public.

much to do in area; basic amenities; outdated design. $\boxed{\$}$ *Rooms from: ISK13,998* ✉ *451 Breiðavík* ☎ *456–1575* ⊕ *breidavik. is* ⥱ *38 rooms* ⊚⏐ *Free Breakfast.*

★ Radagerdi Guesthouse
$$ | **B&B/INN** | This is the very picture of a Nordic guesthouse on the coast—the design is minimalist and on point, breakfast is included, and there's a terrace area for taking in the scenery. **Pros:** free breakfast; beautiful terrace area; modern design. **Cons:** shared bathrooms in some rooms; small rooms; loud plumbing. $\boxed{\$}$ *Rooms from: ISK24,600* ✉ *Aðalstræti* ☎ *456–1560* ⊕ *www.radagerdi.net* ⥱ *11 rooms* ⊚⏐ *Free Breakfast.*

Nightlife

★ Flak
BREWPUBS | In true remote Iceland fashion, this space wears many hats, and to call Flak a pub would be a disservice. Sure, they serve up beers brewed near and far, but it's also a great seafood restaurant and often displays art.

✉ *Eyrargata, Patreksfjörður* ☎ *456–0145* ⊕ *www.flakflak.is.*

Hólmavík

220 km (137 miles) east of Patreksfjörður.

Hólmavík is the repository of Iceland's witchcraft and sorcery history, and not just because of its museum. In the 17th century, this shepherding and fishing community was also the country's center of witch-hunting. Today, Hólmavík offers essentials like restaurants, gas stations, a grocery store, and a few hotels.

GETTING HERE AND AROUND
There are two to four buses between Reykjavík and Hólmavík on Strætó routes every week, depending on the season. There is also a bus route to and from Ísafjörður two to three times a week, depending on the weather. It's easiest to visit by car.

Sights

★ The Museum of Icelandic Witchcraft and Sorcery

HISTORY MUSEUM | If you find the ancient world of Icelandic witchcraft intriguing, this museum is a must-visit. Inside you'll find artifacts with morbid histories, exhibits with terrifying stand-ins, and a pair of necropants with a background so chilling we'll leave you to discover it yourself. ⊠ *Höfðagata 8–10* ☎ *897–6525* ⊕ *www. galdrasyning.is* 🎫 *ISK 1,200.*

★ Sheep Farming Museum

OTHER MUSEUM | **FAMILY** | You only have to drive around the country for a few minutes to understand what an important role sheep play in the Icelandic economy. The Sheep Farming Museum has been a local and visitor favorite since it opened in 2002. If the season is right, after learning all about the industry (specifically the Strandir region), you can meet some of the farm's lambs and help feed them. ☎ *451–3324* ⊙ *Closed Sept.–May.*

★ The Sorceror's Cottage

OTHER MUSEUM | **FAMILY** | The Sorceror's Cottage is a sight to behold, even if you don't have time to enjoy the museum inside. Just a quick drive from the Museum of Icelandic Witchcraft and Sorcery, this cottage serves as the second part of the main museum. You'll learn all about how people lived in the 17th century and why sorcery became such a huge part of life here. ⊠ *Strandavegur* ☎ *897–6525* ⊕ *www.galdrasyning.is* 🎫 *ISK 1,250.*

Restaurants

★ Café Riis

$$$ | **PIZZA** | This restaurant is often packed with locals and travelers, which is a true testament to how great it is. Café Riis serves up a mean fish soup, as well as pizza that some have called the best in Iceland. **Known for:** tasty seafood soup; delicious pizza options; cozy interior.

⒮ *Average main: ISK3,200* ⊠ *Hafnarbraut 39* ☎ *451–3567* ⊕ *www.caferiis.is.*

Restaurant Galdur

$$$ | **SCANDINAVIAN** | **FAMILY** | Located next to the Museum of Icelandic Witchcraft and Sorcery, Galdur is a counter-style restaurant that serves local dishes. It's a tad on the expensive side (even by Icelandic standards), but the dishes remain worth the price tag. **Known for:** excellent lamb stew; Reykjavík-level standards in a small town; convenient to the witchcraft museum. ⒮ *Average main: ISK3,500* ⊠ *Hoefdagata 10* ☎ *451–3525* ⊕ *galdrasyning.is.*

🛏 Hotels

Finna Hotel

$ | **B&B/INN** | One of the very few options for lodging in Hólmavík, the Finna Hotel has basic amenities; if you're not looking for luxury, you'll find it perfectly suitable. **Pros:** breakfast included in room rate; affordable rates; beautiful surroundings. **Cons:** no storage in rooms; thin walls; can be hard to find. ⒮ *Rooms from: ISK13,900* ⊠ *Borgarbraut 4* ☎ *451–3136* ⊕ *www.finnahotel.is* 🛏 *17 rooms* ⏏ *Free Breakfast.*

Hotel Laugarholl

$ | **HOTEL** | The geothermal swimming pool is the biggest draw at this remote hotel. **Pros:** proximity to natural sights and witchcraft museum; free breakfast; geothermal swimming pool. **Cons:** some shared bathrooms; basic amenities; outdated decor. ⒮ *Rooms from: ISK18,629* ⊠ *511 Kaldrananeshreppur* ☎ *451–3380* ⊕ *www.laugarholl.is* 🛏 *16 rooms* ⏏ *Free Breakfast.*

Drangsnes

30 km (19 miles) east of Hólmavík.

Drangsnes is best known as the access point for Grímsey Island, a fantastic destination for bird-watching, arctic snorkeling, and golfing. While there aren't many museums or activities around this fishing village, the community swimming pool shouldn't be missed. There are also plenty of hiking trails through Drangsnes to keep you busy if you decide to spend some time here.

GETTING HERE AND AROUND

Weather permitting, visitors can drive from Hólmavík to Drangsnes on Route 61, which turns into Route 645. To the north is a winding road that takes you past dramatic views of the coast. From Drangsnes you can take a boat to Grímsey Island.

Sights

★ Drangses Hot Tubs

HOT SPRING | Like most communities in Iceland, Drangses has a local hot spring. There are three different tubs on-site of varying temperatures, and they are fantastic—free to the public and each one with a beautiful view of the ocean. Just be sure to follow cultural protocol and shower before entering the water. You won't find large crowds at these hot pots. ✉ *Drangsensvegur, Drangsnes.*

★ Grímsey Island

ISLAND | Take a 10-minute boat ride from the Drangses harbor to Grímsey for some serious bird-watching. You can even see puffins here if you come in the right season (usually the warmer, summer months). There's also a golf course, bike rentals, arctic snorkeling, sea fishing, and more. It's the perfect day trip from Drangses and the main reason why people find themselves in the area.

★ Kerling the Cliff

NATURE SIGHT | You have to know the story to truly appreciate this place: according to local lore, Kerling was a troll woman who, along with two other trolls, wanted to turn the Westfjords into an island. As they started digging, they realized they had nowhere to shelter from the sun as it rose. Kerling did not make it out of the sunlight in time, turned to stone, and sits here still in the form of this cliff. The troll women created many little islands behind them, one of which is known today as Grímsey. ✉ *Drangsnes.*

Restaurants

Malarkaffi

$$$ | SEAFOOD | FAMILY | Serving locally sourced seafood and lamb dishes, Malarkaffi is also popular for its memorable location with a veranda that overlooks the surrounding fjord. Note that this restaurant is closed during the wintertime. **Known for:** stunning views; catch of the day; variety of lamb dishes. [$] *Average main: ISK3,600* ✉ *Grundargata 17, Drangsnes* ☎ *853–6520* 🌐 *www.malarhorn.is* 🕓 *Closed Oct.–mid-May.*

Hotels

★ Malarhorn

$$ | B&B/INN | FAMILY | Although there's hardly any lodging in Dragsnes, Malarhorn really hits a home run when it comes to variety, as guests have a choice between three houses: House 1, with 10 double rooms that have private patios and bathrooms; House 2, with four double rooms that share a living room and kitchen; and House 3, with a family-size room, a two-bedroom apartment, four double rooms, and a superior double room with private entrance. **Pros:** cozy rooms; variety of room options; some rooms have patios. **Cons:** only option in the village; some rooms have shared bathrooms; restaurant closed during the wintertime. [$] *Rooms from: ISK22,400* ✉ *Grundargata 17* ☎ *853–6520* 🌐 *www.malarhorn.is* 🛏 *21 rooms* 🍴 *No Meals.*

Chapter 7

AKUREYRI

Updated by
Hannah Jane Cohen

👁 Sights	🍴 Restaurants	🛏 Hotels	🛍 Shopping	🍸 Nightlife
★★★☆☆	★★★☆☆	★★★☆☆	★★★☆☆	★★★☆☆

WELCOME TO AKUREYRI

TOP REASONS TO GO

★ **Gateway to the north:** The town makes a great base for exploring the northern wonders of Mývatn, Tröllaskagi, and the Jökulsárgljúfur canyon.

★ **Art:** Lıstagil is an entire street dedicated to the arts.

★ **Culture:** This thriving cultural hub has a rich literary heritage, unique museums, and a growing number of cosmopolitan dining options.

★ **Events:** The Arctic Open, Gásir Medieval Trading Weekend, the Summer Arts Festival, and the Iceland Winter Games are all held here.

★ **Winter sports:** Akureyri is home to Iceland's best ski resort, a short drive from the town center.

The capital of the north and Iceland's second-largest urban area, Akureyri is a small but growing city with nature on all sides.

1 Akureyri. Find all the necessities here plus a strong dose of cultural appeal including museums, great food, a top-notch performance venue, and more.

2 Rural Akureyri. The cultural and culinary delights of Akureyri continue south of the town center into Eyjafjarðarsveit. To the north, rural areas extend along both sides of the Eyjafjörður fjord where views across glittering waters, framed by green pastures and snowcapped mountains, are embellished by breaching whales, soaring birds, and the occasional iceberg.

Bakki

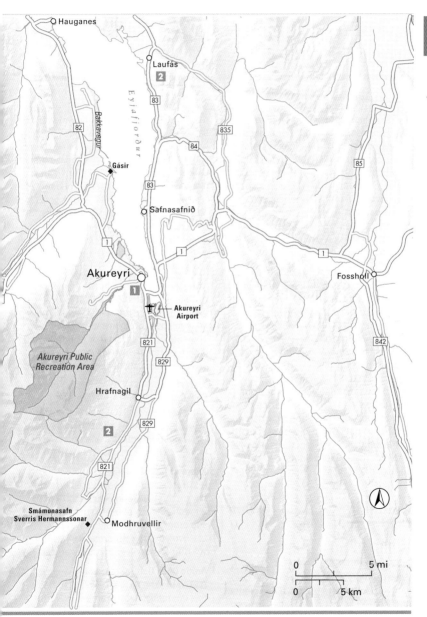

Centrally located, at the head of the lengthy Eyjafjörður fjord, Akureyri is the true heart of North Iceland, as every one of its red heart-shaped traffic lights attests.

It's often referred to as "Iceland's second city" but with a population of fewer than 20,000 residents, this northern capital is still very much a town—albeit one with impressive infrastructure and facilities, including an international airport and docking facilities for large cruise ships. Nestled between the northeast and northwest regions of the country, it's also an excellent base for day trips to the surrounding areas of Mývatn, the Tröllaskagi peninsula, and Jökulsárgljúfur.

Sheltered from ocean winds and cradled by mountains on three sides, Akureyri is as pretty as a postcard. Amid rich vegetation and a collection of late 19th-century wooden houses, the twin spires of a modern Lutheran church—rising on a green hill near the waterfront—provide an impressive focal point. There are plenty of cultural attractions and activities on offer to keep you engaged and entertained. It is also home to one of the world's most northerly botanical gardens and one of the country's best ski resorts. To the south is the pyramid-shaped rhyolite mountain Súlur, and beyond that is Kerling, the highest peak in the region.

Planning

When to Go

Warm and dry in the summer, with cold, snow-laden winters, Akureyri has plenty of seasonal sights and activities to keep

you engaged and entertained. The summer brings longer daylight hours with sensational displays of the midnight sun while the winter sees frequent northern lights activity, plus the occasional extraordinary appearance of *glitský*, or "glitter clouds" (polar stratospheric clouds). Akureyri's wealth of trees and vegetation is impressive, given its proximity to the Arctic Circle, and come fall—with its glorious golden tones and blazing reds—the town acquires a remarkable color palette.

Although Akureyri generally enjoys more hospitable weather than Reykjavík, winter here is much colder—with heavy snowfall beginning as early as October. The driest time of the year is in May, and it gets warmest in July. For up-to-date weather information, visit ⊕ *www.vedur. is.*

FESTIVALS

Along with several national holidays celebrated annually, Akureyri has a few family-friendly festivals and sports events unique to the town.

Akureyri Town Festival

FESTIVALS | Akureyri celebrates its birthday on the weekend closest to August 29 with a series of exhibitions, concerts, and other family-friendly activities. ⊠ *Akureyri* ⊕ *www.northiceland.is/en/ what-to-see-do/events/akureyrarvaka-1.*

Arctic Open Golf Tournament

FESTIVALS | The Akureyri Golf Club hosts this international tournament in North

Iceland, where golfers get to play under the midnight sun. ⊕ *www.arcticopen.is.*

Donald Duck Ski Competition

FESTIVALS | Hotels in Akureyri fill up quickly during this annual kids' skiing event at the Hlíðarfjall ski resort at the end of April. ⊕ *www.visitakureyri. is/en/see-and-do/events-festivals/ donald-duck-children-ski-competition-april.*

Ein Með Öllu

FESTIVALS | The biggest bank holiday weekend of the year in Iceland, the Merchant's weekend (officially known as Verslunarmannahelgin in Icelandic) was originally made to give shopkeepers an official summer vacation. But this explanation has been lost to time as now the weekend—which is always the first weekend of August—is simply known as the biggest party weekend of the year throughout the country. To celebrate, most towns in Iceland throw their own festivities, from Reykjavík's Innipúkinn indie music festival to Ísafjörður's Mýrar-bolti mud football championship. The biggest celebration is in the Westman Islands, called Þjóðhátíð í Eyjum (the Festival of the Nation). Ostensibly a music festival, it's much more well-known for its buckwild drunken wildness. Akureyri's iteration, meanwhile, is called Ein Með Öllu—the classic phrase one uses to order a hot dog in Icelandic. It's more of a family-friendly affair than Þjóðhátíð, as along with the requisite concerts, markets, and parties, there's also quite a bit of kid-centered entertainment, so don't be afraid to bring the tots along. As befits the city, there are also often special art events and workshops. ⊕ *www. northiceland.is/en/what-to-see-do/events/ einmedollu.*

Iceland Winter Games

FESTIVALS | The biggest winter festival in Iceland holds several international snow-sport competitions, including freeskiing, skiing, and snowboarding. ✉ *Akureyri* ⊕ *www.icelandwintergames.com.*

Medieval Trading Weekend at Gásir

FESTIVALS | Each July, the historic trading post site of Gásir is brought back to life during a lively reenactment festival where people dress up in medieval Viking costumes and host fun, old-fashioned activities. ⊕ *www.minjasafnid.is/is/gasir.*

Summer Arts Festival

FESTIVALS | Taking place during the last week of June through July, the Summer Arts Festival celebrates everything art with concerts, exhibitions, and other events. ✉ *Akureyri* ⊕ *www.visitakureyri.is.*

Getting Here and Around

AIR

Akureyri is home to Iceland's only other international airport outside of Reykjavík. Iceland's primary carrier, Icelandair operates several 45-minute flights daily between Reykjavík and Akureyri. Internationally, Niceair offers two weekly direct flights year-round from Akureyri to Copenhagen and Tenerife South in the Canary Islands.

From Akureyri, Norlandair has scheduled flights to local destinations Þórshöfn , Vopnafjörður, and Grímsey. They also operate a scheduled flight to Nerlerit Inaat (Constable Point) on the east coast of Greenland.

CONTACTS Akureyri Airport. ✉ *Urðargil 15, Akureyri* ☎ *424-4000* ⊕ *www.isavia.is/en/ akureyri-airport.*

AIRPORT TRANSFERS

Akureyri is located just 3 km (just under 2 miles) outside of the city center. The Akureyri Airport Bus connects the airport with all major areas of Akureyri, ending at the Hamrar campsite. Rides begin at ISK 800 and last 35 minutes. Tickets can be bought in advance online or via cash and card on the bus.

Taxis are also available at the airport or can be ordered by phone. Rides from the airport cost ISK 2,000 to the town center and ISK 3,000 to the northern perimeters of town.

7

Akureyri PLANNING

Additionally, the airport is only a 30- to 45-minute walk from the town center on a beautiful paved walkway along the coastline.

CONTACTS Akureyri Airport Bus. ✉ *Akureyri* ⊕ *www.sysli.is.* **Akureyri Taxi.** ✉ *Akureyri* ☎ *461–1010.*

BUS

Strætó offers bus service from Reykjavík to Akureyri, with stops along the way. Akureyri also has a free CityBus service operated by Strætó, with six routes running on weekdays from around 6:30 am to 11 pm and one (CityBus 6) on weekends from noon to 7 pm.

In addition, SBA Norðurleið offers bus service from Reykjavík to Akureyri as well as tours of the region, including excursions to Mývatn and Detifoss.

CONTACTS SBA Norðurleið. ☎ *550–0700* ⊕ *www.sba.is.* **Strætó.** ☎ *540–2700* ⊕ *www.straeto.is.*

CAR

It's 386 km (240 miles) from Reykjavík to Akureyri along the Ring Road (Route 1), a 4½-hour drive at least. As one of the main destinations in Iceland, most major car rental companies have facilities at the airport.

Whether you plan on using Akureyri as a base to explore the wild north or just for a quiet weekend away, having a car in Akureyri is both extremely recommended and extremely easy. As evident by the city's famous heart-shaped red lights, the capital of the north is a friendly place for drivers. The streets are well-marked and parking spots are plentiful. Most wonderfully, parking is always—unlike Akureyri's southern rival Reykjavík—free.

Just keep in mind though that while the town center is plowed and cleared during the winter snows, many of the surrounding residential streets are not. Icelanders are used to driving in these perilous conditions, but if you lack experience on slippery roads, take caution.

TAXI

Taxi company BSO has a taxi stand on Strandgata (opposite the HOF building) that's open 24 hours. Typical fares are around ISK 2,500.

CONTACTS BSO. ⊕ *www.bso.is.*

Restaurants

Iceland's northern capital has a collection of classy restaurants and charismatic coffeehouses, the latter concentrated mainly in the town center and near the trendy Listagil, a street exclusively dedicated to art, culture, and excellent food.

Hotels

Year-round accommodation options are diverse in Akureyri—ranging from small cottages to quality hotels in the town center, with a growing number of great-value rural stays on offer, too. Book well in advance if you're planning to visit during the summer or if your stay coincides with any of the town's events, especially the winter festivals.

RESTAURANT AND HOTEL PRICES

Restaurant prices in the reviews are the average cost of a main course at dinner, or if dinner is not served, at lunch. Hotel prices in the reviews are the lowest cost of a standard double room in high season. Restaurant and hotel reviews have been shortened. For more information, visit Fodors.com.

What it Costs in ISK			
$	$$	$$$	$$$$
RESTAURANTS			
under ISK 1,500	ISK 1,500– 2,999	ISK 3,000– 4,000	over ISK 4,000
HOTELS			
under ISK 20,000	ISK 20,000– 29,999	ISK 30,000– 45,000	over ISK 45,000

Nightlife

It might not have the cosmopolitan clout of the capital, but unlike Reykjavík, where bars and clubs come and go as quickly as the seasons, Akureyri's hot spots are still standing after many years of service. Sjallinn, the town's oldest club, has been hosting bands, dances, discos, and club nights since the 1960s.

Activities

Akureyri is a magnet for those who love the great outdoors, especially golfers and bikers, and the town and its surrounding area offer an increasing range of sightseeing services and activities. A growing number of companies specialize in everything from whale-watching to horseback riding. A scenic seafront path extends from the airport to the town center, featuring the attractive "Rendez-vous Bridge," an excellent spot for fishing or a photo op.

Akureyri has also invested in a 7-km (4½-mile) paved biking and hiking path between the town center and the Jólagarðurinn (Christmas Garden) south of the town. In addition, Akureyri is home to Jaðar, the world's most northerly 18-hole golf course and the site of the annual Arctic Open, when golfers from around the world compete under the midnight sun.

Shopping

There's better shopping in Akureyri than in most other towns outside Reykjavík, with many temptations along the pedestrians-only Hafnarstræti. The Glerártorg Square shopping mall 1 km (½ mile) is north of the town center where the Glerá river passes under Route 1.

Tours

Ferðafélag Akureyrar (*Touring Club of Akureyri*)
ADVENTURE TOURS | The Touring Club of Akureyri is the go-to group for hiking and cross-country-skiing trips in and around Akureyri. Their calendar of seasonal hikes includes tours to impressive local peaks like Mt. Súlur (3,750 feet) and Mt. Kerling (5,045 feet). ⊠ *Strandgata 23* ☎ *462–2720* ⊕ *www.ffa.is.*

Imagine Iceland Travel
ADVENTURE TOURS | This Akureyri-based provider offers a range of day tours showcasing all of the north's greatest hits—from Lake Mývatn to the Arctic coastline. They also offer personalized photo tours around the area or, better yet, under the northern lights. ⊠ *Laxagata 4, Akureyri* ☎ *833–5800* ⊕ *www.imagineicelandtravel.is.*

Nonni Travel
ADVENTURE TOURS | Serving the travel industry for over 30 years, Nonni specializes in package tours to Greenland and the Faroe Islands, as well as tours of local natural wonders and historic sites in and around North Iceland and other parts of the country. You can contact them for tailor-made trips and holidays, including mountain-hiking tours out of Akureyri. ⊠ *Brekkugata 5* ☎ *461–1841* ⊕ *www.nonnitravel.is.*

Saga Travel
ADVENTURE TOURS | When the staff are this much fun—some can sing and do handstands—you know you're in for a good time. Saga Travel offers day trips from Akureyri and North Iceland to all the famous natural hot spots on the Arctic coastline and "the Diamond Circle"—including Ásbrygi, Goðafoss, Dettifoss, and Mývatn—with super jeep trips to the northern highlands too. ⊠ Fjölnisgötu 6a, Akureyri 🕾 558–8888 ⊕ www.sagatravel.is.

The Traveling Viking
ADVENTURE TOURS | Horseback riding, kayaking, ice fishing, snowmobiling, and various tours of the region's most famous attractions are available from this operator, which also offers tours of Icelandic film locations where popular TV shows were made. ⊠ Ytri Bakki, Akureyri 🕾 896–3569.

★ Whale Watching Akureyri
BOAT TOURS | In a convenient harborside location by the Hof center, Whale Watching Akureyri operates classic three-hour whale-watching tours on a ship along with express two-hour trips on a RIB speedboat. ⊠ Akureyri 🕾 497–1000 ⊕ www.whalewatchingakureyri.is.

Visitor Information

The official tourist information center is located in Hof—the large round basalt-covered, gray building by the harbor. The staff are helpful and have the latest information on all the city's services, events, lodgings, tours, transportation, and the best places to dine.

CONTACTS Hof Cultural and Conference Center. ⊠ Strandgata 12, Akureyri 🕾 450–1000 ⊕ www.menningarhus.is.

Akureyri

The town has a variety of excellent museums, galleries, and scenic outdoor spaces, such as the botanical gardens and Kjarnaskógur forest. There's also an Akureyri Art Trail highlighting locations where you will find works of public art: Ask at the tourist information desk for a brochure and map.

Sights

★ Akureyrarkirkja
CHURCH | FAMILY | There are 112 steps leading up to Akureyri's main church, which, with its striking facade, is also one of the town's most iconic buildings. Designed by state architect Guðjón Samúelsson, who also designed Hallgrímskirkja in Reykjavík, the church has provided a nice center point for the town since it was built in 1940. Interesting features include the windows, which illustrate moments in Iceland's spiritual history. One window was believed to have been salvaged from Coventry Cathedral, which was destroyed during World War II. ⊠ Near Eyrarlandsvegur, Akureyri 🕾 462–7700 ⊕ www.akureyrarkirkja.is.

Akureyri Museum of Industry
HISTORY MUSEUM | The four exhibition halls at this museum near the airport detail the rather impressive industrial history of the region, which was especially known for producing wool, skins, clothing, and shoes. ⊠ Eyjafjarðarbraut vestri 🕾 462–3600 ⊕ www.idnadarsafnid.is 🖅 ISK 1,500 🕙 Closed Mon.–Wed.

★ Akureyri Swimming Pool
POOL | FAMILY | Akureyri's excellent open-air pool is one of the best in the country. It features water slides, lap and wading pools, an indoor pool, hot tubs, and a steam bath. ⊠ Þingvallastræti 21 🕾 461–4455 ⊕ www.visitakureyri.is 🖅 ISK 1,100.

Did You Know?

Akureyrikirkja, the unmissable main church of Akureyri, was designed by Guðjón Samuelsson, the architect of Hallgrím- skirkja in Reykjavík.

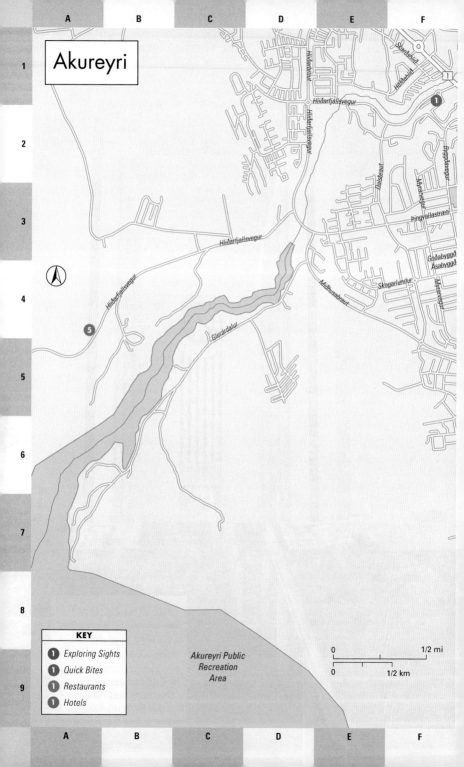

Akureyri

KEY

- **1** Exploring Sights
- **1** Quick Bites
- **1** Restaurants
- **1** Hotels

Akureyri Public
Recreation
Area

0   1/2 mi

0   1/2 km

Akureyri AKUREYRI

7

Sights ▼

1 Akureyrarkirkja	G3
2 Akureyri Museum of Industry	H6
3 Akureyri Swimming Pool	G3
4 Davíðshús	G2
5 Deiglan Gallery	G3
6 Flugsafn Íslands	H8
7 Forest Lagoon	J4
8 Hof	H2
9 Kjarnaskógur Woods	G9
10 Laufás	J4
11 Leikfangahúsið	H5
12 Listasafnið á Akureyri	G3
13 Lystigarður Akureyrar	G3
14 The Motorcycle Museum of Iceland	H6
15 Minjasafnið á Akureyri	H5
16 Nonnahús	H5

Restaurants ▼

1 Akureyri Fish and Chips	G2
2 Bautinn	G3
3 Berlin	G2
4 Bláa Kannan	G3
5 Brynja Ice Cream Shop	H4
6 Café Laut	G4
7 Greifinn	G1
8 Indian Curry House	G2
9 Leirunesti	H5
10 Rub23	G3
11 Strikið	G2

Quick Bites ▼

1 Bakaríið við Brúna	F1

Hotels ▼

1 Hotel Edda	G3
2 Hotel Kea	G3
3 Hotel Kjarnalundur	H8
4 Hotel Norðurland	G2
5 Hrimland Cottages	A4
6 Icelandair Hotel Akureyri	G3

Davíðshús

HISTORIC HOME | David Stefánsson, the owner of this 1940s house, was one of Iceland's most beloved poets and authors and a collector of fine art and rare manuscripts. His library, which is still meticulously preserved, together with all his belongings, is one of the country's most impressive private collections. Look out for several paintings by Jóhannes Kjarval, who was great friends with the author and a frequent guest at the house. ⊠ Bjarkastígur 6, Akureyri ☎ 462–4162 ⊕ www.akmus.is ⊡ ISK 2,000 ⊗ Closed Sept.–May.

Deiglan Gallery

ART GALLERY | Located on Akureyri's famed Listagil art street, the Deiglan Gallery is always worth a stop. Known for having its finger on the pulse of the local art scene, it has multiple exhibitions each month along with a roster of concerts and other various cultural events. ⊠ Kaupvangsstræti 23, Akureyri ☎ 895–3345 ⊕ www.listagil.is ⊡ Free.

★ Flugsafn Íslands

OTHER MUSEUM | FAMILY | Remarkable for several reasons, this aviation museum is home to a beautiful collection of antique aircraft and has been delighting folks with a passion for planes since it opened in 1999. One of its fans is famous actor and pilot Harrison Ford, who tried to purchase an impressive 1960 edition of his favorite plane: the DHC Beaver. The museum also provides an insight into Iceland's aviation history, which traces its roots back to Akureyri in 1937, when Icelandair was founded. ⊠ Akureyri Airport, Akureyri ☎ 461–4400 ⊕ www.flugsafn.is ⊡ ISK 1,500 ⊗ Closed Oct.–Apr.

★ Forest Lagoon

HOT SPRING | Just across the Eyjafjörður fjord from Akureyri city center lies the Forest Lagoon, Akureyri's own geothermal paradise in the Vaðlaskógur forest. With infinity pools, swim-up bars, a cold tub, sauna, bistro, and more, this upscale wooden retreat is warmed only by the interior heat of the mountain on which its carved. Go early for a prime spot to watch the sunrise. ⊠ Vaðlaskógur, Akureyri ☎ 585–0090 ⊕ www.forestlagoon.is ⊡ ISK 5,990.

Hof

PERFORMANCE VENUE | FAMILY | Since it opened in 2010, this basalt-covered house of culture, which lights up with pretty colors in the dark, has become a landmark building and an impressive addition to the picture-postcard view of Akureyri. Apart from housing the local tourist information center, Hof is home to an acoustically sophisticated concert hall and has first-rate facilities for hosting conferences and other cultural events. Its casual restaurant, Gárun Bistro Bar, overlooks the harbor. ⊠ Strandgata 12, Akureyri ☎ 450–1000 ⊕ www.menningarhus.is.

★ Kjarnaskógur Woods

FOREST | FAMILY | Situated on the gentle slopes of Mt. Súlur, 3 km (2 miles) south of Akureyri town center, the impressive Kjarnaskógur woodland is one of Iceland's most enchanting destinations. It is endowed with over a million trees and also features extensive trails and lovely recreational areas. Appealing in every season, the area is a magnet for local athletes as well as families who make great use of the beautifully designed play areas, barbecue facilities, and campground. During the dark winter months, its well-lit trails double as tracks for excellent cross-country skiing. ⊠ Kjarnavegur ☎ 462–4047 ⊕ www.kjarnaskogur.is.

★ Laufás

HISTORIC HOME | FAMILY | This well-preserved 1860s turf farmhouse and parsonage (and now museum) was built in a lovely meadow overlooking the sea. One of the larger examples of its kind in Iceland, Laufás presents an enchanting labyrinth of rooms, each with its own dedicated domestic function—including a "bride's room," which is unique to this particular dwelling. Coffee and kleinur

Lystigarðurinn, the Arctic Botanical Gardens, are home to over 7,000 native and non-native plant species.

(Icelandic doughnuts) are available at the visitors center, where you can also buy jam made from rhubarb grown on-site. ⊠ Greniviksvegur, Akureyri ☎ 463–3196 ⊕ www.minjasafnid.is ✉ ISK 2,000.

Leikfangahúsið
CHILDREN'S MUSEUM | FAMILY | Kids will love this toy museum, but grown-ups might be even more taken with the fascinating collection of 20th-century dolls, toy cars, and superheroes that bring back childhood memories. Located inside the house of an old bookbinder and merchant named Friðbjörn Steinarsson, it doubles as a shrine to "the Independent Order of Good Templars," of which he was a member. ⊠ Aðalstræti 46, Akureyri ☎ 462–4162 ⊕ www.minjasafnid.is ✉ ISK 2,000 ⊙ Closed Oct.–May.

★ Listasafnið á Akureyri
ART MUSEUM | Apart from exhibiting the talents of homegrown artists such as Erró, this modern gallery in the trendy Listagil area of town has hosted collections from some rather impressive names in the world of art, including Rembrandt, Joan Jonas, Matthew Barney, Elina Brotherus, Ange Leccia, Hrafnhildur Arnardóttir (aka Shoplifter), Wolfgang Tillmans, Barbara Probst, and Louisa Matthíasdóttir. ⊠ Kaupvangsstræti 8, Akureyri ☎ 461–2610 ⊕ www.listak.is ✉ ISK 1,900.

★ Lystigarður Akureyrar (Arctic Botanical Gardens)
GARDEN | FAMILY | Located around 30 miles south of the Arctic Circle, Lystigarður Akureyrar is one of the most northern botanical gardens in the world and a paradise of trees, flowers, and shrubs. Established by local women in 1912, with the botanical area opening in 1957, today the garden is home to 430 native and 6,600 non-native plant species, including some rare arctic and exotic plants. It's a short walk from the church on Eyrarlandsvegur. ⊠ Eyrarlandsstofa ☎ 462–7487 ⊕ www.lystigardur.akureyri.is ✉ Free ⊙ Closed Oct.–May

Minjasafnið á Akureyri (*Akureyri Museum*)
ART MUSEUM | The main subjects of this museum are local art and history, which includes the development of the town and surrounding areas since they were settled towards the end of the ninth century. There's a regular schedule of fascinating temporary exhibitions, with seasonal and festive installations too. Iceland's first tree farm was established on the grounds in 1899. ✉ *Aðalstræti 58, 600 Akureyri* ☎ *462–4162* 🌐 *www.akmus.is* 🎟 *ISK 2,000.*

The Motorcycle Museum of Iceland
OTHER MUSEUM | Located 30 minutes from the town center on foot and also accessible by bus, this light-filled museum displays a century's worth of information on Iceland's motorcycle history with well-cared-for bikes from across the world. A quick trip here is perfect for true enthusiasts. ✉ *Krókeyri 2, Akureyri* ☎ *466–3510* 🌐 *www.motorhjolasafn.is* 🎟 *ISK 1,000.*

Nonnahús
HISTORIC HOME | **FAMILY** | This lovely black wooden house is the childhood home of beloved Icelandic children's author Jón Sveinsson, and it's named after his most famous character and literary creation, Nonni. Built in the 1850s, the house is one of the oldest in Akureyri and is well preserved with all original furnishings, along with Jón's bedroom and his personal effects. The walls are lined with illustrations from his many books, and there's also a display of his works in translation. ✉ *Aðalstræti 54, Akureyri* ☎ *462–4162* 🌐 *www.nonni.is* 🎟 *ISK 2,000.*

🍴 Restaurants

Akureyri Fish and Chips
$$ | **FAST FOOD** | This food truck serves up exactly what it says in the title. Stop by for fresh fish, crispy breading, and a heaping pile of fries with all the fixings. **Known for:** memorable fish and chips; quick service; loaded fries with truffle mayo. [$] *Average main: ISK2,200* ✉ *Akureyri* ✥ *Check Facebook page for daily location* ☎ *414–6050* 🌐 *www.facebook.com/akureyriparadise.*

Bautinn
$$$$ | **INTERNATIONAL** | **FAMILY** | Located on one of the main corners of town and in one of its oldest buildings, this family favorite offers generous portions at affordable prices. Popular international favorites (burgers, pasta dishes, and tacos) are served alongside fresh local fish and some Akureyri favorites. **Known for:** crispy fresh fish-and-chips; prime people-watching location; deliciously over-the-top burgers. [$] *Average main: ISK4,290* ✉ *Hafnarstræti 92, Akureyri* ☎ *462–1818* 🌐 *www.bautinn.is.*

★ **Berlin**
$$ | **CAFÉ** | Hungry locals and visitors all come to Berlin (no relation to the city or German food) for the eggs, bacon, and baked tomatoes served on thick crusty bread with a side of juicy fruits. For those with a sweet tooth, the Belgian waffles will no doubt hit the spot. **Known for:** all-day breakfast; hearty portions; waffles with whipped cream and caramel sauce. [$] *Average main: ISK2,200* ✉ *Skipagata 4, Akureyri* ☎ *772–5061* 🌐 *www.berlinakureyri.is* 🕒 *No dinner.*

★ **Bláa Kannan**
$$ | **CAFÉ** | Pretty enough to be featured on picture postcards of Akureyri's town center, this beautiful blue building with red turrets is the perfect spot in any season to grab a coffee and watch the world go by. The interior, with weathered wooden beams and chandeliers, gives off a supercozy vibe—the perfect setting for a simple savory brunch plate, a soup, or a nice sweet treat. **Known for:** happy marriage cake (a traditional dessert in Iceland made with rhubarb); the best coffee in Akureyri; brunch plate. [$] *Average main: ISK2,590* ✉ *Hafnarstræti 96, Akureyri* ☎ *461–4600.*

Brynja Ice Cream Shop

$ | **ICE CREAM** | **FAMILY** | Akureyri's most famous ice cream parlour has been dishing up everyone's favorite scoop since 1939. Legend has it they use a special secret ingredient, and people have traveled from as far away as China to get a taste. **Known for:** the "bragðarefur"—a mix of candy and soft-serve ice cream; iconic Akureyri first date location; popular on Saturdays thanks to half-off candy. $ *Average main: ISK700* ✉ *Aðalstræti 3, Akureyri* ☎ *462–4478* ⊕ *www.facebook. com/brynjuis.*

Café Laut

$$ | **CAFÉ** | **FAMILY** | The botanical garden's café has a striking design that features an oversized pitched roof with two walls constructed entirely of large glass panels arranged into a geometric collage. It's a welcome stop after a long walk through the gardens and serves up decent coffee, surprisingly artisanal desserts, and light sandwiches. **Known for:** chocolate treats; relaxing views out over the Botanical Gardens; open-faced sandwiches. $ *Average main: ISK1,690* ✉ *Eyrarlandsvegur 30, Akureyri* ☎ *461–4601* ⊗ *Closed Oct.–Apr.*

Greifinn

$$$$ | **PIZZA** | **FAMILY** | The quality fare at this family-friendly establishment is well worth the five-minute walk from the town center. Known mostly for exceptional takeout pizzas, Greifinn is also the go-to place for family dinners. **Known for:** reservations highly recommended; pizza to-go; one of the most popular restaurants in Akureyri. $ *Average main: ISK4,690* ✉ *Glerárgata 20, Akureyri* ☎ *460–1600* ⊕ *www.greifinn.is.*

Indian Curry House

$$$ | **INDIAN** | Indian classics with both meat and veggie options are served up at this colorful addition to Akureyri's international culinary scene—it might just be the most northern Indian restaurant in the world. For those looking for a deal, their lunch specials offer a hefty discount. **Known for:** classic Indian favorites; large portions; thrifty lunch specials. $ *Average main: ISK3,000* ✉ *Ráðhústorg 3, Akureyri* ☎ *461–4242* ⊕ *www.curry.is* ⊗ *Closed Mon. in winter.*

Leirunesti

$$ | **FAST FOOD** | Although others claim to have the best burger in town, locals know that Leirunesti is the real deal thanks to its famous Akureyringur Burger, stuffed with fries in the middle—order it on its own for ISK 1,950 or as a combo with soda and extra fries for ISK 2,590. Also try the deep-fried hot dog with fries and melted cheese, another specialty that draws in both locals and out-of-towners. **Known for:** best burger in town; incredible views in all directions; fast food–style cuisine. $ *Average main: ISK1,900* ✉ *Leiruvegur, Akureyri* ☎ *461–3008* ⊕ *www.leirunesti.is.*

★ Rub23

$$$$ | **FUSION** | This Akureyri restaurant takes its name literally, with chefs who use their signature "magic pepper" rub and a variety of others to enliven fish, lamb, and beef dishes. There are excellent sushi options too, and it's one of the few places in Iceland where you can sample real Icelandic wasabi (fresh wasabi is actually grown locally in Iceland, whereas previously the wasabi you would eat here was an imitation). **Known for:** "festival" tasting menus; steak, whether that's tenderloin or tuna; bespoke spice rubs. $ *Average main: ISK5,000* ✉ *Kaupvangsstræti 6, Akureyri* ☎ *462–2223* ⊕ *www.rub23.is.*

★ Strikið

$$$$ | **ICELANDIC** | The views from this attractive fifth-floor restaurant are just as excellent as the food and service. The menu focuses on Icelandic ingredients but doesn't mind borrowing from around the world. **Known for:** heavenly langoustine maki; delightful views of the whole fjord; fancy take on the all-you-can-eat brunch. $ *Average main: ISK4,690* ✉ *Skipagata 14, 5th fl., Akureyri* ☎ *354/462–7100* ⊕ *www.strikid.is.*

Coffee and Quick Bites

★ Bakaríið við Brúna

$ | **BAKERY** | **FAMILY** | Akureyri's favorite bakery gets a lot of business from locals but still flies under visitors' radar. Like most Icelandic bakeries, the shelves are stacked with Danish pastries, freshly baked bread, sandwiches, and cakes—but the quality here puts them a cut above the rest. **Known for:** best kleinur (traditional Icelandic twisted doughnuts) in Iceland; gooey chocolate snúður, the Icelandic take on cinnamon buns; freshly baked bread. Ⓢ *Average main: ISK998* ✉ *Dalsbraut 1, Akureyri* ☎ *461–2700.*

🛏 Hotels

Hotel Edda

$ | **HOTEL** | For most of the year, this building provides dormitory housing for high-school kids, but during the summer months, it's transformed into a modern hotel with beautiful accommodations. **Pros:** beautiful views over the bay; close to the town swimming pool; right next to the botanical garden. **Cons:** steep walk from the town center; no common kitchen or fridge; older section has shared bathrooms. Ⓢ *Rooms from: ISK15,000* ✉ *Thorunnarstraeti, Akureyri* ☎ *444–4900* ⊕ *www.hoteledda.is* ➴ *204 rooms* ⦿ *No Meals.*

Hotel Kea

$$$ | **HOTEL** | Opened in 1944, the Hotel Kea has clean and comfortable guest rooms with leather furniture and businesslike decor. **Pros:** great location; helpful staff; good on-site restaurant. **Cons:** bland decor; some rooms are small; furnishings in some areas look dated and worn. Ⓢ *Rooms from: ISK43,000* ✉ *Hafnarstræti 87–89, Akureyri* ☎ *460–2080* ⊕ *www.keahotels.is* ➴ *104 rooms* ⦿ *Free Breakfast.*

★ Hotel Kjarnalundur

$$ | **HOTEL** | Perched on the hillside next to the gorgeous Kjarnaskógur forest (about 2 miles from the town center), this fabulous hotel provides evergreen respite year-round to those who love nature, hiking, and beautiful views. **Pros:** access to nature; focus on wellness; free use of hot tubs and saunna. **Cons:** 2 miles from the town center; some doubles have twin beds; uphill walk from the main road. Ⓢ *Rooms from: ISK27,000* ✉ *Hotel Kjarnalundur, Akureyri* ☎ *460–0060* ⊕ *www.kjarnalundur.is* ➴ *66 rooms* ⦿ *Free Breakfast.*

Hótel Norðurland

$$$ | **HOTEL** | Located in the center of town, this hotel is close to restaurants, bars, cafés, and shops. **Pros:** centrally located; good lobby bar; free Wi-Fi. **Cons:** no restaurant; slightly faded decor; no elevator. Ⓢ *Rooms from: ISK33,000* ✉ *Geislagata 7* ☎ *462–2600* ⊕ *www.hotel-nordurland.is* ➴ *41 rooms* ⦿ *Free Breakfast.*

Hrimland Cottages

$$$$ | **HOUSE** | **FAMILY** | A practical base for those planning a self-catering winter ski-ing trip, these modern and stylish cottages just off the mountain road to Hlíðarfjall ski resort offer sensational views over the town and fjord. **Pros:** heated floors; beautiful decor; access to skiiing. **Cons:** three miles from town center; two-night minimum stay; expensive. Ⓢ *Rooms from: ISK59,000* ✉ *Hálönd Hlíðarfjalli, Akureyri* ☎ *866–2696* ⊕ *www.hrimland.is* ➴ *16 cottages* ⦿ *No Meals.*

★ Icelandair Hotel Akureyri

$$$ | **HOTEL** | This classy hotel is designed to offer more than just a practical base; it's somewhere you can hang out, relax, socialize, and dine. **Pros:** right next to the town's main swimming pool; lovely views in rooms; short walking distance from town center. **Cons:** steep hill between the hotel and town center; no baths, only showers; breakfast not included. Ⓢ *Rooms from: ISK32,000* ✉ *Þingvallar-stræti 23, Akureyri* ☎ *518–1000* ⊕ *www.icelandairhotels.com/en/hotels/akureyri* ➴ *99 rooms* ⦿ *No Meals.*

☻ Nightlife

★ Götubarinn

BARS | Located on the main shopping street, this wine bar and nightclub is a go-to spot for televised live sports. It also has a piano on the lower level for impromptu drunken sing-alongs. ☒ *Hafnarstræti 96, Akureyri* ☎ *462–4747.*

Græni Hatturinn

LIVE MUSIC | A great live music venue and bar in the north of Iceland, Græni Hatturinn ("the Green Hat") has been hosting some of Iceland's best melody makers since it opened its doors in 1999. Located on a side street off Hafnarstræti in one of the town's oldest houses, its primary mission is to provide a place to experience live rock, jazz, metal, pop, and a variety of other genres. The sound of bands sending it large and loud can often be heard spilling out from its basement doors. ☒ *Hafnarstræti 96, Akureyri* ☎ *461–4646.*

Ölstofa Akureyrar

BARS | Fans of Akureyri's famous craft beer producers, Einstök, will love this place, which has a brewer's lounge dedicated to the award-winning label. You can play darts or watch live sports in this cozy pub while enjoying either a local draft beer or a bottle from their impressive global selection. ☒ *Kaupvangsstræti 23, Akureyri* ☎ *896–3093* ⊕ *www.facebook. com/olstofak.*

★ R5

BARS | Stop by for a nice evening drink at this gem of a bar, where the excellent staff serve up a superb selection of craft beers and some fun anecdotes, too. The vibe is as chill as the beverages, but warmed throughout by the timber, tungsten lights, and honey-color decor. ☒ *Ráðhústorg 5* ☎ *412–9933* ⊕ *www. r5.is.*

◉ Shopping

Eymundsson

BOOKS | There's an Eymundsson bookstore staffed by bibliophiles in almost every major town in Iceland, and the Akureyri location sits on one of the hot corners of town where the main high street meets the trendy Listagil street, which leads up to the church. Here you'll find all the latest titles along with a few classics, in both Icelandic and English, plus an excellent selection of magazines. Their superb in-house coffee shop is Te & Kaffi. ☒ *Hafnarstræti 91–93, Akureyri* ☎ *540–2180* ⊕ *www.penninn.is.*

Flóra

CRAFTS | This lovely concept studio/store presents a beautiful array of goods made by local artists, farmers, designers, and more. They aim to promote fair trade, support local culture, and encourage creativity through workshops, events, and exhibitions. Hours can vary. ☒ *Eyrarlandsvegur 3, Akureyri* ☎ *661–0168.*

Folda-Anna

SOUVENIRS | This shop has been selling woolens, knitting kits, sheepskin rugs, and other souvenirs to locals and visitors for more than 20 years. It's a great place to get a traditional Icelandic woolen sweater. ☒ *Hafnarstræti 100* ☎ *461–4120.*

Fornbókabúðin Fróði

BOOKS | There's a treasure trove of secondhand books here, with around 85% Icelandic titles and quite a few books in English, too. Among the romance novels and pulp fiction you'll find the occasional rare classic, with some dating back to the 1700s. The owner, Olga, has been running the shop for over 30 years, but now in her 80s, she has passed the baton to a couple of charming young Brits named Stu and Ren, who run it on her behalf. ☒ *Kaupvangsstræti 19, Akureyri* ☎ *456–6345* ⊕ *www.facebook. com/fornbokabud.*

66°North

MIXED CLOTHING | The ultimate Icelandic heritage brand, 66°North has managed to stay trendy with both cool fashionistas and their rural grandparents. Their Akureyri location, smack dab in the middle of downtown, offers all their classic wares, from their iconic Workman's hat to their popular Jökla parka. Pick one up and watch as suddenly everyone starts speaking Icelandic to you. ⊠ *Hafnarstræti, Akureyri* ☎ *535–6600* ⊕ *www.66north. com.*

★ Sjoppan

SOUVENIRS | Product designer Almar Alfreðsson converted the entryway of his family home on the trendy Listagil art street to create the smallest design shop in Iceland. The 40-square-foot space houses a curated selection of interesting products by local designers and artists, with items by foreign designers as well. The general theme is cool, playful, and humorous. Ring the bell for service. ⊠ *Kaupvangsstræti 21, Akureyri* ☎ *354/864-0710* ⊕ *www.sjoppanvoruhus. is.*

🏃 Activities

Akureyri Golf Club

GOLF | Perhaps the world's northernmost 18-hole course, this golf club also hosts the Arctic Open golf tournament, which is held annually around the longest day of the year in the midnight sun. ⊠ *Eikarlundur 18* ☎ *462–2974* ⊕ *www.gagolf. is* 🎫 *ISK 1,000 for a day pass* 🏌 *Par 71; greens fees ISK 8,500.*

Hlíðarfjall Ski Resort

SKIING & SNOWBOARDING | **FAMILY** | It's only a seven-minute drive to Akureyri's ski resort, which is set on the slopes of Hlíðarfjall mountain. There are seven lifts to 26 well-groomed ski runs and two ski lodges that offer light refreshments. Although experienced skiers may find the elevation for downhill runs limited, the slopes here are regularly slammed with fresh snow from December to April, and the scenery is spectacular. Skis and snowboards are available to rent. ⊠ *Akureyri* ☎ *462–2280* ⊕ *www. hlidarfjall.is* 🎫 *ISK 5,800 for a day pass.*

Rural Akureyri

Although most think of Akureyri mainly as the town center and its surrounding urban areas, the greater Akureyri region extends well into the surrounding countryside on both sides of the fjord and deep into the southern valley. Most urban addresses have postcodes 600 and 603; rural addresses have the 601 postcode.

Sights

Gásir

OTHER ATTRACTION | **FAMILY** | Located 5 km (3 miles) north of Akureyri, on the western shores of Eyjafjörður fjord, Gásir was the most important trading post in Iceland during the middle ages. Locals joke that it was the Keflavík of its time, but today it's a heritage site that springs to life every year in the third week of July for a lively reenactment festival where people dress up in medieval Viking costumes, host fun old-fashioned activities, and sell all sorts of handcrafted wares. ⊠ *Hörgár in Eyjafjörður, Dagverðareyrarvegur, Akureyri* ☎ *462–4162* ⊕ *www.gasir.is.*

Safnasafnið

ART GALLERY | **FAMILY** | The Icelandic Folk and Outsider Art Museum is an unconventional exhibition space in Svalbarðsströnd, a 10-minute drive from Akureyri town center. This museum owes its endearing qualities to an emphasis on artists outside the cultural mainstream. Its curators are known to scour the country looking for quality pieces from both known and unknown artists. ⊠ *Svaðbarðsströnd* ☎ *461–4066* ⊕ *www. safnasafnid.is.*

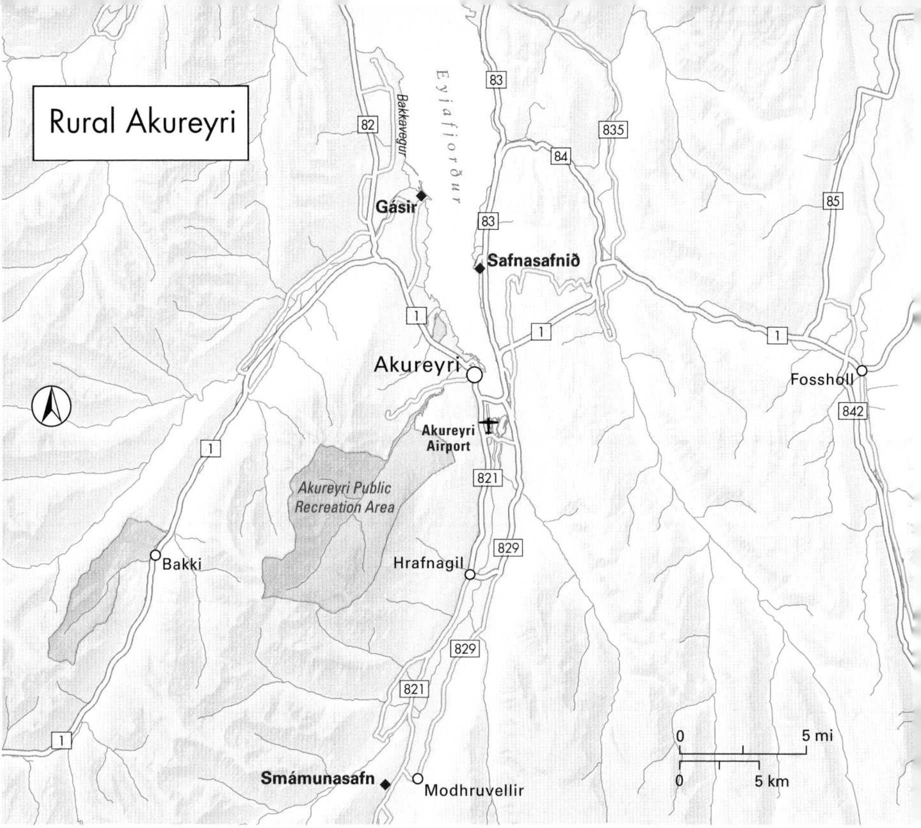

★ **Smámunasafn**

OTHER MUSEUM | FAMILY | A remarkable collection of "small things" is exhibited at this museum, which is dedicated to Sverri Hermansson, a local carpenter who took it upon himself at the age of seven to start collecting, well, stuff. Beginning with a set of pencils, Sverri ended up accumulating more than 20,000 unique items over 80 years—mostly tools and other instruments associated with his craft as a tradesman. ✉ *Sólgarði, Akureyri* ☎ *463–1261* 🌐 *www.esveit.is/smamunasafnid* 🎫 *ISK 1,500* 🕒 *Closed Sept.–May, but tours can be scheduled upon request.*

🍴 Restaurants

★ **Hælið Cafe**

$$ | CAFÉ | FAMILY | In addition to superb coffee and homemade pastries, this excellent vintage hospital–themed café offers a dose of 1940s-style respite—as well as a hint of theater—in a lovely, detailed setting in the countryside. Run by actress Maria Pálsdóttir, the café doubles as an exhibition center dedicated to patients of "the Great White Plague" (tuberculosis). **Known for:** Icelandic marriage cake; themed decor; delicious chocolate cake. [$] *Average main: ISK1,800* ✉ *Kristnes, Eyjafjarðarsveit, Akureyri* ☎ *780–1927* 🌐 *www.haelid.is* 🕒 *Closed weekdays Sept.–May.*

Holtsel

$ | **ICE CREAM** | **FAMILY** | Just a 20-minute drive south of Akureyri lies this idyllic dairy farm. While you can get some local meat and other wares here, the real draw is their homemade ice cream, which will have you swearing off the grocery store stuff. **Known for:** ice cream, ice cream and more ice cream; charming farm store; the ability to pet a cow while eating ice cream. [$] *Average main: ISK900* ✉ *Finnastaðavegur, Akureyri* ✥ *Eyjafjarðarsveit* ☎ *866–1618* 🌐 *www.holtsel.is.*

Hotels

Skjaldarvík

$$ | **HOTEL** | **FAMILY** | A gorgeous rural setting coupled with a warm and welcoming vibe makes this an attractive lodging option, especially for horseback-riding fans. **Pros:** good homemade food; quiet rural location; hot tub. **Cons:** shared bathrooms; not within walking distance of the town center; no public transport. [$] *Rooms from: ISK24,900* ✉ *Skjalkarvík, Akureyri* ☎ *552–5200* 🌐 *www.skjaldarvik.is/en* 🕓 *Closed Nov.–Apr. (except for group reservations)* 🛏 *28 rooms* 🍴 *Free Breakfast.*

Shopping

Jólagarðurinn (*The Christmas Garden*)

OTHER SPECIALTY STORE | **FAMILY** | Located just south of Akureyri in a fairy-tale-inspired house decorated with giant candy canes and trimmed with faux frosting, Jólagarðurinn is not the place for grinches. The inside is packed to its pretty little rafters with an impressive display of Christmas goods, and the smell of burning embers mingles delightfully with those of peppermint, cinnamon, and smoked lamb. Icelandic Christmas music blends romantically with the tick-tock of Black Forest cuckoo clocks and the sound of wood crackling on an open hearth, fueling an atmosphere that should have your heart bursting with Yuletide joy, even in the middle of summer. ✉ *Slétta, Eyjafjarðarsveit* ☎ *463–1433* 🌐 *www.northiceland.is.*

Activities

goHusky Dogsledding Tours

SNOW SPORTS | Whether you want to dog sled on fresh snow or do a nice hike in the forest with the pups, goHusky has you covered. For those that don't want to jump on the sled, they also offer a petting and pictures experience for only ISK 4,000. ✉ *Glæsibær 3, Akureyri* ☎ *898–9355* 🌐 *www.gohusky.is.*

Pólarhestar

HORSEBACK RIDING | This family-run business has been offering horseback-riding trips from the Akureyri area since 1985, and hour-long to multiday tours can be arranged year-round. Along with sleeping-bag accommodation, made-up beds are often available as well. ✉ *Grýtubakki II, Akureyri* ☎ *896–1879* 🌐 *www.polarhestar.is.*

Skjaldarvík

HORSEBACK RIDING | **FAMILY** | This family-friendly horseback-riding service offers hour-long tours of lovely rural Akureyri with superb panoramic views. Tours are from ISK 11,900 and include hot tub access and light treats after. Round-trip pickups can be arranged from Akureyri town center (also included in the price). ✉ *Skjaldarvík, Akureyri* ☎ *552–5200* 🌐 *www.skjaldarvik.is.*

Chapter 8

NORTH ICELAND

8

Updated by
Hannah Jane Cohen

⊙ Sights   🍴 Restaurants   🛏 Hotels   🛍 Shopping   🍸 Nightlife

★★★☆☆   ★★☆☆☆   ★★☆☆☆   ★☆☆☆☆   ★☆☆☆☆

WELCOME TO NORTH ICELAND

TOP REASONS TO GO

★ **The Diamond Circle:** The 160-mile circuit covers some of the region's best sights and attractions, including Goðafoss Waterfall, Mývatn (which includes Lake Mývatn, Dimmuborgir lava field, and Hverir geothermal area) and Jökulsárgljúfur Canyon (which includes Dettifoss Waterfall, the Hljóðaklettur rock formations, and Ásbyrgi Canyon).

★ **The Arctic Coast Way:** Iceland's first official touring route stretches 900 km (650 miles) and includes Drangey Island and the Arctic Henge.

★ **Geothermal hot spots and luxury spas:** Mývatn Nature Baths, Geosea Geothermal Sea Baths, and the beer bath spa are just a few ways to experience ultimate relaxation in a stunning natural setting.

★ **Húsavík:** The whale-watching capital of Iceland has also recently embraced its role as the setting of the Netflix Eurovision movie.

1 Hvammstangi. An official starting point for the 500-mile Arctic Coast Way touring route.

2 Vatnsnes. A place to dine, spot seals, and marvel at the Hvítserkur sea stack.

3 Blönduós. Home to nature and a textile museum.

4 Varmahlíð. Perfect for whitewater rafting and horseback riding.

5 Sauðárkrókur. The location of the fascinating 1238 Battle of Iceland exhibition.

6 Hólar. A medieval political base known for its striking cathedral.

7 Hofsós. Home to a famous swimming pool.

8 Siglufjörður. "Sigló" for short, this is the site of the Herring Era Museum.

9 Ólafsfjörður. A sleepy fishing town that's worth a visit despite its quiet.

10 Dalvík. The perfect place to celebrate the annual summer festival, Fiskidagurinn Mikli.

11 Grímsey. The true north of Iceland, this is the only part of the country transected by the Arctic Circle.

12 Hrísey. A quiet island perfect for bird-watching.

13 Húsavík. The best spot for whale-watching in all of Iceland.

14 The Mývatn Region. Where out-of-this-world geological wonders abound.

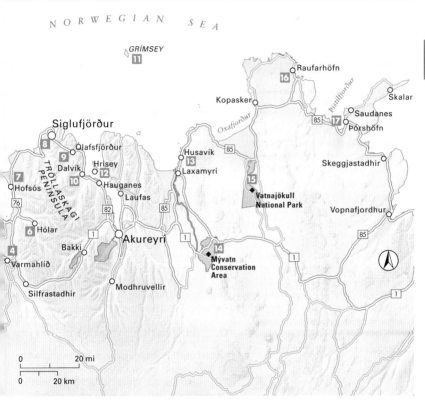

15 Jökulsárgljúfur. The northern entrance to Vatnajökull National Park, a glacier-filled UNESCO World Heritage site that you have to see to believe.

16 Raufarhöfn. Iceland's northernmost town on the mainland and home to the Arctic Henge sculpture.

17 Þórshöfn. A fishing town in the cove of Lónafjörður.

Existing on the edge of the Arctic Circle, the vast expanse of North Iceland resonates peacefully with cool, pristine beauty. Despite its northern location, the region enjoys a warmer, drier climate than the south, with land, lakes, and rivers positively bursting with life.

Stretching from the seal colonies of Vatnsnes in the west to the whale-watching capital of Húsavík in the east and beyond, the region offers an extraordinary expanse of historic, geological, and cultural landscapes with an extensive coastline of snow-capped mountains, deep fjords, and salmon-rich rivers.

The convoluted coastline is dotted with both sleepy hamlets and busy fishing villages, where local chefs have access to the freshest produce possible. To feed the imagination between destinations, roads wind through striking valleys overshadowed by misty mountains and marvelous landmark attractions, where the likes of Ásbrygi have inspired legends of mythical creatures. Farther inland, shimmering glacial rivers are marked by striking waterfalls cutting through canyons and dividing valleys that seem to grow greener with every passing year. As you move closer to the interior, you'll find historic volcanic areas such as Krafla and its active geothermal areas that bubble and hiss with belching mud pots, steaming fumaroles, and smoldering lava fields.

In addition, because it's so far north, the region is illuminated with a different intensity of light across all seasons and is especially famous for its waltzing northern lights, glimmering ice clouds (nacreous), and glorious Arctic summer sunsets that blaze on the horizon until dawn.

MAJOR REGIONS

The Northwest. Northwest Iceland encompasses a host of natural wonders, with an enticing blend of waterfalls, mountains, and superb coastal scenery to lure you off the main road. From the stunning views in Vatnsnes, whose coastline shelters countless bobbing seals, to the Saga-age landscapes in and around the Skagafjörður fjord, northwestern Iceland will beguile visitors.

Tröllaskagi. Neither nestled nor tucked between its adjacent fjords; the spectacular Tröllaskagi peninsula presents an epic new chapter of fairy-tale landscapes marked by tall, snowcapped peaks, rivers rich with salmon, and the postcard-pretty villages of Siglufjörður, Ólafsfjörður, and Dalvík. With its abundance of snow, it's also a magnet for skiers. From Hofsós, this sparsely populated region is accessed by continuing on Route 76, which winds around the coastline, cutting dramatically through steep mountain slopes and occasionally disappearing into dark mountain tunnels.

The Northeast. The remote and sparely populated Northeast of Iceland is an expansive region with villages and attractions dotting its coastal and inland areas. It features superb scenery, diverse landscapes, and charming towns, including the geologically rich Jökulsárgljúfur and Mývatn, and whale-watching mecca Húsavík. In its farthest corners, small coastal towns Þórshöfn and Raufarhöfn exist in misty isolation, attracting wildlife to its driftwood-laden beaches, and photographers to the impressive Arctic Henge. While it may not be endowed with famous volcanoes such as Eyjafjallajökull, with Krafla and its geothermal areas located at the core, this beautiful region still beats, albeit quietly, with a molten heart. This region is also where you can start a tour of the Diamond Circle, which includes Lake Mývatn, Dettifoss Waterfall, Ásbyrgi Canyon, and the town of Húsavík.

Planning

When to Go

North Iceland is a land of many faces, with each season bringing on drastic changes in this remote oasis. Summer is temperate, with clear blue skies, pastures of vivid green grass, and sparkling seas dominating the far reaches of the country. It's the most popular time to visit, and for good reason. Temperatures are much higher here than in the south, and warmer weather means the farthest areas of this unbridled land are free of ice and accessible, making trips up into the fjords or down into the Highlands safe, spectacular, and easy for adventurers of all abilities.

Winter brings out an equally alluring aspect of the north: the Aurora Borealis. In its perpetual near-darkness—and vastly unpopulated areas—the north of Iceland provides a Northern Lights experience unlike any other. Along with this, though, is unpredictable weather and hazardous conditions—so plan in advance and always check the safety conditions before you venture out.

Getting Here and Around

AIR

North Iceland is serviced by a number of small regional airports. The largest is in Akureyri, where Icelandair, Niceair, and Norlandair offer flights to and from both domestic and international destinations.

Within the north, Norlandair offers domestic flights from Akureyri to Þórshöfn and Grímsey. Eagle Air, flying out of the Reykjavík domestic airport, flies a few times weekly (depending on the season) to the tiny Húsavík airport.

CONTACTS Akureyri Airport. ⊠ Urðargil 15, Akureyri ☎ 424–4000 ⊕ www.isavia. is/en/akureyri-airport. **Grímsey Airport.** ⊠ Grímseyjarflugvöllur ⊕ www.isavia. is/en/grimsey-airport. **Húsavík Airport.** ⊠ Húsavík ☎ 464–1253 ⊕ www.isavia. is/en/husavik-airport. **Þórshöfn Airport.** ⊠ Þórshöfn ☎ 468–1420 ⊕ isavia.is/en/ thorshofn-airport.

BOAT

North Iceland is blessed with two beautiful islands, Grímsey and Hrísey, which are both reachable via ferry.

Most famous as Iceland's toe into the Arctic Circle, Grímsey is reached via the Sæfari ferry from the port of Dalvík (27 miles north of Akureyri). It's a 3-hour journey each way that costs ISK 4,000 each way. In winter, there are 3 to 4 departures weekly, which is then upped to 5 in the summer months. The ferry departs at 9 am from Dalvík, stays at Grímsey all day, and then sets off back to the mainland at 5 pm.

Despite being less famous, Hrísey island, which is located in the Eyjafjörður fjord north of Akureyri, is also worth a visit. Hrísey is accessed from Árskógssandur (22 miles north of Akureyri), where scheduled ferry crossings by Sævar Ferry are operated daily every two hours from 7 am until 11 pm. The boat trip takes about 15 minutes and costs ISK

1,700. There is also one ferry per week to Hrísey from Dalvík, which leaves on Thursdays at 6:30 pm.

CONTACTS Sævar Ferry. ☎ *695–5544 For Hrísey schedule, 458–8970 For Grímsey schedule* ⊕ *www.hrisey.is.*

BUS

Strætó operates scheduled services to and from the larger towns in the north including Hvammstangi, Blönduós, Varmahlíð, Sauðárkrókur, Hólar, Hofsós, Siglufjörður, Ólafsfjörður, Dalvík, Akureyri, Húsavík, and Mývatn.

CONTACTS Strætó. ⊕ *www.straeto.is.*

CAR

With limited bus services, traveling by car is sometimes the only option. Roads are generally in good condition, but it's always best to check ahead for conditions and any road closures at ⊕ *www.road.is.*

Restaurants

Expect to find traditional Icelandic cuisine and excellent home-baked desserts inside cozy cafés. There are only a few options in each town, but hearty seafood and lamb dishes are often available.

Hotels

Converted farmhouses and other repurposed buildings make up most of the lodging options in this region. Some hotels are located on horse farms.

RESTAURANT AND HOTEL PRICES

Restaurant prices in the reviews are the average cost of a main course at dinner, or if dinner is not served, at lunch. Hotel prices in the reviews are the lowest cost of a standard double room in high season. Restaurant and hotel reviews have been shortened. For full information, visit Fodors.com.

What it Costs in ISK

	$	$$	$$$	$$$$
RESTAURANTS				
	under ISK 1,500	ISK 1,500– 2,999	ISK 3,000– 4,000	over ISK 4,000
HOTELS				
	under ISK 20,000	ISK 21,000– 29,999	ISK 3,000– 45,000	over ISK 45,000

Safety

You won't find fences or guard rails in Iceland, although for the sake of health and safety there are signs stating dangers. Just like the rest of the country, North Iceland is full of beautiful places, but some of them can be dangerous. Always make sure to heed warning signs, especially around cliffs, caves, beaches, and geothermal areas. The weather is another safety issue in this region, especially during the winter, so dressing appropriately for the conditions is a must. The most dangerous consideration for tourists in Iceland, though, are the roads. In addition to those distracting wonders of nature, including the northern lights and blinding low winter sunshine, driving conditions in Iceland are unique. So it's imperative to take time to prepare. There are several websites dedicated to teaching people about driving in Iceland with fun tutorials. The following websites offer useful information on driving safely in Iceland: ⊕ www.safetravel.is and ⊕ www.road.is.

Visitor Information

CONTACTS Visit North Iceland. ☎ *462– 3300* ⊕ *www.northiceland.is.*

Hvammstangi

*196 km (122 miles) north of Reykjavík,
202 km (125 miles) west of Akureyri.*

Renewed investment in tourism has put Hvammstangi on the map as a great base for exploring the Vatnsnes peninsula to its north and other attractions in the north, south, and west of Iceland. The town itself has a great restaurant, coffee shop, and wool factory, in addition to the Icelandic Seal Center.

In June 2019, Hvammstangi became one of the official starting points of the Arctic Coast Way touring route—a 500-mile trip along the coastline of North Iceland taking in both the best of the beaten and off-the-beaten tracks.

GETTING HERE AND AROUND

Driving is the best way to get to Hvammstangi, but Strætó operates the 57 bus service between Reykjavík and Akureyri, which stops at Hvammstangi.

VISITOR INFORMATION

There's a tourist information center at Selasetur Íslands (also known as the Icelandic Seal Center) with maps featuring all the places of interest in the region.

Sights

Kolugljúfur

CANYON | If you don't mind treading in troll territory, a short 5 km (3 mile) detour off the Ring Road (Route 1) on Route 715 brings you to the striking and relatively unknown Kolugljúfur canyon, where torrents of water from the Víðidalsá river plunge into a tiered gorge. The canyon is named after the legendary lady troll named Kola who supposedly made her home there and feasted on the salmon in the river. ⊠ *Kolugljúfur Canyon.*

★ Selasetur Íslands
(*Icelandic Seal Center*)

OTHER MUSEUM | Iceland's only seal museum features a fun and informative exhibition detailing all the seals of the Arctic and North Atlantic with information on Iceland's seal colonies and why seals are such a significant part of Icelandic culture, tradition, and folklore. ⊠ *Strandgata 1, Hvammstangi* 📞 *451–2345* ⊕ *www.selasetur.is* 🎫 *ISK 1,200* 🕐 *Closed weekends late Sept.–May.*

Restaurants

Bakki Restaurant

$$$$ | **SCANDINAVIAN** | The chef here is a supporter of the sustainable food movement and sources almost all supplies from local Icelandic farmers. All the veggies, salads, and berries are picked from the greenhouses next door. **Known for:** lamb prime rib; great burgers; delicious seafood soup. $ *Average main: ISK4,200* ⊠ *Skeggjagata 1, Hvammstangi* 📞 *519–8600* ⊕ *www.hotellaugarbakki.is.*

★ Sjávarborg Restaurant

$$$ | **SEAFOOD** | Seashells, driftwood, and nautical knickknacks are cleverly incorporated in this well-designed space, where large windows overlook the bay. Here you can dine on some hearty seafood dishes while enjoying a spot of whale-watching; humpbacks and killer whales are often seen breaching in the bay. **Known for:** fresh fish of the day; great views; tasty seafood soup. $ *Average main: ISK3,500* ⊠ *Strandgata 1, Hvammstangi* 📞 *451–3131* ⊕ *www.sjavarborg-restaurant.is.*

Hotels

Gauksmýri Lodge

$$ | **HOTEL** | This friendly lodge, which used to be a horse farm, offers homey accommodations in a beautiful location **Pros:** beautiful setting; kind service; great home-cooked meals at on-site restaurant. **Cons:** small rooms; thin walls;

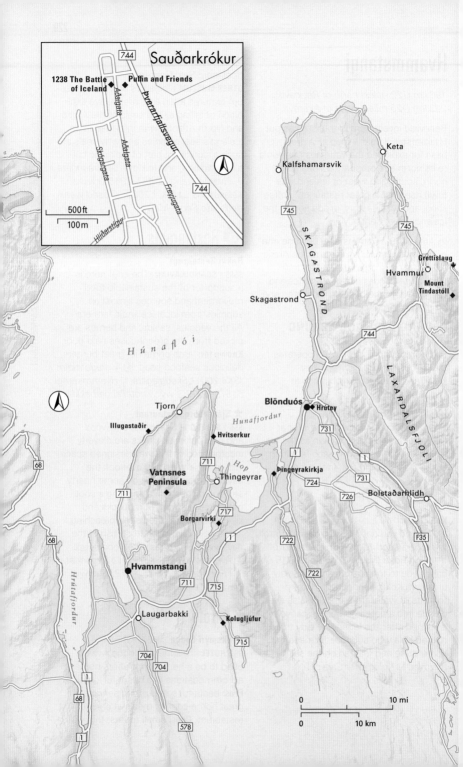

Sauðarkrókur

744

1238 The Battle of Iceland

Puffin and Friends

Aðalgata

Skógargata

Aðalgata

Þverárfjallsvegur

Freyjugata

744

Hlíðarstígur

500 ft
100 m

Keta

Kalfshamarsvik

745

745

S K A G A S T R O N D

Grettislaug

Hvammur

Mount
Tindastóll

Skagastrond

744

L A X A R D A L S F J O L I

H ú n a f l ó i

Tjorn

Hunafjordur

Blönduós

Hrútey

Illugastaðir

731

Hvítserkur

1

711

Hop

Þingeyrakirkja

731

Vatnsnes
Peninsula

Thingeyrar

724

726

68

711

Borgarvirki

717

Bolstaðarhlidh

1

722

68

722

Hvammstangi

F35

Hrútafjordur

711

715

Laugarbakki

Kolugljúfur

704

715

704

0   10 mi

0   10 km

578

1

68

1

NORWEGIAN SEA

see Tröllaskagi map

Siglufjordhur

Thonglabakki

76

Fell

MALMEY

Olafsfjordhur

Drange
Island

Dalvik

Hrisey

Hrappstadhakot

Grenivik

Hofsós

Grafarkirkja

Laufas

Sauðarkrókur
see inset
at left

76

748

Gestastofa Sútarans

Hólar

Akureyri

764

76

Miklavatn
Nature
Reserve

75

Glaumbær

Viðimýri
Turf Church

Varmahlíð

1

1

Reykjafoss

Fosslaug

Bakki

1

Silfrastaðir

1

752

The
Old Stable

Modhruvellir

Northwest

location might be too remote for some. [$] *Rooms from: ISK22,700* ✉ *Gauksmýri* ☎ *831–1411* 🌐 *www.facebook.com/sveitasetrid.gauksmyri* 🛏 *24 rooms* 🍴 *Free Breakfast.*

Hótel Laugarbakki

$$$ | **HOTEL** | This lodging option retains the exterior of the 1970s school it used to be, but the inside has been completely remodeled, and no expense was spared in the design. **Pros:** great location; good on-site restaurant; close to a fishing river. **Cons:** austere exterior; not in walking distance of the town center; a/c can be loud when windy. [$] *Rooms from: ISK31,214* ✉ *Laugarbakki, Hvammstangi* ☎ *519–8600* 🌐 *www.hotellaugarbakki.is* 🛏 *56 rooms* 🍴 *Free Breakfast.*

Shopping

★ Bardúsa

CRAFTS | Colorful handknit Icelandic sweaters and other woolens join a handsome exhibition of locally made handicrafts and art at Bardúsa. But the real draw is an old 1900s grocery store and hardware shop hidden in the back of the building, left entirely untouched since the last century. It features an impressive collection of vintage goods and sundries still sitting on the shelves and hanging from the walls and ceiling. The upstairs rooms are dedicated to a merchants' museum. ✉ *Brekkugata 4, Hvammstangi* ☎ *845–0586.*

KIDKA Wool Factory

MIXED CLOTHING | If you want to make sure your Icelandic woolen goods are truly made in Iceland, then the KIDKA wool shop is your best bet. The wool is not only processed here, but this is also where the goods are designed and manufactured. They run workshops (for a fee) and offer complimentary tours of the factory, where you can learn the secret of how they make their wool so soft and fluffy. ✉ *Höfðabraut 34, Hvammstangi* ☎ *451–0060* 🌐 *www.kidka.com.*

Vatnsnes Peninsula

40 km (25 miles) north of Hvammstangi.

For a long time, this peninsula was frequently bypassed by travelers heading north or south on the Ring Road, but thanks to its population of playful seals that you can see up close as well as the photo-worthy sea stack Hvítserkur and a growing number of other tourist attractions, more visitors are taking the 50-mile detour around Vatnsnes.

GETTING HERE AND AROUND

Strætó operates the 57 bus service from Reykjavík to Akureyri and vice-versa, stopping at Hvammstangi, which is the closest one can get via public transportation to the Vatnsnes peninsula. It's therefore imperative to have a car if you wish to see all the sites and remote wonders the peninsula offers.

To get to the peninsula, turn off Route 1, then take Highway 72 to Hvammstangi and then Highway 711 around the peninsula circling back to Route 1. Note that portions of Highway 711 and the smaller Vatnsnes roads 717 and 716 are still gravel and can be in poor condition, especially during the winter months.

VISITOR INFORMATION

CONTACTS Tourist Information Center. ✉ *Brekkugata 2, Hvammstangi* ☎ *451–2345* 🌐 *www.selasetur.is/en/tourist-info.*

Sights

Borgarvirki

NATURE SIGHT | A quick and tempting diversion can be found by taking Route 717 off Route 1 and driving 9 km (just under 6 miles) to Borgarvirki, an outstanding natural fortress made of basalt strata. Standing 177 meters (580 feet) above sea level with superior views over the vast plains, you can let your imagination run wild here. Legend has it that Vikings once used this geological wonder as a real fort. ✉ *Borgarvirki.*

Hvítserkur is a legendary sea stack in northwest Iceland.

★ Hvítserkur

NATURE SIGHT | This legendary 15-meter sea stack is shaped remarkably like a giant rhino drinking from the sea. Fueling imaginations since time immemorial, Hvítserkur is said to have been a night troll caught in the sunrise while making its way to the old convent at Þingeyrar to complain about the bells. Hvítserkur translates to "white shirt" and refers to the white color from the accumulation of bird droppings. To reach this obligatory photo op, turn off Route 711 north of Ósvar. A trail leads from the parking lot to a viewing platform. ⊠ *Vatnsnesvegur*.

Illugastaðir

FARM/RANCH | This farm on the western coast of the Vatsnes peninsula, just off Route 711, has a trail from the parking lot that leads to a viewing platform with excellent views of Strandir, where you can observe seals at play. Apart from being a seal-watching paradise, the location is the setting of a historic murder case in Iceland, which was dramatized in Hannah Kent's award-winning novel, *Burial Rites*. Note that the area is home to a large population of eider ducks and is closed to visitors from May 1 to June 20 during their nesting period. ⊠ *Illugastaðir*.

Hotels

Ósar Hostel

$ | HOTEL | Right next to the Hvítserkur sea stacks, this spot on Route 711 is an old converted farmhouse surrounded by lovely countryside views. **Pros:** five-minute walk to Hvítserkur; close to seal colonies; lovely countryside views. **Cons:** shared bathrooms; thin walls; basic amenities. $ *Rooms from: ISK16,000* ⊠ *Vatnsnesvegur* ☎ *862–2778* ⊕ *www. facebook.com/osarhostel* ⤳ *19 rooms* ⦿❙ *No Meals*.

Blönduós

144 km (89 miles) west of Akureyri, 58 km (36 miles) northeast of Hvammstangi.

Most people drive straight through this small town and administrative center or use it as a stop to refuel. If you have some time to spare, though, there's a particularly romantic nature spot to explore, a food-lover's haven, and an excellent museum.

GETTING HERE AND AROUND

This town is best served by car, but Strætó runs the 57 bus service between Reykjavík and Akureyri, with a stop at Blönduós.

Sights

Hrútey

ISLAND | Easily accessible just off the main road, Hrútey Island is located in the middle of the glacial Blanda River. Dense with trees and vegetation after an extensive reforestation program, the island is now home to a thriving population of birds. A small footbridge connects to the island, which is closed to the public from April 20 to June 20 to protect nesting birds from being disturbed. ⊠ *Þjóðvegur, Blönduós* ☾ *Closed mid-Apr.–mid-June.*

★ Textile Museum

OTHER MUSEUM | The famed Textile Museum in Blönduós is all about the *þráður* or the "thread," and uses this theme to weave together a cohesive and inventive exploration of Icelandic textiles. Stop by to learn about Iceland's beautiful national costumes, the history of the Icelandic sweater, or the intricacies of embroidery, or just check out which local textile designer is currently showcasing their wares there. ⊠ *Árbraut 29, Blönduós* ☎ *452–4067* ⊕ *www.textile.is* 🎟 *ISK 1,500.*

★ Þingeyrakirkja

CHURCH | A 6.3-km (4-mile) detour off the Ring Road on Route 721 leads to Þingeyrakirkja, a unique 1877 church constructed of basalt and limestone and located in a picturesque setting next to the lovely Lake Hóp. Make sure you visit this attraction when it's open so you can marvel at the interior, which features a 15th-century altarpiece and an extraordinary dome-shaped, midnight-blue ceiling, covered with countless golden stars. Next to the church is a visitor center offering light refreshments. ☎ *895–4473* ⊕ *www.thingeyraklausturskirkja.is* ☾ *Interior closed Sept.–May.*

Restaurants

Teni Restaurant & Café

$$ | ETHIOPIAN | Located next to a swimming pool, Teni Restaurant & Café is an appealing café where you can fill up on traditional Icelandic dishes or something a little more exotic from Ethiopia, where the owner and chef are from. Portions can be generous here—particularly for Iceland—so arrive hungry. **Known for:** great place to stop along the Ring Road; only Ethiopian restaurant in the North; large portions. $ *Average main: ISK2,350* ⊠ *Húnabraut 2, Blönduós* ☎ *452–4040* ⊕ *www.facebook.com/tenirestaurant.*

🛏 Hotels

★ Brimslóð Atelier Guesthouse

$$$ | HOTEL | This sleek, minimalist boutique hotel has put Blönduós on the map as a culinary destination, as its owners are also authors of the fabulous Icelandic cookbook *Into the North.* The hotel also hosts workshops on Iceland's food history and intimate dinners by a super-sized window that frames epic sunsets during the summer and regular displays of northern lights in the darker months. **Pros:** authentic Icelandic experience; great place to mingle with locals;

fantastic food. **Cons:** books up quickly; not all rooms have ocean views; some rooms have shared bathrooms. [$] *Rooms from: ISK32,000* ✉ *Brimslóð 10A, Blönduós* ☎ *899–1199* 🌐 *www.brimslodguesthouse.is* 🛏 *10 rooms* 🍴 *Free Breakfast.*

Hótel Húni

$$ | HOTEL | This countryside hotel feels worlds away, thanks to the panoramic views of Lake Svínavatn that you can enjoy from the large swimming pool. **Pros:** beautiful remote setting; nice on-site restaurant; swimming pool with awesome views. **Cons:** not all rooms have private bathrooms; quite far from the main highway; campsites next door can get noisy. [$] *Rooms from: ISK22,500* ✉ *Húnavallaskóli, Blönduós* ☎ *691–2207* 🌐 *www.hotelhuni.com* 🛏 *28 rooms* 🍴 *Free Breakfast.*

Varmahlíð

50 km (31 miles) southeast of Blönduós.

Located at the junction between Route 1, which continues to Akureyri, and Route 75 to Sauðárkrókur, Varmahlíð, with a convenient gas station and general store, is a great pit stop. Those seeking thrilling outdoor activities might want to stay longer and explore the white-water rafting conditions on the East-Glacier and West-Glacier rivers or the area's superb horseback riding tours. Activities are concentrated on Route 752.

GETTING HERE AND AROUND

Driving is the best way to explore this region, but Strætó runs the 57 service from Reykjavík to Akureyri daily, which stops at the N1 gas station in Varmahlíð.

VISITOR INFORMATION

CONTACTS Varmahlíð Regional Information Center. ✉ *Varmahlíð* ✥ *Located in the wooden house with the traditional turf roof, next to the local store* ☎ *455–6161.*

Sights

Fosslaug

HOT SPRING | Close to the Reykjafoss waterfall, this heated natural pool is a popular destination for travelers in the area, so you might have to share it with strangers, especially if you're visiting in the summer. Go after midnight or at the crack of dawn if you want to enjoy it on your own. A short trail off Route 752 leads to this hidden gem. ✉ *Varmahlíð.*

★ Glaumbær

MUSEUM VILLAGE | North of Varmahlíð on Route 75, Glaumbær is an excellent example of traditional Icelandic turf farms and features a church and several buildings, some of which date back to the 18th century. Among its fascinating artifacts is a beautifully crafted willow-root basket said to have been made by the legendary outlaw Fjalla-Eyvindur. Adding to its historical significance is the fact that Glaumbær is an ancient farmstead (existing long before the buildings we see today) and was once home to Guðríður Þorbjarnardóttir, the first European white woman to travel to America. ✉ *Glaumbær, Varmahlíð* ☎ *453–6173* 🌐 *www.glaumbaer.is* 🎟 *ISK 1,700* 🕐 *Closed late Oct.–Mar. except by request.*

The Old Stable

FARM/RANCH | This unusual turf-house stable is the only one of its kind known to exist in Iceland. It's just one of the attractions at Lýtingsstaðir, which also offers horseback riding and self-catering accommodation in cottages located just below the Old Stable. ✉ *Lýtingsstaðir, Varmahlíð* ☎ *893–3817* 🌐 *www.lythorse.com* 🕐 *Closed Sept.–Apr.*

Reykjafoss

WATERFALL | A short trail off Route 752 leads to this enchanting little waterfall, one of the lesser-photographed spots in Iceland. It is not only lovely to look at, but it also provides a relaxing natural soundtrack to those taking a dip in the nearby Fosslaug natural pool. ⊠ *Reykja-foss, Varmahlíð.*

Víðimýri Turf Church

CHURCH | Set in a peaceful meadow with pastures for grazing horses, Víðimýri Church (off Route 1) is one of only six preserved turf churches in Iceland. The beautiful building constructed of thick sod and driftwood is still used as a parish church, but also opens its doors to visitors daily (between 9 am and 6 pm) during the summer. ⊠ *Víðimýrarkirkja, Varmahlíð ⊙ Interior closed Sept.-May.*

Restaurants

★ Áshús

$$$ | ICELANDIC | Glaumbær's cozy tea room is an unforgettable stop, particularly after a meander around the historical grounds. Either get their soup, cakes, and coffee buffet or just order something á la carte. **Known for:** every traditional Icelandic pastry there is; top-tier pancakes; looks like grandma's house, tastes like grandma's secret family recipes. $ *Average main: ISK3,100 ⊠ Glaumbær, Varmahlíð ☎ 453–6173 ⊕ www.glaumbaer.is/is/en/ashus-tea-room-cafe ⊙ Closed late Sept.–early May.*

Hótel Varmahlíð Restaurant

$$$ | SCANDINAVIAN | You don't have to be a hotel guest to dine here, and as the only place for miles where you can get a decent sit-down meal, you should book well in advance. The menu features lots of Icelandic dishes boasting the use of fresh, locally sourced ingredients from the so-called "Skagafjörður food chest." The decor is modern and inviting. **Known for:** lighty salted cod; local lamb; chocolate cake for dessert. $ *Average main: ISK3,700 ⊠ Laugarvegur, Varmahlíð ☎ 453–8170 ⊕ www.hotelvarmahlid.is ⊙ Closed winter except by appointment.*

Hotels

★ Hestasport Cottages

$$ | HOUSE | Perched on a hilltop above the town center, this collection of cabins is beautifully decorated, and has all the amenities you need for a self-catering holiday. **Pros:** lovely location; close to local places of interest; communal stone hot stub. **Cons:** limited public transport; self-catering so no dining on-site; 2 km walk to the reception. $ *Rooms from: ISK27,000 ⊠ Vegamót, Varmahlíð ☎ 453–8383 ⊕ www.riding.is/cottages ⇥ 7 rooms.*

Hótel Varmahlíð

$$$ | HOTEL | Conveniently located just off the main road in the town center, this family-run hotel is an excellent base for exploring the region. **Pros:** central location; great restaurant; close to hiking trails. **Cons:** small bathrooms are badly ventilated; books up quickly during the summer; pricey option for the area. $ *Rooms from: ISK32,000 ⊠ Laugavegur, Varmahlíð ☎ 453–8170 ⊕ www.hotelvar-mahlid.is ⇥ 19 rooms* ⦿| *Free Breakfast.*

Shopping

Alþýðulist

SOUVENIRS | Based in the same delightful turf-topped store as the information center, Alþýðulist (which translates to "folk art") sells lots of colorful woolens, souvenirs, and handmade crafts proudly produced in the Skagafjörður area. ⊠ *Varmahlíð, Varmahlíð ☎ 453–7000 ⊕ www.facebook.com/althydulist.*

🏃 Activities

★ Hestasport

HORSEBACK RIDING | This company specializes in horseback riding tours, and their reputation as the best in the region is well earned. The owners are fun and friendly and have recruited a fabulous team of experienced guides to help provide true quality service. They offer a number of short riding tours, extended wilderness expeditions into the highlands and combo horseback riding and river rafting tours in addition to tongue-in-cheek seasonal trips such as "Game of Horses." ⊠ *Skagafjarðarvegur, Varmahlíð* ☎ *453–8383* ⊕ *www.riding.is.*

Lýtingsstaðir

HORSEBACK RIDING | This farm off Route 752, around 20 km (12 miles) southeast of the town center, offers a range of horseback riding tours, from short one- to three-hour excursions (ISK 7,000–18,000) to extended multiday trips. They also provide an affordable horseback riding and self-catering accommodation package "Stop & Ride," which costs ISK 83,000 for two people for one week. ⊠ *Lýtingsstaðir, Varmahlíð* ☎ *893–3817* ⊕ *www.lythorse.is.*

★ Viking Rafting

WHITE-WATER RAFTING | **FAMILY** | This company takes its fun seriously, offering exciting river-rafting tours that combine the stunning scenery of river-cut canyons with the roaring sound of nature and torrents of dashing adventure. Family trips on the more gentle currents of the West Glacial River (Vestari-Jökulsá) are available as well as white-water action adventures on the so-called Beast of the East (Austari-Jökulsá). Make sure to try the hot spring hot chocolate that's offered after most trips. ⊠ *Skagafjarðarvegur, Varmahlíð* ☎ *823–8300* ⊕ *www.vikingrafting.is.*

Sauðárkrókur

25 km (16) miles north of Varmahlíð.

The curious name of this town, which was first settled by Vikings in the 9th century, is translated to "River-sheep-hook" and originates from the local Sauðá River. Home to the second largest population in North Iceland along with the occasional wandering polar bear, the town prospers on an economy based on

The Öxnadalur ◉ Valley

Those bypassing the northern coastline and heading straight to Akureyri from this region take Route 1 from the junction at Varmahlíð, which continues east over Öxnadalsheiði mountain pass and into Öxnadalur valley. This striking valley is noted for being the birthplace of national poet Jónas Hallgrímsson (1807–1845) born at Hraun farm, and also for the extraordinary serrated peaks of Mt. Hraundrangi (3,527 ft) on the northern side of the valley.

industry, agriculture, and more recently, tourism. Its latest attraction, 1238 The Battle of Iceland, is based on a bloody chapter of Iceland's Saga Age history. Sauðárkrókur is also the gateway to the birdwatching paradise that is Drangey Island.

GETTING HERE AND AROUND

Located 16 miles north of Varmahlíð on Route 75, Sauðárkrókur is served by Stræto bus route number 57 from Akureyri and Reykjavík, stopping at the N1 gas station on Sauðamýri. Having a car is still the best way to explore the region.

TOURS

★ Drangey Tours

BOAT TOURS | Daily boat tours to Drangey (ISK 14,900) are offered during the summer (June 1–August 20), leaving from the Sauðárkrókur marina. From the landing point fitted with a small floating jetty, a vertigo-inducing path with rope for handrails winds 180 meters (590 feet) to the top. The views are extraordinary. The company also offers sailing trips around Drangey (ISK 9,500) for those who want to skip the hike. ⊠ *Hesteyri* ☎ *821–0090* ⊕ *www.drangey.net.*

Sights

★ Drangey Island

ISLAND | With sheer vertical drops on all sides, Drangey rises sharply out of the sea, creating one of the region's most iconic images. To the south of the island is a remarkable sea stack named Kerling ("old woman" in Icelandic) and farther east is the island Málmey. Besides hosting a legion of diving birds (puffins, guillemots, and auks), Drangey was once the home of legendary Saga hero Grettir, who spent the last three years of his life there in exile. The remains of his turf house can still be seen on the island. ⊠ *Drangey, Skagafjörður.*

Grettislaug

HOT SPRING | This legendary bathing hot spot at the end of Route 748 was constructed with natural stone. The area has excellent views of Drangey Island and is a superb place to relax after a long hike while watching a sensational summer sunset. Changing facilities and showers are available for a small fee next to the pool. There's also a campsite and a small café. ⊠ *Reykir Grettislaug* ⓢ *ISK 2,000.*

Mount Tindastóll

MOUNTAIN | Legend has it that a small lake on top of this landmark mountain occasionally produces magical wishing stones, but the real treasure is the glorious views from the top, where you will also find a cairn named Unicorn (Einhyrningur). Access to the marked hiking trail leads from Skógarhvammur off Route 745. The mountain also has a skiing area (⊕ *www.skitindastoll.is*) during the winter. ⊠ *Tindastóll, Skogarhvammur.*

Puffin and Friends

OTHER MUSEUM | Climate change, global warming, and other issues affecting the Atlantic puffin population are issues covered at this excellent museum, which also features the taxidermied corpse of an unfortunate polar bear that found its way to Iceland in 1986. They also have footage of whales and a sensational 360 VR experience of the northern lights and the vertigo-inducing cliffs of Drangey Island. ⊠ *Aðalgata 24, Sauðárkrókur* ☎ *892–7707* ⊕ *www.facebook.com/puffinandfriends* ⓢ *ISK 1,900.*

★ 1238 The Battle of Iceland

HISTORY MUSEUM | This Sauðárkrókur attraction, enhanced by VR technology, presents an immersive exhibition based on the legendary and bloody chapter of Iceland's history known as the Age of the Sturlungs (1220–1264), which marked the end of Iceland's independence. At the on-site restaurant Grána Bistro, you can fill up on good local food. ⊠ *1238 The Battle of Iceland, Aðalgata 21* ☎ *588–1238* ⊕ *www.1238.is* ⓢ *ISK 3,450.*

🍴 Restaurants

★ Grána Bistro

$$ | **CAFÉ** | Located within the 1238 Battle of Iceland museum, this restaurant not only serves some delightful fare but also acts as Skagafjörður's premier concert venue, bringing both famous and small-time artists to play in the remote countryside. They also have a small store with gifts and souvenirs. **Known for:** lots and lots of cakes; simple salads, soups, and sandwiches; only concert venue in the surrounding area. ⓢ *Average main: ISK2,000* ⊠ *Aðalgata 21* ☎ *588–1238* ⊕ *www.facebook.com/granabistro.*

Hard Wok Cafe

$$$ | **ASIAN FUSION** | There's an unusual ensemble of Asian and Mexican dishes at the Hard Wok Cafe, with a few international fast food favorites like pizza and burgers thrown into the mix. While you wait for your meal you'll hear '80s classics and get to appreciate framed quotes by the likes of Captain Jack Sparrow and Bob Marley. **Known for:** "Wok On The Wild Side" chef's surprise menu; local hotspot; quirkiest menu in rural northern Iceland. ⓢ *Average main: ISK3,000* ⊠ *Aðalgata 8* ☎ *453–5355* ⊕ *www.facebook.com/Hard.Wok.Cafe.Island.*

Kaffi Krókur

$$$ | **INTERNATIONAL** | This appealing restaurant set in a historic town building from 1890 offers a menu of traditional Icelandic dishes with a variety of international favorites, including pizza, pasta, and a grill menu with burgers. If you can't decide what to order, the fish of the day is always a star. **Known for:** the pepper cheeseburger; historic setting; always excellent fish of the day. $ *Average main: ISK3,600* ⊠ *Aðalgata 16* ☎ *453–6454* ⊕ *www.kkrestaurant.is.*

Coffee and Quick Bites

Sauðárkróksbakarí

$ | **BAKERY** | A port in any weather, this lovely little bakery-cum-café on the main street has great coffee and lots of tasty pastries and cakes. They also serve daily delicious soups and a variety of ready-made sandwiches. **Known for:** Icelandic marriage cake; perfect for a quick meal; tasty sandwiches. $ *Average main: ISK500* ⊠ *Aðalgata 5* ☎ *455–5000* ⊕ *www.saudarkroksbakari.net.*

Hotels

Hótel Tindastóll

$$ | **HOTEL** | Occupying a lovely old Norwegian timber house from 1884 with exposed beams and low ceilings, Hotel Tindastóll (named after the town's mountain) generates a cozy, yesteryear atmosphere, warmed throughout with a palette of mustard, peach, cherry, and apple green. **Pros:** outdoor hot tub; romantic atmosphere; comfortable beds. **Cons:** old house with thin walls; steep stairs; small bathrooms. $ *Rooms from: ISK23,800* ⊠ *Lindargata 3* ☎ *453–5002* ⊕ *www.arctichotels.is* ⇆ *20 rooms* ⦿ *Free Breakfast.*

Hólar

31 km (19 miles) east of Sauðárkrókur.

With a striking cathedral at its center, Hólar is one of Iceland's most important historical sites and was considered for many years to be the capital of the north. Founded as a diocese in 1106, it became a significant medieval political base and center of learning, but it is most famous for being the last stronghold of Catholicism in Iceland, a source of great religious conflict during the Reformation, and home of Iceland's last Catholic bishop, Jón Árnason, who was beheaded along with his two sons in 1550. Hólar is also home to a small agricultural university specializing in aquaculture, equine studies, and rural tourism.

GETTING HERE AND AROUND

Tucked away off the beaten path of the already remote North, you can reach Hólar via the small Highway 767, a turnoff from Tröllaskagi's famed Arctic Coast Way on Highway 76. Located 320 km (199 miles) away from Reykjavík, the four-hour drive begins on the Ring Road, Highway 1. Once at Blönduós, turn north onto Highway 74 and then right onto Highway 744. At Sauðárkrókur, continue on to Highway 75 and then make a left onto Highway 76, which will lead to the turnoff onto Highway 767 and Hólar.

Expect an hour-and-a-half drive if you approach from the opposite direction from Akureyri. Start on the Ring Road until you see the Highway 76 turn-off just before Varmahlíð. Make a right and then continue north until you see Highway 767.

There is no public transportation to or within Hólar; the nearest stop is Strætó's Route 57 bus stop in Sauðárkrókur, which is a little less than 30 minutes away. It's therefore absolutely necessary to have a car if you want to visit the historical region.

Sights

Auðunarstofa

HISTORIC HOME | Built using 14th-century building methods, Auðunarstofa is a reconstruction of an unusual 14th-century bishop's residence. The original building was brought from Norway around 1316 by a Norwegian man named Auðun Rauði Þorbergsson and erected at Hólar where he was a bishop (1313–1322). The building was reconstructed using wood from Norway in 2002. ⊠ *Auðunarstofa, Hólar í hjartadalur.*

Hóladómkirkja

CHURCH | Iceland's oldest stone cathedral, Hóladómkirkja, was constructed in 1763 using local basalt and red sandstone. The striking steeple was added in 1950 as a memorial to the last Catholic bishop of Hólar, Jón Árnason. Apart from its impressive cherrywood and oak altarpiece dating from 1520, the cathedral contains several unique treasures, including a 1584 Bible, a 1620 portrait of Hólar bishop, a 16th-century crucifix, and a 17th-century baptismal font made of soapstone. ⊠ *Hóladómkirkja, Hólum í Hjaltadal* ☎ *453–6300* ⊕ *www.kirkjan.is.*

Nýibær

HISTORIC HOME | A well-preserved 19th-century turf farmhouse, Nýibær is located next to the university buildings. Maintained by the National Museum of Iceland since 1956, the house is open to visitors daily from 8 am to 6 pm. ⊠ *Nýibær, Hólar í hjartadalur* ☎ *530–2200* ⊕ *www.thjodminjasafn.is.*

Hofsós

27 km (16 miles) north of Hólar.

Hofsós is a small settlement established in the 1500s on the eastern shore of the Skagafjörður fjord. There are two main reasons people visit Hofsós: one is for the fabulous outdoor swimming pool with terrific views of the fjord, and the other is rooted in history and curiosity. For many North Americans with ties to Iceland, Hofsós is a place of pilgrimage where they can visit the town's famous emigration museum and find out about their Icelandic ancestors.

GETTING HERE AND AROUND

Hofsós is located just off Highway 76 on the Arctic Coast Way, 327 km (203 miles) from Reykjavík. From the western Ring Road, it can be reached by turning north onto Highway 74 at Blönduós and then making a quick right onto Highway 744. Continue on this road to Sauðárkrókur and Highway 75, then make a left onto Highway 76 and continue north until you see the well-marked Hofsós signs.

From Akureyri, it's simply a two-hour drive starting north to Dalvík on Highway 82, which will eventually turn into Highway 76 after Ólafsfjörður. Continue on around the peninsula—and make sure to be careful in the tunnels—until you get to Hofsós.

There is unfortunately no public transportation to Hofsós or within the town itself. The closest bus pickup is Strætó's Route 57 stop in Sauðárkrókur, which is still a 30-minute drive away from Hofsós. A car is highly, highly recommended in order to make your trip around Hofsós a spectacular one.

Sights

Grafarkirkja

CHURCH | For a quick fix of turf-topped delight visit Grafakirkja (also known as Gröf), a tiny yet fetching chapel dating from around the late 1600s. Maintained by the National Museum of Iceland since 1939, Gröf is the oldest church in Iceland. ⊠ *Grafarkirkja, Deildardalsvegur.*

Hofsós Swimming Pool

POOL | FAMILY | The unlimited sea views over the fjord from this open-air swimming pool are especially pretty during the summer months. As it lacks shelter from the north, it can get somewhat choppy when the wind picks up. ✉ *Suðurbraut, Hofsós* ☎ *455–6070* ⊕ *sundlaugar.is/en/ sundlaugar/hofsos/* 🖃 *ISK 1,090.*

Icelandic Emigration Center
HISTORY MUSEUM | Also known as Vesturfarasetrið in Icelandic, this permanent exhibition documents the mass emigration of Icelanders to the New World during the late 19th and early 20th centuries. At least 20% of the Icelandic population at that time headed west to make a home in North America, resulting in many modern-day Americans with Icelandic heritage. The exhibition also details the fates of those who left and offers a genealogy service. ✉ *Kvosin, Hofsós* ☎ *453–7935* ⊕ *www.hofsos.is* ۞ *Closed Sept.–May.*

Siglufjörður

60 km (37 miles) north of Hofsós.

Beautifully situated in a steep-sided fjord and surrounded by lofty mountains, Siglufjörður, or "Siglo" as it's lovingly referred to by locals, spent more than a century as one of Iceland's most significant fishing towns. At its peak during the first half of the 20th century, it was the herring capital of the world and home to more than 3,000 people. Its cultural heritage is now preserved at the award-winning Herring Era Museum.

Although it still operates as a fishing town, its new focus on tourism has seen much investment over the past few years, with a growing number of shops and services opening. It has a superb 9-hole golf course and is a great base for a series of first-rate hiking trails across the Tröllaskagi peninsula.

GETTING HERE AND AROUND
Siglufjörður is best reached by car, but Strætó operates bus service 78 to Siglufjörður from Akureyri (70 minutes)

with three trips daily (Monday–Friday) and one service on Sunday.

FESTIVALS
Folk Music Festival
MUSIC FESTIVALS | For one week a year, the entire town of Siglufjörður becomes a haven of folk music, with musicians from all around the world gathering to put on workshops, lectures, and more concerts than you can count. Don't miss any of the traditional Icelandic shows—there's nothing like the timbre of the old *rímur* melodies. ☎ *467–2300* ⊕ *siglofestival. wpcomstaging.com.*

VISITOR INFORMATION
CONTACTS Tourist Information Center. ✉ *Gránugötu 24* ☎ *464–9100* ⊕ *www. visittrollaskagi.is.*

Sights

★ The Folk Music Center
OTHER MUSEUM | For the perfect soundtrack to your Siglufjörður visit, head to the Folk Music Museum, where you can listen to some traditional folk music and try your hand at a range of antique Icelandic instruments, such as the fiddle and drone zither. ✉ *Norðurgata 1* ☎ *467–2300* ⊕ *www.facebook.com/ thjodlagasetur/* 🖃 *ISK 1,000; free with ticket to Herring Era Museum* ۞ *Closed Sept.–May except by advance request.*

★ The Herring Era Museum
HISTORY MUSEUM | The glorious herring fishing history of Siglufjörður is well preserved in five old harborside buildings at this superb museum. Covering the entire period of the town's glory days, these beautifully curated exhibition spaces offer a remarkable glimpse into an industry that once generated more than a quarter of the country's export income. A visit to this museum also gives you free admission to the Folk Music Museum. ✉ *Snorragata 10* ☎ *467–1604* ⊕ *www. sild.is* 🖃 *ISK 2,200* ۞ *Closed Oct.–Apr. except by appointment.*

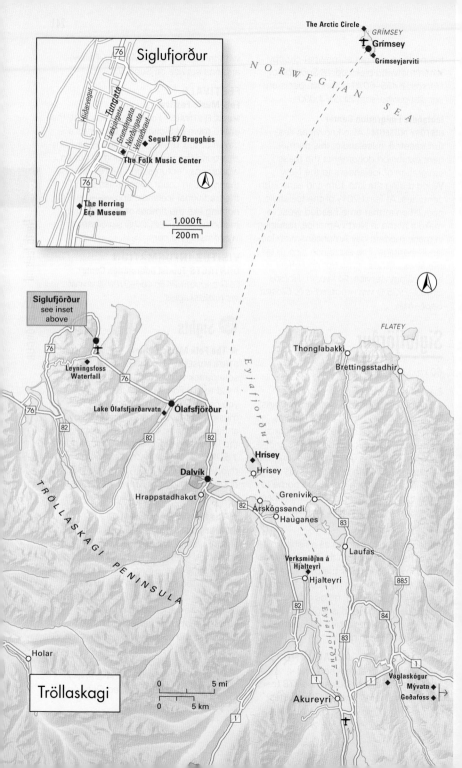

Siglufjörður

76

Hlíðarvegur
Tungata
Lækjagata
Grundargata
Norðurgata
Vetrarbraut

Segull 67 Brugghús

The Folk Music Center

76

The Herring
Era Museum

1,000ft
200m

The Arctic Circle
GRÍMSEY
Grímsey
Grímseyjarviti

NORWEGIAN SEA

FLATEY

Siglufjörður
see inset
above

76

Leyningsfoss
Waterfall

76

Lake Ólafsfjarðarvatn

Ólafsfjörður

82

82

82

Thonglabakki

Brettingsstadhir

Eyjafjörður

Hrísey

Hrísey

Dalvík

Hrappstadhakot

82

Grenivik

Árskógssandi

Hauganes

83

Laufas

Verksmiðjan á
Hjalteyri

Hjalteyri

885

Eyjafjörður

82

84

83

Holar

TRÖLLASKAGI PENINSULA

Tröllaskagi

0   5 mi

0   5 km

1

Akureyri

1

Vaglaskógur

Mývatn

Goðafoss

1

★ **Leyningsfoss Waterfall**

WATERFALL | A waterfall in a forest is a rare treat in Iceland, and while it might be only a few meters tall, the lovely Leyningsfoss is nonetheless impressive. A short walk on one of the delightful forest trails leads to this enchanting spot, where you can sit down on one of the wooden benches and enjoy a few moments of pure bliss. ✉ *Skarðsdalsskógur.*

Segull 67 Brugghús

BREWERY | A family runs this craft beer brewery whose name is a compound of their favorite number and the word for "magnet" in Icelandic. The building was formerly a fish factory and the largest workplace in town. They offer tours of the brewery, where you can sample brews and see how they're made. ✉ *Vetrarbraut 8–10* ☎ *863–2120* 🌐 *www.segull67.is* 🎫 *ISK 3,000 for a one-hour tour* 🕒 *Closed Sun.–Wed.*

Restaurants

Kaffi Rauðka

$$$ | **PIZZA** | Even if you aren't hungry, a trip to this eatery—located in the so-bright-you-can't-miss-it red house right on the Siglufjörður harbor—isn't a wasted one, thanks to its spectacular views. But if you are hungry, the pizzas are filling and the cakes are sweet. **Known for:** prime outdoor drinking locale for a sunny day; amazing views out to the ocean; huge pizza portions. [$] *Average main: ISK3,000* ✉ *Gránugata 19* ☎ *461–7733* 🌐 *www.raudka.is.*

★ **Siglunes Guesthouse Restaurant**

$$$ | **MOROCCAN** | Reserve a table at this restaurant run by award-winning Moroccan chef Jaouad Hbib, who arrived at this remote northern town in 2016. The menu changes every few weeks and often features local ingredients. **Known for:** tajine, tajine, and more tajine; ever-changing menus; vegetarian-friendly options. [$] *Average main: ISK3,950* ✉ *Lækjargata 10* ☎ *467–1222* 🌐 *www.hotelsiglunes.is* 🕒 *Closed Mon.*

★ **Sunna Restaurant**

$$$$ | **SCANDINAVIAN** | Fine dining enhanced by glorious views over the marina and fjord create a memorable experience at Sunna. Standouts on the menu include the lamb fillet and pan-fried cod, but save some room for the white chocolate mousse, a sweet, tangy dessert with lime pear that fizzes delightfully on your tongue. **Known for:** fresh seafood; surprisingly affordable multi-course menu; nice wine list. [$] *Average main: ISK4,890* ✉ *Snorragata 3* ☎ *461–7730* 🌐 *www.siglohotel.is.*

Coffee and Quick Bites

★ **Fríða Chocolate Café**

$ | **CAFÉ** | For a true chocolate high, visit Frida—aka the chocolate temptress of the north—who sells exceptional handmade chocolates in her delightful coffee shop. The decor is stylish, from the cartoon-covered walls of the bathroom to all the featured works of art, but the chocolates are the star attractions here, with some surprising flavors like blue cheese and beer. **Known for:** some of the best chocolate in Iceland; delicious hot chocolate; Belgian waffles. [$] *Average main: ISK980* ✉ *Túngata 40a* ☎ *896–8686* 🌐 *www.frida.is.*

Hotels

The Herring House Guesthouse

$ | **HOTEL** | Endowed with great views of the town and surrounding mountains, plus a lovely garden, this guesthouse has four modern and stylish rooms with shared facilities and a cozy garden cottage. **Pros:** good breakfast; hot tub; blackout curtains in rooms. **Cons:** shared bathrooms; breakfast not included in the price; cottage shower is outdoors. [$] *Rooms from: ISK18,000* ✉ *Hlíðarvegur 1* ☎ *517–4300* 🌐 *www.theherringhouse.com* 🛏 *4 rooms* 🍴 *No Meals.*

★ Sigló Hótel
$$$ | **HOTEL** | There's a touch of class, but not a trace of pretension at Sigló Hótel, which is named after the endearing title given to the town by its locals. **Pros:** beautiful design; great views; superb cocktail bar and restaurant. **Cons:** a bit of a walking distance from the car park; no driveway leading to the entrance; not all rooms overlook the marina. [$] *Rooms from: ISK32,900* ✉ *Snorragata 3* ☎ *461–7730* 🌐 *www.keahotels.is/siglo-hotel* 🛏 *64 rooms* 🍴 *Free Breakfast.*

Siglunes Guesthouse
$ | **HOTEL** | Located in an old 1934 building that once housed the town's first hotel, this guesthouse has a number of well-appointed rooms with wall art and vintage furnishings. **Pros:** central location; superb restaurant; affordable prices. **Cons:** not all rooms have bathrooms; no televisions; small rooms. [$] *Rooms from: ISK18,000* ✉ *Lækjargata 10* ☎ *467–1222* 🌐 *www.hotelsiglunes.is* 🛏 *19 rooms* 🍴 *No Meals.*

Activities

Sigló Golf
GOLF | It might be challenging to keep your eye on the ball when you're surrounded by such glorious views, especially during the summer when the midnight sun lingers on the horizon. Siglufjörður's 9-hole golf course (designed by award-winning architect Edwin Roald Rögnvaldsson) presents an excellent improvement to the gravel mines that once occupied the space. Sigló Hotel has special offers on golf and accommodation packages. ☎ *461–7730* 🌐 *www.siglogolf.is* 🎟 *From ISK 6,500* ⛳ *9 holes, 3,000 yards, par 35.*

Skarðsdalur Ski Resort
SKIING & SNOWBOARDING | Four lifts service 5½ km (3½ miles) of well-groomed ski slopes at this modest ski resort. With elevations reaching 630 meters, it might not satisfy the seasoned international skier, but it does have spectacular views. The longest trail is 1½ km (1 mile). Skis and snowboards are available to rent at reasonable prices (ISK 5,500 a day). This is also a great destination during the summer, where you can frame an epic shot of the town and surrounding mountains. ✉ *Skarðsvegur* ☎ *878–3399* 🌐 *www.skardsdalur.is* 🎟 *ISK 4,000.*

Top Mountaineering
KAYAKING | This is the go-to company for kayaking trips and hiking in Siglufjöður and the remarkable surrounding areas of Fljót and Heðinsfjörður. They accommodate all levels of ability. ✉ *Hverfisgata 18* ☎ *898–4939* 🌐 *www.topmountaineering.is.*

Viking Heliskiing
SKIING & SNOWBOARDING | The co-founders of Viking Heliskiing are World Cup and Olympian competitors but now run multiday skiing tours in the extraordinary, fairy-tale peaks of Tröllaskagi. They have 256 landing points and around 500 routes including "Thor," a run that offers a higher-than-heaven ski high from the summit of Vikurhirna (1,200 meters) into Heiðinsfjörður Valley. ✉ *Sigló Hotel, Snorragata 3* ☎ *846–1674* 🌐 *www.vikingheliskiing.com.*

Ólafsfjörður

17 km (10 miles) southeast of Siglufjörður.

The sleepy little fishing town of Ólafsfjörður, where fishing has been practiced for nearly a century, is tucked between sheer-sloped, tall mountains, with the fairytale-like Lágheiði highland pass rising to the south. Located so far north and with only basic services and facilities, it's no surprise that less than 1,000 people make their home here. If you have time to spare, the town offers stunning views, and the surrounding nature makes great company any time of year.

GETTING HERE AND AROUND

From Siglufjörður, Route 76 leads through the stunning uninhabited Héðinsfjörður fjord via a couple of modern mountain tunnels exiting into Ólafsfjörður. The route from Dalvík into Ólafsfjörður (Route 82), which exits from the belly of a 3½-km (2-mile) long mountain tunnel at ear-popping heights, provides a more dramatic entrance with brilliant views of the fjord. There's a viewing platform where you can stop to take a photo.

Strætó bus service 78 from Akureyri stops in Ólafsfjörður three times a day (Monday–Friday) with one service running on Sunday.

VISITOR INFORMATION

CONTACTS Visitor Center. ⊠ *Fjallabyggð Library, Ólafsvegur 4* ☎ *464–9215.*

Sights

Lake Ólafsfjarðarvatn

BODY OF WATER | The town's beautiful lake, which freezes over to perfection during the winter, is not only a great place to go ice-skating, it's also a peculiar natural wonder listed in the Nature Conservation Register due to its layer of freshwater that floats on top of a body of denser seawater. ⊠ *Ólafsfjarðarvatn.*

Natural History Museum of Ólafsfjörður

OTHER MUSEUM | Located in Pálshús, one of the oldest buildings in town, the Natural History Museum of Ólafsfjörður features a permanent exhibition entitled *The Desire to Fly*, which focuses on Iceland's diverse bird life mixed with elements addressing the human desire to fly. ⊠ *Pálshús, Strandgata 4, Ólafsfjörður* ☎ *466–2255* ⊕ *www.palshusmuseum.is* ⊠ *ISK 1,500* ⊘ *Closed Sept.–mid-May.*

 Restaurants

Kaffi Klara

$$ | CAFÉ | At Kaffi Klara, you can fill up on hearty traditional Icelandic food with langoustine pizzas and open-face sandwiches. It's owned by avid foragers, so it's highly likely that a tasty harvest of blueberries and other fruits of the land could be flavoring your food. **Known for:** gluten-free chocolate; plokkfiskur (fish stew); traditional Icelandic cooking lessons. $ *Average main: ISK2,500* ⊠ *Strandgata 2, Ólafsfjörður* ☎ *466–4044* ⊕ *www.kaffiklara.is.*

Activities

★ Fairytale at Sea

BOATING | This family-run tour operator based in Ólafsfjörður offers thrilling two-hour tours onboard Yamaha Waverunners. The tours (ISK 29,900) take participants to marvelous sights impossible to see from land, including the extraordinary sea cliffs around Tröllaskagi, where legions of busy birds go about their day. Custom tours are also available. ⊠ *Fairytale at Sea, Ólafsvegur 2, Ólafsfjörður* ☎ *833–4545* ⊕ *www.fairytale.is.*

Dalvík

18 km (11 miles) south of Ólafsfjörður.

Tucked away between the glimmering Arctic Ocean and the gorgeous mountains of Tröllaskagi, Dalvík is a small town with a large fishing and commercial port. It also serves as the departure point of the Sæfari ferry to Grímsey island. Although the town is actively growing its cultural charm, ambitiously inviting the whole country for the annual fish-themed summer feast, Fiskidagurinn Mikli, its primary industries are fishing, fish processing, and trading.

The route (82) to Akureyri from Dalvík winds through some of the region's prettiest rural landscapes framed by snow-topped peaks, with a growing number of tourist attractions to tempt you off the main road. Places of interest include the brewery beer spa at Árskogssandur (also a departure point for the ferry to Hrísey), Hauganes, and Hjalteyri.

GETTING HERE AND AROUND
This town is best reached by car. Strætó bus service 78 from Akureyri stops in Dalvík three times a day (Monday–Friday) with one service running on Sunday.

FESTIVALS
Fiskidagurinn Mikli
FESTIVALS | Dalvík's annual Fiskidagurinn Mikli celebrates the fishing industry with a free seafood buffet and live entertainment. Held on the second Saturday in August, guests can enjoy live music, art, traditional Icelandic seafood, and outdoor activities like canoeing, whale watching, horseback riding, and more. ☎ 897–9748 ⊕ www.fiskidagurinnmikli.is.

TOURS
Tours and activities to pursue in and around Dalvík include whale-watching, skiing, and horseback riding in Svarfaðardalur Valley or swimming in the local pool. There are also several excellent hiking trails around Dalvík listed in the locally available Gönguleiðir í Dalvíkurbyggð brochure and map.

Arctic Sea Tours
BOAT TOURS | This local company offers a traditional three-hour whale-watching adventure (ISK 9,990), shorter express RIB boat trips (ISK 15,990), and a special Midnight Sun whale-watching trip (ISK 15,990) from May to early July. ⊠ Hafnarbraut 22 ☎ 771–7600 ⊕ www.arcticseatours.is.

Bergmenn Mountain Guides
ADVENTURE TOURS | The country's only UIAGM-IFMGA certified mountain guides, Bergmenn Mountain Guides specializes in ski touring, ski mountaineering, heli-skiing, ice climbing, and alpine climbing. They organize customized trips and also offer training and courses. ⊠ Klængshóll Lodge ☎ 858–3000 ⊕ www.bergmenn.com.

Ektafiskur
SPECIAL-INTEREST TOURS | Guided by the King of Baccalá himself Elvar Reykjalin, this fun tour takes you around the family-run Ektafiskur fishery in the nearby town of Hauganes, where salted cod has been prepared since 1940. It also includes membership to the Rotten Shark Club—and yes, you do have to try some to get your certificate. Contact in advance to schedule a visit. ⊠ Hafnargata 6, Akureyri ☎ 466–1016 ⊕ www.ektafiskur.is/en ⊡ ISK 2,000 (8 people minimum).

Whale Watching Hauganes
BOAT TOURS | The oldest whale-watching tour operator in Iceland started as a sea-angling tour company in 1989 and expanded to whale-watching in 1993. Two different whale-watching tours, one a traditional journey and the other a sea-angling combo, are offered daily from the town of Hauganes. The most commonly sighted whales are humpbacks and minkes. There are also regular sightings of harbor porpoises and white-beaked dolphins. ⊠ Hafnargata 2 ☎ 867–0000 ⊕ www.whales.is ⊡ ISK 10,600.

VISITOR INFORMATION
The tourist information center also houses a café, library, exhibition space, and events hall.

CONTACTS Tourist Information Center. ⊠ Menningarhúsið Berg., Goðabraut 8 ☎ 460–4900 ⊕ www.dalvikurbyggd.is.

Sights

Berg Menningarhús

VISITOR CENTER | The Berg Culture House is a modern building in the center of town, with a concert hall, art exhibitions, and conference facilities. It is also home to the town's library, a coffee shop, and the tourist information/visitor center. ✉ *Goðabraut 8* ☎ *823–8616* 🌐 *www.dalvikurbyggd.is.*

★ Bjórböðin Beer Spa

OTHER ATTRACTION | With unlimited ice-cold Kaldi beer on tap within arm's reach, you won't be tempted to slurp your beer bathwater. Not that you could, anyway, as the freshly run beer in these stylish kambala tubs is not for drinking. It's made with a blend of geothermal water and young unfermented beer with added brewer's yeast, rich in skin-conditioning B vitamins and minerals. They add some essential oils and beer soap, which creates a mildly fragrant foam on the top. After your 25-minute bath, plush carpets, warm blankets, and day beds await for post-bath relaxation. The spa is located in the town of Árskógssandi, just south of Dalvik. ✉ *Ægisgata 31, Árskógssandi* ☎ *414–2828* 🌐 *www.bjorbodin.is* 🎟 *ISK 11,900.*

Bruggsmiðjan Kaldi Brewery

BREWERY | Learning about how beer is made does not take away the pleasure of drinking it, and at Kaldi, Iceland's first microbrewery, you can do both. You even get to keep your glass as a souvenir. Make sure to call and schedule an appointment in advance. The brewery is located in the town of Árskógssandi, just south of Dalvik. ✉ *Öldugata 22, Árskógssandi* ☎ *466–2505* 🌐 *www.bruggsmidjan.is* 🎟 *ISK 2,500.*

★ Byggðasafnið Hvoll

OTHER MUSEUM | At the Dalvík Folk Museum, you can find out about the town's most celebrated locals, including Jóhann Svarfdælingur, the 2.25-meter (7-feet 4½-inch) tall "Viking Giant," who was for many years the tallest man in the world. A few of the rooms upstairs are dedicated to his life as a side-show performer and film star, and feature some of his custom-made clothes, costumes, and specially made furniture. ✉ *Karlsrauðatorg* ☎ *460–4928* 🌐 *www.dalvikurbyggd.is* 🎟 *ISK 950* 🕓 *Closed Sept.–May.*

Hauganes Sea Baths

OTHER ATTRACTION | **FAMILY** | Located 15 minutes from Dalvik, several marine containers are now employed as hot tubs installed on the black sand beach at Hauganes, providing a delightful beach spa experience and a great place to warm up after a cool sea swim. There are two traditional tubs and then one that's been remade into a ship's hull for the kids. Showers and changing facilities are next to the tubs. ✉ *Aðalgata 2* 🌐 *www.visithauganes.is* 🎟 *ISK 1,000.*

Verksmiðjan á Hjalteyri

ART GALLERY | An old abandoned herring factory has found new life as a contemporary art center, showcasing several eclectic exhibitions each year. The collective behind the gallery has a fantastic eye for up-and-coming talent and exhibitions that spark conversation. It's located in the tiny village of Hjalteyri, about 20 minutes south of Dalvik. ✉ *Hjalteyri* ☎ *461–1450* 🌐 *www.verksmidjanhjalteyri.com* 🕓 *Closed Mon.*

Restaurants

Á Gregors

$$$ | **ICELANDIC** | Fish and lamb are the name of the game at this casual eatery, which is perfect for a filling dinner after a day of sightseeing. Despite its humble exterior, the cooking here is expert. **Known for:** great outdoor seating; expertly cooked lamb fillet; perfectly smoked salmon. [$] *Average main: ISK3,900* ✉ *Goðabraut 3* ☎ *847–8846* 🕓 *Closed Mon.–Wed. in winter.*

★ Baccalá Bar

$$ | **SEAFOOD** | An attention-attracting Viking ship decked out with colorful shields acts like a visual ringmaster for this fabulous Hauganes restaurant, drumming up business for their fishy fare. Tasty seafood dishes and baccalá (salted codfish)–themed meals star on the menu alongside the seaside views. **Known for:** outrageously good fish and chips; amazing views out to the ocean; baccalá pizza. [$] *Average main: ISK2,800* ✉ *Hafnargata 6* ☎ *620–1035* 🌐 *www.ektafiskur.is.*

★ Gísli, Eiríkur, Helgi

$$ | **CAFÉ** | There is a glorious jumble of vintage ski wear, old leather saddles, and other knickknacks to engage your curiosity in this small-town café, which is just as charming as the children's story it's named after: *The Brothers From Bakki.* The famous local storybook (about three brothers who build a house with no windows and tried to carry sunshine into the house using their hats) makes for a great read while you wait for your order. **Known for:** exellent fish soup; cakes that look almost too good to eat; homey interior filled with antiques. [$] *Average main: ISK2,190* ✉ *Grundargata 1* ☎ *865–8391* 🌐 *www.facebook.com/bakkabraedurkaffi.*

Hotels

★ Dalvík HI Hostel

$ | **HOTEL** | They might have hostel prices, but the accommodation options here are far superior and full of local character. **Pros:** central location; delightful vintage furniture; access to garden sauna and hot spring. **Cons:** shared bathrooms; no on-site dining; decor might be too old-fashioned for some. [$] *Rooms from: ISK14,691* ✉ *Hafnarbraut 4* ☎ *699–6616* 🌐 *www.hostel.is/hostels/dalvik-hi-hostel* 🛏 *11* 🍴 *No Meals.*

Activities

Skíðasvæði Dalvíkur

SKIING & SNOWBOARDING | The ski resort at Böggvisstaðafjall mountain in Dalvík is one of the five top places to ski in North Iceland, and so close to the town center you can walk there. It has two lifts servicing several well-maintained slopes of varying difficulty. It also has a good cross-country skiing track and well as a lodge offering sleeping bag accommodation for up to 30 people. Ski and snowboard rentals are available as well. ✉ *Brekkusel* ☎ *466–1010* 🌐 *www.skidalvik.is* 🎟 *ISK 3,600 (day pass).*

★ Strýtan Dive Center

DIVING & SNORKELING | Located out of Hjalteyri, this company specializes in scuba diving tours, including a remarkable dive to the Strýtan hydrothermal chimney, the only one in the world that isn't too deep for scuba divers to explore (others are between 2,000 and 6,000 meters deep). The dive, which is featured in the BBC TV show *Forces of Nature,* requires advanced open-water diver and dry suit experience. ✉ *Hjalteyri* ☎ *862–2949* 🌐 *www.strytan.is.*

Grímsey

41 km (26 miles) north of Dalvík.

Grímsey Island is the true north of Iceland and the only part of the country transected by the Arctic Circle. To mark the spot, there's a giant concrete sphere monument that's rolled to a new location once a year to reflect the changing position of the Arctic Circle. The main incentive for visitors to Grímsey is to tick the "I've-crossed-the-Arctic-Circle" box off their bucket list, but the island, as any of its 80 inhabitants will tell you, has a charming mix of culture and nature to offer too. It's also the only place in Iceland where the sun stays visible for 24 hours during the summer solstice.

GETTING HERE AND AROUND

Grímsey Island is only accessible via a three-hour ferry from Dalvík or a 25-minute flight from Akureyri. Ferry trips are certainly the most scenic option and are available all year long via the Ferry Sæfari, though availability differs depending on the season. Flights, meanwhile, are the quicker choice. Norlandair offers weekly flights to the island from Akureyri all year.

At only two square miles, Grímsey is an easily walkable island once you get here. Outside of the small village area, the other famed parts of the island, such as the Orbis et Globus Arctic Circle Marker or the Grímsey Lighthouse, are reachable via well-marked hiking trails, as are puffin grounds and other coastal wonders. Be sure to wear comfortable shoes on your trip as you're bound to get a lot of steps in.

For those looking for more adventure, it is sometimes possible to rent bikes once on the island, which can make your journey to Grímsey's sites much quicker. Ask the information center for the latest on bike rentals.

FESTIVALS

Summor Solstice Festival

CULTURAL FESTIVALS | **FAMILY** | Each Summer Solstice, the residents of Grímsey throw a large festival to celebrate the Midnight Sun. There's live music, scavenger hunts, a "soup crawl." and their annual ball. Expect to stay up late. ✉ *Grímsey Island* 🌐 *www.facebook.com/solsticegrimsey.*

TOURS

Arctic Trip

ADVENTURE TOURS | This local company is operated by a passionate, nature-loving team who collectively know everything there is to know about Grímsey. They can arrange everything from diving, sightseeing, and snorkeling tours to sea angling and bird-watching excursions. ✉ *Kiðagili 7* ☎ *848–1696* 🌐 *www.arctictrip.is.*

👁 Sights

The Arctic Circle

PUBLIC ART | To mark the location where the Arctic Circle transects the island, the Orbis et Globus (Circle and Sphere) was commissioned and installed in 2017. The artwork, which is a 3-meter concrete sphere, was designed by Kristinn E. Hrafnsson in collaboration with Studio Grandi. The orb is moved once a year to reflect the changing position of the Arctic circle. The 3.7-km walk from the harbor to the Arctic Circle is a three-hour round trip. ✉ *Grímseyjargata.*

Grímseyjarviti

LIGHTHOUSE | Built in 1937, the bright yellow Vitinn lighthouse, with its picturesque surroundings, is a lovely destination at any time of the day, but is especially pretty on an Arctic summer's evening. The pleasant 2-km (1.25-mile) walk to the lighthouse takes around 25 minutes. ✉ *Grímseyjarviti.*

🍴 Restaurants

Krían

$$$ | **BISTRO** | Named after the arctic tern, Krían is the only restaurant on the island. They serve simple traditional Icelandic dishes and standard international favorites like hamburgers; it's also one of the few places in Iceland where you can try puffin. **Known for:** rare Icelandic specialities like puffin; the only restaurant on the island; big portions. [$] *Average main: ISK3,690* ✉ *Hafnargata* ☎ *467–3112* 🌐 *www.facebook.com/krianrestaurant.*

🛏 Hotels

Básar Guesthouse

$ | **B&B/INN** | Located in a lovely old house next to the airport, Básar is a clean and comfortable no-frills guesthouse with helpful and friendly hosts. **Pros:** location next to the airport; pretty sea views; free, fast Wi-Fi. **Cons:** shared bathroom; low ceilings; windy location. [$] *Rooms from:*

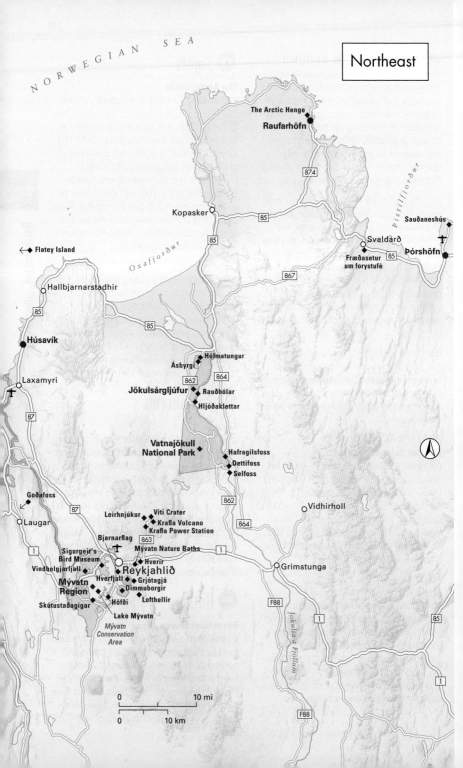

Northeast

NORWEGIAN SEA

The Arctic Henge
Raufarhöfn

874

Kopasker

85

Öxafjörður

85

867

← Flatey Island

Hallbjarnarstadhir

Þistilfjörður

Sauðaneshús

Svaldarð

Þórshöfn

Fræðasetur
um forystufé

85

Húsavík

85

85

Laxamyri

87

Hólmatungur

Ásbyrgi

862   864

Jökulsárgljúfur

Rauðhólar

Hljóðaklettar

Vatnajökull
National Park

Hafragilsfoss

Dettifoss

Selfoss

Goðafoss

87

862

Laugar

864

Vidhirholl

Leirhnjúkur   Víti Crater

Krafla Volcano

Krafla Power Station

Bjarnarflag

863

Mývatn Nature Baths

1

Sigurgeir's
Bird Museum

Hverir

Grimstunga

Vindbelgjarfjall

Reykjahlíð

Hverfjall   Grjótagjá

Mývatn
Region

Dimmuborgir

Höfði   Lofthellir

Skútustaðagigar

Lake Mývatn

Mývatn
Conservation
Area

F88

1

85

Jökulsá á Fjöllum

0   10 mi

0   10 km

F88

1

ISK16,000 ✉ 611 Grímsey ☎ 467–3103 🌐 www.gistiheimilidbasar.is 🛏 8 rooms 🍴 Free Breakfast.

Gullsól Guesthouse

$ | **B&B/INN** | The "Golden Sun" guesthouse is conveniently located right next to the harbor with fresh, modest rooms and a shared guest kitchen. **Pros:** affordable rates; convenient location; superb views. **Cons:** small rooms; shared bathroom; no breakfast. [$] *Rooms from: ISK13,000 ✉ Sólberg ☎ 467–3190 🌐 www.gullsol.is 🛏 6 rooms 🍴 No Meals.*

Shopping

Búðin

GENERAL STORE | The island's only supermarket is well stocked with supplies and also with that good old-fashioned community spirit from the golden age of the local retailer. ✉ *Hafnargötu 19, Grímsey* ☎ *898–2058.*

Hrísey

10 km (6 miles) off the coast of Dalvík.

Hrísey is the small island located in the middle of the fjord that gave Eyjafjörður (island fjord) its name. Content to be ignored by the outside world, residents of Hrísey love the simple life and have maintained a culture where old habits and traditions are of high importance. About 200 people still live in Hrísey, where a modest collection of shops and services can be found, in addition to a museum and a swimming pool.

With no predators on the island, Hrísey is home to around 40 different bird species, which can be observed at a bird-watching house by the Lambhagatjörn pond. At only 7½ km (4.6 miles) in length, the island is easy to navigate on foot. There are several marked trails of varying lengths with information signs on the flora, bird life, and geology.

GETTING HERE AND AROUND

Hrísey is accessed from the small town of Árskógssandur (13 km [8 miles] south of Dalvík), where scheduled ferry crossings to and from the island are operated daily every two hours from 7 am until 11 pm. The boat trip takes about 15 minutes and costs ISK 1,700.

VISITOR INFORMATION

The Hrísey Tourist Information Center is located inside the House of Shark Jörundur.

CONTACTS Tourist Information Center. ✉ *Norðurvegur 17* ☎ *695–0077* 🌐 *www.visithrisey.com.*

Sights

The House of Shark Jörundur

OTHER MUSEUM | Inside the island's oldest house, historically renovated to match its original style, is a surprisingly interesting exhibition on the history of shark fishing in Iceland. The Hrísey Tourist Information Center is also here. ✉ *Norðurvegur 3* ☎ *695–0077* 🌐 *www.hrisey.is* 🕒 *Closed in winter except by appointment.*

Restaurants

Verbúðin 66

$$ | **SEAFOOD** | This charming harborside restaurant is open daily during the summer and by appointment throughout the rest of the year. Using locally grown ingredients, this restaurant serves popular fish dishes, a soup of the day, burgers, and a selection of cakes. **Known for:** tasty fish and chips; Verbúðin burger and fries; excellent fish soup. [$] *Average main: ISK2,600 ✉ Sjávargata 2 ☎ 467–1166 🌐 www.facebook.com/verbudin66.*

Húsavík

75 km (47 miles) northeast of Akureyri, 119 km east of Dalvik.

It might compete with Siglufjörður for the most picturesque town in North Iceland, but for whale-watching adventures, Húsavík is the undisputed capital (it was also the site where NASA astronauts trained before going to the moon in the 1960s). Characterized by a collection of colorful houses, this charming town, framed by majestic snow-topped peaks, is not only a busy fishing port but also a thriving commercial center for the surrounding rural areas. Húsavík also found fame as the setting for the 2020 Netflix movie *Eurovision: The Story Of Fire Saga*, and even lent its name to the Oscar-nominated song "Húsavík." Since the success of the film, the town has wholeheartedly embraced its new reputation as the Eurovision capital of Iceland—even opening up a themed bar and an exhibit in a local hotel dedicated to the famous music contest.

GETTING HERE AND AROUND

Driving is the best way to get to this town. Strætó also runs the number 79 bus service from Akureyri to Húsavík three times a day on weekdays and twice on Sundays.

Eagle Air operates year-round flights between Reykjavík airport and Húsavík airport in Aðaldalur around 7½ miles south of the town center.

TOURS

★ Gentle Giants

BOAT TOURS | With cheery staff and guides, you are in good company at Gentle Giants, who offer classic whale-watching tours (ISK 10,790) in an old wooden fishing boat. For a bit more excitement you can take their Big Whale Safari on a RIB speedboat to look for puffins and larger whales (ISK 19,790). They also offer combo whale-watching and horse-riding tours (ISK 19,900),

sea angling (ISK 16,900), sea kayaking (ISK 19,900), and a trip to Flatey island (ISK 29,900). ⊠ *Garðarsbraut, Húsavík* ☎ *464–1500* ⊕ *www.gentlegiants.is.*

North Sailing

BOAT TOURS | One of the largest whale-watching tour companies based at the harbor, North Sailing has an impressive fleet of old wooden fishing boats and schooners, two of which have been modified with an electric engine to offer an eco-friendly carbon-neutral whale-watching experience. Tours start from ISK 10,990 for a classic whale-watching experience, with more expensive options with puffins (ISK 12,990) or horse-riding (ISK 18,900). ⊠ *Hafnarstétt 1, Húsavík* ☎ *464–7272* ⊕ *www.northsailing.is.*

VISITOR INFORMATION

CONTACTS Visit Húsavík. ⊠ *Húsavík* ⊕ *www.visithusavik.is.*

 Sights

Flatey Island

ISLAND | Once home to a small community, Flatey, or Flat Island, is now inhabited only during the summer, mostly by birds and those who love watching them. A sanctuary to at least 30 different species, it has a large population of cute puffins and swooping, scalp-pecking arctic terns. Gentle Giants and North Sailing offer tours to the island, which is 14.7 nautical miles northwest of Húsavík in Skjálfandi Bay. ⊠ *Flatey, Húsavík.*

★ Geosea Geothermal Sea Baths

POOL | This beautiful infinity pool offers sensational Arctic views of the shimmering Skjálfandi Bay and the Flateyjarskagi Peninsula. While you relax in the geothermally heated seawater, you can wave to folks on whale-watching tours sailing by and point with excitement at large whales breaching in the bay. The mineral-rich water is said to help with skin conditions such as psoriasis. Towel, swimsuit, and bathrobe rentals are available. ✉ *Vitaslóð 1, Húsavík* ☎ *464–1210* 🌐 *www.geosea.is* 🎫 *ISK 5,500.*

Húsavík Öl

BREWERY | Inspired by adventures in European taprooms, the owner of Húsavík Öl traveled to Newcastle in the United Kingdom to learn the art of brewing beer before setting up his microbrewery and taproom in Húsavík. Located in the old Gamla Mjólkurstöð cheese factory, Húsavík Öl now produces a range of tasty IPAs, including their signature brew Skjálfandi, named after the glacial river. ✉ *Héðinsbraut 4, Húsavík* ☎ *789–0808* 🌐 *www.facebook.com/husavikol* 🕒 *Closed Sun.–Wed.*

★ Húsavík Whale Museum

OTHER MUSEUM | This excellent museum is entirely dedicated to whales with a number of splendid installations. The center provides detailed information on the whale's habitat along with its biology and ecology. Learn about the species in the North Atlantic in detail, as well as whale stranding and natural history. The facility also includes a full and intact skeleton of a 25-meter-long blue whale. ✉ *Hafnarstétt 1* ☎ *414–2800* 🌐 *www.hvalasafn.is* 🎫 *ISK 2,200.*

★ Húsavíkurkirkja

CHURCH | A unique and unusually large church by Icelandic standards, Húsavíkurkirkja is the town's most iconic landmark attraction and focal point of postcards and images. It was built to accommodate the entire community at the time it was built in 1907 and still serves the public with regular services and ceremonies. Some residents modeled for the large altar painting depicting the resurrection of Lazurus, but not everyone was happy with the result. ✉ *Húsavík Church, Garðarsbraut 11, Húsavík* ☎ *464–1317* 🌐 *www.husavikurkirkja.is.*

Skrúðgarður Park

CITY PARK | **FAMILY** | This leafy, scenic town park is complete with a babbling brook, duck pond, and some exotic tree species such as the Manchurian cherry. It's perfect for an afternoon stroll in any weather but is particularly charming in the summer, which comes with the soundtrack of quacking ducks. ✉ *Garðarsbraut, Húsavík.*

🍴 Restaurants

★ Fosshotel Húsavík Restaurant

$$$$ | **SCANDINAVIAN** | Located inside the Fosshotel Húsavík, this beautifully designed restaurant is a convenient place for guests to dine, although you don't need to be a guest to eat here. While their main menu offers traditional first rate Icelandic fare, they also have pizzas and great burgers. **Known for:** hits-the-spot burgers; great arctic char; creative pizza menu. [$] *Average main: ISK4,500* ✉ *Ketilsbraut 22, Húsavík* ☎ *464–1220* 🌐 *www.islandshotel.is/hotels-in-iceland/fosshotel-husavik.*

Gamli Baukur

$$$ | **SEAFOOD** | This attractive old harborside restaurant made mainly of driftwood serves some of the heartiest meals in town, featuring a blend of burgers and pasta with an emphasis on seafood and traditional Icelandic dishes. It can get lively under the low beams of the nautical-inspired tavern, especially when there's live music playing. **Known for:** role in Eurovision Netflix movie; post-whale-watching lunches; fun atmosphere with live music. [$] *Average main: ISK3,800* ✉ *Hafnarstétt 9, Húsavík* ☎ *464–2442* 🌐 *www.gamlibaukur.is.*

★ Jaja Ding Dong

$$$ | **PIZZA** | The quiet enclave of Húsavík found worldwide fame in 2020 with the release of the Netflix film *Eurovision Song Contest: The Story of Fire Saga,* which told the dramatic tale of two

Húsavík musicians who dream of winning the famous contest. Named after a song from the film, this themed café pays homage to the hit in a delightfully cheesy manner. **Known for:** questionable copyright infringement; outdoor seating worthy of a pop star; pizza that deserves 12 points. $ *Average main: ISK3,250* ✉ *Laugarbrekka, Húsavík* ☎ *463–3399* ⊕ *www.facebook.com/jajahusavik* ⊗ *Closed Mon. and Tues.*

Salka Restaurant
$$$ | **SCANDINAVIAN** | Built in 1883, this appealing old wooden building once housed the town's first co-op and was the heart and soul of the community. It's now home to a lovely restaurant, where its historic presence is augmented by a lively crowd of locals and tourists getting their fill. **Known for:** lightly salted cod; grilled lamb; nice outdoor seating on sunny days. $ *Average main: ISK3,500* ✉ *Garðarsbraut, Húsavík* ☎ *464–2551* ⊕ *www.facebook.com/salkarestaurant.*

Hotels

★ **Fosshotel Húsavík**
$$ | **HOTEL** | Your first impression of this hotel will be one of lofty sophistication, as among the modern, stylish design features in the lobby and lounge are giant felted balls that hang from the ceiling. **Pros:** fun whale theme throughout; good, central location; nice harbor views. **Cons:** not all rooms have harbor views; breakfast is not included; no hot tub. $ *Rooms from: ISK24,392* ✉ *Ketilsbraut 22, Húsavík* ☎ *464–1220* ⊕ *www.islandshotel.is/hotels-in-iceland/fosshotel-husavik* ⊗ *Closed Dec.–Feb.* ⊷ *110 rooms* ❢ *No Meals.*

Húsavík Cape Hotel
$$ | **HOTEL** | This homey hotel features a large library in the dining room and a quirky theme, which journeys between astronauts and the *Eurovision Song Contest*—two of Húsavík's claims to fame. **Pros:** fun Eurovision exhibition;

complimentary coffee and cookies; close to pool and other attractions. **Cons:** some rooms are small; not all rooms have great views; some of the bathrooms need upgrading. $ *Rooms from: ISK25,000* ✉ *Explorers House, Laugarbrekka 26, Húsavík* ☎ *463–3399* ⊕ *www.husavikhotel.com* ⊷ *19 rooms* ❢ *Free Breakfast.*

Mývatn Region

74 km (46) miles east of Akureyri, 56 km south of Húsavík.

Packed with geological marvels and teeming with life, Mývatn is a truly extraordinary destination featuring an unusual combination of remarkable ecology, geothermal activity, and volcanic landscapes. The lake (the area's star attraction) at the center of the region is admired for its bird population, especially during the summer, when it explodes with countless species. Those who know their birds will be able to spot Northern divers, red-necked phalaropes, Slavonian grebes, red-throated divers, merlins, and the occasional gyrfalcon.

Mývatn translates as Midge Lake and comes from the swarms of midges that descend upon the lake during the summer. While the midges don't bite, they are attracted to carbon dioxide and tend to make a beeline for your nose and mouth.

GETTING HERE AND AROUND
Driving is a great way to visit this region, and many travelers head here after spending time in Akureyri. From Akureyri, Route 1 continues through the modern Vaðlaheiðargöng (roughly 5 miles) mountain tunnel which opened in 2018. While the tunnel shortens the travel distance by around 10 miles, the toll is ISK 1,500, which must be paid within three hours of entering the tunnel; otherwise, the price jumps to ISK 2,500. Fees are paid via ⊕ *www.tunnel.is.*

Alternatively, you can save yourself some money and time, and continue along the east side of the Eyjafjörður fjord on Route 83 (which cuts through some of the region's most spectacular scenery). Route 84 over the Víkurskarð pass joins up with Route 1 on the other side of the mountain.

Bus service 56 runs once daily on Mondays, Tuesdays, Fridays, and Sundays from Akureyri to Egilsstaðir, stopping at Reykjahlíð in Mývatn. The journey from Akureyri takes just over an hour, and from Eglisstaðir, two hours.

The main route delivers you to Reykjahlíð, the small village and central hub of Mývatn (on the northeast shore of the lake), where there are several accommodation options and services, including a petrol station, supermarket, and information center. Reykjahlíð is also the start of a well-marked trail connecting some of Mývatn's best sights, such as Grjótagjá, Hverfell, and Dimmuborgir.

TOURS

Several excellent tour companies operate in Mývatn with horseback-riding tours, Superjeep, and sight-seeing trips by plane. Strýtan, the dive center based in Hjalteyri, offers the fabulous Warm Water Adventure day tour to Mývatn, where you get to swim in some of the region's lesser-known geothermal places.

★ Geo Travel
ADVENTURE TOURS | This company specializes in guided Super Jeep tours, snowmobiling, and bespoke trips to the region's main attractions. The company also offsets its carbon footprint by planting thousands of trees in the Geo Travel Forest. ☒ *Geiteyarströnd, Mývatn* ☎ *464–4442* ⊕ *www.geotravel.is.*

Mýflug Air
AIR EXCURSIONS | In business since 1985, Mýflug offers spectacular sightseeing flights of Mývatn, the northern highlands, the Arctic Circle, and more. For one- to two-hour flights, prices range from ISK 23,000 to ISK 74,000. ☒ *Reykjahlíð Airport, Mývatn* ☎ *464–4400* ⊕ *www.myflug.is.*

Mývatn Tours
GUIDED TOURS | This well-established local tour bus company with more than 30 years of experience specializes in 4WD bus tours to Askja in the Highlands (ISK 25,900). They also offer combo tours with Askja and whale watching or the nature baths, as well as various other regional experiences. ☒ *Arnarnes, Mývatn* ☎ *861–1920* ⊕ *www.myvatntours.is.*

Safari Horse Rental
SPECIAL-INTEREST TOURS | In the lovely rural area next to Sel-Hotel Mývatn, Safari Horse Rental offers one- to two-hour tours along Lake Mývatn, around the spectacular pseudocraters, and on old horse roads through lava landscapes. Tours range from ISK 9,000 to 14,000; private tours cost around ISK 5,500 extra. ☒ *Safafri, Alftagerdi 3, Mývatn* ☎ *464–4203* ⊕ *www.safarihorserental. com* ⊗ *Closed Oct.–Jan.*

VISITOR INFORMATION

CONTACTS Mývatn Visitor Centre. ☒ *Skútustaðir* ☎ *464–4460* ⊕ *www.visitmyvatn. is.*

 # Sights

There's such a concentration of impressive sights in Mývatn that you should definitely set aside a couple of days to explore the area. With each season also offering dramatically different visions of nature, you might want to return for the glorious fall palette or the magical winter wonderland edition.

Bjarnarflag
FACTORY | As you drive east from Reykjahlíð toward the Krafla Geothermal Area, you'll encounter a striking turquoise lake, blemished by industrial pipes and bright yellow and red warning signs. As inviting as it may seem, the steaming blue water here is strictly not for bathing. The site

is a small geothermal station providing power for the local region and water for the nearby Jarðböðin Nature Baths. ⊠ *Rte 1, Mývatn* ☎ *515–9000* ⊕ *www. landsvirkjun.com.*

★ Dimmuborgir (*Dark Castles*)

NATURE SIGHT | FAMILY | Southwest of Hverfjall is this mesmerizing lava field known as Dimmuborgir, or "Dark Castles," a labyrinth of tall and twisted formations where you can choose between short and longer signposted routes through the eerie yet enchanting landscape. The best views are available in September when the fiery reds and oranges of the dwarf birch trees contrast brilliantly with the jagged black peaks, crags, and crevices within. It's also fun to visit during the holiday season when the Icelandic Yule Lads take up residence in Dimmuborgir's many hiding spots. ⊕ *www.visitmyvatn.is.*

★ Goðafoss

WATERFALL | North Iceland's landmark waterfall dazzles with its symmetrical torrents, cascading thunderously into an impressive canyon cut through a 7,000-year-old lava field. Conveniently located just off the main road, Goðafoss (Waterfall of the Gods) is renowned not only for its beauty, but also for the Saga Age legend that gave it its name. As the story goes, in 1000 AD, Þorgeir of Ljósavatn decided that Iceland would peacefully adopt Christianity and cast the pagan idols into the falls. ⊠ *Goðafoss, Goðafoss.*

Grjótagjá

CAVE | No amount of ice can cool down this steamy attraction, a fact the producers of *Game of Thrones* discovered when they tried to film an equally steamy scene there with actors Kit Harrington and Rose Leslie. Long before the Grjótagjá cave became a famous film location, its water-filled chasm was a popular place to bathe, until the Krafla Fires of the 1970s and '80s turned up the heat. Although the water still looks tempting,

it's too hot to take a dip, and it may well be years before it cools down enough for a comfortable soak. ⊠ *Grjótagjá Cave, Mývatn.*

★ Höfði

NATURE SIGHT | One of the main stops on the lake circuit, Höfði is an impressive nature spot, where peculiar twisted lava formations rise out of the water like giant gnarled fingers. It's particularly pleasant during the summer, when the scenery is busy with blooming vegetation and colorful waterfowl. Look out for loons, the beautiful birds known to nest in the area. ⊠ *Höfði, Höfði, Mývatn.*

Hverfjall

TRAIL | Proceed along the eastern shore of Lake Mývatn to this 1,300-foot-high ash cone, several hundred feet from the road. Two paths lead to the top. The outer walls of this volcanic crater are steep, but the ascent is easy. The walk around the top of the crater is about 1.8 miles. ☎ *464–4460* ⊕ *www.visitmyvatn.is.*

Hverir

NATURE SIGHT | Next to the Námaskarð Mountain Ridge, on the eastern side of the Ring Road, are the bubbling, gray-mud sulfur springs of Hverir, boiling like a witch's cauldron in the strange red-and-yellow valleys. Hike around this fascinating area, but remember to step carefully. Though the sulfurous vapors smell like rotten eggs, the fumes are generally harmless. ⊠ *Grand Island, NE-2 660, Mývatn* ⊕ *www.visitmyvatn.is.*

Krafla Power Station

FACTORY | Those curious about how geothermal heat is cleverly converted into electricity should not miss the exhibition at the Krafla Power Station, off Route 863. Brought online in 1977, the plant has a power generation capacity of 500 GWh p.a. (gigawatt hours per annum), enough electricity to power 60,000 homes for an entire year. ⊠ *Krafla Power Plant, Mývatn* ☎ *515–9000* ⊕ *www.landsvirkjun.com* ⊗ *Visitor center closed Sept.–May.*

Krafla Volcano

VOLCANO | Not to be confused with the mountain of the same name, this volcano's rise to blazing fame arrived with the dramatic Krafla Fires episode (1975–1984), when huge curtains of lava spewed from a system of fissures inside its huge caldera. The volcano is part of the Greater Krafla Volcanic System, and its caldera, located at the center, has a sizable 10-km (6-mile) wide ring that is difficult to see from the ground. Located within the caldera is the Krafla Geothermal Area, home to the bubbling mud fields of Hverir and the Mývatn Nature Baths. There is also a power station on Route 863 where you can learn about how geothermal energy is cleverly converted into electricity. ⊠ *Krafla, Mývatn.*

Kirkja

NATURE SIGHT | Among the mysterious arches, gates, and caves of Dimmuborgir, the best known is the Kirkja (church), resembling a Gothic chapel (it's marked by a sign, lest you miss it). Don't wander off the paths, as Dimmuborgir is a highly fragile environment. ⊠ *Dimmuborgir, Mývatn* ☎ *354/464–4460* ⊕ *www.visitmyvatn.is.*

★ Lake Mývatn

BODY OF WATER | An aqueous gem amid mountains and lava fields, Lake Mývatn is fed by cold springs in the lake bottom and warm springs in the northeastern corner. The shallow lake—it's 37 square km (14 square miles) yet averages only 8 feet deep—teems with birds and insects, including the swarming midges for which the lake is named. These tiny flies are essential in the bird food chain.

Waterfowl migrate long distances to breed at Mývatn: 115 species of bird have been spotted in the area, including 28 duck species. Indeed, the lake has Europe's greatest variety of nesting ducks, including some—the harlequin duck and Barrow's goldeneye—found nowhere else in Europe. Dozens of other kinds of waders, upland birds, and birds

of prey also nest here. Be sure to stay on established trails and pathways, as nests can be anywhere. During summer you might find a head net useful to protect yourself against the huge midge swarms. ☎ *464–4460* ⊕ *www.visitmyvatn.is.*

Leirhnjúkur

NATURE SIGHT | A surreal mix of still-smoldering lava fields, bubbling solfataras (volcanic craters emitting sulfurous gas), and steam vents can be seen at Leirhnjúkur, which sits on top of a vast magma chamber, with some parts as close as 3 km (1.9 miles) to the surface. From the car park, a circular footpath leads around the area with sensational views over the impressive volcanic landscapes. The terrain outside of the marked trail is hazardous, especially in the high-temperature regions, so don't be tempted to wander off. Good walking boots are essential. ⊠ *Leirhnjúkur, Mývatn.*

★ Lofthellir

CAVE | This masterpiece of nature was discovered by a farmer who was out looking for his sheep. He crawled through a small opening inside a cave to discover an underground realm of peculiar ice sculptures. Tours to Lofthellir are operated directly from Mývatn with Geo Travel (ISK 29,900). Getting to Lofthellir involves a very bouncy 45-minute drive on a rugged track southeast of Hverfjall, followed by a 25-minute walk across a ropey lava field. And, yes, just like the farmer, you will have to crawl through a small opening to get to this frozen treasure. ⊠ *Lofthellir, Mývatn.*

★ Mývatn Nature Baths

HOT SPRING | The north's answer to the Blue Lagoon, the Mývatn Nature Baths contain a unique blend of minerals, silicates, and geothermal micro-organisms. Much paler (and less green) than its southern counterpart, this nature bath has lovely views over the lake that are especially enchanting at sunset. It's a warm and wonderful place to relax, and if it gets too hot you can order an in-bath

Lofthellir Cave and its strange ice formations are over 3,500 years old.

glass of cold beer. ⊠ *Jarðbaðshólar, Mývatn* ☎ *464–4411* ⊕ *www.myvatnnaturebaths.is* ◿ *ISK 5,900.*

★ Sigurgeir's Bird Museum
OTHER MUSEUM | Mývatn, with its feast of midges, is a paradise for birds and well known for its abundance of waterfowl. At Sigurgeir's Bird Museum, located in an impressive turf-topped circular building by the lake, an exhibition of the country's most extensive private collection of taxidermy birds is on display, featuring specimens of nearly every species known to breed in Iceland. ⊠ *Ytri-Neslönd, Mývatn* ☎ *464–4477* ⊕ *www.fuglasafn.is* ◿ *ISK 2,200.*

Skútustaðagígar
NATURE SIGHT | On the south side of Lake Mývatn (easily accessible on foot), there is a cluster of beautifully formed pseudo-craters situated close to Skútustaðir. Not real volcanic craters, they are the result of violent steam explosions created when hot lava flows into a body of water, a rare phenomenon outside of Iceland. ⊠ *Mývatn* ✛ *One of the first things you will see when you enter the Mývatn area; 2-min walk from Hotel Gigur.*

★ Vaglaskógur
FOREST | Providing plenty of leafy respite from the vast treeless expanses of Iceland, the Vaglaskógur forest off Route 836 in Fnjóskadalur is one of the few original birch forests surviving Iceland's "Little Ice Age" and the settlers' needs for building materials and fuel. Trees here cover 300 hectares of land and are unusually tall, ranging from 5 to 10 meters. Listening to "Vor í Vaglaskógi" by rock band Kaleo is a must when visiting this ancient national treasure. ⊠ *Vaglaskógur Forest* ☎ *470–2000* ⊕ *www.skogur.is.*

Vindbelgjarfjall
MOUNTAIN | The marked trail to the cairn-topped summit of Mount Windbag—an appropriately named 529 meter (1,735 feet) peak—takes around 30 minutes to hike and zigzags through thickets of heather and up steep scree slopes. The wind warning is in the title, so dress appropriately and wear decent walking boots, as the scree slopes are slippery.

For the sweeping views of the lake and craters from the top, it's well worth the time and effort. Access is via a gravel parking lot off Route 1. ✉ *Rte. 1, Mývatn.*

Víti Crater

NATURE SIGHT | Its name means "hell" in Icelandic, but this crater lake with its brilliant turquoise pool looks more like heaven. The ancient belief that volcanoes were the gateways to the netherworld of eternal damnation inspired the name of this beauty and, confusingly, another crater lake of the same name in Askja. A path from the car park leads around the rim. ✉ *Mývatn* ✣ *2.3 km from the power plant; about 12.5 km from the main road (Rte. 1).*

🍴 Restaurants

Daddi's Pizza

$$$ | **PIZZA** | If you're exhausted after a long day of driving between all the wonders of the Mývatn region, Daddi has you covered. This small hole-in-the-wall pizza place is a local favorite and offers quick delectable bites. **Known for:** perfect end to a day of sightseeing; New York pizza–style portions; unique smoked trout pizza. [$] *Average main: ISK3,500* ✉ *Vogar, Mývatn* ☎ *773–6060* 🌐 *www.daddispizza.com.*

Gamli Bærinn

$$$ | **BISTRO** | There's a lively, old-fashioned tavern vibe going on at this "Old Farm," where you can enjoy a cold beer and a pub lunch in the comfort of one of their velvet-upholstered, vintage wooden chairs. The menu features a range of popular classics like burgers and fish and chips, with a few local specials thrown in like Icelandic flatbread and meat soup. **Known for:** country bistro-style; Icelandic classics; friendly atmosphere. [$] *Average main: ISK3,980* ✉ *Reykjahlíð, Mývatn* ☎ *464–4270* 🌐 *www.icelandairhotels.com/is/hotelin/myvatn/veitingar/gamli-baerinn* ⏲ *Closed Oct.–July.*

Kaffi Sel

$ | **CAFÉ** | The terrific views of Stakhólstjörn pond and the Skútistðagígur pseudocraters are reason enough to visit this no-frills café, but the homemade fare comes in at a close second. Along with their delightful meat soup and cakes, they also offer a cozy selection of souvenirs and beer brewed onsite. **Known for:** great beer brewed on-site; delicious meat soup; chocolate cake for dessert. [$] *Average main: ISK1,600* ✉ *Skútustaðir 2, Mývatn* ☎ *464–4164* 🌐 *www.myvatn.is* ⏲ *Closed Oct.–May.*

★ **Vogafjós Cowshed Café**

$$$$ | **SCANDINAVIAN** | Those who appreciate dairy will love this place, which serves super-fresh whole milk and cream to go with your coffee and delicious (although ridiculously overpriced) home-baked cakes. The café has big windows with such satisfying views of the lush surroundings that you might be tempted to stay for the free refills (filter coffee only). **Known for:** excellent Vogafjós cake; as fresh as you can get dairy products (you can even see the cows while you dine); farm-to-table dishes. [$] *Average main: ISK4,500* ✉ *Vogafjós, Mývatn* ☎ *464–3800* 🌐 *www.vogafjosfarmresort.is.*

🛏 Hotels

Fosshotel Mývatn

$$$ | **HOTEL** | Inside this colossal property designed by award-winning architects, rooms are a well-measured blend of contemporary, executive, and comfort with warm and soothing natural tones to make you feel both important and relaxed. **Pros:** great views; good restaurant on-site; lovely decor. **Cons:** food is pricey; not centrally located; only south-facing rooms have lake view (and they cost extra). [$] *Rooms from: ISK36,000* ✉ *Grímsstaðir, Mývatn* ☎ *453–0000* 🌐 *www.islandshotel.is/hotels-in-iceland/fosshotel-myvatn* 🔑 *92 rooms* 🍽 *No Meals.*

★ Hótel Laxá

$$$$ | HOTEL | Modern, minimalist, and trying its best to blend into the landscape with turf grass rooftops, Laxá has a focus on sustainability and low-impact design. **Pros:** comfortable beds; good sound insulation; gorgeous design. **Cons:** not centrally located; large price difference between the summer and winter; small bathrooms. $ *Rooms from: ISK41,400* ✉ *Olnbogaás, Mývatn* ☎ *464–1900* ⊕ *www.hotellaxa.is* ⟿ *80 rooms* ❑ *Free Breakfast.*

Icelandair Hotel Mývatn

$$$$ | HOTEL | Formerly Hotel Reynihlíð, the area's leading hotel where the cast and crew of *Game of Thrones* stayed during filming, this spot is still on the fancy end of the spectrum, with Icelandair's signature design of modern Nordic-chic, combined with upcycled vintage wares and local art. **Pros:** central location; great restaurant and bar; Game of Thrones pedigree. **Cons:** rooms can get hot; expensive during high season; rooms are on the small side. $ *Rooms from: ISK52,000* ✉ *Reynihlid, Mývatn* ☎ *444–4000* ⊕ *www.icelandairhotels.com/en/hotels/myvatn* ⟿ *59 rooms* ❑ *No Meals.*

Sel Hótel Mývatn

$$$ | HOTEL | It might not be winning any accolades for design, but Sel Hótel Mývatn is a great base with comfortable rooms perfect for exploring the Mývatn area; it's located right next to the extraordinary Skútustaðagígur pseudocraters, one of the region's main attractions. **Pros:** great location; helpful and friendly staff; large rooms. **Cons:** hot water has strong sulphur smell; can get too hot in the rooms; lots of midges in the summer. $ *Rooms from: ISK35,090* ✉ *Skútustaðir 2, Mývatn* ☎ *464–4164* ⊕ *www.myvatn.is* ⟿ *58 rooms* ❑ *Free Breakfast.*

Vogafjós Farm Resort

$$ | RESORT | The attractive country-style log cabin look here is super cozy, but not the most soundproof; thankfully most of the clientele at this rural resort are nature-loving tourists, who, after a long day of hiking and exploring, tend to be good at sleeping. **Pros:** close to natural attractions; friendly staff; excellent restaurant. **Cons:** no lake views; noise tends to travel; small rooms. $ *Rooms from: ISK29,500* ✉ *Vogafjós, Mývatn* ☎ *464–3800* ⊕ *www.vogafjosfarmresort.is* ⟿ *26 rooms* ❑ *Free Breakfast.*

Vatnajökull National Park–Jökulsárgljúfur

60 km (37 miles) southeast of Húsavík, 76 km (47 miles) northeast of Mývatn.

Established in 2008, UNESCO World Heritage Site Vatnajökull National Park spans a huge area that encompasses nearly 14% of all of Iceland. While several main points of interest (including the famed Vatnajökull glacier) are located in the park's southeast, there are still points of entry and important nature sites to explore in the park's north. The park is composed of four territories, the northernmost of which was previously designated as Jökulsárgljúfur National Park. Pronounced "yur-kul-tsowr-gl-yoo-ver", this tongue-twisting natural wonder translates as Glacial River Canyon, which sums up its essential features.

The deep 120-meter (394-foot) rugged canyon, extends 24 km (15 miles) south of the legendary Ásbyrgi glacial canyon toward the highlands and is divided by an impressive stretch of the mighty Jökulsá á Fjöllum glacial river. It's renowned for its wondrous rock formations (Hljóðaklettar) and thunderous falls, such as Dettifoss, Europe's most powerful waterfall. Jökulsárgljúfur has separate boundaries but is connected to the rest of the park via the Jökulsá á Fjöllum glacial river, fed by the northern tongues of the immense Vatnajökull Glacier.

GETTING HERE AND AROUND

Driving is the best way to visit this part of Vatnajökull National Park, whether by renting your own car or with a tour group. Coming from the north off Route 85, the upland roads between Ásbyrgi and Dettifoss (Routes 862 and 864) run south to Dettifoss.

TOURS

The are several tour operators servicing the beautiful Jökulsárgljúfur with drop-off and pick-up services available, too.

Fjallasyn

BUS TOURS | This company offers shuttle services to and from the Húsavík Airport, Húsavík town center, and other locations including Ásbyrgi, Dettifoss, Akureyri, and Mývatn. Shuttles between different areas in the Vatnajökull National Park as well as around the area can be booked privately as well. ⊠ *Smiðjuteigur 7, Reykjahverfi, Húsavík* ☎ *464–3940* ⊕ *www.fjallasyn.is.*

Nordic Natura

DRIVING TOURS | This company operates shuttles between Húsavík and Ásbyrgi and also offers drop-offs and pick-ups for hikers between Ásbyrgi, Vesturdalur, Hólmatungur, and Dettifoss. Be sure to book in advance (and let them know if you're traveling with a bike). They also have airport shuttles from Ásbyrgi to the Húsavík Airport. ⊠ *Dettifossvegur* ☎ *862–7708* ⊕ *www.nordicnatura.is.*

VISITOR INFORMATION

Located at the mouth of the Jökulsárgljúfur canyon, Ásbyrgi Visitor Centre has a tourist information center, an exhibition on the area, a campsite, and a small souvenir shop.

CONTACTS Gljufrastofa–Ásbyrgi Visitor Centre. ⊠ *Ásbyrgi* ☎ *470–7100* ⊕ *www. vatnajokulsthjodgardur.is.*

Sights

★ Ásbyrgi

CANYON | Legend has it that this extraordinary, horseshoe-shaped landmark is the hoofprint of Odin's giant eight-legged horse, Sleipnir. Alternatively, it could have been created by a massive ancient glacial flood, although no reliable eyewitnesses were around at the time to confirm either story, so we'll never know for sure. From the car park, several trails of varying lengths meander through the well-vegetated areas; the shortest and most popular trail (1 km) leads to the serene, green Botnstjörn Pond. ⊠ *Ásbyrgi, Ásbyrgi* ☎ *575–8400* ⊕ *www.vatnajokulsthjodgardur.is.*

★ Dettifoss

WATERFALL | Europe's most powerful waterfall dispatches an average flow of 193 meters cubed per second with a breathtaking force that makes the earth vibrate beneath your feet. The immense column of white-foaming water thunders over a 45-meter (147 feet) drop creating a magnificent and formidable vision of the sheer force of nature. Expect to see terrific rainbows when the sun is shining. From the parking lot off Route 862, there's a 15-minute trail through otherworldly rocky plains. Dettifoss can also be viewed from the east side of the falls off Route 864 as well but this road can often be hazardous in winter so it's vital to check road conditions before setting out. ⊠ *Dettifoss, Dettifoss (west side), Ásbyrgi* ☎ *575–8400* ⊕ *www.vatnajokulsthjodgardur.is.*

Hafragilsfoss

WATERFALL | If you still have a thirst for photogenic waterfalls, head north from Dettifoss on Route 864 on the eastern side of the river (Jökulsá á Fjöllum) to Hafragilsfoss, the sister waterfall to Dettifoss, which plunges dramatically off an 18-meter (59-foot) drop. ⊠ *Hafragilsfoss.*

★ Hljóðaklettar

NATURE SIGHT | The "Echo Cliffs" is an extraordinary labyrinth of rock formations, located on the west side of Jökulsárgljúfur canyon off Route 862. There are two trails from the parking lot to this remarkable attraction: one is a short (1 km) there-and-back path leading to a magnificent rock named The Troll, and another longer trail (3 km [1.85 miles]) takes a ring around the areas and is more challenging. The name of the attraction comes from the honeycomb textures of the rocks, which act as sound processors amplifying the reverberating sound of the river. ✉ *Hljóðaklettar, Ásbyrgi* ☎ *575–8400* ⊕ *www.vatnajokulsthjodgardur.is.*

★ Hólmatungur

NATURE SIGHT | An extraordinary episode of nature can be found at Hólmatungur where unique rock formations frame a verdant, well-vegetated oasis bustling with cascading waterfalls and clear-water springs. Hólmatungur is accessed via Route 887. Nordic Natura offers drop-offs and pick-ups for those wishing to hike in the area. ✉ *Hólmatungur, Ásbyrgi* ☎ *354/575–8400* ⊕ *www.vatnajokulsthjodgardur.is.*

Rauðhólar

NATURE SIGHT | The trail to this remarkable row of red scoria craters starts from the parking lot just past the Vesturdalur campsite—don't be confused by the popular site in Heiðmörk near Reykjavík with the same name. The footing can be tricky in places, but otherwise it's not too challenging. The rocky path winds enchantingly through remarkable basalt structures with unusual natural patterns. ✉ *Ásbyrgi* ☎ *575–8400* ⊕ *www.vatnajokulsthjodgardur.is.*

Selfoss

WATERFALL | Plenty of people stop to see the famed Dettifoss waterfall, but most sleep on its sister, Selfoss, which is located just slightly upstream and a short hike away from the Dettifoss parking area. A panoramic spot filled with small tumbling cascades of glacial water, it's surrounded by some spectacular basalt cliffs to awaken your inner geologist. ✉ *Ásbyrgi* ☎ *575–8400* ⊕ *www.vatnajokulsthjodgardur.is.*

Raufarhöfn

71 km (44 miles) northeast of Vatnajökull National Park.

Iceland's northernmost mainland town is located on the driftwood-laden shingle shores of the Melrakkaslétta peninsula. The now sparsely populated town was once at the heart of the herring industry, with a prosperous economy and a thriving population. When the fish disappeared, the population diminished to fewer than 300 people, and the town is now most famous for its Arctic Henge. The town has modest accommodation options and services with a swimming pool, campsite, and café. Dotted around the area is a treasure trove of lovely lakes and ponds ideal for fishing and bird-watching.

GETTING HERE AND AROUND

Without public transport or flights, you need a car to reach Raufarhöfn, which is accessed by Route 870 or Route 874.

VISITOR INFORMATION

The local swimming pool by Skólabraut is home to the town's information center.

Sights

The Arctic Henge

PUBLIC ART | Inspired by Stonehenge in England, the Arctic Henge is an impressive work of art, albeit incomplete, located atop a desolate hill in Raufarhöfn. Featuring a 10-meter-tall stone archway at the center and surrounded by four smaller arches, the attraction is designed to behave like a sundial, but one that also frames the sun and other celestial sources of light such as the auroras. The unfinished Arctic Henge is rooted in

Icelandic mythology sourced from the ancient Eddic poem, Völuspá (the prophecy of the seeress), and once complete, it will feature a giant sunlight-scattering crystal and a circular perimeter of stone pillars, each symbolic of one of the 72 dwarfs of Völuspa. The stones are easy to spot once you get to the town of Raufarhöfn. ✣ *Take Rte. 85 northeast out of Húsavík; after you pass Ásbyrgi, take Rte. 874 junction east until just before you reach Kópasker.*

🍴 Restaurants

★ Kaupfélagið Raufarhöfn

$$ | CAFÉ | Glorious in its haphazardness, this welcoming café is also a bar and gallery exhibiting and selling various paintings, handicrafts, knitwear, and a selection of homemade jams and preserves. It's a happy blend of old, upcycled, and new, featuring lots of driftwood and an entire wall dedicated to a quirky collection of teapots, pans, and kitchenware. **Known for:** great souvenirs; quality hamburgers; delightful homemade cakes. [$] *Average main: ISK2,200* ✉ *Aðalbraut 24* ☎ *849–3536* ⏲ *Closed Mon.*

🛏 Hotels

Hotel Northern Lights

$$ | HOTEL | The best accommodation option in the area, this hotel has clean, warm, and comfortable rooms, with a basic no-frills design; the lounge and dining area with a bar and sea-view terrace are a step up from the rooms, which have a dormitory feel to them, as the building was initially constructed to accommodate people working in the fishing industry. **Pros:** extensive views of the fishing village; good on-site restaurant; comfortable beds. **Cons:** two flights of stairs up to the entrance; outside of building is not very attractive; breakfast costs extra. [$] *Rooms from: ISK28,000* ✉ *Aðalbraut 2* ☎ *465–1233* 🌐 *www.hotelnordurljos.is* 🛏 *15 rooms* 🍴 *No Meals.*

Þórshöfn

62 km (39 miles) southeast of Raufarhöfn.

Þórshöfn is a small but lively fishing town, generating an edge-of-the-earth type of fascination. Nestled in the cove of Lónafjörður within the broad Þistilfjörður fjord, it's surrounded by pristine beauty and is a magnet for those who love to explore the road less traveled. Apart from the usual selection of shops and services, Þórshöfn has a domestic airport, modest accommodation options, and is home to the best restaurant in the northeast corner of Iceland, Báran.

An excellent base for bird-watchers, Þórshöfn is also the launch point for excursions to Langanes, a narrow peninsula and bird paradise boasting the largest colony of gannets in northeastern Iceland.

GETTING HERE AND AROUND

You can fly to Þórshöfn with Norlandair, which operates scheduled flights from Akureyri five days a week on Monday, Tuesday, Thursday, Friday, and Sunday. Þórshöfn Airport is located on the Langanes peninsula, approximately 2 miles north of Þórshöfn.

Otherwise, a car is indispensable in this corner of Iceland, as there is no public transportation in these remote areas. Þórshöfn is roughly 180° into the Ring Road, marking the halfway point between the eastern and western routes heading north—it's about three hours away from Akureyri on Highway 85.

VISITOR INFORMATION

CONTACTS Tourist Information Center. ✉ *Langanesvegi 2* ☎ *468–1220* 🌐 *www.langanesbyggd.is.*

Sights

Fræðasetur um forystufé

OTHER MUSEUM | There's an exhibition on a rare breed of remarkable sheep unique to Iceland here at the Leader Sheep Center. This breed can herd other sheep, sense danger, predict the weather, and navigate—they always find their way home. The wool, which is said to be stronger and softer than regular wool, is for sale, as are other woolen souvenirs and products at the shop. ✉ *Svalbarð 1* ☎ *852–8899* 🌐 *www.forystusetur.is* 🕒 *Closed Sept.–May. except by appointment.*

Sauðaneshús

HISTORIC SIGHT | On the way to Langanes, around 7 km (4.3 miles) north of Þórhöfn, make a quick stop at this charming little restored stone vicarage from 1879, which houses a folk museum and café. ✉ *Rte. 869* ☎ *464–1860* 🌐 *www.husmus.is* 🕒 *Closed Mon. and Sept.–May.*

Restaurants

★ **Báran Restaurant**

$$$ | **SCANDINAVIAN** | The fresh flavors of Icelandic seafood and lamb feature in several superb dishes served at Báran, a welcoming bar and restaurant where the prices are affordable and the quality is high. Its harborside location adds atmospheric charm to the welcoming candlelit interior, where old historical annals, some dating back to the 19th century, have been incorporated into the decor. **Known for:** one of the best burgers in Iceland; historic charm; relaxing waterfront terrace. [$] *Average main: ISK3,700* ✉ *Eyrarvegur 3* ☎ *468–1250* 🌐 *www.baranrestaurant.is/en.*

Hotels

★ **Grásteinn Guesthouse**

$$ | **B&B/INN** | For a little rural respite in a remote location with sea views, head to Grásteinn, where you can combine the thrill of the great outdoors with a stylish, boutique design and all the creature comforts you need. **Pros:** great breakfast delivered to the cottage; private beach area; charming garden. **Cons:** farm experience isn't for everyone; not in walking distance of the town; far away from all amenities. [$] *Rooms from: ISK20,700* ✉ *Holt* ☎ *895–0834* 🌐 *www.grasteinnguesthouse.is* 🛏 *9 rooms* 🍴 *Free Breakfast.*

Sandur Guesthouse

$ | **HOTEL** | Conveniently located next to the best restaurant in town (Báran), this cozy harborside guesthouse offers comfortable accommodations in an old renovated townhouse. **Pros:** convenient location; great host with connections to area activities; fantastic connected restaurant. **Cons:** budget rooms have shared bathrooms; old house with squeaky floors; narrow staircase. [$] *Rooms from: ISK18,000* ✉ *Eyrarvegur 8* ☎ *862–9697* 🌐 *www.sandurguesthouse.com* 🛏 *8 rooms* 🍴 *No Meals.*

Activities

Þórshöfn Kayak

KAYAKING | This kayaking company offers guests of the Sandur Guesthouse brief sessions (ISK 5,000) for beginners and families and, for the more experienced kayakers, rentals located in the nearby harbor. Guided trips include a run along striking low cliffs to the lighthouse and tours to places rich in bird life. ✉ *Eyrarvegur 3* ☎ *862–9697* 🌐 *www.sandurguesthouse.com/kayaking* 🎟 *From ISK 5,000.*

THE HIGHLANDS

Updated by
Carolyn Bain

 Sights
★★★☆☆

 Restaurants
★☆☆☆☆

 Hotels
★★☆☆☆

 Shopping
☆☆☆☆☆

 Nightlife
☆☆☆☆☆

WELCOME TO THE HIGHLANDS

TOP REASONS TO GO

★ **Sigöldugljúfur Canyon:** This super-photogenic canyon, lined with waterfalls, is an oasis of luminous color.

★ **The Kerlingarfjöll mountain range:** The heart of the Highlands, geothermal wonder is on full display here, with awesome trails for exploration.

★ **Hveravellir Nature Reserve:** A welcoming place to hike, rest, refuel, and soak in warm waters.

★ **Askja Caldera:** Get ready for an immense show of volcanic power, set in a stunningly desolate landscape.

★ **Holuhraun lava field:** Walk on some of Iceland's spikiest and newest lava, fresh from a 2014 eruption.

This chapter is divided into driving routes, not towns. And for good reason: there are actually no towns in the Highlands. Travelers generally tackle Iceland's interior by following a specific route, and we have these ordered as they are traveled, with their highlights listed as you would encounter them along the way.

1 Kjölur Route. An ancient trail forged by Vikings (Route 35), it's home to the mountains and hot springs of Kerlingarfjöll.

2 Sprengisandur Route. Also known as Route F26, this is the longest of the Highland routes between north and south Iceland. Here you'll see Sigöldugljúfur Valley and Aldeyarfoss Waterfall.

3 Askja Route. Glorious mountains, volcanic crater lakes, and lava landscapes await you on this drive from the north to the Askja caldera (Routes F88 and F910).

4 Kverkfjöll Route. Emerging from the Vatnajökull glacier, routes F905, F910, and F902 take you to the Kverkfjöll ice caves and the hot springs of Hveradalur.

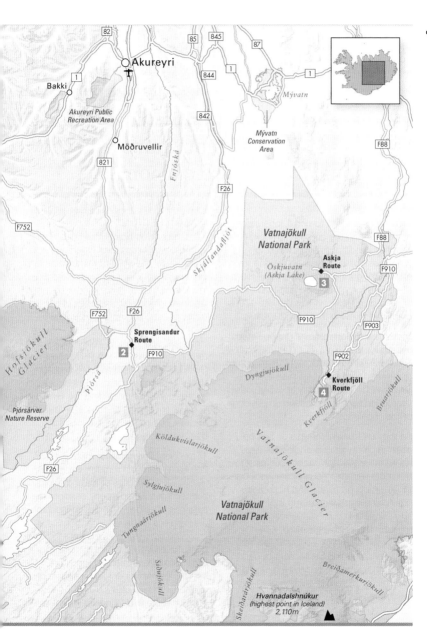

In complete contrast with the more fertile and inviting lowland regions of the country, this desolate heart of Iceland presents a formidable vision of otherworldly terrain, where vast deserts of black lava and pumice-peppered sand are enlivened by shimmering rivers, snowcapped mountains, and the occasional lonely heroic bloom.

Although it's home to park rangers and tourists during the summer, the extreme weather conditions of this howling wilderness have prevented anyone from truly making it their home—that is, with the exception of outlaw Fjalla-Eyvindur and his wife Halla, who in the late 1700s managed to dwell there for 20 years.

Today, the region remains unpopulated, except for the Hveravellir Nature Reserve and Kerlingarfjöll Mountain Resort, which are staffed year-round, as well as the Highland Center Hrauneyjar, which offers year-round accommodations on the edge of the Highlands.

As the last true wilderness of Europe offering plenty of challenging terrains, it's an attractive summer destination for the more determined explorer, especially for experienced hikers and horseback riders (and a growing number of cyclists). The restricted travel season for the four main routes—Sprengisandur, Kjölur, Askja, and Kverkfjöll—falls somewhere between June and September depending on the weather, but even during the summer, explorers should be prepared for sudden extreme conditions, including snowstorms.

MAJOR REGIONS

With misty blue mountains, steaming hot springs, and landscapes where legends were made, the ancient **Kjölur** route (also called Kjalvegur in Icelandic) offers an impressive mix of raw, untamed beauty, fascinating geology, and tales of evil trolls, ghosts, and notorious outlaws—it might even be the resting place of the Holy Grail according to some fables. The region stretches 173 km (107 miles) from Gullfoss in the south to the Blöndulón Valley in the north, featuring a series of impressive sights including the Hveravellir geothermal area and the star attraction of the Kjölur route, the Kerlingarfjöll mountain range.

The ancient **Spengisandur** route extends 240 km (150 miles) through the rugged glacial-cut wilderness of Iceland's uninhabited interior—so utterly desolate that splashes of color within this monochrome masterpiece are few and far between. From the southern end, a detour to Sigöldugljúfur canyon followed by Iceland's largest lake Þórisvatn form an impressive prelude to the unfolding empire of oblivion. Nýidalur offers a welcome splash of color at the midway point, where a well-worn trail leads to the popular Vonar-skarð (Pass of Hope) hiking area.

The route to **Askja,** an impressive volcanic region in the northern Highlands, presents a raw and powerful exhibition of intoxicating scenery, starring Iceland's national mountain, Herðubreið, the enchanting Herðubreiðarlindir Highland oasis, and the razor-sharp, super-black expanse of the Holuhraun lava field, created during the six-month-long Bárðarbunga eruption of 2014. A hike to the Askja caldera, featuring the Öskjuvatn crater lake and the pearly blue geothermal waters of Víti, delivers a sensational chapter of nature at its best.

A rare geological wonder where you can see the dramatic interplay of fire and ice at work, the **Kverkfjöll** mountain range will reward you with an afternoon of lasting impressions and an education in geology. Highlights of the area include the Hvannalindir Highland oasis, the Kverkfjöll ice caves, and the sensational mountain valley Hveradalur, where an expanse of steaming volcanic vents contrasts with the view of a cool, blue glacial lagoon.

Planning

When to Go

Really, the only time to even consider visiting this region is in summer (June to September), when the rough and unpaved Highland roads (known as F-roads, as *fjall* means mountain in Icelandic) are open to travel for four-wheel-drive vehicles.

The mountain roads open at different times according to location, and dates vary yearly. The exact dates depend on the state of snow cover and road conditions after the spring melt. The Icelandic Road and Coastal Administration (IRCA) has detailed information about mountain roads and opening dates on its website (⊕ *www.road.is*).

Some parts of the highlands are accessible in winter on tours in Super jeeps (large, modified four-wheel-drive vehicles) driven by locals experienced in navigating the terrain.

Getting Here and Around

The Highlands remain relatively untouched by man and free of modern infrastructure. In fact, those very same rocky routes and mountain passes forged by the first settlers over 1,000 years ago are still the main thoroughfares today, albeit now mainly recreational. Although you can hike and cycle the old Highland routes or traverse them on horseback, the most comfortable and most convenient form of transport is a high-clearance four-wheel-drive vehicle or bus.

Public Transport (⊕ *www.publictransport. is*) provides comprehensive information on all forms of public transport in Iceland, including the Highlands. In addition to the Public Transport PDF, there are several others you can download with specific information on cycling, camps and huts, and other useful info.

AIR
You can't reach the Highlands via plane, but just flying over the region makes for a gorgeous spectacle. Apart from domestic flights with Icelandair to Akureyri and Egilsstaðir, which fly directly over the highlands and double as sightseeing flights on clear days, there are a couple of tour companies offering helicopter tours and sightseeing flights to the highlands including Mýflug Air (⊕ *www.myflug.is*) and Circleair (⊕ *www.circleair.is*).

BUS
There is extremely limited bus service in the Highlands. There is usually a summer service along the Kjölur route, connecting Reykjavík with Gullfoss, Kerlingarfjöll, and Hveravellir.

Bus and tour companies will usually be happy to customize a private tour for small groups to the region.

CAR

A car is the best way to see this region, but just keep in mind that driving in the Highlands can be more challenging than you expect, and you may need to ford several unbridged rivers. The best option is to go on a tour with an experienced driver. Those determined to drive the Highlands themselves may want to start with Kjölur (Route 35), which is the least demanding route (there are no rivers to ford) but still requires four-wheel drive. Although you could potentially traverse Kjölur with regular two-wheel drive, car rental companies strictly forbid this, and the insurance would not cover any damages. It would also be a very bumpy, uncomfortable journey. All the other highland routes require robust, high-suspension four-wheel-drive vehicles.

⚠ **Those driving in the Highlands should know that sandstorms can strip the paint off a car. Check with your rental car company to make sure you are covered for this sort of damage if you do decide to drive yourself.**

Restaurants

Dining options are few and far between in the Highlands. Apart from the Highland Center Hrauneyjar (close to the southern end of the Sprengisandur route); Hveravellir, the Kerlingarfjöll Mountain Resort; Árbúðir (on the Kjölur route); and Fjalladýrð at Möðrudalur (for the Askja and Kverkfjöll routes), there are no places to eat out or even buy food. Always make sure to bring enough food and water for your journey.

Hotels

Except for the Highland Center Hrauneyjar, Hveravellir, and the Kerlingarfjöll Mountain Resort, accommodation options in the Highlands are mostly limited to mountain huts and cabins with basic facilities and dormitory-style sleeping-bag bunks and mattresses.

RESTAURANT AND HOTEL PRICES
Restaurant prices in the reviews are the average cost of a main course at dinner, or if dinner is not served, at lunch. Hotel prices in the reviews are the lowest cost of a standard double room in high season. Restaurant and hotel reviews have been shortened. For full information, visit Fodors.com.

What it Costs in ISK

	$	$$	$$$	$$$$
RESTAURANTS				
	under ISK 1,500	ISK 1,500–2,999	ISK 3,000–4,000	over ISK 4,000
HOTELS				
	under ISK 20,000	ISK 20,000–29,999	ISK 30,000–45,000	over ISK 45,000

Safety

This region of Iceland is still a true wilderness, so it's strongly recommended to visit with an experienced guide or on a tour group, especially if you don't have much experience navigating the outdoors. If you plan on traveling in the Highlands on your own, visit the Safetravel website (⊕ *www.safetravel.is*) before setting out, and monitor road conditions, weather, and any alerts. Visitors should also leave a detailed travel plan with Safetravel and rent a Personal Location Beacon (PLB), which they can provide.

Tours

Fjalladýrð
ADVENTURE TOURS | Along with great food and accommodation, Fjalladýrð also offers several superb Highland tours in

the summer, including a Super jeep day tour to Kverkfjöll with a glacier hike to Hveradalur valley. The trip takes around 13–14 hours and costs ISK 41,900. ☒ *Möðrudalur, Akureyri* ☎ *894–8181* ⊕ *www.fjalladyrd.is.*

Geo Travel
ADVENTURE TOURS | This company offers day trips by Super jeep to Askja from Mývatn for ISK 49,900. Tours are available from mid-June through September. Bring your own food and water and a good pair of hiking boots. The tour includes a walk on the Holuhraun lava field, which will shred trainers, sneakers, or other unsuitable footwear. ☒ *Geiteyarströnd, Mývatn* ☎ *464–4442* ⊕ *www.geotravel.is.*

Kjölur Route

2½ km (1½ miles) north of Gullfoss to the start of the route in the south, 30 km (19 miles) southeast of Blönduós to the start of the route in the north.

One of the two main routes through Iceland's desolate interior, the legendary Kjölur (pronounced *kyer -ler*, and also referred to as Kjalvegur in Icelandic) is the only Highland road with bridged rivers. Running spectacularly between the Langjökull and Hofsjökull glaciers, and reaching an altitude of 700 meters (2,300 feet) at its highest point, Kjölur is an ancient trail forged by small Viking armies during the Settlement Age. With its incredible vistas and rocky passes, this dramatic route has over the years garnered an eerie reputation as a haunted highway and is plagued with stories of ghosts, trolls, and notorious outlaws. It is also believed to be the location of a secret chamber filled with treasure and possibly the Holy Grail, hidden by the Knights Templar with the help of Snorri Sturluson.

GETTING HERE AND AROUND
Traveling from either end of Kjölur, the 173 km (107 miles) stretch of mountain track is best suited for those with robust four-wheel-drive transport with good clearance and suspension. From the southern end, Kjölur is accessed by continuing on the road past Gullfoss, and exits in Blöndudalur Valley in the north, between the towns of Varmahlíð and Blönduós. The route, which is a six- to eight-hour drive, is open only from mid-June to September. As the most frequently traveled Highland route, Kjölur has scheduled bus services during the summer months.

Operated by Gray Line, the scheduled bus service leaves Reykjavík four times a week, on Sunday, Monday, Wednesday, and Friday. The service stops at Gullfoss, Árbúðir, Kerlingarfjöll, and Hveravellir before turning around and heading back to Reykjavík. It does not connect with northern towns such as Akureyri.

TOURS
A few operators offer tours on the Kjölur route, including Íshestar and Eldhestar, which both organize excellent multiday horseback-riding tours. Mountaineers of Iceland offers snowmobiling tours on Langjökull glacier, with pick-up from Gullfoss car park in a Super jeep for a cool ride across the southern part of the Kjölur route.

VISITOR INFORMATION
The Kjölur route runs through the north and south territories so both Visit North Iceland (⊕ *www.northiceland.is*) and Visit South Iceland (⊕ *www.south.is*) provide visitor information.

Ferðafélag Íslands (⊕ *www.fi.is*) has detailed information on a 41 km (25-mile) self-guided hut-to-hut hike along part of the trail between Hveravellir and Hvítárnes.

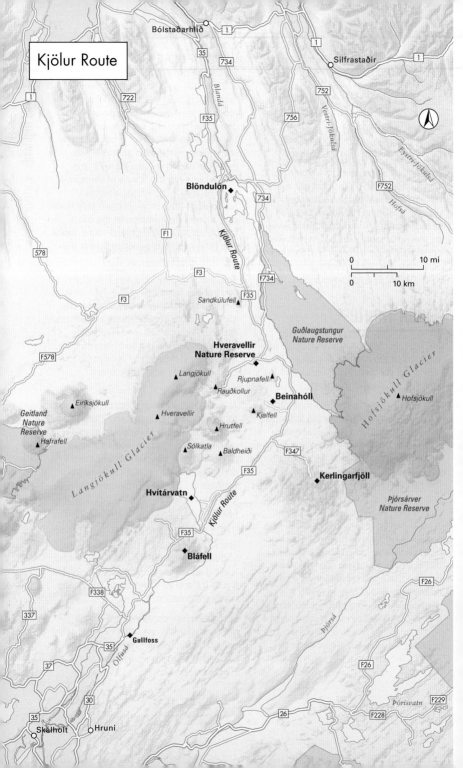

Sights

Sights and points of interest on Kjölur follow the south–north route and appear in the order in which you would encounter them when traveling from the entry road past Gullfoss waterfall in South Iceland to Blöndudalur Valley between Varmahlíð and Blönduós in the North.

Bláfell

MOUNTAIN | As the old Icelandic saying goes, distance makes the mountains blue. Rising on the horizon as you drive north, Bláfell is a magnificent 1,204-meter (3,950-foot) mountain steeped in myth, legend, and tales of hidden treasure. A trail off the main road leads to the Fremastaver mountain hut, which makes an excellent base for those planning to climb the mountain—it's a long but rewarding hike. ⊠ *Bláfell, Kjölur*

Hvítárvatn

BODY OF WATER | A glacier outlet from the Langjökull ice cap occasionally calves into Hvítárvatn (White River Lake), an 84-meter-deep glacial lagoon filled to the brim with milky-blue water. Accessed via a turnoff on Route 35, the whole area—featuring an oasis of vegetation with marshy plains and the haunted old Sæluhúsið cabin—creates a captivating scene. ⊠ *Hvítárvatn.*

★ Kerlingarfjöll

MOUNTAIN | The star attraction of the Kjölur route, the Kerlingarfjöll mountain range features steaming hot springs and a span of beautiful rhyolite mountain slopes topped with several dramatic glacier-speckled peaks, the highest rising to 1,477 meters (4,846 feet). The area is popular with hikers and has great trails of varying lengths and difficulty, with steps and trails climbing the slopes to give access to dramatic, other-worldly panoramas. To reach the mountain cluster, turn off Route 35 onto Route F347 and drive for 10 km (6 miles), where you'll reach the Kerlingarfjöll Mountain Resort. You can hike along a canyon from here

to reach the mountains, or continue on a rough gravel road for 5 km (3 miles) to reach a parking lot in an area known as Hveradalir. ⊠ *Kerlingarfjöll* ⊕ *www.kerlingarfjoll.is.*

Beinahóll

MONUMENT | There are many chilling stories of unfortunate folks who perished in the Highlands; one tale tells of brothers named Bjarni and Einar Halldórsson, who were caught in a snowstorm northeast of Kjalfell mountain and tragically died along with their horses and sheep. Their bones were found years later in a place since dubbed Beinahóll (Bone Hill) and found around 21 km (13 miles) south of Hveravellir, off Route F35. The Wilderness Centre in East Iceland features an exhibition on this legendary event.

★ Hveravellir Nature Reserve

HOT SPRING | This historic oasis at the halfway point of the Kjölur route is also one of Iceland's best-known geothermal areas, featuring the luminous Bláhver hot spring and a silica-encrusted fumarole called Öskuhólshver (Screaming Spring). A highlight of the Kjölur route, Hveravellir has mountain cabins with modern private rooms, sleeping-bag accommodations, and a service center with a restaurant, plus access to a geothermal pool for bathing. Trails in the area lead to some unexpected treasures, such as the Þjófadalir hidden valley. Stay on the boardwalks while exploring the hot springs. ⊠ *Hveravellir* ⊕ *www.hveravellir.is.*

Blöndulón

BODY OF WATER | North of Hveravellir and the Kjalhraun lava field is the expansive, milky-green Blöndulón lagoon—a man-made lake formed when the Blanda river was dammed together with the source of the river Kolkukvísl for the Blanda hydroelectric power plant, which came online in 1991. The lagoon forms the third-largest lake in Iceland. ⊠ *Blöndulón* ⊕ *www.landsvirkjun.com.*

Hotels

Apart from the more modern services at Hveravellir and Kerlingarfjöll Mountain Resort, which both offer private rooms and decent meals, other lodging options in this area of the Highlands are basic mountain huts with dormitory-style sleeping-bag accommodations, shared facilities, and self-catering. The only other site that offers food is Árbúðir, where there is a small café and shop.

Árbúðir

$ | HOTEL | An excellent place to stay by the Svartá river, this mountain hut operated by Gljásteinn has beds for 30 people and stable facilities for those traveling by horse. **Pros:** good showers with hot water; on-site shop and café with food and drinks; great views. **Cons:** basic facilities; shared rooms; can get crowded. $ *Rooms from: ISK7,000* ✉ *Árbúðir* ☎ *895–9500* ⊕ *www.gljasteinn.is* ⤴ *30 beds* ⦿| *No Meals.*

Hveravellir

$$ | HOTEL | A convenient stop on the Kjölur route, Hveravellir sees lots of traffic, not just for its impressive geothermal features and bathing pool, but also for its refreshments and accommodation options, which include camping and mountain cabins: one with sleeping-bag spaces for up to 30 people and a newer building with private rooms, made-up beds, and breakfast. **Pros:** private rooms available; good food; free Wi-Fi. **Cons:** shared bathrooms; basic rooms; area can get windy. $ *Rooms from: ISK29,900* ✉ *Hveravellir* ☎ *452–4200* ⊕ *www.hveravellir.is* ⤴ *6 private rooms, 30 dormitory-style beds* ⦿| *Free Breakfast.*

★ Kerlingarfjöll Mountain Resort

$$$$ | HOTEL | Over the years, this remote mountain complex has featured a campsite and A-frame huts alongside a low-key restaurant in a beautiful setting, but now it's enjoying a complete overhaul under the guiding hand of Blue Lagoon, getting new life as an upscale hotel with lodges, a glamping area, a campsite, and lagoons tapping into the local geothermal waters. **Pros:** hot-spring lagoons; only truly upscale option in the region; proximity to Kerlingarfjöll mountains. **Cons:** pricey; rebuild happening in stages; rough road access. $ *Rooms from: ISK48,000* ✉ *Kerlingarfjöll Mountain Resort* ☎ *664–7878* ⊕ *www.kerlingarfjoll.is* ⤴ *150 rooms* ⦿| *No Meals.*

Sæluhúsið

$ | HOTEL | Not to be confused with the mountain hut of the same name in the north by Jökulsá í Fjöllum, this two-story crofter cottage was built in 1930 and is the oldest lodging operated by Ferðafélag Íslands (Iceland Touring Association); it's listed on their website under "Hvítárnes." The second floor is said to be occupied by the ghost of a woman who prefers to haunt young men. **Pros:** splendid views; reliable running water; kitchen with stove. **Cons:** all shared rooms; no showers; no food available to purchase. $ *Rooms from: ISK6,500* ✉ *Hvítárnes Hut* ☎ *655–0173* ⊕ *www.fi.is* ⤴ *30 dormitory-style beds* ⦿| *No Meals.*

Activities

HORSEBACK RIDING

Íshestar

HORSEBACK RIDING | This company organizes excellent multiday horseback-riding tours along the Kjölur route for experienced riders. ✉ *Sörlaskeið 26, Hafnarfjörður* ☎ *555–7000* ⊕ *www.ishestar.is.*

Sprengisandur Route

69 km (43 miles) northeast of Hella to the start of the route in the south, 34 km (21 miles) east of Akureyri to the start of the route in the north.

Longer and even more foreboding than Kjölur, the ancient Sprengisandur route (Route F26) once drove fear into the hearts of even the bravest Vikings, who

Within Sigöldugljúfur canyon, waterfalls cascade over ravine walls.

would travel great distances on horse-back to avoid using it. Those who did brave the barren wasteland would ride hard, "springing" across the sands on their horses to outrun any foul spirits or menacing phantoms.

Today the route will take you to some of the country's most desolate yet gorgeous areas, including the vast Sigöldugljúfur canyon.

GETTING HERE AND AROUND
Leading from the Þjórsárdalur valley in the south, this route traverses a vast deserted expanse between Hofsjökull and Vatnajökull ice caps, exiting in the north on Route 842, near Goðafoss waterfall. There are also two other exits/approach points: Route F752 in the village of Varmahlíð in Skagafjörður and the particularly scenic F821 in Eyjafjörður. Unlike the Kjölur route, Sprengisandur has many unbridged rivers and can only be crossed using appropriate four-wheel-drive transport with good clearance and suspension. The route is accessible

usually from early July until early September, depending on the weather.

TOURS
Gray Line Iceland
BUS TOURS | There are no scheduled tours or bus routes through Sprengisandur. However, Gray Line Iceland can arrange private tours for large and small groups. ✉ *Grayline Iceland, Klettagarður 4, Reykjavík* ☎ *540–1313* ⊕ *www.grayline.is.*

VISITOR INFORMATION
Although it's not an official visitor information center, the Iceland Touring Association (also known as Ferðafélag Íslands) is one of the best sources of information on traveling in the Highlands. Check road conditions with the Icelandic Road and Coastal Administration before traveling this route by calling 1777 or checking the website.

CONTACTS Ferðafélag Íslands. ✉ *Mörkinni 6, Reykjavík* ☎ *568–2533* ⊕ *www.fi.is.* **The Icelandic Road and Coastal Administration.** ✉ *Suðurhraun 3, Garðabær, Reykjavík* ☎ *522–1000* ⊕ *www.road.is.*

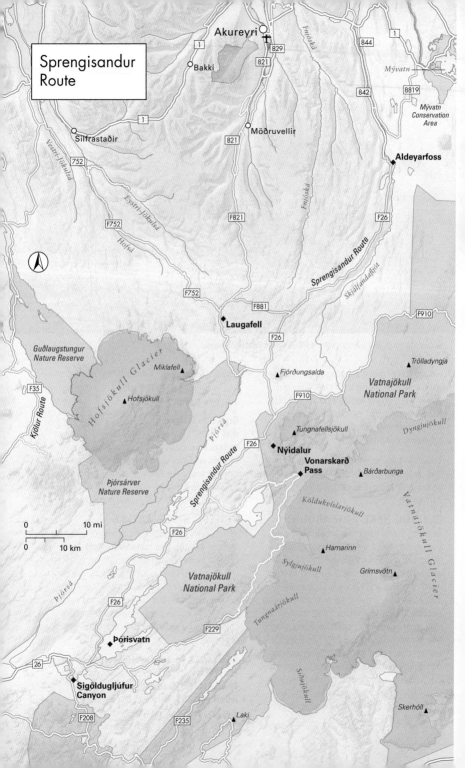

Sights

Sights listed on the Sprengisandur route follow the access road in South Iceland, starting in Þjórsárdalur valley and heading north.

★ Sigöldugljúfur Canyon
CANYON | An awesome flash of beauty and color in an otherwise bleak landscape, Sigöldugljúfur Canyon Features a parade of waterfalls toppling over a stretch of ravine walls, vibrant with green vegetation, into a luminous blue river. Combined, these elements create an enchanting fairy-tale scene worthy of any picture postcard. To get here, turn off Route 26 and take the F208 south to Landmannalaugar. From the junction, it's about 8 kilometers (5 miles) to a small parking area for the canyon, and you walk the rest of the way (approximately 15 to 20 minutes) to view the spectacle. Ask at Hrauneyjar for specific directions; the trail from the parking lot to the canyon is not marked. ✉ *Sigöldugljúfur Canyon.*

Þórisvatn
BODY OF WATER | As the largest lake in Iceland, Þórisvatn has a surface area of around 88 square km (about 33 square miles). Serving as a reservoir, the lake increased in size when water was diverted from the Kaldakvísl river for a hydroelectric plant. The scenic lake lies to the east of Route F26 around 18 kilometers (11 miles) northeast of Hrauneyjar Highland Center. ✉ *Þórisvatn.*

Nýidalur
VISITOR CENTER | In the remote desert between glaciers Hofsjökull and Tungnafellsjökull, Nýidalur is one of the main stops on the Sprengisandur route and an outpost with sleeping-bag accommodation. It's a great base camp for people trekking the Vonarskarð Pass. For bookings, contact Ferðafélag Islands. ✉ *Nýidalur* ☎ *568–2533 Ferðafélag Íslands (for bookings)* 🌐 *www.fi.is.*

★ Vonarskarð Pass
TRAIL | A highlight of the Sprengisandur route, the "Pass of Hope" is a hiking trail between the Tungnafelljökull and Vatnajökull glaciers with stunning panoramic views. Ask at Nýidalur for updates on conditions before setting out on this trail, as meltwater from glaciers can make crossing streams difficult. ✉ *Vonarskarð.*

Laugafell
MOUNTAIN | On the Eyjafjörður exit via F821, 25 km (15 miles) west of the main Sprengisandur route, Laugafell is a mountain oasis with a steaming hot spring on its northwestern slopes. Close by are naturally heated mountain huts with sleeping-bag accommodations and a fantastic geothermal pool to relax in. ✉ *Laugafell.*

★ Aldeyarfoss
WATERFALL | Fed by the icy waters of the glacial river Skjálfandafljót, Aldeyarfoss (near Goðafoss in the north) presents a terrific torrent of white water surging over a strange chasm of twisted basalt columns with enough thunderous force to vibrate the surrounding rock. It's a powerful and impressive grand finale at your journey's end. ✉ *Aldeyarfoss.*

Restaurants

The Highland Center Hrauneyjar
$$$$ | **ICELANDIC** | The restaurant at the Highland Center Hrauneyjar caters to both hotel guests and visitors, offering home-cooked cuisine like leg of lamb and pan-fried salmon. An attached grill offers a variety of cheaper burgers and grilled sandwiches with later opening hours. **Known for:** strekkingur (hamburger with egg, bacon, mushooms, and cheese); skyr dessert with blueberries; stunning Northern Light sightings. [$] *Average main: ISK4,500* ✉ *The Highland Center Hrauneyjar* ☎ *487–7782* 🌐 *www.thehighlandcenter.is.*

Hotels

The Highland Center Hrauneyjar

$$$ | HOTEL | Open year-round and accessible via a paved road, Hrauneyjar offers simple hotel rooms and one of the only restaurants in the region. **Pros:** no light pollution so good northern lights viewing; free Wi-Fi; pretty decent food. **Cons:** small rooms; very pricey for the accommodations; no self-catering facilities. [$] *Rooms from: ISK34,160* ✉ *The Highland Center Hrauneyjar* ☎ *487–7782* 🌐 *www.the-highlandcenter.is* 🛏 *51 rooms* 🍴 *Free Breakfast.*

Nýidalur

$ | HOUSE | Ferðafélag Íslands (also known as the Iceland Touring Association) maintains this campsite and two mountain huts in the Nýidalur Valley. **Pros:** superb views; clean showers and toilets; warden on-site in summer. **Cons:** shared bathrooms; toilets and showers in a different building; can get crowded. [$] *Rooms from: ISK10,200* ✉ *Nýidalur Mountain Hut* ☎ *860–3334* 🌐 *www.fi.is* 🛏 *79 beds, 2 mountain huts* 🍴 *No Meals.*

Activities

HORSEBACK RIDING

Eldhestar

HORSEBACK RIDING | This company runs multiday horseback-riding tours of Sprengisandur starting at Mount Hekla in South Iceland and ending in Eyjafjörður in North Iceland. The tour is for experienced riders and is accompanied by a free-running herd of horses. ✉ *Eldhestar ehf, Vellir, 816 Ölfus* ☎ *480–4800* 🌐 *www.eldhestar.is.*

Askja Route

117 km (73 km) east of Akureyri, 33 km (21 miles) east of Mývatn.

The Askja route is the rock star of the Icelandic interior, threading together a series of impressive sights: including picture-perfect Herðubreið, "Queen of the Icelandic Mountains"; the Herðubreiðarlindir Highland oasis; the dramatic new Holuhraun lava field; and Askja, a spectacular central volcano. Askja is responsible for creating a myriad of marvels including the deepest freshwater lake in Iceland, Öskjuvatn, and the sensational Víti crater lake, which is filled with lagoon-blue geothermal water. The attractions are numerous, but you can pack them into a single day of travel, as either a trip from Akureyri or Mývatn or as a detour from the route between Egilsstaðir and Mývatn.

The area is part of the vast Vatnajökull National Park, and more information can be found on the park's website (🌐 *www.vjp.is*).

GETTING HERE AND AROUND

Although Askja is one of the more popular routes in the Highlands, there is no public bus service in the region. Just like Mordor, one does not simply walk (or drive) to Askja: the best option is to take a tour with an experienced operator.

Roads are open in summer from around mid-June to mid-September, but only for appropriate large, high-suspension four-wheel-drive vehicles. If the main route to Askja (F88) is closed—which it sometimes is—head east to Möðrudalur and take the F905 followed by the F910 to Drekagil. Take the F894 from Drekagil past Svarthöfði (where NASA trained their astronauts) up to the car park and

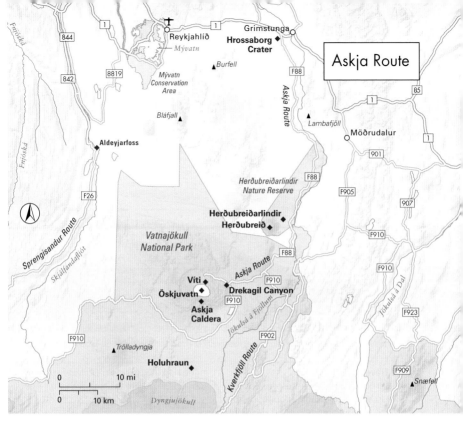

start the 2.4-km (1½-mile) walking trail to Öskjuvatn Lake and Víti. Note that there may still be snow on the trail in June, so bring appropriate footwear.

TOURS
Circle Air
AIR EXCURSIONS | Based in Akureyri, this company runs helicopter tours of Askja for ISK 55,500. ✉ Akureyri Airport ☎ 588–4000 ⊕ www.circleair.is.

Ferðafélag Akureyrar (Touring Club of Akureyri)
GUIDED TOURS | For hiking tours and mountain hut bookings, contact Ferðafélag Akureyrar. Its website outlines details for the five-day Askja Trail hike. ✉ Strandgata 23, Akureyri ☎ 462–2720 ⊕ www.ffa.is.

Fjalladýrð
ADVENTURE TOURS | To take the route to Askja from Möðrudalur in the east, Fjalladýrð offers Super Jeep tours for ISK 39,000. ✉ Möðrudalur ☎ 471–1858 ⊕ www.fjalladyrd.is.

Geo Travel
ADVENTURE TOURS | The guides at Geo Travel lead superb, super-bouncy Super Jeep day tours with the added bonus of visiting the recent Holuhraun lava field for ISK 49,900. ✉ Geiteyarströnd ☎ 464–4442 ⊕ www.geotravel.is.

Mývatn Tours
GUIDED TOURS | This company runs a classic 12-hour trip from Mývatn to Askja in a four-wheel-drive bus for ISK 22,900. ✉ Mývatn ☎ 861–1920 ⊕ www.myvatn-tours.is.

One of the main attractions of the Kjölur route, Hveravellir is also one of Iceland's best-known geothermal areas.

Saga Travel

GUIDED TOURS | Based in Akureyri, Saga Travel is one of the leading tour operators of North Iceland and runs great day tours covering all the highlights. The Super Jeep tour to Askja and Holuhraun is ISK 49,900. ✉ *Torfunefsbryggja, Akureyri* ☎ *558–8888* ⊕ *www.sagatravel.is.*

⊙ Sights

Sights and points of interest listed for the Askja Route follow the access road from North Iceland, starting at the turn-off from the Ring Road (Route 1) onto road F88. They are listed in the order you would encounter them as you travel south to Askja.

Hrossaborg Crater

NATURE SIGHT | This remarkable 10,000-year-old crater, or "tuff ring," was formed by the explosive meeting of red-hot magma and cold groundwater. Its shape, which is reminiscent of an amphitheatre, was put to good use as a shelter for horses before it was used as a location in the hit 2013 sci-fi film *Oblivion* starring Tom Cruise. ✉ *Hrossaborg, Mývatn.*

★ Herðubreiðarlindir

NATURE SIGHT | A little piece of heaven can be found at Herðubreiðalindir, where the spring-fed river Lindaá waters wildflowers and lush vegetation. As one of the main stops on the Askja Trail, the area is home to a campsite and a rangers' station, in addition to the charming little Þorsteinsskáli hut operated by Ferðafélag Akureyrar. There are some lovely short hikes around the oasis and a trail to what is believed to be the remains of a hideout built by famous outlaw Fjalla-Eyvindur. According to legend he sheltered here, in the winter of 1774, surviving on raw horse meat and angelica roots. ✉ *Herðubreiðarlindir, Mývatn* ⊕ *www. vatnajokulsthjodgardur.is.*

★ Herðubreið

MOUNTAIN | If you've seen postcards of Iceland, you might already be familiar with the beautiful symmetrical form of this 1,682-meter (5,518-foot) table mountain. Standing alone in the vast

Ódáðahraun lava field, Herðubreið (meaning "the broad-shouldered") is a national favorite and dubbed "Queen of the Icelandic Mountains."✉ *Herðubreið* ⊕ *www.vatnajokulsthjodgardur.is.*

Drekagil Canyon

CANYON | A highlight of the Dyngjufjöll massif that surrounds the Askja caldera, the "Dragon Gorge" is a gnarly canyon that resembles a dragon from certain angles. When the river running through the canyon is shallow enough, a relatively short hike leads to a lovely waterfall. Drekagil is a basecamp for trails leading to Askja, Öskjuvatn, and Víti, with a mountain hut, a rangers' station, and camping facilities. There's water available, but you'll need to bring food supplies. ✉ *Drekagil* ☎ *462–2720 Ferðafélag Akureyrar (for bookings), 842–4357 ranger station* ⊕ *www.ffa.is.*

★ Askja Caldera

NATURE SIGHT | A large caldera in the center of a volcanic system with many fissures, Askja is one of the most stunning sights in all of Iceland. Although it has a history stretching back 700,000 years, the topography seen today—the pristine blue Öskjuvatn lake and Víti crater—is the result of a massive 1875 volcanic episode that produced more ash than any other in Iceland's history. It blanketed 3,861 square miles, wiping out livestock and forcing many to migrate to North America. The hike to Öskjuvatn lake and Víti crater is around 3 km (2 miles) from the Vikraborgir car park, where you'll also find well-maintained toilet facilities. ✉ *Askja* ⊕ *www.vatnajokulsthjodgardur.is.*

Öskjuvatn

BODY OF WATER | A rare instance of true beauty in the bleak highlands, this lake on the southern part of the Askja caldera formed when a magma chamber collapsed in on itself (a subsidence cauldron) after the devastating volcanic event of 1875. At approximately 220 meters (722 feet) deep, the lake is one of the deepest in Iceland and still growing. ✉ *Öskjuvatn.*

Víti

HOT SPRING | On the other side of a narrow ridge from Öskjuvatn lake, Víti (meaning "hell") was formed during the same 1875 eruption. With its milky-blue warm water, it's both a visual treat and an opportunity to take a dip in a geothermal pool of mineral-rich water. The trail down to the water is steep and can be slippery, so exercise caution. The water temperature is around 30°C (86°F) but is usually warmer in the middle. Beware of gravel and rocks falling from the sides. The hike to the Víti crater is around 3 km (2 miles) from the Vikraborgir car park—the same trail leading to Askja and Öskjuvatn.

★ Holuhraun

NATURE SIGHT | A relatively new addition to the desolate heart of Iceland's northern interior, the Holuhraun lava field is the result of a six-month-long volcanic event that began in August 2014. By the time it was over it had produced Iceland's most significant lava flow in over 200 years, with the 1,600-meter-long fissure spewing out enough lava to completely cover 85 square km (33 square miles). A marked trail leads through a small section of the lava field on the northern edge close to the parking area. The new lava is particularly sharp, so wear hiking boots (not sneakers) and be careful. To reach Holuhraun follow the F910 south of Askja. Stop at the rangers' station at Drekagil first for safety information and more detailed directions. ✉ *Holuhraun.*

 # Hotels

Dreki

$ | **HOTEL** | Ferðafélag Akureyrar, or the Touring Club of Akureyri, operates mountain cabins by the Drekagil canyon on the eastern side of the Dyngjufjöll mountains (accessed by mountain route F88 from the north and F910 from the east). **Pros:** running water; cozy atmosphere; superb views. **Cons:** shared bathrooms; shared bedrooms; no food supplies. $ *Rooms* *from: ISK9,000 ✉ Drekagil ☎ 462–2720 for reservations 🌐 www.ffa.is 🛏 55 dormitory-style beds 🍴 No Meals.*

Þorsteinsskáli

$ | **HOTEL** | Located in the gorgeous Herðubreiðarlindir oasis off the main route (F88), this lovely little cabin operated by the Ferðafélag Akureyrar (Touring Club of Akureyri) is around 60 km (37 miles) south of Hrossaborg. **Pros:** hot running water; epic views; kitchen and dining area. **Cons:** shared rooms; shared bathrooms; no food supplies. [$] *Rooms from: ISK8,000 ☎ 462–2720 for reservations 🌐 www.ffa.is 🛏 25 dormitory-style beds 🍴 No Meals.*

Activities

Askja Trail

HIKING & WALKING | Known as "Öskjuvegurinn" in Icelandic, this five-day trail traverses the Ódáðahraun lava field and leads through a cluster of star attractions famous for their raw, untamed appeal. It might leave you with tired legs, but also with a great sense of accomplishment and lots of lasting impressions. Contact Ferðafélag Akureyrar for information and to book your mountain cabin accommodation. ☎ *462–2720* 🌐 *www.ffa.is.*

Kverkfjöll Route

80 km (50 miles) east of Mývatn.

The impressive northern edge of the Kverfjöll massif emerges from the icy extremities of the Vatnajökull glacier and stands proud between the Dyngjujökull and Brúarjökull glacial tongues; a smaller third tongue, Kverkjökull descends spectacularly right down the middle. Its tallest peak, Skarphéðinstindur, breaks through the icy surface to reach 1,936 meters (6,353 feet), and at the base hot geothermal waters emerge, forming dramatic ice caves. The trails around the area weave together a series of stunning sights that feature river gorges, hot springs, volcanic fissures, ice caves, and sparkling glacier-fed lagoons.

GETTING HERE AND AROUND

Kverkfjöll is accessed via several different highland roads, but the main starting point is in the northeast at Möðrudalur, off Route 1. Follow Route 901 to the F905, F910, F903 for the stop at Hvannalindir, and then onto the F902, which takes you all the way to the Kverkfjöll base camp and the Sigurðarskáli mountain cabin. The route to Kverkfjöll opens around mid-June or later, depending on weather and road conditions.

TOURS

There are few tour operators servicing this route. Your best best is Fjalladýrð, based at Möðrudalur, which offers a 14-hour tour from Möðrudalur to Kverkfjöll for ISK 41,900.

Sights

Sights and points of interest listed for the Kverkfjöll Route follow the road south from the most common access point, Möðrudalur Farm in northeast Iceland. They are listed in the order you would encounter them as you travel south to Kverkfjöll using routes F905, F910, F903, and finally F902.

★ **Möðrudalur**

FARM/RANCH | **FAMILY** | The starting point of the Kverkfjöll route, Möðrudalur (on Route 901) is Iceland's highest farmstead, at 469 meters (1,539 feet). With sweeping views of magnificent Herðubreið, this remote sheep farm dates back to the Saga age. It was an important waypoint for Icelanders for many years—and it still is, providing excellent farm-fresh food and accommodation for weary travelers. At Möðrudalur you will find a petting area where you can get close up to arctic foxes, the quaint Fjallakaffi restaurant and café, camping, a guesthouse, and upscale hotel rooms. They also offer superb day

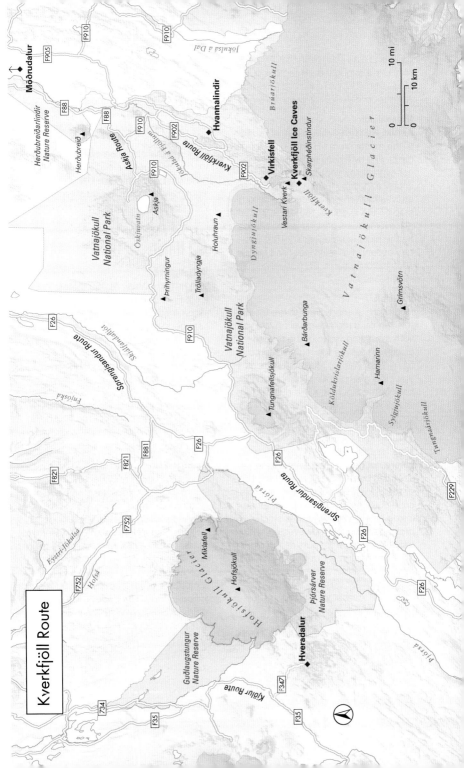

Kverkfjöll Route

tours and activities. Note that Route 901 may close during the winter: check road access on 🌐 www.road.is. ✉ *Möðrudalur, Mývatn* ☎ *894–8181* 🌐 *www.fjalladyrd.is.*

Hvannalindir

NATURE PRESERVE | This splash of green in the monochrome Highlands is a true oasis. Fed by Lindaá river springs and rich with alpine vegetation—especially angelica (*hvönn*), from which the location derives its name—the area is a delightful stop on the Kverkfjöll route (F903). The discovered ruins of what is believed to be the hideout of legendary 18th-century outlaws Fjalla-Eyvindur and Halla adds historic charm. ✉ *Hvannalindir, Hvannalindir.*

Virkisfell

MOUNTAIN | A short climb to the top of this Highland mountain will reward you with sweeping views of the rugged glacier-cut realms the region is famous for. A 2-km (1-mile) marked trail leads up to Virkisfell (1,109 meters) from the back of the Sigurðarskáli mountain hut. ✉ *Virkisfell.*

★ Kverkfjöll Ice Caves

NATURE SIGHT | A combination of opposites results in the Kverkfjöll ice caves, where hot geothermal waters emerge, sculpting dramatic ice caves at the base of the glacier. Because of the unstable conditions inside the caves, venturing inside (at any time of year) is strictly prohibited. You can, however, enjoy the beauty of them from outside. Inquire at Sigurðarskáli hut about free, ranger-led tours of the area. ✉ *Kverkfjöll Ice Caves.*

Hveradalur

MOUNTAIN | From the Sigurðarskáli mountain hut, the 12-km (7½-mile) round-trip hike up to Hveradalur (meaning "valley of the hot springs") takes nine hours. Not an easy hike by any measure—there's an unrelenting 2-km (1-mile) steep climb—it makes a memorable episode for the more determined explorer, with rewarding views of a spectacular glacial lagoon and a mountainside steaming with countless hot springs. ✉ *Hveradalur Kverkfjöll*

🛏 Hotels

★ Fjalladýrð

$$$ | **HOTEL** | **FAMILY** | At 469 meters (1,539 feet), Fjalladýrð is the highest farmstead accommodation in Iceland, and a night here gets you a little closer to the stars and offers even better views of the northern lights in winter. **Pros:** good mix of sleeping options for all budgets; on-site petting farm; great restaurant. **Cons:** some rooms have shared bathrooms; can be busy; no northern lights wake-up call. [$] *Rooms from: ISK36,800* ✉ *Möðrudalur, Mývatn* ☎ *894–8181* 🌐 *www.fjalladyrd.is* 🛏 *22 rooms* 🍴 *No Meals.*

Sigurðarskáli

$ | **HOUSE** | A large mountain cabin, Sigurðarskáli provides basic sleeping-bag accommodations for up to 75 people, as well as toilets, showers, cooking facilities, and a campsite. **Pros:** close to a number of great hiking routes; well-maintained facilities; hot water. **Cons:** shared accommodations; no warden during the winter; toilets are in an outside building. [$] *Rooms from: ISK8,500* ✉ *Sigurðarskáli* ☎ *863–9236* 🌐 *www.ferdaf.is* 🛏 *75 dormitory-style beds* 🍴 *No Meals.*

Chapter 10

EAST ICELAND AND THE EASTFJORDS

10

Updated by
Carolyn Bain

Sights	Restaurants	Hotels	Shopping	Nightlife
★★★★☆	★★☆☆☆	★★☆☆☆	★★☆☆☆	☆☆☆☆☆

WELCOME TO EAST ICELAND AND THE EASTFJORDS

TOP REASONS TO GO

★ **Stuðlagil Canyon:** Discover the beauty of this gorgeous narrow gorge of basalt columns with a glacial river running through it.

★ **Lagarfljót River:** Circumnavigating this legend-filled river-slash-lake makes an ideal day trip, with perfect pit stops that include forest walks and waterfall trails.

★ **Seyðisfjörður:** The east's prettiest fjord town is nestled among mountains and blooming with color and creativity.

★ **Jökulsárlón Glacier Lagoon:** At this ethereally beautiful lagoon that truly puts the 'ice' in Iceland, you can take a boat ride among icebergs.

★ **Svartifoss:** One of Iceland's best known waterfalls is just one of many reasons to stop in the Skaftafell region of mighty Vatnajökull National Park.

1 Vopnafjörður. A picturesque village on the northeast coast settled in the late 1800s.

2 Borgarfjörður Eystri. The former haunt of artist Kjarval with inspiring vistas and plentiful puffins.

3 Jökuldalur. Where you will find many waterfalls and the superb Stuðlagil Canyon.

4 Egilsstaðir. Home to an international airport and Vök Baths.

5 Fljótsdalur Valley. A valley framed by the Highlands with enchanting forests and beautiful lakes.

6 Seyðisfjörður. East Iceland's cultural capital.

7 Mjóifjörður. A remote, near-empty fjord between Seyðisfjörður and Neskaupstaður.

8 Neskaupstaður. A town with a socialist past and unparalleled scenery.

9 Eskifjörður. Home to the world-famous spa mine, Helgustaðanáma.

10 Reyðarfjörður. The longest and widest of the Eastfjords.

11 Fáskrúðsfjörður. Also known as Búðir, a town with a strong tie to France.

12 Stöðvarfjörður. A place to discover rare and beautiful multicolored stones and minerals.

13 Breiðdalsvík. A cozy coastal town with a microbrewery.

14 Djúpivogur. A fishing village that's home to Búlandstindur mountain.

15 Snæfellsöræfi. The Snæfell Wilderness on the eastern side of Vatnajökull National Park.

16 Höfn. A great place to stop along the Ring Road with incredible mountain views.

17 Vatnajökull National Park–Skaftafell. The most visited region of Vatnajökull National Park, a UNESCO World Heritage site.

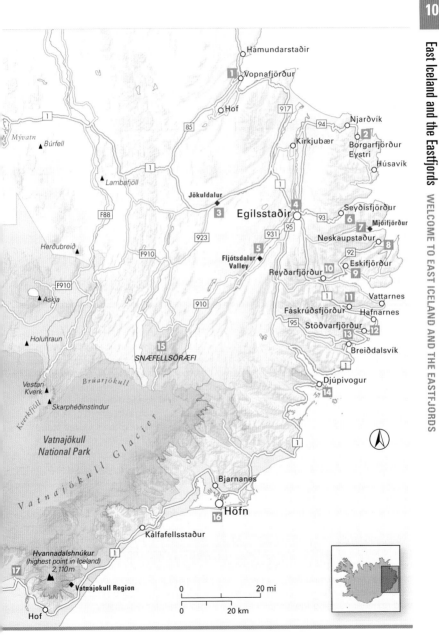

East Iceland, also known as the land of dragons, is one of the least-visited regions of the country. While the thought of fire-breathing mythical monsters might have kept out the visitors during medieval times, it's more likely the distance from the capital that scares people off these days. But with regular short flights to Egilsstaðir from Reykjavík and a growing number of excellent travel services operating in the region, East Iceland is more accessible than you might imagine these days.

Travelers who go the extra distance discover an empire of unique wonders where the land is marked by greater dimensions: mountains are steeper, lakes are longer, fjords are deeper, and with Hallormsstaðaskógur, Iceland's largest forest, located at the region's heart, the East is indisputably greener.

Apart from the superior scenery of the highland wilderness around Snæfell—crowned king of all mountains in Iceland—and the Eastfjords, dotted with charming fishing villages and surprising cultural attractions, the East is blessed with countless waterfalls, salmon-rich rivers, and fertile lands loaded with wild mushrooms and berries. It's also the primary habitat of the highly prized bird of prey, the gyrfalcon, and the only place in Iceland where you can witness herds of wild reindeer roaming the land.

From Vopnafjörður in the north to Djúpivogur in the southeast, roads weave in and out of a spectacular series of long, narrow fjords, divided by sheer mountains, streaked with streams of racing water, and dotted with pretty fishing villages. Visiting every fjord entails a 410-mile trip that often involves steep elevations and dramatic descents. If you don't have time to thread your way through every fjord, inland Route 95 plus 939 from **Egilsstaðir** bypasses 358 miles, taking you directly to **Djúpivogur**.

While driving through the **Eastfjords**, you will likely encounter signage and information boards referring to the **Fjarðabyggð** region, which combines seven villages in the fjords of Mjóifjörður, Norðfjörður, Eskifjörður, Reyðarfjörður, Fáskrúðsfjörður, Stöðvarfjörður, and Breiðdalsvík into a single municipality.

Planning

When to Go

Summer shines in East Iceland, often with temperatures that are warmer than in Reykjavík. Outdoor activities are in full swing under the midnight sun, including hiking, biking, and kayaking. The visiting birds arrive in spring and depart at the end of summer, then fall brings a sense of coziness and a celebration of the harvest. Winter can be a cozy time for seeing the sights, with reindeer appearing at lower altitudes and mountains looking picturesque under fresh snow. There are a couple ski areas that are particularly popular around Easter, when daylight hours increase.

Getting Here and Around

AIR
The region's main airport, Egilsstaðir Airport is located less than a five-minute drive from the Egilsstaðir town center beside Lagarfljót lake. There are daily flights connecting Egilsstaðir with Reykjavík, while smaller airports at Vopnafjörður and Hornafjörður also have connections to Akureyri or Reykjavík. Starting in summer 2023, German airline Condor will be flying once a week from Frankfurt direct to Egilsstaðir. Vopnafjörður Airport serves the northeast region with flights to and from Akureyri Airport five times a week, operated by Norlandair. Hornafjörður Airport services one-hour flights to and from Reykjavík operated by Eagle Air.

CONTACTS Egilsstaðir Airport. ⌧ Miðvangur 2, Egilsstaðir ☎ 424–4000 ⊕ www.isavia.is. **Hornafjörður Airport.** ⌧ Höfn ☎ 478–1250 ⊕ www.isavia.is. **Vopnafjörður Airport.** ⌧ Vopnafjörður ☎ 424–4080 ⊕ www.isavia.is.

BOAT
East Iceland is the only part of the country connected to mainland Europe by ferry. The Smyril Line service sails weekly between Hirtshals in northern Denmark to Seyðisfjörður, via the Faroe Islands.

CONTACTS Smyril Line. ⌧ Yviri við Strond 1, Tórshavn ☎ 470–2803 ⊕ www.smyrilline.is.

BUS
Strætó operates the daily bus service 51 between Mjódd in Reykjavík and Höfn with a change at Vík. The journey time is approximately seven hours. The 56 service between Akureyri and Egilsstaðir operates four times a week and takes 3½ hours. Within East Iceland is a network of local bus routes connecting small towns, primarily to and from the hub town of Egilsstaðir.

CONTACTS Strætó. ⌧ Reykjavík ☎ 540–2700 ⊕ www.straeto.is.

CAR
Having a car is by far the best way to explore this region, with the opportunity to follow lakeshores and winding fjord roads, stopping at various points of interest you encounter. Road conditions are generally good, but it is a priority to keep to the Ring Road (Route 1), which is open and accessible year-round. It's good to be aware that there are gravel roads accessible only in summer (but open to regular cars) as well as F-roads in the highland areas that are only accessible by four-wheel-drive. The best way to check road conditions when you travel is by visiting ⊕ www.road.is.

Restaurants

Restaurants in the east of Iceland use local ingredients: lots of fresh fish, seafood, and lamb, most of it traditional Icelandic, Scandinavian, or New Nordic cuisine. There are continental/Icelandic fusions and plenty of popular international classics such as burgers and pizza, too.

You'll also find dishes featuring reindeer and the East's renowned larch bolete mushrooms.

Hotels

There are three main types of accommodations in Iceland: modern and minimalist hotels; repurposed schools or institutions; and old townhouses with vintage furnishings.

RESTAURANT AND HOTEL PRICES
Restaurant prices in the reviews are the average cost of a main course at dinner, or if dinner is not served, at lunch. Hotel prices in the reviews are the lowest cost of a standard double room in high season. Restaurant and hotel reviews have been shortened. For full information, visit Fodors.com.

What it Costs In ISK			
$	$$	$$$	$$$$
RESTAURANTS			
under ISK 1,500	ISK 1,500–2,999	ISK 3,000–4,000	over ISK 4,000
HOTELS			
under ISK 20,000	ISK 20,000–29,999	ISK 30,000–45,000	over ISK 45,000

Tours

★ Wildboys
ADVENTURE TOURS | Run by experienced guides Skúli Júlíusson and Óskar Ingólfsson, Wildboys leads hiking tours to East Iceland and the Highlands, including to magnificent Stórurð close to Borgarfjörður Eystri; the king of Icelandic mountains Snæfell; and Hafrahvammar Canyon. ☎ 864–7393 ⊕ www.wildboys.is.

Visitor Information

Good information about East Iceland can be found on the region's tourism website (⊕ www.east.is). For Southeast Iceland in particular, check out ⊕ www.south.is and ⊕ www.visitvatnajokull.is. The Vatnajökull National Park website (⊕ www.vjp.is) is also rich in detail about the huge nature reserve.

Vopnafjörður

215 km (134 miles) east of Akureyri, 128 km (80 miles) north of Egilsstaðir.

A series of beautiful waterfalls, coastal cliffs, and black sand beaches are found around Vopnafjörður, a picturesque village on the country's northeast coast, settled in the late 1800s. A trading post with its prosperity rooted in the fishing industry, the town is flanked by lush valleys, divided by two of Iceland's best salmon rivers, Hofsá and Selá. It's also home to *Dreki* (dragon), one of Iceland's legendary four "landvættir" ("land wights," or, protectors) featured on the national coat of arms.

GETTING HERE AND AROUND
There are five weekly flights from Akureyri to Vopnafjörður. There are no public buses that serve Vopnafjörður.

VISITOR INFORMATION
CONTACTS Visit Vopnafjordur. ⊕ www.visitvopnafjordur.com.

Sights

★ Bustarfell
HISTORY MUSEUM | The striking row of crimson-painted gables topped with green turf set this traditional dwelling apart from others in Iceland. It's now a museum offering unique insight into farming practices and domestic life from the beginning of the 18th century through the mid-20th century, and

visitors can marvel at a collection of artifacts, including handmade chess pieces and baby booties knitted with human hair. Homebaked goodies and coffee are available at the on-site café. It's open daily from June to September, and by request at other times. ⊠ *Bustarfell* ✛ *12.4 miles southwest of Vopnafjörður in Hofsárdalur* ☎ *855–4511* ⊕ *www. bustarfell.is* 🎟 *ISK 1,200.*

Gljúfursárfoss

WATERFALL | One of the hidden treasures of Vopnafjörður, Gljúfursárfoss is a striking waterfall off Route 917. A path from the stop at the Gljúfursá river leads to an observation deck where you can witness a single torrent plunging 150 feet (46 meters) down a ravine lined with vibrant moss. ⊠ *Gljúfursárfoss, Vopnafjörður.*

Hellisheiði

SCENIC DRIVE | The mountain road (Route 917) between Vopnafjörður and Egilsstaðir crosses over Hellisheiði plateau leading to ear-popping and vertigo-inducing heights before descending down the other side. From here you can see superb panoramic views of Héraðsflói Bay and the black sands of Héraðssandur. Route 917 is usually closed during the winter; you can check its status before setting off on the website ⊕ *www.road.is.*

★ Selárdalslaug

POOL | Located on the banks of the shimmering, salmon-rich Selá river, 12 km (7½ miles) north of Vopnafjörður, the Selárdalslaug swimming pool has a geothermally heated lap pool and hot tub. ☎ *473–1499* 🎟 *ISK 970.*

Skjólfjörur

BEACH | A popular destination for locals and families, Skjólfjörur beach is a short walk from Route 917. Look out for the Ljósastapi rock pillar, lovingly dubbed the Elephant (*Fíllinn*) by locals. **Best for:** sunset; walking. **Amenities:** none. ⊠ *Skjólfjörur.*

Activities

Strengur Angling Club

FISHING | Vopnafjörður is home to the bountiful Hofsá (King Charles III's favorite) and Selá rivers, two of Iceland's most exclusive salmon rivers, which are both managed by the Strengur Angling Club. They also arrange fishing on the Sunnudalsá river, a tributary of Hofsá. ⊠ *Reykjavík* ⊕ *www.strengurangling.is.*

Borgarfjörður Eystri

133 km (83 miles) southeast of Vopnafjörður, 70 km (43 miles) northeast of Egilsstaðir

Borgarfjörður Eystri is a realm of rugged elements, with hiking trails leading to marvels of nature such as Stórurð and Hvítserkur. The main settlement, known as Bakkagerði, is home to around 100 people. It's not surprising that Iceland's most famous artist, Kjarval, hails from this visually stunning place. As added appeal, it's also one of the best places in Iceland to see puffins.

For the best hiking routes pick up a copy of the widely available area hiking map, called *Borgarfjörður Eystri & Víknaslóðir Hiking Map—Trails of the Deserted Inlets.*

GETTING HERE AND AROUND

The best way to get here is by car; you can take Route 94 north from Egilsstaðir. The local bus company Straeto also operates a weekday bus service between Borgarfjörður and Egilsstaðir.

Sights

Álfaborg

NATURE SIGHT | According to Icelandic folklore, the Elf Queen herself is said to reside on the rocky hill Álfaborg (Kingdom of the Elves), located south of the campsite next to the village. ⊠ *Álfaborg, Borgarfjörður Eystri.*

Lindarbakki is an oft-photographed house in Borgarfjörður Eystri.

Dyrfjöll

MOUNTAIN | While en route to Borgar-fjörður Eystri look out for the magnificent mountain range Dyrfjöll, featuring a remarkable gap in the middle; the name translates to "Door Mountain," with the gap being viewed as a door. Reaching heights of up to 3,727 feet, it's an ambitious setting even for experienced hikers, but the views from the top are extraordinary.

★ Hafnarhólmi

NATURE SIGHT | A superb spot for bird-watching, at Hafnarhólmi, you can climb a the staircase leading up to a viewing platform to see puffins up close without risking life and limb on the cliffs. You'll also see other seabirds such as kittiwakes and fulmars. About 10,000 pairs of puffins nest here from mid-April through mid-August, then spend the winter at sea. ⊠ *Hafnarhólmi, Rte 947.*

Hvítserkur

MOUNTAIN | Not to be confused with the sea stack of the same name on the Vatnsnes Peninsula in northwest Iceland, the Hvítserkur of the east is a distinctive mountain. Dark streaks (basaltic dykes) run across its bright surface, making it look like a work of art. ⊠ *Hvítserkur* ✛ *9 miles south of Borgarfjörður Eystri on Rte 946.*

Lindarbakki

HISTORIC HOME | This eye-catching private residence has red gables and a matching chimney poking out of its well-groomed turf top. ⊠ *Lindarbakki, Borgarfjörður Eystri.*

★ Stórurð

NATURE SIGHT | Set aside five to seven hours for the round-trip hike to Stórurð, where giant moss-topped boulders form islands within pools of vibrant green water. To reach Stórurð, which translates to "giant boulders," take the trail from the Vatnsskarð pass: it takes around 2½ hours. A round-trip is approximately 9 miles with an elevation of between 1,640 to 1,968 feet. For guided tours with transport from Egilsstaðir, contact the tour company Wildboys. ⊠ *Stórurð.*

Hotels

★ Blábjörg

$ | **HOTEL** | This guesthouse is an old renovated fish factory with rooms that share bathrooms; all are furnished in a minimalist style and the rooms with sea views are most recommended. **Pros:** hot tubs overlooking the sea; on-site spa; shared kitchen and good on-site restaurant. **Cons:** remote location; doubles have twin beds pushed together; shared bathrooms. [$] *Rooms from: ISK19,040* ✉ *Blábjörg* ☎ *472–1180* 🌐 *www.blabjorg.is* 🛏 *11 rooms, 4 apartments* 🍴 *Free Breakfast.*

Egilsstaðir

74 km (46 miles) southwest of Borgarfjörður Eystri.

Considered the capital of East Iceland, Egilsstaðir is the region's main hub for trade, transport, and travel, with a concentration of shops and services and a growing number of attractions, such as Vök Baths. It also has a busy airport that can accommodate international flights. While it might not be the cultural hotspot of the east—that title belongs to Seyðisfjörður—the town, which is located right next to the legendary Lagarflót lake and surrounded by pretty woodlands, isn't without its charms.

GETTING HERE AND AROUND

Flights from Reykjavík to Egilsstaðir are operated daily by Icelandair. The town is also a major stop on local bus routes operated by Strætó. There's a bus from Akureyri four times a week, but no direct services from Reykjavík.

Sights

Baðhúsið Spa

OTHER ATTRACTION | You don't have to be a guest at the Lake Hotel to enjoy the lovely Baðhúsið Spa. Located on the ground floor with a view of the lake, Baðhúsið has an indoor hot tub, sauna, and cold pool, plus relaxation areas indoors and outside. ✉ *Baðhúsið, Egilsstöðum 1-2* ☎ *471–1114* 🌐 *www.lakehotel.is* 🎟 *ISK 4,000.*

Fardagafoss

WATERFALL | A pretty waterfall with a history that includes tales of hidden gold, trolls, and secret tunnels, Fardagafoss is a tempting detour for travelers on Route 93 to Seyðisfjörður. Located approximately 5 km (3 miles) from Egilsstaðir, just off the main road, the hike up to the falls takes around 30 minutes. Though it's relatively easy, it can get steep in places. From the top you can enjoy extensive views over Egilsstaðir, Lagarfljót, and the snow-capped Snæfell peak. ✉ *Egilsstaðir.*

Minjasafn Austurlands

HISTORY MUSEUM | Two permanent exhibitions detail the history of reindeer and rural life in East Iceland at Minjasafn Austurlands, the East Iceland Heritage Museum. They also have several rotating exhibitions throughout the year. ✉ *Minjasafn Austurlands, Laufskógar 1* ☎ *471–1412* 🌐 *www.minjasafn.is* 🎟 *ISK 1,200* 🕒 *Closed Sat.–Mon. in Sept.–May.*

★ Vök Baths

HOT SPRING | At Vök Baths, cool design meets warm natural inspiration. Designed by the award-winning Basalt Architects, this sublime soaking spot has two infinity pools that float atop Urriðavatn lake, drawing on the pure, warm water flowing from the ground. On the lakeshore, you'll find more warm pools, a steam bath and sauna, and a bistro that showcases local ingredients. ✉ *Vök, Vök við Urriðavatn* ☎ *470–9500* 🌐 *www.vokbaths.is* 🎟 *From ISK 5,990.*

Restaurants

Askur Pizzeria

$$ | **PIZZA** | A simple, stylish space, Askur Pizzeria pumps out a menu of 12-inch pizzas with toppings that range from

standard (ham and pineapple) to unexpected (wild goose and red-onion jam). It's attached to Askur Taproom, which serves craft beers from the Austri label (brewed on-site) in a relaxed, fun setting. **Known for:** attached brewery with craft beers; spicy BOBA pizza topping; vegan options. $ *Average main: ISK2,700* ✉ *Fagradalsbraut 25* ☎ *470–6070* 🌐 *askurpizzeria.is.*

Bókakaffi Hlöðum

$$ | **CAFÉ** | This spot has been in business since 1973, first as a bookstore and now as a homey café. Friday and Saturday afternoons feature a fantastic cake buffet, with some old-school Icelandic specialties. **Known for:** weekend cake buffet; lamb chop in breadcrumbs; savory pancakes. $ *Average main: ISK2,500* ✉ *Bókakaffi Hlöðum, Helgafelli 2* ✣ *Across the river from Egilsstaðir in Fellabær* ☎ *471–2255* 🌐 *www.bokakaffi.is* 🕓 *Closed Sun.*

★ **Eldhúsið**

$$$$ | **ICELANDIC** | White tablecloths, vintage-style crockery, and antiques add to the neoclassic tone of Eldhúsið restaurant, where you can enjoy beautifully plated meals made from local ingredients. You can't go wrong with the fish of the day, beef reared on the surrounding farm, or the homemade ice creams and sorbets. **Known for:** lunchtime beef burger; beef tenderloin and beef cheek; beef rib eye and béarnaise. $ *Average main: ISK5,590* ✉ *Eldhúsið, Egilsstöðum 1-2* ☎ *471–1114* 🌐 *www.lakehotel.is.*

★ **Nielsen**

$$$ | **ICELANDIC** | Helmed by the former head chef at Reykjavík restaurant Dill, Nielsen is the first Icelandic eatery to be awarded a Michelin star. The chef does wondrous things with the fine produce, all grown, caught, farmed, and foraged in the restaurant's radius. **Known for:** reindeer tartare; pan-fried cod; creative vegetarian dishes. $ *Average main: ISK3,000* ✉ *Tjarnabraut 1* ☎ *471–2001* 🌐 *www.nielsenrestaurant.is* 🕓 *Closed Sun. and Mon. No lunch Sat.*

🛏 Hotels

★ **Gistihúsið–Lake Hotel Egilsstaðir**

$$$ | **HOTEL** | This historic lakeside farm saw the town grow up around it and began offering guesthouse services in 1884. **Pros:** open all year; excellent restaurant; lakeside views. **Cons:** extra charge for the spa (ISK 2,000); hot water smells of sulphur; on the expensive side. $ *Rooms from: ISK33,840* ✉ *Gistihúsið–Lake Hotel Egilsstaðir* ☎ *471–1114* 🌐 *www.lakehotel.is* 🕓 *Closed mid-Dec.–early Jan.* 🛏 *50 rooms* 🍴 *Free Breakfast.*

Hótel Eyvindara

$$ | **HOTEL** | Located in a lovely wooded area about 2 miles from the town center, Hótel Eyvindara has annex rooms with private bathrooms and terraces, in addition to rooms within the main building. **Pros:** outdoor hot tubs; charming woodland location; views of northern lights during winter. **Cons:** compact fluorescent lighting; away from the town center; breakfast costs extra. $ *Rooms from: ISK27,500* ✉ *Hótel Eyvindara, Eyvindará II* ☎ *471–1200* 🌐 *www.eyvindara.is* 🛏 *34 rooms* 🍴 *No Meals.*

Icelandair Hótel Hérað

$$$ | **HOTEL** | This modern, Nordic-chic hotel has large portrait windows in the lounge that frame the cliffs outside, and a sculpture by Icelandic artist Aðalheiður S. Eysteinsdóttir in the lobby. **Pros:** central location; good breakfast; delicious on-site restaurant. **Cons:** not all rooms have good views; lots of large tour groups; expensive breakfast (ISK 3,400) not included in room price. $ *Rooms from: ISK44,000* ✉ *Miðvangur 1-7* ☎ *471–1500* 🌐 *www.icelandairhotels.com* 🛏 *60 rooms* 🍴 *No Meals.*

Shopping

★ Fjóshornið

FOOD | At Fjóshornið, you can buy fresh, local dairy products like skyr, cheese, and yogurt straight from the farmer. The shop also has a cozy café where you can treat yourself to waffles, cakes, and bagels. ⊠ *Fjóshornið, Egilsstaðir 1 Eiðar* ☎ *471–1508* ⊕ *www.facebook.com/ fjoshorn.*

★ Hús Handanna

CRAFTS | This local art and design shop can be found in a central spot in town. Stop by to browse the souvenir-worthy handicrafts from local artists and designers. ⊠ *Hús Handanna, Miðvangur 1-3* ☎ *471–2433* ⊕ *www.hushandanna.is.*

Jökuldalur

54 km (33 miles) west of Egilsstaðir.

Translated as "Glacier Valley," Jökuldalur is divided by the mighty Jökla (Jökulsá á Dal) river, and lies northwest of the Fljótsdalur Valley. It's known for its abundance of waterfalls and the remarkable Stuðlagil Canyon, which was under the radar until relatively recently and now understandably features on many travelers' itineraries.

GETTING HERE AND AROUND

Driving is the easiest way to get here. You can take Route 923, 33 miles northwest of Egilsstaðir off Route 1.

◉ Sights

Sænautasel

FARM/RANCH | In July and August, Sænautasel—a restored lakeside turf farm with pleasant green surroundings dating back to 1843—serves excellent coffee, homebaked *lummur* (oatmeal pancakes), and a welcoming splash of color in the otherwise desolate landscapes of the area. Apart from the evacuation period caused by the eruption of Askja in 1885,

it was inhabited until 1943. Sænautasel is said to be the inspiration for the main character's home in the novel *Independent People*, written by Nobel Prize–winning Icelandic writer Halldór Laxness. ⊠ *Sænautasel* ⊕ *www.facebook.com/pg/ Saenautasel* ☉ *Closed Oct.–May.*

★ Stuðlagil Canyon

CANYON | Once a hidden gem of the east, this is an incredible narrow canyon whose main feature is basalt rock columns. The Jökla river runs through the gorge, with its water colored bright blue-green in the right conditions, making for a truly memorable sight.

A newly built observation platform offers the most accessible views of the canyon. The platform is accessed about 19 km (12 miles) from the Ring Road on Route 923, on the farm known as Grund. You will find parking spaces, toilets, and stairs to the platform. There is an excellent view down into the gorge and over the basalt columns, but you cannot get down into the canyon from this side. To hike to the canyon's east side, drive south of the Ring Road on Route 923 about 14 km (9 miles) to the farm known as Klaustursel. From the second parking area, not far from Stuðlafoss waterfall, it's a 2½ km (1½ mile) hike to reach the access point for entering the canyon. It's not too challenging a hike: there is a clear tractor trail to follow and the ground is uneven but not very steep (but it may be muddy). When you reach the area to go into the gorge, it gets rocky and uneven, so go slow and keep in mind that the rocks can be wet and slippery. This is a very popular spot for visitors, so you'll likely be sharing the space with others. You can explore the columns at the water's edge before retracing your steps to the car park.

Note that there are two parking lots at Klaustursel. The first is by a bridge and walking from there to the canyon is about 5 km (3 miles) one way. The second car park is 2½ km further along a rough road that isn't kind to small 2WD

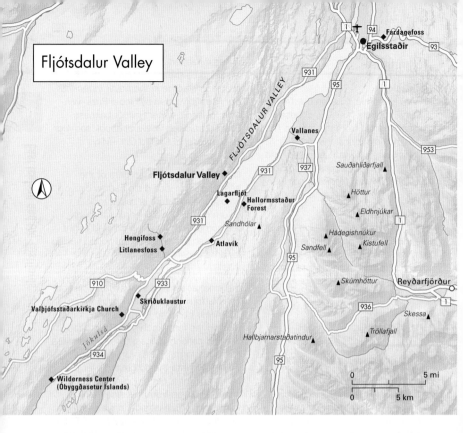

Fljótsdalur Valley

vehicles (so 4WD is advised to reach it).
✠ *Turn south off Rte. 1 onto Rte. 923*
⊕ *www.studlagil.is.*

Rjúkandi

WATERFALL | A roadside waterfall off Route
1, Rjúkandi is a great place to stop and
stretch your legs. A short trail from the
parking lot leads to the delightful falls
with views of the Jökuldalur Valley. ✠ *50
km (30 miles) northwest of Egilsstaðir on
the Ring Road (Rte. 1).*

Fljótsdalur Valley

*56 km (353 miles) southwest of
Egilsstaðir.*

Those eager to see the Eastfjords often
bypass this stunning location and miss
out on some of the region's most impressive scenery. The valley, in which you

could easily spend a week, is loaded with
places of beauty and splendor. Here the
enchanting Hallormsstaðaskógur forest
borders the legendary Lagarfljót lake.
Framed in the south by the Highlands
where reindeer wander, and crowned
farther in the distance by the glorious
snow-encrusted peak of Snæfell, the
area is a true masterpiece of nature with
several cultural and culinary destinations,
too.

GETTING HERE AND AROUND

From Egilsstaðir, your best option is to
drive south on Route 95 and then take
Route 931, which circumnavigates
Lagarfljót lake. The entire circular route
around Fljótsdalur, including a visit to the
Wilderness Center at the far end of the
valley (accessed on Route 934), is 114
km (71 miles).

Sights

Atlavík

NATURE SIGHT | A wooded cove on the shores of Lagarfljót, Atlavík is a popular picnic spot and summer destination, especially for young weekend revelers and those on the lookout for the legendary lake monster (the famous "Lagarfljót-sormurinn," Iceland's version of the Loch Ness Monster). There's a camping area on-site and pedal boats for hire during the summer months. ⊠ *Atlavík* ⊘ *Closed during winter.*

★ Hallormsstaður Forest

FOREST | Iceland's first national forest was established in 1905 and now provides 740 hectares of leafy respite along the eastern banks of Lagarfljót. Home to 85 tree species, 40 km (25 miles) of marked trail paths, an arboretum, hotel, campsites, and children's play areas, Hallormsstaður is a delightful destination where you can even forage for wild berries and edible mushrooms, including the tasty larch bolete. ⊠ *Hallormsstaður Forest.*

★ Hengifoss

WATERFALL | This waterfall plunges 128 meters (420 feet) over a sheer drop into a glorious gorge with an unusual striped appearance, thanks to its red clay and black basalt. The 2½ km (1½ miles) path from the car park (off Route 931) leads to the falls and takes around 40 to 60 minutes, with some relatively steep sections. The superb Litlanesfoss waterfall can be found halfway up the trail. ⊠ *Hengifoss.*

★ Lagarfljót

BODY OF WATER | The legendary Lagarfljót river-lake is famous for its elusive Loch Ness–like resident "Lagarfljótsormurinn," part of local lore since the annals of 1345. The 140 km (87-mile) stretch of water, known as Lögurinn lake at its widest point, is fed by the glacial waters of Jökulsá í Fljótsdal river originating in Vatnajökull glacier; the glacier's sediment gives the water its milky appearance. With a bridge across the water on Route 931, it's possible to drive around the lake 70 km (44 miles), stopping at several impressive natural sites such as Hallormsstaður forest and Hengifoss waterfall, and cultural hot spots like Skriðuklaustur and the Wilderness Center, which is a few additional miles down the valley. ⊠ *Lagarfljót.*

Litlanesfoss

WATERFALL | Located on the trail to Hengifoss waterfall, the Litlanesfoss waterfall plunges 100 feet (30 meters) over a wall of symmetrical basalt columns. It's a perfect prelude to the area's star attraction, Hengifoss. ⊠ *Litlanesfoss.*

★ Skriðuklaustur

HISTORIC HOME | This striking two-story mansion with its distinctive basalt stone walls and turf top was the former home of beloved Icelandic author Gunnar Gunnarsson. Designed by German architect Fritz Höger, the house was an ambitious and expensive project taking 64 construction workers 33,000 working hours to complete. When Gunnar moved to Reykjavík in 1948, he donated the building to the nation "to be forever owned by the Icelandic people." It is now run as an educational museum featuring exhibitions on the 16th-century ruins of the old monastery found on the property, as well as the life and works of Gunnar Gunnarson, along with rotating art exhibitions. Home to the fabulous Klausturkaffi restaurant, it's also the best lunch option you will find for miles around. ⊠ *Skriðuklaustur* ✛ *3 miles south of Hengifoss off Rte 933* ☏ *471–2990* ⊕ *www.skriduklaustur.is* ⊘ *Irregular opening hours Nov.–Mar.*

★ Vallanes

FARM/RANCH | This farm is home to Iceland's premium organic brand "Móðir Jörð" (Mother Earth), which specializes in growing barley, fresh vegetables, and herbs. They also produce a range of preserves, chutneys, and fermented vegetables. On-site there's a shop and a stylishly rustic café, generally open from May to September. They also offer accommodations in a private apartment or cottage. ✉ *Vallanes* ☏ *471–1747* ⊕ *www.vallanes.is.*

Valþjófsstaðarkirkja Church

CHURCH | The 12th-century Valþjófsstaður door, a rare, beautifully carved Icelandic treasure that's now on display at the National Museum in Reykjavík, originates from Valþjófsstaður at the southern end of Fljótsdalur Valley, off Route 933. The door, which depicts a knight on horse-back slaying a dragon to free an enslaved lion and an inscription of medieval runes, was installed in a stave church that stood for centuries at Valþjófsstaður before a new church was built there in 1966. The modern church features a perfect replica of the medieval artwork installed as an interior door. ✉ *Valþjófsstaðarkirkja.*

★ Wilderness Center (Óbyggðasetur Íslands)

OTHER ATTRACTION | FAMILY | A year-round haven on the edge of the eastern Highlands, complete with a hot spring spa and a restored barn dedicated to night-sky viewing, the Wilderness Center is a destination for the more determined explorer looking for an old-fashioned, authentic Icelandic experience. Servic-es include unique accommodation and bespoke horseback riding and hiking tours, plus mountain bike rentals. The main draw of the center, however, is the award-winning exhibition on forces of nature and Iceland's fascinating folklore. ✉ *Wilderness Center, Norðurdalur í Fljótsdal* ☏ *440–8822* ⊕ *wilderness.is* 🎫 *Exhibition ISK 2,800.*

 Restaurants

★ Klausturkaffi

$$$ | ICELANDIC | While enjoying the exhibi-tions at Skriðuklaustur, you might get dis-tracted by the delightful aromas wafting

from the inviting in-house restaurant. If you follow your nose, you'll discover a lovely farmhouse-style dining area serving a buffet of lamb stew, reindeer pie, quiche, and potato salad, all made from mostly local ingredients. **Known for:** seafood soup; reindeer pie; cake buffet for dessert. $ *Average main: ISK3,990* ✉ *Skriðuklaustur* ☏ *354/471–2990* ⊕ *www.skriduklaustur.is* 🕐 *No dinner.*

 Hotels

Hótel Hallormsstaður

$$$ | HOTEL | Located in Iceland's largest national forest with views over Lagarfljót lake, Hótel Hallormsstaður offers spa-cious, comfortable rooms with modern Scandinavian design and furnishings in a palette of woodsy tones. **Pros:** beautiful location; two great restaurants; close to local attractions. **Cons:** location prone to fog in the mornings; not served by public transport; expensive. $ *Rooms from: ISK32,900* ✉ *Hótel Hallormsstaður* ☏ *471–2400* ⊕ *www.foresthotel.is* 🕐 *Closed Oct–Apr.* ➮ *92 rooms* 🍽 *Free Breakfast.*

★ Wilderness Center (Óbyggðasetur Íslands)

$ | RESORT | This appealing 19th-century historically restored old farmstead offers the unique opportunity to "sleep in a museum" with the option of staying in a Landowner's Suite, rooms in the old farmhouse, or in "bed closets," unique dorm-style beds with authentic, yester-year feel. **Pros:** great scenery; authentic traditional experience; excellent outdoor activities. **Cons:** old house, so sound car-ries; remote location; very small rooms. $ *Rooms from: ISK19,200* ✉ *Norðurdalur in Fljótsdalur* ☏ *440–8822* ⊕ *wilderness. is* ➮ *11 rooms* 🍽 *No Meals.*

Seyðisfjarðarkirkja is known as the Blue Church.

Seyðisfjörður

27 km (17 miles) east of Egilsstaðir.

Whether by land or sea, Seyðisfjörður, the cultural capital of East Iceland, makes a dramatic first impression. From Egilsstaðir the road winds to giddy heights and over a highland pass before weaving alongside racing waterfalls as you head into the town. Arriving by sea (with the ferry service Norröna) offers a different but no less stunning prelude as you sail along the 17 km (11-mile) fjord. With its small collection of colorful houses clustered around its tiny center and its iconic blue church, you might not want to leave.

GETTING HERE AND AROUND
Local public buses operated by Strætó run daily except Sunday between Egilsstaðir and Seyðisfjörður.

The Smyril Line ferry to Seyðisfjörður operates weekly from mid-March through late November on a route that begins in Hirtshals in northern Denmark, stopping at Tórshavn in the Faroe Islands. It takes 36 hours to sail from Denmark to the Faroe Islands, and 19 hours from the Faroes to Iceland. Prices vary with the season, whether you are traveling with a car/campervan/motorcycle/bike (as many do in summer), and what sort of sleeping cabin you opt for. You can also book a stopover in the Faroe Islands as part of your trip.

CONTACTS Smyril Line. ✉ *Yviri við Strond 1, Tórshavn* ☏ *470–2803* ⊕ *www.smyrill-ine.is.*

VISITOR INFORMATION
CONTACTS Visit Seyðisfjörður. ✉ *Ferjuleira 1* ☏ *472–1551* ⊕ *www.visitseydisfjordur.com.*

Sights

Rainbow Road
NEIGHBORHOOD | Found on many a postcard of Seyðisfjörður (along with many an Instagram feed), the town's pride-inspired Rainbow Road, as it has been lovingly

dubbed, is much smaller in reality but nonetheless charming. ⊕ *The street's original name is Norðurgata.*

Seyðisfjarðarkirkja

CHURCH | Follow the rainbow-brick road to this striking pale-blue church, an old landmark attraction built in the town center in 1920. The church is open during the summer months for regular concerts and events. An unusual white sculpture next to the church was made from the girders of a factory that was flattened in an avalanche in 1996. ✉ *Bjólfsgata* 🌐 *www.blaakirkjan.is.*

Skaftfell Art Center

ART GALLERY | There's a continual blossoming of creativity at Skaftfell, a center dedicated to visual and contemporary art. Located on the first floor above the Skaftfell bistro, the center features a large gallery exhibiting the works of both local and international artists. It also hosts art courses and workshops, and has a communal space for artists and a lovely artist residence on the top floor. ✉ *Austurvegur 42* ☎ *472–1632* 🌐 *www.skaftfell.is.*

Tvísöngur

PUBLIC ART | A short uphill trail (a 15-minute walk) off Hafnargata on the east side of town leads up the mountainside and this musical sculpture called Tvísöngur. Designed by German artist Lukas Kühne, the series of interconnected concrete domes resonates with specific tones from the traditional, five-tone Icelandic harmony. The views are glorious. ✉ *Tvísöngur.*

Restaurants

Aldan

$$$$ | **FUSION** | The house restaurant of Hotel Aldan is a lively spot for breakfast, lunch, and dinner, especially during the summer. The menu features a fusion of Icelandic cuisine with a bit of continental influence and is big on fish fresh from the fjord. **Known for:** local cod; Icelandic lamb; reindeer burger. [$] *Average main: ISK4,200* ✉ *Norðurgata 2* ☎ *472–1277* 🌐 *www.hotelaldan.is.*

Bistro Skaftfell

$$ | **PIZZA** | Pizza dominates the menu at Bistro Skaftfell, a charming place to dine located in the same building as the Skaftfell Art Center and furnished in the spirit of the late artist Dieter Roth, the art icon of Seyðisfjörður. The regularly updated menu also features soups, brownies, and cakes. **Known for:** great pizzas, including lobster pizza; arty vibes; vegetarian and vegan options. [$] *Average main: ISK2,500* ✉ *Austurvegur 42* ☎ *472–1633* 🌐 *skaftfell.is/en/bistro.*

★ Norð Austur Sushi&Bar

$$$ | **JAPANESE FUSION** | Winning high-pedigree accolades for its food that creatively fuses fresh local fish with Japanese techniques and flavors, Norð Austur is worth booking ahead for. It is open in the summer only and is in high demand for its beautifully presented morsels, creative cocktails, and cozy atmosphere. **Known for:** omakase for the table; sake and Japanese whiskey; maki rolls. [$] *Average main: ISK3,400* ✉ *Norðurgata 2* ☎ *787–4000* 🌐 *www.nordaustur.is* ⏲ *Closed Mon. and Tues.*

Hotels

Hotel Aldan

$$$ | **HOTEL** | Spread across three properties, Hotel Aldan takes up much of the town: the reception and restaurant are located next to the famous Rainbow Road while the guestrooms are found in fjordside Snæfell (also known as the Old Post Office) and the renovated Old Bank. **Pros:** central location; good restaurant; comfy beds. **Cons:** breakfast in a different building; Snæfell rooms are smaller; old houses where sound carries. [$] *Rooms from: ISK36,300* ✉ *Hotel Aldan* ☎ *472–1277* 🌐 *www.hotelaldan.is* 🛏 *23 rooms* 🍴 *No Meals.*

★ **Við Lónið Guesthouse**

$$$ | **HOTEL** | An absolute gem of a guesthouse, Við Lónið has gorgeous rooms featuring either beautiful views over the fjord or the sweet and charming scene over Rainbow Road. **Pros:** lovely views of the fjord from private balconies; central location; "Spa of Iceland" toiletries. **Cons:** old house so sound can carry between rooms; breakfast not included; no kitchen facilities. [$] *Rooms from: ISK38,000* ✉ *Norðurgata 8* ☎ *899–9429* 🌐 *www.vidlonidguesthouse.is* 🛏 *8 rooms* 🍴 *No Meals.*

Shopping

★ **Blóðberg**

CRAFTS | There are many visual treats in the creative village of Seyðisfjörður, and this beautiful black-and-white painted building, formerly owned by famous artist Dieter Roth, is a piece of art in itself. Inside is home to Blóðberg, which sells a curated selection of Icelandic products with works of art and design. The word "blóðberg" means Arctic thyme, a beautiful purple flower common in Iceland. ✉ *Norðurgata 5* ☎ *822–5258.*

Activities

Stafdalur Ski Area

SKIING & SNOWBOARDING | The scenic Stafdalur ski resort on the road into Seyðisfjörður has three lifts and offers easy to intermediate skiing and cross-country trails. The ski season is December to May. ✣ *On Fjarðarheiði heath, 10 miles from Egilsstadir on the way to Seyðisfjörður, off Rte. 93* ☎ *845–2690* 🌐 *www.stafdalur.is.*

Mjóifjörður

38 km (24 miles) southeast of Egilsstaðir.

From 1,312 feet above sea level the descent into Mjóifjörður, the 11-mile long "narrow" fjord between Seyðisfjörður and Neskaupstaður, is jaw-dropping; the landscape is striped with giant basalt steps that the locals say is are stairways for trolls. The fjord was once home to more than 200 people, most of whom worked at the old whaling station at Asknes, but now there are fewer than 15 residents.

GETTING HERE AND AROUND

There are no public bus services to Mjóifjörður. Route 953, off Route 1 from Egilsstaðir, is open only from May to October, depending on the weather. During the winter, boat services from Neskaupstaður operate twice a week to connect the fjord with the rest of the country.

Sights

Brekkuþorp

TOWN | One of several places in Iceland claiming to be the country's smallest village, Brekkuþorp (Hill Village) is home to only 14 year-round residents, and the road in and out of the fjord is closed during winter. Among the few amenities, the tiny settlement has a church as well as a summertime guesthouse, campsite, and café in the old school building. There's also a small dock for boats. A boat service operates twice weekly trips from Brekkuþorp to Neskaupstaður in all seasons. ✉ *Brekkuþorp.*

Dalatangi

LIGHTHOUSE | As far east as you can go in Iceland by car, Dalatangi is located at the very end of the road through Mjóifjörður with sensational views over the sea-licked cliffs out towards the North Atlantic. At Dalatangi there are two lighthouses, both some of the oldest in Iceland. The small, older building was constructed of basalt in 1895, while the larger, bright orange house, which is still in use, was built in 1908. The road is rough out here, so a vehicle with 4WD is recommended. ✉ *Dalatangi* ✣ *Around 9 miles east of Brekkuþorp on the northern side of the fjord.*

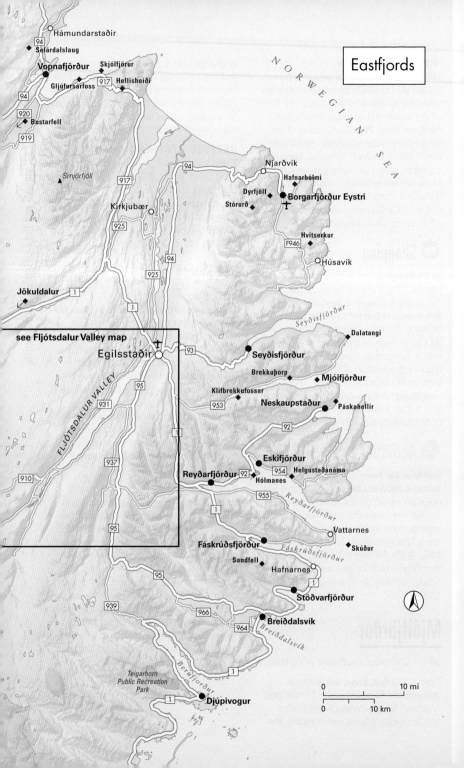

Eastfjords

Hámundarstaðir

94
Selárdalslaug
Vopnafjörður   Skjólfjörður
917   Hellisheiði
Gljúfursárfoss
94
920
Bustarfell
919

Smjörfjöll
917

Kirkjubær
925

Jökuldalur   1

NORWEGIAN SEA

94
Njarðvík
Hafnarhólmi
Dyrfjöll
Stórurð   **Borgarfjörður Eystri**

Hvítserkur
F946
Húsavík

94
925

see Fljótsdalur Valley map

Egilsstaðir
93
Seyðisfjörður
Dalatangi
Seyðisfjörður

Brekkuþorp
Klifbrekkufossar   **Mjóifjörður**
953
Neskaupstaður   Páskahellir
92

Eskifjörður
954   Helgustaðanáma
Reyðarfjörður   92
Hólmanes
955   *Reyðarfjörður*

Vattarnes
Skúður
Fáskrúðsfjörður   *Fáskrúðsfjörður*
Sandfell
Hafnarnes
1

95   FLJÓTSDALUR VALLEY
931
937
910
95

Stöðvarfjörður

939
966   **Breiðdalsvík**
964   *Breiðdalsvík*

*Teigarhorn
Public Recreation
Park*
1
Djúpivogur

0   10 mi
0   10 km

Hofsárgljúfur Canyon

CANYON | Stop at the bridge on the way to Dalatangi to view the terrific torrent of water known as the Heljarfoss waterfalls thundering down through the Hofsárgljúfur canyon. The stop is just under two miles past the Brekkuþorp village. ✉ *Hofsárgljúfur.*

★ **Klifbrekkufossar**

WATERFALL | One of the highlights of Mjóifjörður, Klifbrekkufossar waterfall impressively cascades 90 meters (295 feet) over a series of ledges into a delightful dell carpeted with a springy growth of blueberry scrub. Klifbrekkufossar is accessed just off the right-hand side of the main Mjóafjarðarvegur road (Route 953) descending into the fjord; it's 16 km (10 miles) from the turn-off from the Ring Road. Keep in mind that Route 953 is closed in the winter, from October to late May (weather dependent). ✉ *Klifbrekkufossar.*

Prestagil

CANYON | Look out for the landmark known as Prestagil (which translates as "the priests' ravine") while descending the winding road into Mjóifjörður. According to an old folk tale, a gruesome ogress once lived here; she would lure men of the cloth into the ravine and make a meal of their holy flesh. ✉ *Mjóifjörður* ✣ *Located on the southern side of Mjóifjörður.*

🍴 Restaurants

Sólbrekka Cafe

$ | **CAFÉ** | The only dining stop in this fjord, Sólbrekka Cafe serves light refreshments and coffee (with free refills), and they have a cake buffet on Sunday. On display are old photos from life in the valley. **Known for:** great cake buffet; decent coffee; only restaurant on the fjord. [$] *Average main: ISK1,000* ✉ *Sólbrekka* ☎ *899–7109* 🌐 *www.mjoifjordur.weebly.com* 🕒 *Closed mid-Aug.–mid-June.*

🛏 Hotels

Sólbrekka Guesthouse

$ | **HOUSE** | Located within the old village school, Sólbrekka Guesthouse offers basic accommodations (mainly bunk beds) for a limited period during the summer. **Pros:** great views; close to hiking routes; bike rental available. **Cons:** shared bathrooms; breakfast needs booking in advance; no other meals available. [$] *Rooms from: ISK10,000* ✉ *Sólbrekka* ☎ *899–7109* 🌐 *www.mjoifjordur.weebly.com* 🕒 *Closed Sept.–May* 🛏 *5 rooms, 2 cottages* 🍴 *No Meals.*

Neskaupstaður

23 km (14 miles) southeast of Eskifjörður.

Located on the northern shores of Norðfjörður, the friendly town of Neskaupstaður is home to almost 1,500 people, qualifying it as one of the biggest communities in East Iceland. Often overlooked because of its remote location, the town offers magnificent scenery and fascinating history. It's one of the few towns in Iceland where life and the town's strong economy still depend almost entirely on fishing and fish processing.

GETTING HERE AND AROUND

Continue northeast of Eskifjörður on Route 92 to reach the town. The 5-mile tunnel leading to Neskaupstaður provides a more convenient, but less thrilling entrance than the old tunnel via the Oddsskarð mountain pass, which reached heights of 2,313 feet above sea level. Buses operated by Strætó operate daily except Sunday, connecting Egilsstaðir with Eskifjörður and Norðfjörður.

Sights

★ Fólkvangur Neskaupstaðar

CITY PARK | For some easy romantic walks, head to Neskaupstaður public park, a peat-rich nature reserve on the far east of town on the north side of the fjord with superb vistas. There are several trails (a bit boggy in places), one of which leads to Páskahellir (Easter Cave). ✉ *Fólkvangur Neskaupstaðar.*

Páskahellir

CAVE | A pleasant trail leads through the Fólkvangur Neskaupstaðar nature reserve to reach Páskahellir (Easter Cave in English), where, according to legend, the sun can be seen dancing on Easter morning. Remarkable holes in the cave are impressions left by trees covered with lava in an ancient volcanic episode that occurred around 12 million years ago. The views east towards Barðsneshorn with the red rhyolite glow of Rauðaberg are worth stopping to take in. Be cautious when descending the steps to the cave; they can get slippery with sea spray. ✉ *Páskahellir.*

Safnahúsið

OTHER MUSEUM | You'll find three museums under one roof here at Safnahúsið. Tryggvasafn features an impressive collection of exotic-looking paintings by local artist Tryggvi Ólafsson, who was born in the town in 1940. Sjóminja-og Smiðjumunasafn is an impressive collection of historical maritime artifacts while Náttúrugripasafnið is the museum of natural history with an eclectic exhibition of taxidermy birds, fish, and other life forms. ✉ *Egilsbraut 2* ☎ *470–9000* 🎟 *ISK 1,700* 🕒 *Closed Sept.–May.*

Restaurants

Beituskúrinn

$$$ | SCANDINAVIAN | There's a ramshackle appeal to this converted old fishing hut located by the waterfront (its name translates to "the Bait Shack"). Meals served under the low-beamed ceilings decorated with nautical salvage are tasty and the service is quick, but the real draw of this place is the epic views of the fjord. **Known for:** pop-up menus from local and visiting chefs; lobster pizza; lunch buffet. $ *Average main: ISK3,000* ✉ *Egilsbraut 26* ☎ *477–1950* 🌐 *www.beituskurinn.is.*

Hotels

Hildibrand Apartment Hotel

$$ | HOTEL | Located in a functional block in the center of town, this modern hotel offers 15 spacious, well-appointed apartments, all with private balconies overlooking the sea. **Pros:** retro restaurant on-site; delicious bakery; nice views from balconies in apartments. **Cons:** water isn't geothermally heated; no elevator; some rooms are in another building. $ *Rooms from: ISK24,500* ✉ *Hafnarbraut 2* ☎ *477–1950* 🌐 *www.hildibrandhotel.com* 🛏 *29 rooms, 15 apartments* 🍴 *No Meals.*

Activities

★ Skorrahestur

HORSEBACK RIDING | Not many leave Neskaupstaður without hearing about Doddi, the singing, horseback-riding hiking guide from Skorrahestur who entertains guests with his extensive local knowledge and story-telling skills. One-hour horseback-riding tours (ISK 9,500) and seven-day tours, including farm accommodation and meals, are available from mid-May to September. Additionally, there's also the option of a two-hour guided hike (ISK 15,500) in the mountains, with stories and pancakes included. The family also has a cozy guesthouse on the property. ☎ *477–1736* 🌐 *www.skorrahestar.is.*

Eskifjörður

23 km (14 miles) southwest of Neskaupstadur.

Wedged between the towering 985-meter (3,232-foot) Hólmatindur peak and the mountains known as the "East Iceland Alps," the town of Eskifjörður is a thriving village on the northern shore known for its maritime history and the famous spar mine, Helgustaðanáma.

GETTING HERE AND AROUND

The town is northeast of Reyðarfjörður on Route 92; this route continues east to Neskaupstaður. Local buses run by Strætó connect Egilsstaðir, Reyðarfjörður, Eskifjörður, and Neskaupstaður (Norðfjörður).

TOURS

Tanni Travel

GUIDED TOURS | Based in Eskifjörður, Tanni Travel offers day tours and multiday offerings in the local area and beyond with excursions all around the east and the eastern highlands. They can also design tailor-made tours. ✉ *Strandgata 14* ☎ *476–1399* 🌐 *www.tannitravel.is.*

Sights

Helgustaðanáma

MINE | Follow the coastal road past Mjóeyri, and continue southeast (around 4½ miles) to reach Helgustaðanáma, an old Iceland spar mine. These types of "spars" in Iceland are actually crystallized calcium carbonate, called "silfurberg" in Iceland. A short trail from an information board leads up to the opening. Iceland spar's unusual light-polarizing properties and the Nicol prisms made from it were crucial components for microscopes and instruments measuring optical activity, and the site was mined from the 16th until the 21st century. It's a popular belief that Iceland spar was used by Vikings as "sunstones" to help them navigate. Small pieces of Iceland spar lie around the entrance, but it is strictly forbidden to take it. ✉ *Helgustaðanáma.*

★ **Hólmanes**

MOUNTAIN | The road from Reyðarfjörður leads around the Hólmanes peninsula, which is overlooked by the towering 985-meter (3,232-foot-high) Hólmatindur peak. There's a parking area with benches and viewing platform if you want to pull over and take a photo. The hike to the top of Hólmatindur is challenging, but the views are incredible. There's also a popular and easy two-hour trail that loops around the nature reserve. Look out for eider ducks, geese, and other birdlife, which make their home there during the summer. ✉ *Hólmanes.*

Restaurants

★ **Randulffssjóhús**

$$$$ | **SCANDINAVIAN** | At this boathouse on the water's edge (built in 1890), you can enjoy gourmet dishes like spotted catfish and crispy reindeer meatballs. The interior is furnished with an impressive collection of maritime artifacts, and the soundtrack is of old Icelandic fishing songs. **Known for:** shark, dried fish, and brennivín; fish soup; authentic fisherman's living quarters upstairs. [$] *Average main: ISK4,500* ✉ *Strandgata 96* ☎ *477–1247* 🌐 *www.randulffssjohus.is* 🕒 *Closed Sept.–May.*

Hotels

Hotel Eskifjörður

$$ | **HOTEL** | Located in the former town bank, Hotel Eskifjörður has modern, bright rooms and all the facilities you would expect: en suite bathrooms, TVs, hairdryers, and Wi-Fi. **Pros:** wine cellar in former bank vault; central location; discount for winter stays. **Cons:** small rooms; not all rooms have sea views; breakfast additional cost. [$] *Rooms from: ISK27,000* ✉ *Strandgata 47* ☎ *476–0099* 🌐 *www.hoteleskifjordur.is* 🛏 *17 rooms* 🍴 *No Meals.*

★ Mjóeyri Cottages

$$$ | HOUSE | The cluster of small wooden cottages by the shore on the east side of the fjord belongs to Mjóeyri—a local family-run travel service offering accommodations and activities. **Pros:** gorgeous setting; well-equipped cottages; hot tub in a converted boat. **Cons:** some shared bathroom; small rooms; guesthouse not well sound-insulated. $ *Rooms from: ISK35,000 ⌂ Strandgata 120 ☎ 477–1247 mobile, 696–0809 landline ⊕ www.mjoeyri.is ➪ 5 rooms, 10 cottages* ⋈ *No Meals.*

Activities

SKIING

Bergmenn Mountain Guides

SKIING & SNOWBOARDING | For an off-piste adventure in the Land of Dragons, Bergmenn Mountain Guides (based in Dalvík, North Iceland) offers a seven-day ski tour in the Eastfjords, with a touring base at Mjóeyri. ⌂ *Dalvík ☎ 858–3000 ⊕ www.bergmenn.com.*

Oddsskarð

SKIING & SNOWBOARDING | Located in the "East Iceland Alps" above Eskifjörður, Oddsskarð might not be the most famous ski resort in Iceland, but with elevations reaching 840 meters (2,755 feet), the views are hard to beat. Skiers and snowboarders visiting Oddsskarð can enjoy around 9 km (5½ miles of slopes); 2½ miles are classified as difficult. They're served by three lifts, and the area is a gateway to backcountry skiing. The ski area usually opens in December and is in full operation until April or early May, depending on snowfall. ⌂ *Oddsskarð ☎ 833–5888 ⊕ www.visitfjardabyggd.is/oddsskard.*

Reyðarfjörður

34 km (21 miles) south of Egilsstaðir.

The longest of the Eastfjords, Reyðarfjörður, which served as an allied base during World War II, is closely associated with Alcoa, the world's biggest aluminum corporation. Alcoa produces 360,000 tons of aluminum annually in its smelter, which opened just outside of the town in 2007. Also the primary location for the popular British TV show *Fortitude*, Reyðarfjörður is a leading port for freight exports and boasts the second largest population in the Fjarðabyggð region.

GETTING HERE AND AROUND

Local buses operated by Strætó connect Reyðarfjörður with Egilsstaðir twice daily (except Sunday).

Sights

Icelandic Wartime Museum

HISTORY MUSEUM | The sight of several restored army trucks parked within the vicinity of some old Nissen barracks might look out of place in the small town of Reyðarfjörður, but they serve as a reminder of Iceland's history with the allied forces during the Second World War, when 4,000 soldiers descended on the small town, outnumbering locals by more than three to one. The vintage trucks and buildings are now part of Íslenska Stríðsárasafnið (War Museum), an exhibition featuring images and other memorabilia from the wartime period. ⌂ *Íslenska Stríðsárasafnið, Heiðarvegur 37 ☎ 470–9063 ⊕ stridsarasafn.fjardabyggd.is ⌸ ISK 1,700 ⊙ Closed Sept.–May.*

🍴 Restaurants

★ Sesam Brauðhús

$$ | BAKERY | There's a good selection of quality bread and pastries at Sesam, an artisanal bakery in the middle of town that also serves coffee and cake. Each weekday there's a good-value lunch special that's popular with locals (Friday is pizza day). **Known for:** pizza Fridays; draumaterta cake (soft, white cake on a bed of meringue with chocolate cream); lunch dish of the day. $ *Average main:*

Sandfell is a 743-meter-high rhyolite mountain.

ISK1,900 ✉ Hafnargata 1 ☏ 475–8000 ⊕ www.sesam.is ☉ Closed Sun.

Tærgesen

$$$ | **EUROPEAN** | Large portions of comfort food (think burgers, pizzas, and more expensive meat and fish dishes) are served under low timber ceilings at Tærgesen, a family-run restaurant and guesthouse located in a lovely old building dating back to 1870. Tærgesen was the filming location for the Midnight Sun Hotel in the British TV thriller *Fortitude*. **Known for:** great pizza; fillet of lamb dijon; butter-fried trout. $ *Average main: ISK3,000* ✉ *Búðargata 4* ☏ *470–5555* ⊕ *www.taergesen.com.*

 Hotels

Tærgesen

$$ | **B&B/INN** | An old iron-clad, black timber house dating back to 1870, Tærgesen has been offering charming accommodations since 1938. **Pros:** historic building; central location; good restaurant. **Cons:** shared bathrooms in guesthouse;

noise between rooms; small rooms. $ *Rooms from: ISK24,000* ✉ *Búðargata 4* ☏ *470–5555* ⊕ *www.taergesen.com* ⌖ *17 rooms* ⊚*| Free Breakfast.*

Fáskrúðsfjörður

50 km (31 miles) southeast of Egilsstaðir.

Also know as Búðir, the town of Fáskrúðsfjörður has a strong French influence (you'll see signs in French in addition to Icelandic). Fáskrúðsfjörður's French heritage—which you can learn more about at the French Museum (Frakkar á Íslandsmiðum)—dates back to the 17th century when Bretagne fishermen were lured to the east coast of Iceland by its rich fishing waters. In the years until World War I, it's estimated that up to 5,000 fishermen from the continent lost their lives in the famously perilous waters around Fáskrúðsfjörður. Many of those who perished are buried in the French Graveyard.

GETTING HERE AND AROUND

The town is located just off the Ring Road, about 18½ (11 miles) south of the junction to Reyðarfjörður. Strætó operates weekday buses between Norðfjörður (Neskaupstaður) and Fáskrúðsfjörður, and between Breiðdalsvík and Fáskrúðsfjörður.

Sights

Frakkar á Íslandsmiðum

HISTORY MUSEUM | One of the perks of staying at Fosshotel Eastfjords is that you get free admission to Frakkar á Íslandsmiðum (aka the French Museum). The installations, which are based on the history of the French fishermen in Fáskrúðsfjörður, are located in the old Doctor's House and French Hospital, which are now part of the hotel. The main attraction, a captivating replica of the sailors' quarters, is located in the underground passage connecting the two buildings. ✉ *Hafnargata 12* ☎ *475–1170* 🌐 *www.visitfjardabyggd.is* 🎫 *ISK 2,200.*

Sandfell

MOUNTAIN | A distinctive rhyolite mountain on the south side of the fjord, Sandfell beckons experienced hikers. It's a steep round-trip hike to the 1,157-meter (3,796-foot) summit that can be done in around five hours. ✥ *A trail from Stóra-Sandfell farm leads to the summit.*

Skrúður

ISLAND | While exploring Fáskrúðsfjörður, you'll see the island of Skrúður at the mouth of the fjord. The island is known for its large caves—the biggest in East Iceland, in fact, and home to a thriving bird population. Its other resident is Skrúðsbondi, a mythical giant. ✉ *Skrúður, Fáskrúðsfjörður.*

Restaurants

★ **L'Abri**

$$$$ | EUROPEAN | The menu at waterside L'Abri is full of fish and meat dishes with the usual emphasis on locally sourced ingredients, and a twist on French classics like French onion soup and steak frites. The decor is modern and minimalist, featuring vintage photos of life in the town, but the best feature is the epic views of the fjord, where you might see a whale swimming by or even catch a show of the northern lights. **Known for:** fantastic views of the fjord; a few French menu classics; good-value 3-course set menu. [$] *Average main: ISK5,500* ✉ *Hafnargata 11-14* ☎ *470–4070* 🌐 *www.islandshotel.is* 🕒 *Closed Nov.–Apr.*

Hotels

★ **Fosshotel Eastfjords**

$$$$ | HOTEL | Spread across four of the town's historic buildings, the Fosshotel Eastfjords is one of the best lodging options in the region. **Pros:** quiet atmosphere; free admission to the French Museum; good on-site restaurant. **Cons:** low ceiling in some rooms on the top floor; breakfast is extra; not all rooms have sea views. [$] *Rooms from: ISK43,500* ✉ *Hafnargata 11-14* ☎ *470–4070* 🌐 *www.islandshotel.is* 🕒 *Closed Nov.–Apr.* 🛏 *47 rooms* 🍴 *No Meals.*

Stöðvarfjörður

27 km (17 miles) southeast of Fáskrúðsfjörður.

A woman named Petra with a lifelong love of petrology has helped put Stöðvarfjörður on the map as a modern-day tourist attraction, thanks to Petra's Stone Collection. The beautiful fjord with spectacular surroundings is famous for its remarkable variety of colorful rocks and minerals, including many rarities which can be observed at Steinasafn Petru.

GETTING HERE AND AROUND

The Ring Road cruises right around the fjord, passing through the village. Strætó operates a weekday bus between Fáskrúðsfjörður and Breiðdalsvík, stopping in Stöðvarfjörður.

Sights

★ **Petra's Stone Collection**

OTHER MUSEUM | A highlight of the region, Petra Sveinsdóttir's stone collection was borne of her lifelong fascination with rocks, stones, and minerals. Installed in her family home and expanded throughout the garden, the exhibition was 80 years in the making and features obsidian (volcanic glass), colorful jasper fusions, amethyst, agate, and solid quartz. ✉ *Fjarðarbraut 21* ☎ *475–8834* 🌐 *www.steinapetra.is* 🎟 *ISK 1,500* 🕒 *Closed Sept.–May.*

Breiðdalsvík

19 km (12 miles) southwest of Stöðvarfjörður.

Resting beneath some rather lofty mountains and neighboring rugged black-sand beaches, Breiðdalsvík is a tiny, cozy coastal town just off the Ring Road. Thanks to the rise of microbrews in Iceland, this town of only around 140 people has a great brewery, Beljandi Brugghús. It's also home to the renowned salmon fishing river, Breiðdalsá, found in the scenic inland valley known as Breiðdalur.

GETTING HERE AND AROUND

At Breiðdalsvík, the Ring Road (Route 1) continues south to Djúpivogur, while Route 95 cuts inland through Breiðdalur north to Egilsstaðir. Strætó operates weekday bus services north to Fáskrúðsfjörður and south to Höfn via Djúpivogur.

VISITOR INFORMATION

CONTACTS Visit Breiðdalsvík. ✉ *Sólvellir 14, Breiðdalsvík* ☎ *470–0000* 🌐 *www.breiddalsvik.is/en.*

Sights

★ **Beljandi Brugghús**

BREWERY | You might have already tried the Beljandi pale ale during your travels in the east, but at the bar and microbrewery where it's made you can sample even more craft beers from the collection, incluiding the Skuggi (Shadow) porter, Spaði (Spade) IPA, or Sauður (Sheep) brown ale. Group tours of the brewery are available even when the bar is closed; call ahead for a reservation. ✉ *Sólvellir 23* ☎ *866–8330* 🌐 *www.facebook.com/beljandibrugghus* 🕒 *Closed Oct.–May.*

Hotels

Hótel Breiðdalsvík

$$ | **HOTEL** | Rooms under the bright blue roof of Hótel Breiðdalsvík are comfortable and bright. **Pros:** central location; Finnish-style sauna; good breakfast included. **Cons:** limited views; bathrooms on the small side; not all rooms have a balcony. [$] *Rooms from: ISK29,000* ✉ *Sólvellir 14* ☎ *470–0000* 🌐 *www.breiddalsvik.is* 🛏 *46 rooms* 🍴 *Free Breakfast.*

Shopping

Kaupfjélagið

GENERAL STORE | Time stands still at Kaupfjélagið, the old general store in Breiðdalsvík, where vintage stock is still on display. Today it sells groceries, toiletries, preserves, and other conveniences. You can also buy coffee and light meals. ✉ *Sólvellir 25, Breiðdalsvík* ☎ *475–6670* 🌐 *www.breiddalsvik.is.*

Djúpivogur

61 km (38 miles) southwest of Breiðdalsvík.

Every town in the Eastfjords has its most revered mountain, and in Djúpivogur the title belongs to Búlandstindur—a prominent 1069-meter (3,507-foot-high) peak in the shape of an almost-perfect pyramid. The fact that Djúpivogur is a fishing village will surprise no one, but because its maritime activities date back to 1589, Djúpivogur is home to the oldest port in the country. The town, which is visited frequently by wandering reindeer and curious seals, is now attracting more tourists, inspiring a new cultural focus and an alternative source of income. It's also the only place in Iceland to adopt the Cittaslow movement, a sustainable philosophy inspired by the "slow food" movement originating in Italy.

GETTING HERE AND AROUND

There are local bus services: Strætó connects Djúpivogur with Breiðdalsvík and Höfn once daily (no services on Tuesday and Saturday).

Sights

Eggin í Gleðivík

PUBLIC ART | A series of giant bird eggs known as the Eggs of Merry Bay are lined up along the waterfront in Djúpivogur, waiting to give you a lesson in ornithology. Each of the highly polished stone eggs, created by Icelandic artist Sigurður Guðmundsson, represents and honors one of the 34 bird species native to East Iceland. ✉ *Víkurland* ✣ *Head northwest on Víkurland—the road along the waterfront northwest of the village.*

Restaurants

★ **Hótel Framtíð Restaurant**

$$$$ | **EUROPEAN** | Stop for pizza at this cozy restaurant overlooking the harbor, or try something a little more exotic like wild goose breast. Whether it's trout, salmon, haddock, or plaice, the catch of the day is always delicious, as is the soup. **Known for:** grilled lobster tails; seafood soup; catch of the day. [$] *Average main: ISK5,000* ✉ *Vogaland 4* ☎ *478–8887* 🌐 *www.hotelframtid.com.*

Hotels

Bragðavellir

$$$ | **HOUSE** | Set amid big, bucolic landscapes about 13 km (8 miles) south of Djúpivogur, Bragðavellir is a family-run farm with a collection of cozy timber cottages, with one or two bedrooms. **Pros:** close to nature; on-site restaurant and tours; friendly farm animals. **Cons:** rooms have two single beds pushed together; restaurant only open June to August; basic furnishings. [$] *Rooms from: ISK34,000* ✉ *Djupivogur* ☎ *478–8240* 🌐 *www.bragdavellir.is* 🛏 *6 cottages* 🍴 *No Meals.*

Hótel Framtíð

$$ | **HOTEL** | The main building of Hótel Framtíð, which means Future Hotel, was once a store and then a post office before it was converted into a hotel in 1987. **Pros:** comfortable beds; pretty harbor views; great restaurant. **Cons:** breakfast is additional cost; decor lacks character; some rooms have shared bathrooms. [$] *Rooms from: ISK29,800* ✉ *Vogaland 4* ☎ *478–8887* 🌐 *www.hotelframtid.com* 🛏 *50 rooms* 🍴 *No Meals.*

Snæfellsöræfi

92 km (57 miles) southwest of Egilsstaðir.

Southwest of Egilsstaðir, the extraordinary and formidable highland realms of Snæfellsöræfi—the Snæfell Wilderness—occupy the eastern territory of Vatnajökull National Park, with the mountain Snæfell presiding majestically over the region. The remote location attracts a wealth of

wildlife, including wild-roaming reindeer and the pink-footed goose. Here, you're also likely to encounter the gyrfalcon, a bird of prey and the largest of the falcon species.

Roads built to facilitate the construction of the Kárahnjúkar dam and the hydro-electric power plant have dramatically improved access to this area, with a surfaced road (Route 910) leading from the south end of Fljótsdalur valley up to the north side of Snæfellsöræfi, and west towards the location of the dam. However, you will still need a vehicle with 4WD to access the F909 mountain road to Snæfell, Eyjabakkajökull, and the surrounding landmark attractions within the national park. Note that road F909 is only open in summer, from about June to mid-September (weather conditions permitting). You can check the status of the road at ⊕ www.road.is.

GETTING HERE AND AROUND
There are no public transportation services to this destination. You will need your own wheels. Tours of the area are available from the tour company Wild Boys (⊕ www.wildboys.is).

VISITOR INFORMATION
Snæfellsstofa Visitor Centre
VISITOR CENTER | Smart, modern and sustainable, Iceland's first BREEAM-certified building is the service and visitor information center for travelers exploring the remote eastern territory of Vatnajökull National Park. Inside the equally modern interior, there's an exhibition on the region and a small shop selling maps and locally made souvenirs. ⊠ Skriðuklaustur ☎ 470–0840 ⊕ www.vjp.is.

Sights

Bjálfafell
VIEWPOINT | On the way to Eyjabakka-jökull, take the right turn at the Bjálfafell signpost for truly spectacular views over the pristine wilderness west of Snæfell known as Vesturöræfi. Here you can see the broad edge of the Brúarjökull glacier tongue to the west, and Eyjabakkajökull to the east. ⊠ Bjálfafell ⊕ www.vjp.is.

★ Eyjabakkajökull
NATURE SIGHT | South of Snæfell is the spectacular Eyjabakkajökull, the north-easternmost glacial outlet of Vatnajökull glacier. It's a bumpy 50-minute ride from the Snæfell mountain hut all the way down to the edge of the glacier, but well worth traveling the few extra miles. The F909 mountain route is only suitable for vehicles with 4WDs. At the end of the road, there's a car park and a visitors' trail (marked out annually depending on changes to the glacier). ⊠ Eyjabakkajökull ⊹ 18.2 km south from Snæfellsskáli mountain hut on Rte. F909 ⊕ www.vjp.is.

★ Snæfell
MOUNTAIN | Dubbed the king of all mountains in Iceland, Snæfell, which translates as "snow mountain," is Iceland's highest peak not sitting under a glacier, with a summit reaching 1,833 meters (6,014 feet). While its status as a "probably extinct" volcano is still a topic for debate, no one disputes its beauty. Those visiting Snæfell, which is part of Vatnajökull National Park, may encounter wild reindeer who have made the deserted expanses around the mountain their primary habitat. The route to the rangers' hut at the base of the mountain is accessible only by vehicles with 4WD. ⊠ Snæfell ⊹ 7½ miles on Rte. 909 from the junction off Rte. 910 to the ranger's hut at the base of the mountain ⊕ www.vjp.is.

Hotels

★ Laugarfell
$ | **B&B/INN** | This spot is the perfect base for several excellent hiking trails, including the Waterfall Circle, plus there are two tempting stone pools filled with hot spring water. **Pros:** lovely hot springs; proximity to nature; accessible without 4WD in summer. **Cons:** shared bathrooms

and showers; breakfast not included in the price; small rooms. $ *Rooms from: ISK14,000* ✉ *Laugarfell* ☎ *773–3323* ⊕ *www.laugarfell.is* ⊗ *Closed Oct.–mid-May* ⇌ *28 beds* ⦿❙ *No Meals.*

Snæfellsskáli

$ | HOUSE | Operated by the national park rangers who live on-site in summer, this mountain hut on the northwest side of Snæfell sleeps up to 45 people in a large dorm-style room, with just mattresses on the floor (no beds). **Pros:** peaceful location; truly in the wilderness; great place to see gyrfalcons. **Cons:** shared rooms; shared bathrooms; far away from any services. $ *Rooms from: ISK4,500* ✉ *Snæfellsskáli* ☎ *842–4367* ⊕ *www.vjp.is* ⇌ *45 beds* ⦿❙ *No Meals.*

Höfn

104 km (65 miles) south of Djúpivogur.

With views of Europe's largest ice cap and its tantalizing glacier tongues descending the valleys between mountains, Höfn, a sleepy port and fishing village in southeast Iceland, has arguably the most impressive backdrop in the country. The largest commercial center servicing the region with a thriving agricultural and farming community, Höfn provides a significant pit stop on the Ring Road where you can rest, repose, and stock up on some essentials.

GETTING HERE AND AROUND

Strætó operates the daily bus service 51 between Mjódd in Reykjavík and Höfn with a bus change at Vík. The same company operates local buses in East Iceland, including bus 94 operating five times a week (not Tuesday and Saturday) connecting Höfn, Djúpivogur, and Breiðdalsvík.

⊙ Sights

★ Stokksnes

VIEWPOINT | Featured in marketing images, advertisements, TV shows, and countless wedding shots, the view of Vestrahorn mountain on the Stokknes peninsula, east of Höfn, is one of the most iconic in Iceland. The best place to frame a snapshot is by the gate of the old U.S. radar station. The peninsula is also home to the Viking Cafe and a remarkable, never-used film set of a Viking village. ✉ *Höfn.*

Viking Village

TOWN | Sitting in the shadow of the iconic Vestrahorn mountain in Stokksnes is a remarkable replica of a Viking village. The landowners, who also run the Viking Cafe, charge a small entrance fee to the village. The enclosure with its collection of grass-topped wooden houses was built in 2010 as a film set for a movie that was never finished. It's in varying states of disrepair thanks to the weather, but still fun to explore. ✉ *Viking Village, Höfn* ⊹ *3 miles east from the junction to Höfn on Rte., 1 turn right onto a gravel track just before the Vestrahorn mountain. Turn left at the Viking Cafe.* 🎫 *ISK 900.*

🍴 Restaurants

★ Íshúsið Pizzeria

$$$ | PIZZA | The town's old icehouse, which was once a storeroom for glacier ice used to keep the local fresh catches cool, is now a popular harborside pizzeria serving up soups and salads but mainly stone-baked pizzas. You'll find classic pizza toppings along with langoustine. **Known for:** excellent fish and chips; lobster soup; good variety of pizzas. $ *Average main: ISK3,500* ✉ *Heppuvegur 2a, Höfn* ☎ *354/478–1230* ⊕ *www.ishusidpizzeria.is.*

★ Pakkhús

$$$$ | ICELANDIC | Based in an old warehouse made of scrap wood, Pakkhús makes good use of the area's supply of fresh seafood, especially the langoustine, which they are primarily known for (often referred to as 'lobster' in Iceland). Their menu also features duck, lamb, and beef, with some tempting desserts too. **Known for:** langoustine tails; créme bruleé flavored with licorice; grilled fillet of lamb. $ *Average main: ISK5,000 ⊠ Krosseyjarvegur 3, Höfn ☎ 478–2280 ⊕ www.pakkhus.is.*

Viking Cafe

$$ | CAFÉ | This small café operated by the landowners of Viking Village in Stokksnes serves coffee, light meals, and snacks. Pay here to explore the Viking Village and access iconic views of Vestrahorn mountain. **Known for:** beautiful mountain views; photogenic surroundings; decent coffee. $ *Average main: ISK1,500 ⊠ Viking Cafe, Horni, Höfn ☎ 478–2577 ⊕ www.vikingcafe.is.*

Hotels

★ Fosshotel Vatnajökull

$$$$ | HOTEL | Höfn is a popular overnight stop on any Ring Road adventure, and this branch of the Fosshotel chain is a modern, stylish place with epic glacier views. **Pros:** happy hour in the bar from 6 pm; good on-site restaurant; incredible views. **Cons:** 9 miles outside of Höfn; expensive; breakfast not included in all rates. $ *Rooms from: ISK57,500 ⊠ Lindarbakki, Höfn ☎ 478–2555 ⊕ www.islandshotel.is ⊗ Closed Dec. and Jan. ⊐ 66 rooms � ❍� No Meals.*

★ Milk Factory

$$ | HOTEL | Evidence that Icelanders will renovate almost any building to turn it into a guesthouse, the Milk Factory was once—you guessed it—a milk factory and the stylish redesign has resulted in 17 modern, minimalist rooms, including family rooms that sleep four (with beds on a mezzanine level). **Pros:** breakfast included; free tea and coffee; gorgeous mountain views. **Cons:** no glacier views; no kitchen facilities; a mile away from habor dining. $ *Rooms from: ISK27,000 ⊠ Dalbraut 2, Höfn ☎ 478–8900 ⊕ www.milkfactory.is ⊐ 17 rooms ❍� Free Breakfast.*

Vatnajökull National Park–Skaftafell

135 km (84 miles) west of Höfn.

This is the region that puts the "ice" in Iceland. The area is dominated by the incredible Vatnajökull ice cap, the largest in Europe, which covers a staggering 7,700 square kilometers (close to 3,000 square miles). At its thickest, the ice is 950 meters (more than 3,100 feet), and under that mass of ice are seven volcano systems (yes, this is indeed the land of fire and ice). The ice cap also has around 40 outlet glaciers—frozen rivers of ice you see dripping down the mountains as you drive along the Ring Road from Höfn to Skaftafell. You can even access these glaciers for adventures such as glacier walks, snowmobiling, boat rides among the icebergs, and more.

When established in 2008, Vatnajökull National Park covered roughly 13% of Iceland, encompassing not only the entirety of Vatnajökull, Europe's largest ice cap, but also the stunning wilderness areas of Skaftafell in the south and Jökulsárgljúfur in the north.

Over time, the park's boundaries have grown. With the more recent additions of Lakagígar, Langisjór, Krepputunga, and Jökulsárlón to the national park, the area, which was inscribed as a UNESCO World Heritage Site in July 2019, now covers over 14,967 square kilometers or 57,80 square miles (as of September 2021), edging close to 15% of Iceland. Much of it lies in uninhabited highland areas.

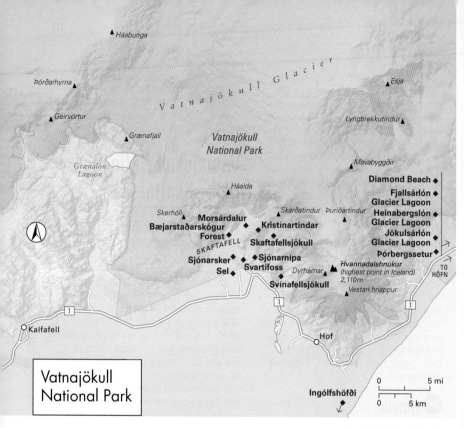

Vatnajökull National Park

Within this massive park—Western Europe's largest—you'll find spectacular displays of nearly every geological feature and landscape Iceland has to offer: horse-shoe-shaped cliffs, thundering waterfalls, endless glacier tongues, active volcanoes, otherworldly lava fields, and more. A number of the park's natural attractions are unique sights, such as Dettifoss, the most powerful waterfall in Europe (found in North Iceland); Hljóðaklettar, a series of curious volcanic plugs; and Snæfell, the highest freestanding mountain in Iceland.

By far the most popular region of the park is Skaftafell, which receives more than 500,000 visitors each year, who come to hike its numerous scenic trails, marvel at dripping glacier tongues, and take pictures of its most photographed attraction, Svartifoss (aka "Black Falls," so named because of its surrounding black

basalt columns). Illuminated by the rising heights of dazzling white glacial tongues, the area presents a dynamic scene filled with busy streams and beautiful waterfalls. Vast stretches of black sand meet magnificent birchwood forests blooming with wildflowers and lush vegetation. Trails around Skaftafell, which are said to be some of the best in the country, are mostly concentrated on the Skaftafellsheiði heath, where the popular landmark attraction Svartifoss waterfall is located. Another popular trail leads right up to the serrated edge of the Skaftafells-jökull glacial tongue.

All in all, there are five visitor centers for the park, all in lowland areas and easily accessible: Kirkjubæjarklaustur (South Iceland), Skaftafell and Höfn (Southeast Iceland), Skriðuklaustur (East Iceland), and Ásbyrgi (Northeast Iceland). Each of them has an exhibition about the park's nature and cultural heritage. Park services and facilities are outlined on the park website and include basic campgrounds and mountain huts, ranger-led interpretative hikes, and detailed maps. Operating seasons vary, with highland rangers only in place for two to four months over the summer, but year-round rangers can be found in lowland areas.

GETTING HERE AND AROUND

Stræto operates the year-round 51 bus service between Reykjavík and Höfn with stops at several major towns as well as Skaftafell.

Drivers should note that is a service fee for parking in the car park at Skaftafell. The charge is for one day, valid until midnight each day. The cost for a regular car (up to five passengers) is ISK 750 per car. You can pay online (⊕ *www.parka.is*) or using the Parka app.

TOURS

★ Fjallsárlón Iceberg Boat Tours

BOAT TOURS | To get a close-up of the icebergs at Fjallsárlon, you can take a 45-minute private or scheduled boat tour. There are nine departures between 9:30 am and 5:30 pm every day. Tours cost ISK 8,300 per person, and there are a maximum of 10 people on each small zodiac boat. Tours operate from April through October. ✉ *Fjallsárlón, Höfn* ☎ *666–8006* ⊕ *www.fjallsarlon.is.*

★ From Coast to Mountains

GUIDED TOURS | In spring and summer, the remote, 76-meter Ingolfshöfði headland (halfway between Skaftafell and Jökulsárlón) is overrun with nesting birds, including puffins and great skuas. A local family runs fun guided tours here: first, you meet at a departure hut about 1½ mile off the Ring Road (signed), then you board a cart pulled by a tractor for a bumpy ride across 6 km (4 miles) of tidal black sands. There's a relatively steep walk to reach the top of the headland, then you have about 1½ hours to ogle

the birds and the spectacular Vatnajökull views. Needless to say, come dressed for the weather. ⊹ *Look for the sign "Ingolfshöfði 2km", about 3½ km west of Fosshotel Glacier Lagoon* ☎ *894–0894* ⊕ *www.fromcoasttomountains.com* ✉ *ISK 9,750.*

★ Glacier Lagoon Boat Tours

BOAT TOURS | This company offers tours of Jökulsárlón lagoon, where you can sail between the floating icebergs in amphibian boats. Even better are their zodiac tours (operating June to September; ISK 11,000), which get you much closer to the bergs and up to the edge of the glacier where all the calving action takes place. ✉ *Jökulsárlón* ☎ *354/478–2222* ⊕ *www.icelagoon.is* ✉ *ISK 6,000* ⏱ *no tours Dec-Apr.*

★ Icelandic Mountain Guides

ADVENTURE TOURS | IMG has a base by the park's Skaftafell visitor center and offers year-round ice adventures with highly experienced and certified glacier guides, from short and easy glacier walks (ISK 12,500) to a full day on the ice (ISK 26,900). From October to April, when the region's remarkable blue ice caves are accessible, you can combine a glacier walk with an ice cave tour (ISK 14,900) that takes about 3½ hours. All equipment is provided, but come dressed for the ice. ☎ *587–9999* ⊕ *www.mountainguides.is/tours-from-skaftafell.*

★ IceGuide

ADVENTURE TOURS | Based at Flatey Farm (24 miles west of Höfn), IceGuide specializes in glacier-themed tours with thrilling visits to glacier ice caves or kayaking excursions between creaking icebergs on a glacier lagoon, plus glacier walks and hikes too. The company has an excellent reputation and is staffed with a team of knowledgeable and experienced professionals who are likely to share fun anecdotes during tours. ✉ *Höfn* ☎ *354/661–0900* ⊕ *www.iceguide.is.*

VISITOR INFORMATION
Skaftafell Visitor Centre

VISITOR CENTER | Before exploring the area, make sure to stop at the Skaftafell Visitor Centre for a good overview of all the region has to offer. The center is open year-round and staffed with local experts who can give you detailed and up-to-date information about conditions of the trails and roads to attractions, places of interest, and recreational activities. There are bathrooms and a souvenir shop selling books, postcards, and locally handcrafted goods. ⊠ *Skaftafell Visitor Centre, Öraefi* ☎ *470–8300* ⊕ *www.vjp.is.*

 Sights

Bæjarstaðarskógur Forest

FOREST | Lush, leafy heaven can be found at Bæjarstaðarskógur, 22 hectares of vibrant woodland, where the native Icelandic birch trees grow thick and tall between a carpet of wood cranesbill, stone brambles, and meadow buttercups. The challenging 9.8-mile circular hike from Skaftafell Visitor Centre takes you towards Sjónarsker down to Kamgil and across the footbridge over the Morsá river, where a marked trail leads to the forest. ⊠ *Jökulsárlón.*

★ Diamond Beach

BEACH | At the southern end of Jökulsárlón glacier lagoon, a powerful outlet stream carries an endless parade of icebergs under a bridge and into the mouth of the sea, where they are tossed and tumbled in the waves before reaching the black sand shoreline where they dazzle like giant polished diamonds. It's the perfect spot to walk around and just appreciate the stunning scenery. ⊠ *Jökulsárlón.*

Fjallsárlón Glacier Lagoon

NATURE SIGHT | Smaller and considerably colder than Jökulsárlón, Fjallsárlón offers an alternative perspective of iceberg calving activity, and with the snout of the glacier being much closer to the shore,

you don't need a long lens to see the action. Services at the lagoon include boat tours, a modern visitor center, and a restaurant. ⊠ *Fjallsárlón, Jökulsárlón* ✛ *47 km east of Skaftafell and 10 km west of Jökulsárlón.*

★ Heinabergslón Glacier Lagoon

NATURE SIGHT | Nature makes its own music at Heinabergslón, one of several glacier lagoons between Skaftafell and Höfn. A pleasant symphony of chiming candle ice is interrupted now and then by the air-fracturing sound of icebergs crashing as they calve from the serrated edge of the glacier. IceGuide offers kayaking tours on the lagoon, but you can drive there on your own (note this is a gravel road) and follow walking trails in the area. Look for the sign about 3 km (2 miles) west of Flatey Farm. ⊠ *Heinabergslón, Heinabergslón, Höfn* ⊕ *www.vjp.is.*

Ingólfshöfði

NATURE PRESERVE | East of Skaftafell, rising sharply above the vast plains of black sand is Ingólfshöfði, a solitary headland surrounded by sand and sea. In a region of ice, it steals attention from the inland sights. Taking its name from Iceland's first settler, Ingólfur Arnarson, who probably spent his first months here, the location is also a beautiful nature preserve with abundant bird life, especially puffins and skuas who make their home there during nesting season. Visit it on a joyous tour with From Coast to Mountains. ⊠ *Jökulsárlón.*

★ Jökulsárlón Glacier Lagoon

NATURE SIGHT | Literally translated as "Glacier River Lagoon", Jökulsárlón is where you can see large chunks of the glacier tumble and float around in a spectacular ice show. The scenery is so magnificent, it has been used as a location for scenes in some James Bond movies (*A View to a Kill* and *Die Another Day*), as well as *Lara Croft Tomb Raider*. West of the lagoon, on the Breiðamerkur sands, you'll find the largest North Atlantic colony of skua, sizable predatory seabirds that dive-bomb intruders during nesting season. Boat and zodiac rides on the lagoon are hugely popular, but you can spend hours just walking the area and admiring the spectacle. ✉ *Jökulsárlón* ⊕ *www. icelagoon.com.*

Kristínartindar

MOUNTAIN | Some say you haven't truly experienced Skaftafell until you've conquered the twin peaks of Kristínartindar. Standing at 3,212 and 3,694 feet, the views from the vertigo-inducing summits, which are connected by a narrow path along a jagged ridge, are the best in the region, taking in the vast expanse of Skaftafellsjökull, Morsárdalur, and Skeiðarársandur. The trail to Kristínartindar is a challenging six to eight-hour round-trip (approximately 11 miles) from the visitor center. Access is closed usually starting from mid-September and over the winter because of snow, ice, and windy weather. Due to meltwater in the spring, the path stays closed until around May or early June, depending on conditions. ✉ *Jökulsárlón.*

★ Morsárdalur

TRAIL | Time and effort are rewarded with extraordinary views of epic scenery at Morsárdalur, where the silence is frequently interrupted by the formidable, air-fracturing sound of the Morsárjökull glacier cracking and churning in the distance. The valley is also home to Morsárfoss falls, which, at 787 feet, snatched the highest waterfall crown from Glýmur when it was discovered to be at least 100 feet taller. Morsárfoss only became visible in 2007 when Morsárjökull started melting. ✉ *Jökulsárlón.*

Sel

FARM/RANCH | A stop on the popular Svartifoss trail, Sel is a lovely old traditional turf-topped house built by Þorsteinn Guðmundsson in 1912 and occupied until 1946 when it was abandoned. The restored property is now maintained by the National Museum. ✉ *Jökulsárlón.*

★ Skaftafellsjökull

NATURE SIGHT | The 2.3-mile round-rip walk to the Skaftafell outlet glacier is one of the more comfortable options for seeing a glacier, with the trail to the edge of the glacier paved half the way there. Starting from the visitor center, the trip to Skaftafellsjökull takes around 30 minutes each way. The color of the glacier occasionally dazzles in brilliant shades of blue. ✉ *Skaftafellsjökull, Jökulsárlón.*

★ Sjónarnípa

TRAIL | One of the more popular spots to visit in Skaftafell is the Sjónarnípa viewpoint, which is a 4- to 5-mile hike with several challenging sections. It offers glorious views of Skaftafellsjökull glacier. You can either head straight to Sjónarnípa from the visitor center via Austurbrekkur or take a turn-off on the trail up to Svartifoss heading east over the heath. ✉ *Sjónarnípa, Jökulsárlón.*

Sjónarsker

TRAIL | Sjónarsker is a vantage point on the popular Svartifoss–Sel trail around 1,000 feet above sea level. Take the western route up from Svartifoss. From here you are rewarded with superb panoramic views, and with the help of the compass-style locator disk installed there you can quickly identify the surrounding landmarks. ✉ *Höfn.*

★ Svartifoss

WATERFALL | Prepare to have your breath taken away twice by Svartifoss (literally, 'Black Falls'): once by the trail, which is rather steep, and again by the waterfall itself, a wonder of natural architecture. The falls feature a single torrent of water plunging over a wall of symmetrical basalt columns that look like a pipe organ. The mile-long, rubber-lined trail starts from the campsite at Skaftafell. Do not be tempted to drive up the access road—this is for staff only and strictly prohibited. ✉ *Svartifoss, Höfn.*

Svínafellsjökull

NATURE SIGHT | As a filming location for several big-budget films and the wildly popular HBO show *Game of Thrones*, Svínafellsjökull is often referred to as the "Hollywood glacier," attracting countless fans to its formidable icy terrain. More recently, it has been a cause for concern as scientists discovered the glacier was becoming more unstable and too dangerous to warrant any glacier walking activities (so glacier tours take participants to nearby glacier tongues). You can drive the very bumpy access road to the car park giving access to a few trails (on regular terrain, not on ice) for some great close-ups. It's off the Ring Road just east of Skaftafell. ✣ *The rough track to the car park is just over a mile long and full of potholes.*

Þórbergssetur

OTHER MUSEUM | Designed to look like a giant shelf of books, the Þórbergssetur museum is a fitting tribute to the author Þórbergur Þórðarson (1888–1974), whose life and works have been curated into an interesting exhibition. There's a good restaurant here too, specializing in farm-raised arctic char. ✉ *Hali, Suðursveit, Höfn* ✣ *9 miles east of Jökulsárlón* ☎ *478–1078* 🌐 *www.thorbergur.is* 🎟 *ISK 1,000.*

🍴 Restaurants

The Café

$$ | **CAFÉ** | As the only place of shelter at Jökulsárlón Glacier Lagoon, this basic café, resembling a series of pitched roofs, offers light refreshments with sandwiches, soups, hot chocolate, and coffee. There is free Wi-Fi, bathrooms, and a modest selection of postcards and souvenirs. **Known for:** free Wi-Fi; souvenirs to buy; only stop for amenities at the Glacier Lagoon. [$] *Average main: ISK1,500* ✉ *Jökulsárlón* ☎ *478–2222* 🌐 *www.icelagoon.is.*

Glacier Goodies

$$ | **FAST FOOD** | Convenient, fast, and especially welcome after a morning hike on Skaftafellsheiði, Glacier Goodies, located next to the visitor center in Skaftafell, serves a modest menu of tasty, hot meals from their food truck. Just follow your nose. **Known for:** lobster soup; fish-and-chips; deep-fried ice cream. [$] *Average main: ISK2,500* ☎ *847–0037* 🌐 *www.facebook.com/glaciergoodies* 🕒 *Closed mid-Oct.–mid-May.*

Kaffiterían Skaftafelli

$$ | **CAFÉ** | At the large and no-frills Kaffiterían Skaftafelli, next to the Skaftafell Visitor Centre, you can get light lunch of soup or a hot dish like fish or meatballs. They also serve grilled sandwiches, pastries, and cakes, plus snacks for the trails. **Known for:** vegan options; lamb meatballs; fried cod. [$] *Average main: ISK2,200* ✉ *Kaffiterian Skaftafelli, Öræfi, Jökulsárlón* ☎ *830–0094.*

Þórbergssetur Restaurant

$$$$ | **ICELANDIC** | The large restaurant inside the Þórbergssetur museum and cultural center is often busy, as there are limited food options along this stretch of road in Iceland. Even with that pressure, the dishes are always tasty, with a special emphasis on lamb and arctic char raised on the local farm. **Known for:** skyr cheesecake; lamb soup; pan-fried arctic char. [$] *Average main: ISK4,300* ✉ *Hali, Jökulsárlón* ✣ *9 miles east of Jökulsárlón* ☎ *478–1073* 🌐 *hali.is/restaurant.*

🛏 Hotels

★ Fosshotel Glacier Lagoon

$$$$ | **HOTEL** | The stylish and luxurious Fosshotel Glacier Lagoon stands out like a black fortress from its surroundings. **Pros:** good sauna and gym; spacious and modern rooms with great views; good on-site restaurant. **Cons:** expensive; no alternative restaurant options in the area; no shuttle service to nature sights. [$] *Rooms from: ISK59,000* ✉ *Hnappavellir, Jökulsárlón* ☎ *514–8300* 🌐 *www.islandshotel.is* 🛏 *125 rooms* 🍴 *No Meals.*

Index

Photo Credits

Front Cover: Theerayoot Tapina/Getty Images [Description: Godafoss waterfall and magic sky at midnight in Summer,Iceland]. **Back cover, from left to right:** AllaLaurent/iStockphoto. Simon's passion 4 Travel/Shutterstock. Patpongs/iStockphoto. **Spine:** 1Tomm/iStockphoto. **Interior, from left to right:** Supreecha Samansukumal/Shutterstock (1). Patpongs/iStockphoto (2-3). **Chapter 1: Experience Iceland:** Blue Planet Studio/Shutterstock (6-7). Jamen Percy/Shutterstock (8-9). Jeafish Ping/Shutterstock (9). VicPhotoria/Shutterstock (9). Fuzja44/Dreamstime (10). Vadym Lavra/Shutterstock (10). Whatafoto/Shutterstock (10). Promote Iceland (11). Alfiya Safuanova/Shutterstock (11). Ragnar Th./Visit Reykjavík (12). Menno Schaefer/Shutterstock (12). Gestur Gislason/Shutterstock (12). Alec Donnell Luna/CptVibes (12). Ragnar Th Sigurdsson/Promote Iceland (13). JuliusKielaitis/Shutterstock (13). Margouillat photo/Shutterstock (18). Langoustine harbor/lobster harbor (19). Perlan Museum (20). Brooks Walker (20). Arnar Gudmundsson (20). Courtesy of Saga Museum (20). Magnus Elvar Jonsson/Gagarin (21). Olgeir Andresson (22). Einar Gudmann/Svartifoss (22). Standret/Shuterstock (22). DonVictorio/iStockphoto (23). Courtesy of Larry Malvin Photography (23). Erik Mandre/Shutterstock (24). Iam-Photography/iStockphoto (25). **Chapter 3: Reykjavík:** Worldtowalk/istockphoto (55). Martinho Smart/Shutterstock (64). Javen/Shutterstock (81). Nicolae Prisacaru/Shutterstock (90). Badahos/iStockphoto (98). **Chapter 4: Reykjanes Peninsula and the South Coast (with the Golden Circle):** Alexey Stiop/iStockphoto (107). Michael Ver Sprill/iStockphoto (110). Trungsnaps/Shutterstock (111). Filip Fuxa/Dreamstime (111). Elkaphotos/iStockphoto (122). Stastny_Pavel/Shutterstock (137). Jeafish Ping/ Shutterstock (138). Bibhash Banerjee/iStockphoto (146). Chrisdorney/iStockphoto (150). Demerzel21/iStockphoto (155). **Chapter 5: West Iceland and Snæfellsnes Peninsula:** Alexander Erdbeer/Shutterstock (157). Sasha64f/iStockphoto (168). Endorphine/Shutterstock (173). DesiDrew Photography/iStockphoto (179). Alexey Stiop/Dreamstime (182). **Chapter 6: Westfjords:** Kiran Photo/Shutterstock (185). Raulhudson1986/iStockphoto (194). Vitalii Matokha/Shutterstock (196). LouieLea/Shutterstock (200). **Chapter 7: Akureyri:** Standret/Dreamstime (203). Filip Fuxa/Dreamstime (211). Gestur Gislason/Shutterstock (215). **Chapter 8: North Iceland:** Andrij Vatsyk/Shutterstock (223). Blue Planet Studio/Shutterstock (233).. Magnusas/Dreamstime (258). **Chapter 9: The Highlands:** Pyty/Shutterstock (265). Takepicsforfun/Dreamstime (275). Filip Fuxa/Shutterstock (280). **Chapter 10: East Iceland and the Eastfjords:** RbbrDckyBK/iStockphoto (285). Andrea Brandimarte/Shutterstock (292). Parys/Dreamstime (299). Attila JANDI/Shutterstock (307). Saletomic/Dreamstime (318).

Every effort has been made to trace the copyright holders, and we apologize in advance for any accidental errors. We would be happy to apply the corrections in the following edition of this publication.

Notes

Notes

Notes

Notes

Notes

Notes

Notes

Notes

Fodor's ESSENTIAL ICELAND

Publisher: Stephen Horowitz, *General Manager*

Editorial: Douglas Stallings, *Editorial Director;* Jill Fergus, Amanda Sadlowski, *Senior Editors;* Kayla Becker, Brian Eschrich, Alexis Kelly, *Editors;* Angelique Kennedy-Chavannes, *Assistant Editor*

Design: Tina Malaney, *Director of Design and Production;* Jessica Gonzalez, *Senior Designer;* Erin Caceres, *Graphic Design Associate*

Production: Jennifer DePrima, *Editorial Production Manager;* Elyse Rozelle, *Senior Production Editor;* Monica White, *Production Editor*

Maps: Rebecca Baer, *Senior Map Editor;* Mark Stroud (Moon Street Cartography), *Cartographer*

Photography: Viviane Teles, *Senior Photo Editor;* Namrata Aggarwal, Neha Gupta, Payal Gupta, Ashok Kumar, *Photo Editors;* Eddie Aldrete, *Photo Production Intern;* Kadeem McPherson, *Photo Production Associate Intern*

Business and Operations: Chuck Hoover, *Chief Marketing Officer;* Robert Ames, *Group General Manager*

Public Relations and Marketing: Joe Ewaskiw, *Senior Director of Communications and Public Relations*

Fodors.com: Jeremy Tarr, *Editorial Director;* Rachael Levitt, *Managing Editor*

Technology: Jon Atkinson, *Director of Technology;* Rudresh Teotia, *Associate Director of Technology;* Alison Lieu, *Project Manager*

Writers: Carolyn Bain, Hannah Jane Cohen, Erika Owen, John Pearson

Editor: Amanda Sadlowski

Production Editor: Elyse Rozelle

2nd Edition

ISBN 978-1-64097-563-7

ISSN 2644-3465

All details in this book are based on information supplied to us at press time. Always confirm information when it matters, especially if you're making a detour to visit a specific place. Fodor's expressly disclaims any liability, loss, or risk, personal or otherwise, that is incurred as a consequence of the use of any of the contents of this book.

SPECIAL SALES
This book is available at special discounts for bulk purchases for sales promotions or premiums. For more information, e-mail SpecialMarkets@fodors.com.

PRINTED IN CHINA

10 9 8 7 6 5 4 3 2 1

About Our Writers

Australian-born **Carolyn Bain** has written guidebooks and travel features for almost 20 years, and in the process has fallen in love with far too many destinations, from Greek islands to Slovenian mountain villages. After visiting Iceland as many times as possible in the name of research, she finally moved from the bottom of the world to the top in 2017, and now calls Reykjavík home. She updated the Highlands and East Iceland and the Eastfjords chapters this edition.

Hannah Jane Cohen is based out of Iceland by way of New York. An alumna of Columbia University, she began her work within the Icelandic travel industry as the Culture Editor and Listings Director at the *Reykjavík Grapevine,* Iceland's biggest English-language newspaper, where she worked for five years. She's currently writing her first novel. Hannah Jane updated the Reykjanes Peninsula and the South Coast, Akureyri, and North Iceland chapters this edition.

Erika Owen is a Brooklyn-based writer and professional Iceland enthusiast. Her work has appeared in *Vogue, Bon Appétit, Departures,* and *Travel + Leisure,* among other travel and lifestyle publications and websites. She is also the author of *The Art of Flaneuring: How to Wander with Intention and Discover a Better Life*. Erika updated the Reykjavík, West Iceland and Snæfellsnses Peninsula, and Westfjords chapters this edition.

John Pearson is a journalist, longtime Reykjavík resident, and Iceland aficionado, whose love for the Land of Fire and Ice developed over a decade of regularly escaping his native London for lengthy Icelandic wanderings. Realizing that he was finding any excuse to linger longer, he finally hopped over the North Sea to live in Iceland and write about it for the *Reykjavík Grapevine* and the *Iceland Monitor*. He updated the Experience and Travel Smart chapters this edition.